D0841826

The Inside Track to

CAREERS IN ACCOUNTING

BY **Stan Ross**

& James Carberry

DISCARD

Notice to Readers

The Inside Track to Careers in Accounting does not represent an official position of the American Institute of Certified Public Accountants, and it is distributed with the understanding that the authors and publisher are not rendering legal, accounting, or other professional services in the publication. If legal advice or other expert assistance is required, the services of a competent professional should be sought.

ISBN: 978-0-87051-872-0

Publisher: Amy Stainken
Managing Editor: Amy Krasnyanskaya
Acquisitions Editor: Erin Howard Valentine
Developmental Editor: Andrew Grow
Copy Editor: Courtney Paschal
Senior Project Manager: M. Donovan Scott
Cover Design: David McCradden

Contents

Chapter 1: Accounting: A Hot Career Path

Chapter 2: Education: Foundation of a Career

The following interviews are included on the CD-ROM:

   Andriana Mavidis, Student, St. John's University School of Law, New York

   Shirley Maxey, Professor of Clinical Accounting and Management Communication, Leventhal School

     of Accounting, Marshall School of Business, University of Southern California

   Milli Penner, Assistant Dean, Undergraduate Program, Leventhal School of Accounting,

     Marshall School of Business, University of Southern California

Chapter 3: Certification

<u>Chapter 4: Careers in Public Accounting</u>

The following interviews are included on the CD-ROM:

James L. Freer, Retired Vice Chair of People, Ernst & Young Americas

Patrick Henry, Partner, Deloitte & Touche LLP

Philip Holthouse, Co-founder and Partner, Holthouse Carlin & Van Trigt LLP

Denis Joseph, Audit Assistant, Deloitte

Chapter 5: Careers in Corporate Accounting

Chapter 6: Careers in Government Accounting

Chapter 7: Careers in Nonprofit Accounting

Chapter 8: Sole Practitioner: Starting Your Own Business

Chapter 9: Careers in Teaching

Chapter 10: Career Paths: What's Right for You?

Chapter 11: Finding that First Job

Foreword

As the largest membership organization for certified public accountants in the world, the AICPA is dedicated to the future of the profession. Ensuring a pipeline of qualified future CPAs and fostering a strong and diverse work force is a top priority for us. We are proud of our efforts in this area. The 2007–2008 academic year saw the number of accounting graduates at an all-time high of 66,000.

But it is about more than just the numbers for us. Simply put, we have a strong desire to encourage young talent and spread the word about the exciting and rewarding career opportunities available to CPAs. This book is one of the many ways we are reaching out to students to encourage their interest in the profession that has been so rewarding for so many of us.

The author of this book, Stan Ross, has had an incredible career—owed in no small part to his CPA credential. You'll learn about Stan's CPA journey as you read on, but the book is far more than just a chronicle of one notable career. Recognizing the multitude of different ways in which CPAs are putting their talent and skills to work, Stan reached out to colleagues in every corner of the profession and asked them to talk about their career paths. The diverse group of over 50 CPAs that you'll meet in these pages demonstrates that for CPAs the opportunities are truly endless–and as varied as we choose.

For readers who have not yet settled on the CPA path, our hope is that this book will expand your understanding of what CPAs do, help you navigate and explore the opportunities that are available, and put you on the inside track to a rewarding career in accounting.

It is our honor to bring you this important resource and we extend our sincere gratitude to Stan Ross and his team for entrusting AICPA with its publication.

Sincerely—

Barry C. Melancon, CPA
President and CEO
The American Institute of Certifed Public Accountants

Preface

I grew up in a Bronx tenement, about 12 blocks from Yankee Stadium. When I was in high school, I worked part time in a factory that made women's belts. My uncle was an accountant whose clients included the factory owner. On occasion, he would visit the factory. There he was, dressed in a nice looking suit and shirt and tie, comfortably working in the factory office, and there I was, sweating away on the factory floor. It was then and there that I thought I might want to be an accountant. At the time, I didn't really understand what an accountant was, or did, but my uncle seemed to have a great job.

Actually, I had some early experience with accounting. My father died when I was 14, and I helped my mother with the family bookkeeping. In a sense, I was the CFO of our family (although I'm sure I didn't call myself that at the time). I went on to study accounting at Baruch College, part of the City University of New York. Because Baruch was relatively affordable, I and thousands of others from families of modest means were able to have an education.

To earn some income while I was in college, I went into business for myself. I prepared tax returns for individuals and families, charging them according to the complexity of their returns. To help my clients with specific tax questions, I learned to research applicable tax laws and regulations. And to run my fledgling business, I prepared a budget for rent (I was subleasing space) and other expenses—it was an early lesson in business economics. My business started to grow, and I hired some people to work for me. All in all, my business was both a source of income and a learning opportunity.

After I graduated from Baruch, I worked for a small accounting firm that mainly provided auditing and tax services to small businesses. I built on my experience in running my little business to learn how to provide services to the firm's clients. Then I was drafted into the U.S. Army, and I served about two years in the Army's audit agency. It gave me a broader perspective on accounting and auditing—and on life.

Upon completing my Army service, I joined SD Leidesdorf, a large regional accounting firm in the New York area, as an associate junior accountant. At Leidesdorf, I had an opportunity to work for clients who were large public and private companies in different industries, and to travel around the country on engagements. I got a first-hand look at the range of services that an accounting firm offers—services that today are much broader than in my early years as a CPA.

After a while, I found myself looking for a new challenge, and I answered a help wanted ad placed by Kenneth Leventhal & Company, a small Los Angeles-based CPA firm specializing in real estate. I met with Kenneth Leventhal, the founder of the firm, and he persuaded me to move to Los Angeles to join his organization. We provided traditional accounting services to clients, but we differentiated ourselves from competitors by customizing our services to the needs of developers, builders, and other real estate businesses, and by helping our clients solve business problems—such as how to finance multimillion dollar development projects. It proved to be a highly successful business model. By the time the Leventhal firm merged with Ernst & Young in the mid-1990s, I had succeeded Kenneth Leventhal as managing partner, and I became a vice chairman of Ernst & Young. In the process, I developed broad experience in every aspect of the real estate industry.

Years later, I had the honor of delivering a commencement address at Baruch College. As I looked over the students, parents, relatives, and family friends in attendance, I thought back to the day when I first walked through Baruch's doors, and how my accounting degree enabled me to get started on what has been a very rewarding and satisfying career in accounting. I have been fortunate in being able to show my appreciation by endowing the Stan Ross Department of Accountancy at Baruch.

Over the years, I have had the opportunity to meet and get to know a number of students at Baruch, the University of Southern California, and other schools around the country. From my meetings and conversations with students, faculty members, and people in the accounting profession, I became aware of the need for better information on the many career opportunities in accounting. I know when I enrolled at Baruch, I wasn't quite clear about all that accounting had to offer. Out of my early experience, and talking with people, the idea for this book was born.

The purpose of this book is twofold: to assist students in deciding whether they might want to pursue careers in accounting, and to assist students who have decided on accounting as a career but may not be aware of all the career paths in the profession.

Accounting is an exciting field, full of opportunities. But don't take my word for it. This book includes a number of interviews with CPAs who have had interesting, rewarding and successful careers in public accounting, business, government, the not-for-profit sector, entrepreneurship, and other fields.

You can have the same success. To get started, do your own research. Read up on the accounting profession (some books, articles, Web sites, and other resources are listed in the appendix.) Talk to CPAs about their work, and why they decided on careers in accounting. Attend meetings of professional societies for accountants. Consider other careers, and decide whether accounting is right for you. This book will help you with your decision.

If you are interested in accounting, think about where you might want to study for a degree in accounting (or, alternatively, in business with a major in accounting or other degree program). While you are in college, start thinking about the career path in accounting that might be right for you, and how to get started in your career.

It goes without saying that deciding on a career is one of the most important and challenging decisions you will make in life. So invest the time and effort in making the right career choice. And once you start on your career, use every job as a learning opportunity, as I did. If you are open to new challenges, you can have an exciting and rewarding career in the fast-growing accounting profession.

Finally, as you advance in your career, think about giving back. Tutor high school students. Mentor a college student studying for a degree in accounting. Get involved in the profession and the community. Join the AICPA and other professional societies and serve on their committees. Volunteer for the board of a not-for-profit organization. Help to provide a scholarship for a deserving student to study accounting. There are many ways you can give back.

And I wish you much success in your career.

—Stan Ross

Acknowledgments

This book would not have been possible without the help of many people. They include not only those whose interviews appear in the book, but also many others who contributed. All are listed in the contributors section. And to all of you, thank you.

AICPA Leadership

I want to give special thanks to the American Institute of Certified Public Accountants (AICPA) for agreeing to publish this book and for managing the publication process from the editing of the manuscript to the design, layout, production, and marketing of the book. There is a need in the marketplace for a book that informs students and professionals about the many career opportunities in accounting and how to decide on a career path. The AICPA's leadership has made this book possible.

I much appreciate the direction and support provided by the AICPA's dedicated and talented publications team: Amy Stainken, director of publications product development; Erin Valentine, acquisitions editor; and Amy Krasnyanskaya, senior manager of practice and industry publications. Erin Valentine and Amy Krasnyanskaya brought perspective, clarity, and focus to the editing of the manuscript, and the result is an informative, easy-to-read publication. Heather O'Connor, communications manager (and former acquisitions editor), provided editorial guidance early on.

Denny Reigle, the AICPA's director of academic and career development, was of great help with the chapters on education and teaching and in suggesting people to interview. Stephen Winters, the former director of AICPA's specialized communities and firm practice management, provided a step-by-step explanation of CPA credentialing and licensing as well as an overview of other credential programs. Martha Renaud of the AICPA's examination team explained the particulars of the CPA examination process.

Research Support

Rita Ormsby, Baruch College assistant professor and information services librarian, provided valuable research support and answered many questions about careers and other topics. Baruch students (and now graduates) Andriana Mavidis, Eileen Ni, and Rick Smith helped with interviews and research.

Interviewees

Education

Thanks to deans John Elliott of Baruch College, Zicklin School of Business, City University of New York, and Randolph Beatty of the University of Southern California's Leventhal School of Accounting, Marshall School of Business, for their guidance in the planning of this book and their insights on careers in accounting. Ira Solomon, chair of the department of accounting at the University of Illinois, and James Benjamin, head of the accounting department at Texas A&M, discussed the accounting programs at their respective schools and how they prepare students for careers.

For CPAs who are interested in teaching and research, there is a great need for PhD accounting faculty at universities and colleges with accounting programs. Masako Darrough, chair of the Stan Ross Department of Accountancy at Baruch College, discussed why she likes teaching, and how to earn a PhD in accounting. Doyle Z. Williams, executive director of the Accounting Doctoral Scholars Program, discussed its goal of increasing the supply of accounting faculty who are academically qualified and who have recent experience in public accounting in audit and tax.

Diversity

The progress that has been made—and the challenges that remain—in the recruiting, retention, and advancement of women in accounting and business were discussed by Kimberly Fantaci, executive director of the American Woman's Society of Certified Public Accountants, and Lee Lowery, executive director of the American Society of Women Accountants. Misean Reed, manager of diversity, work/life, and women's Initiatives with the AICPA, discussed the AICPA's Women's Initiatives, a program to attract women to accounting and help them to remain in the profession and advance in their careers. Ostine Swan, the AICPA's senior manager of diversity programs and relationships, and staff liaison to the AICPA's Minority Initiatives Committee, discussed the committee's initiatives, including scholarship programs for minority accounting students, workshops for accounting scholars, a fellowship program for minority doctoral students, and publication of an e-book, "CPAs of Color: Celebrating 40 Years." Gregory Johnson, executive director and chief operating officer of the National Association of Black Accountants (NABA), covered the NABA's programs to interest students in accounting, assist them to get started, and help them advance in their careers. Manny Espinoza, CEO of the Association of Latino Professionals in Finance and Accounting (ALPFA), discussed his career in accounting (including international assignments, one a fraud investigation that took him into the Ecuadorian jungle) as well as ALPFA's programs to help professionals pursue careers in accounting and finance.

Deborah Holmes, Ernst & Young's Director of Corporate Responsibility, discussed its initiatives to recruit, retain and assist women to advance in their careers. Billie Williamson, EY's Americas Inclusiveness Officer, explained EY's programs to foster and maintain a diverse and inclusive culture.

Public Accounting

James Turley, chairman and CEO of Ernst & Young, and James Quigley, CEO of Deloitte Touche Tohmatsu, made time in their busy schedules to talk about careers in public accounting, among other topics. Career perspectives were provided by CEOs (or managing partners) of these major public accounting firms: Rick Anderson, Moss Adams; Kenneth Baggett, Reznick; William Hermann, Plante & Moran; Phil Holthouse, Holthouse, Carlin and Van Trigt; Krista McMasters, Clifton Gunderson; Bert Mitchell, Mitchell & Titus; Ed Nusbaum, Grant Thornton; and Charles Weinstein, Eisner LLP.

Corporate

In the corporate world, CPAs can be found at every level from entry positions to senior leadership. Thanks to the following CEOs for taking time to discuss their careers and career opportunities for CPAs in corporations: Thomas Falk, Kimberly Clark; Ted Phillips, Chicago Bears; William Rhodes, AutoZone; and Michael Roth, Interpublic. Joseph Macnow discussed his career and his responsibilities as CFO of Vornado Realty Trust, a leading real estate company.

Government

For the chapter on careers for CPAs in government, the FBI's Office of Public Affairs arranged interviews with Michael Cuff, unit chief of the FBI's Forensic Accountant Unit, and Kamile Narine, accounting section chief. At the IRS, Robert Buggs, chief human capital officer, coordinated interviews with IRS professionals Shannon Dickerson, Winnie Lichtner, and Teresa Edwards, as well as Kathy Petronchak, then IRS commissioner for small business, and now a partner at Deloitte. Jeanette Franzel, director, financial management and assurance, in the U.S. Government Accountability Office (GAO), discussed the GAO's work, her job, and career opportunities for CPAs with the GAO. Michele Mark Levine, director of accounting services with New York City's Office of Management and Budget, discussed her responsibilities and why she decided on a career in government service.

Not-for-profit

Working for not-for-profit organizations provides opportunities for CPAs to serve the community and enjoy satisfying careers. Two CPAs who advanced to senior leadership positions in their organizations talked about their careers: Allan C. Golston, president of the United States Program, Bill and Melinda Gates Foundation; and Amy Coleman, vice president, finance, of the Kresge Foundation.

Starting a CPA Firm

CPAs with an entrepreneurial bent have started their own CPA firms, including my lifelong friend Eugene Price, who started his firm after he graduated from Baruch College. (When we were growing up together in the Bronx, he played a very competitive game of pickup basketball. The drive that led him to start his own business was evident at an early age.) DeAnn Hill got a few years of experience working for CPA firms, then started her own firm at age 24. She discussed the value of serving in leadership positions in community and professional organizations and building networks of colleagues and business associates.

Beyond Accounting

CPAs are leveraging their CPA credentials and professional experience to join or start consulting firms and other businesses. After 30 years of working for the FBI and in public accounting, Ronald Durkin founded a forensic accounting firm that focuses on solving fraud and fraud related issues for its clients. While working in auditing for public accounting firms, CPA Howard Rosenkrantz began doing forensic accounting projects and decided to earn certified fraud examiner certification. He now does intellectual property infringement consulting and forensic investigations for a consulting firm.

Other Contributors

I would not have been able to complete a project of this magnitude without the able support of my longtime associates Karen Correa and Connie Lockhart.

A special thanks to Karen for her countless hours of help in organizing and managing this project, contacting people to arrange interviews and the review of interview drafts, tracking numerous changes to the manuscript, and otherwise keeping this project on track.

Supporting Cast

Kenneth Leventhal, founder of Kenneth Leventhal & Company, my mentor, partner and friend who gave me the opportunity, direction, and support to build a successful career in both accounting and real estate.

Sheldon LaZar, my good friend, who gave me accounting guidance throughout the years.

Gail Carberry, wife of James Carberry, my collaborator on this book. For her patient support through the many hours spent on this project.

My wife Marilyn, who has been with me throughout my entire accounting career, who has supported me through all the ups and downs, who has participated in many of my philanthropic activities, and who was extremely tolerant during the writing of this book.

About the Authors

Stan Ross

Stan Ross is Chairman of the Board of the University of Southern California Lusk Center for Real Estate and Distinguished Fellow of USC's School of Policy, Planning & Development. He is a retired Vice Chairman—Real Estate Industry Services for Ernst & Young LLP, where he was a member of the firm's Management Committee, and former Managing Partner of E&Y Kenneth Leventhal Real Estate Group. He continues his diverse activities in the real estate industry as a consultant and serves on several boards of directors, including The Irvine Company, Forest City Enterprises, and American Jewish University.

Ross is widely recognized for his experience in strategic planning for real estate companies, with expertise in mergers, acquisitions and reorganizations, and the development of creative financial structures. He was involved in the initial organization of the Resolution Trust Corporation (RTC), a government agency that in the 1990s liquidated hundreds of failed savings and loan associations. He was a member of the Auditing Standards Board of the American Institute of Certified Public Accountants (AICPA). Ross is a frequent lecturer at various universities, accounting symposia, and real estate conferences and has written numerous articles concerning real estate and accounting matters. He is a Life Trustee and Governor of the Urban Land Institute and Trustee of Baruch College, from which he graduated in 1956. After graduating from Baruch, he served in the U.S. Army. Ross was awarded an honorary Doctor of Laws degree from Baruch College in 1999. He was inducted into the California Building Industry Foundation's Hall of Fame in 2004. Ross has written *The Inside Track to Careers in Real Estate*, a book published by the Urban Land Institute in 2006. Stan and his wife, Marilyn, have three daughters and twelve grandchildren.

Contributing Author

James Carberry

James Carberry is the principal of Carberry Communications, a business writing and editing service based in the Portland, Oregon, metropolitan area. He has been a corporate writer and editor, a business writer based in Singapore, and, for ten years, a staff reporter of *The Wall Street Journal*. Before joining the Journal, he was a reporter for newspapers in Berkeley and Riverside, California. Carberry is the contributing author of *The Inside Track to Careers in Real Estate*, by Stan Ross. He is a graduate of the University of Missouri School of Journalism. He served in the U.S. Navy.

Contributors

Many people contributed to this book. All of their contributions were important in taking it from concept to publication. (Some titles/organizations may have changed since this book was published.)

Ernest Almonte
Former Auditor General
State of Rhode Island
Providence, Rhode Island

Rick Anderson
Chairman & CEO
Moss Adams LLP
Seattle, Washington

Kenneth Baggett
Managing Principal/CEO
Reznick Group, P.C.
Atlanta, Georgia

Randolph Beatty
Dean
Leventhal School of Accounting
Marshall School of Business
University of Southern California
Los Angeles, California

James Benjamin
Professor
Head of Accounting Department
Mays Business School
Texas A&M
College Station, Texas

Doug Carmichael
Professor
Baruch College
New York, New York,

Lily Chen
Tax Manager
JP Morgan Chase
New York, New York

Amy Coleman
Vice President of Finance
The Kresge Foundation
Troy, Michigan

Susan Crosson
Professor
Coordinator of Accounting
Santa Fe Community College
Gainesville, Florida

Michael Cuff
Unit Chief
Forensic Accounting Unit
Financial Crimes Section
Criminal Investigation Division
Federal Bureau of Investigation
Washington, DC

Masako Darrough
Chair
Stan Ross Department of Accountancy
Baruch College
Zicklin School of Business
New York, New York

Dan Deines
Professor of Accounting
College of Business Administration
Kansas State University
Manhattan, Kansas

Shannon Dickerson
Revenue Agent
Internal Revenue Service
Wheaton, Maryland

Ronald Durkin
Founder and Senior Managing Director
Durkin Forensic, Inc.
San Diego, California

Teresa Edwards
Revenue Agent
Internal Revenue Service
Maitland, Florida

John Elliott
Dean
Baruch College
Zicklin School of Business
New York, New York

Manny Espinoza
CEO
Association of Latino Professionals in
    Finance and Accounting
Los Angeles, California

Thomas Falk
Chairman and CEO
Kimberly Clark
Dallas, Texas

Kimberly Fantaci
Executive Director
American Woman's Society of CPAs
Dayton, Ohio

Jeanette Franzel
Managing Director
Financial Management and Assurance Team
U.S. Government Accountability Office
Washington, DC

James Freer
Vice Chair (Retired)
Ernst & Young
New York, New York

Allan Golston
President
U.S. Program
Bill & Melinda Gates Foundation
Seattle, Washington

Patrick Henry
Partner
Deloitte & Touche LLP
New York, New York

William Hermann
Managing Partner
Plante & Moran
Southfield, Michigan

Conrad Hewitt
Former Chief Accountant
Securities and Exchange Commission
Washington, DC

DeAnn Hill
CPA and Owner
DeAnn Auman Hill CPA
Baxter Springs, Kansas

Deborah Holmes
Global Director of Corporate Responsibility
Ernst & Young LLP
New York, New York

Philip Holthouse
Founder & Partner
Holthouse Carlin & Van Trigt LLP
Santa Monica, California

Mei Hua
Senior Associate
McGladrey & Pullen
New York, New York

Gregory Johnson
Executive Director
National Black Accountants, Inc.
Greenbelt, Maryland

Denis Joseph
Audit Senior Assistant
Deloitte & Touche LLP
New York, New York

Mary-Jo Kranacher
Chair
Department of Accounting & Finance
School of Business & Information Systems
York College
City University of New York, New York
and
Editor-in-Chief
The CPA Journal
New York State Society of CPAs
New York, New York

Amy Krasnyanskaya
Senior Manager
Practice & Industry Publications
American Institute of Certified Public
    Accountants
Durham, North Carolina

Alan Langer
Tax Director
Private Client Advisors Group
Deloitte
New York, New York

Elyse Lerner
Accountant
HBO
New York, New York

Alan B. Levine, CPA
New York, New York

Michele Mark Levine
Director of Accounting Services
Office of Management & Budget
City of New York, New York
New York, New York

Lee Lowery
Executive Director
American Society of Women Accountants
McLean, Virginia

Winnie Lichtner
Group Manager
Internal Revenue Service
Englewood, Colorado

Joseph Macnow
EVP-Finance and Administration,
    CFO and CAO
Vornado Realty Trust
New York, New York

Aaron Maguire
Partner
KPMG
New York, New York

Andriana Mavidis
Law Student
St. John's University School of Law
New York, New York

Shirley Maxey
Professor
Clinical Management Communication and
Director
Master of Accounting and Business Taxation
    programs
Leventhal School of Accounting
USC Marshall School of Business
Los Angeles, California

Krista McMasters
CEO
Clifton Gunderson LLP
Milwaukee, Wisconsin

Bert N. Mitchell
Chairman & CEO
Mitchell & Titus
New York, New York

Kamile Narine
Accounting Section Chief
Finance Division
FBI
Washington, DC

Frank Ng
Tax Controversy and Risk Management
    Services
Ernst & Young and
Former Commissioner
Large and Midsized Business Division
Internal Revenue Service
Washington, DC

Eileen Ni
CPA, Associate II
Barclais USA
New York, New York

Marilyn Neimark
Professor of Accountancy
Baruch College
New York, New York

Ed Nusbaum
CEO
Grant Thornton International Ltd.
Chicago, Illinois

Heather O'Connor
Communications Manager
American Institute of Certified Public
    Accountants
Durham, North Carolina

Rita Ormsby
Assistant Professor
Information Services Librarian
Baruch College
Zicklin School of Business
New York, New York

Joseph Page
Internal Revenue Service (Retired)
Former SBSE (Exam) Territory Manager
Denver, Colorado

Maria Pena
Associate Director
Ernst & Young
New York, New York

Milli Penner
Assistant Dean
Undergraduate Program
Leventhal School of Accounting
USC Marshall School of Business
Los Angeles, California

Kathy Petronchak
Director of Tax Controversy
Deloitte Tax LLP
Washington, D.C. and
Commissioner Small Business/
     Self-Employed (Retired)
Internal Revenue Service
Washington, DC

Ted Phillips
President and CEO
Chicago Bears
Lake Forest, Illinois

Eugene Price
Founder and Senior Partner
RRC Price CPAs
Bardonia, New York

James Quigley
CEO
Deloitte Touche Tohmatsu
New York, New York

Misean Reed
Manager—Diversity, Work/Life & Women's
     Initiatives
American Institute of Certified Public
     Accountants
Durham, North Carolina

Denny Reigle
Director
Academic and Career Development Team
American Institute of Certified Public
     Accountants
Durham, North Carolina

Martha Renaud
Examinations Team
American Institute of Certified Public
     Accountants
Ewing, New Jersey

William Rhodes
Chairman, President and CEO
AutoZone Inc.
Memphis, Tennessee

David Richards
President
Institute of Internal Auditors
Altamonte Springs, Florida

Janet Riesel
Recruiting Director
Ernst & Young
New York, New York

Howard Rosenkrantz
Senior Manager
UHY Advisors
New York, New York

Michael Roth
Chairman and CEO
The Interpublic Group of Companies Inc
New York, New York

Bruce Sherman
Chairman (Retired)
Private Capital Management
Naples, Florida

Rick Smith
Associate, Tax
KPMG, LLP
New York, New York

Ira Solomon
Department Head and R. C. Evans
    Chair of Accountancy
University of Illinois
Champaign, Illinois

Amy Stainken
Director
Publications Product Development
American Institute of Certified Public
    Accountants
Durham, North Carolina

Ostine Swan
Senior Manager
Diversity, Work/Life & Women's Initiatives
American Institute of Certified Public
    Accountants
Durham, North Carolina

James Turley
Chairman and CEO
Ernst & Young
New York, New York

Erin Valentine
Manager, Practice Management Content
Practice & Industry Publications
American Institute of Certified Public
    Accountants
Durham, North Carolina

Igor Vaysman
Associate Professor
Baruch College
Zicklin School of Business
New York, New York

Charles Weinstein
Managing Partner
Eisner LLP
New York, New York

Joseph Weintrop
Stan Ross Professor of Accountancy
Baruch College
New York, New York

Doyle Williams
Executive Director
AICPA Foundation
Durham, North Carolina

Billie Williamson
Americas Inclusiveness Officer
Ernst & Young
New York, New York

Stephen Winters
Former Director of Specialized Communities
    and Firm Practice Management
American Institute of Certified Public
    Accountants
Durham, North Carolina

Dennis Wraase
Chairman and CEO (retired)
Pepco Holdings
Washington, DC

Joseph Yau
Manager
McGladrey & Pullen
New York

Accounting:
The First 10,000 Years

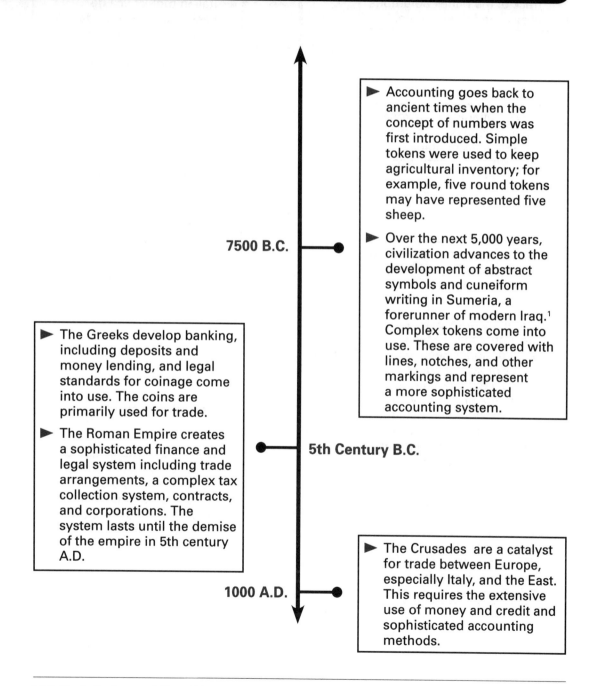

Accounting goes back to ancient times when the concept of numbers was first introduced. Simple tokens were used to keep agricultural inventory; for example, five round tokens may have represented five sheep.

7500 B.C.

Over the next 5,000 years, civilization advances to the development of abstract symbols and cuneiform writing in Sumeria, a forerunner of modern Iraq.[1] Complex tokens come into use. These are covered with lines, notches, and other markings and represent a more sophisticated accounting system.

The Greeks develop banking, including deposits and money lending, and legal standards for coinage come into use. The coins are primarily used for trade.

The Roman Empire creates a sophisticated finance and legal system including trade arrangements, a complex tax collection system, contracts, and corporations. The system lasts until the demise of the empire in 5th century A.D.

5th Century B.C.

1000 A.D.

The Crusades are a catalyst for trade between Europe, especially Italy, and the East. This requires the extensive use of money and credit and sophisticated accounting methods.

---

1 "Who Was the First Accountant?," Texas A&M University. http://acct.tamu.edu/giroux/FIRST.html.

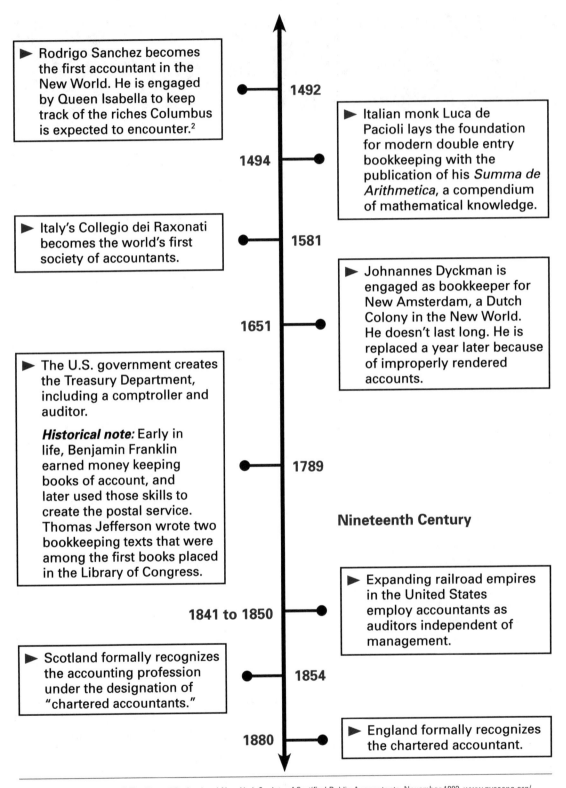

▶ Rodrigo Sanchez becomes the first accountant in the New World. He is engaged by Queen Isabella to keep track of the riches Columbus is expected to encounter.[2]

1492

1494

▶ Italian monk Luca de Pacioli lays the foundation for modern double entry bookkeeping with the publication of his *Summa de Arithmetica*, a compendium of mathematical knowledge.

▶ Italy's Collegio dei Raxonati becomes the world's first society of accountants.

1581

1651

▶ Johnannes Dyckman is engaged as bookkeeper for New Amsterdam, a Dutch Colony in the New World. He doesn't last long. He is replaced a year later because of improperly rendered accounts.

▶ The U.S. government creates the Treasury Department, including a comptroller and auditor.

Historical note: Early in life, Benjamin Franklin earned money keeping books of account, and later used those skills to create the postal service. Thomas Jefferson wrote two bookkeeping texts that were among the first books placed in the Library of Congress.

1789

Nineteenth Century

▶ Expanding railroad empires in the United States employ accountants as auditors independent of management.

1841 to 1850

▶ Scotland formally recognizes the accounting profession under the designation of "chartered accountants."

1854

▶ England formally recognizes the chartered accountant.

1880

2 "A History of Accountancy," *The Trusted Professional,* New York Society of Certified Public Accountants, November 1993. www.nysscpa.org/trustedprof/1103/tp24.htm.

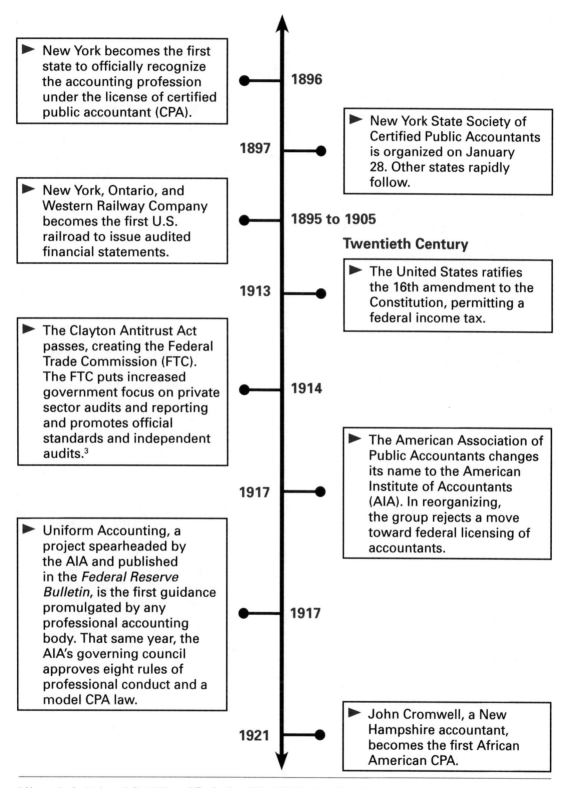

► New York becomes the first state to officially recognize the accounting profession under the license of certified public accountant (CPA).

1896

1897

► New York State Society of Certified Public Accountants is organized on January 28. Other states rapidly follow.

► New York, Ontario, and Western Railway Company becomes the first U.S. railroad to issue audited financial statements.

1895 to 1905

Twentieth Century

1913

► The United States ratifies the 16th amendment to the Constitution, permitting a federal income tax.

► The Clayton Antitrust Act passes, creating the Federal Trade Commission (FTC). The FTC puts increased government focus on private sector audits and reporting and promotes official standards and independent audits.[3]

1914

► The American Association of Public Accountants changes its name to the American Institute of Accountants (AIA). In reorganizing, the group rejects a move toward federal licensing of accountants.

1917

► Uniform Accounting, a project spearheaded by the AIA and published in the *Federal Reserve Bulletin*, is the first guidance promulgated by any professional accounting body. That same year, the AIA's governing council approves eight rules of professional conduct and a model CPA law.

1917

1921

► John Cromwell, a New Hampshire accountant, becomes the first African American CPA.

---

3 "Accounting for the Journal's First 100 Years: A Timeline from 1905 to 2005," Stephanie Moussalli, *Journal of Accountancy.* www.aicpa.org/pubs/jofa/oct2005/timeline.htm.

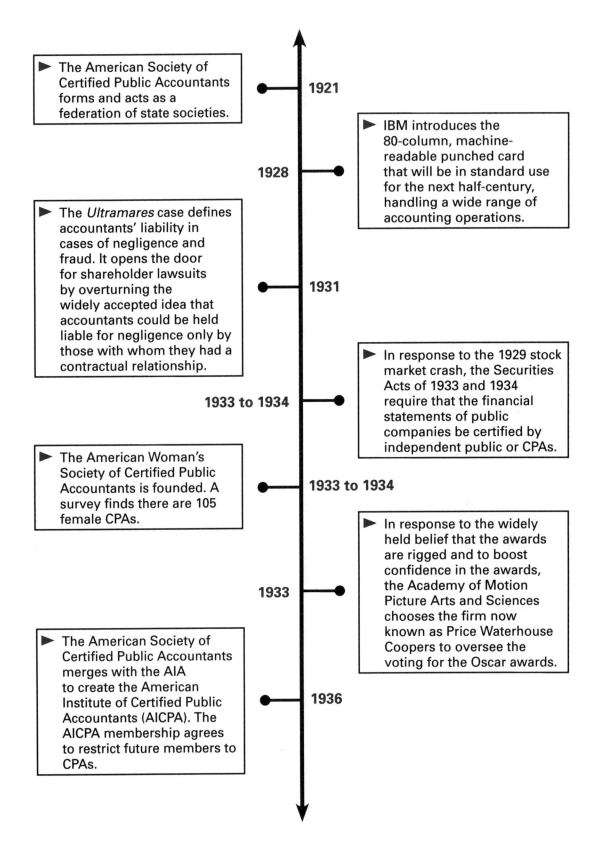

► The American Society of Certified Public Accountants forms and acts as a federation of state societies.

1921

1928

► IBM introduces the 80-column, machine-readable punched card that will be in standard use for the next half-century, handling a wide range of accounting operations.

► The *Ultramares* case defines accountants' liability in cases of negligence and fraud. It opens the door for shareholder lawsuits by overturning the widely accepted idea that accountants could be held liable for negligence only by those with whom they had a contractual relationship.

1931

► In response to the 1929 stock market crash, the Securities Acts of 1933 and 1934 require that the financial statements of public companies be certified by independent public or CPAs.

1933 to 1934

► The American Woman's Society of Certified Public Accountants is founded. A survey finds there are 105 female CPAs.

1933 to 1934

► In response to the widely held belief that the awards are rigged and to boost confidence in the awards, the Academy of Motion Picture Arts and Sciences chooses the firm now known as Price Waterhouse Coopers to oversee the voting for the Oscar awards.

1933

► The American Society of Certified Public Accountants merges with the AIA to create the American Institute of Certified Public Accountants (AICPA). The AICPA membership agrees to restrict future members to CPAs.

1936

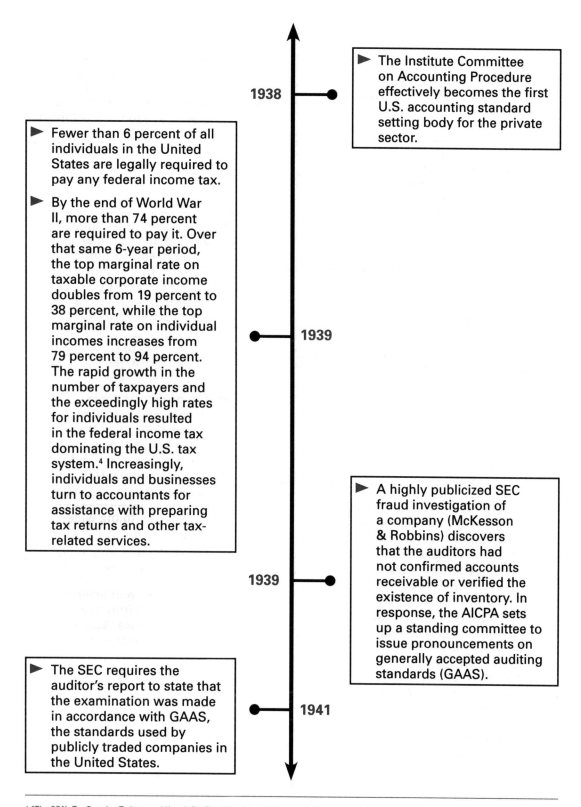

1938

▶ The Institute Committee on Accounting Procedure effectively becomes the first U.S. accounting standard setting body for the private sector.

▶ Fewer than 6 percent of all individuals in the United States are legally required to pay any federal income tax.

▶ By the end of World War II, more than 74 percent are required to pay it. Over that same 6-year period, the top marginal rate on taxable corporate income doubles from 19 percent to 38 percent, while the top marginal rate on individual incomes increases from 79 percent to 94 percent. The rapid growth in the number of taxpayers and the exceedingly high rates for individuals resulted in the federal income tax dominating the U.S. tax system.[4] Increasingly, individuals and businesses turn to accountants for assistance with preparing tax returns and other tax-related services.

1939

1939

▶ A highly publicized SEC fraud investigation of a company (McKesson & Robbins) discovers that the auditors had not confirmed accounts receivable or verified the existence of inventory. In response, the AICPA sets up a standing committee to issue pronouncements on generally accepted auditing standards (GAAS).

▶ The SEC requires the auditor's report to state that the examination was made in accordance with GAAS, the standards used by publicly traded companies in the United States.

1941

---

4 "The CPA's Tax Practice Today—and How It Got That Way," Ray M. Sommerfield and John E. Easton, *Journal of Accountancy*, May 1987.

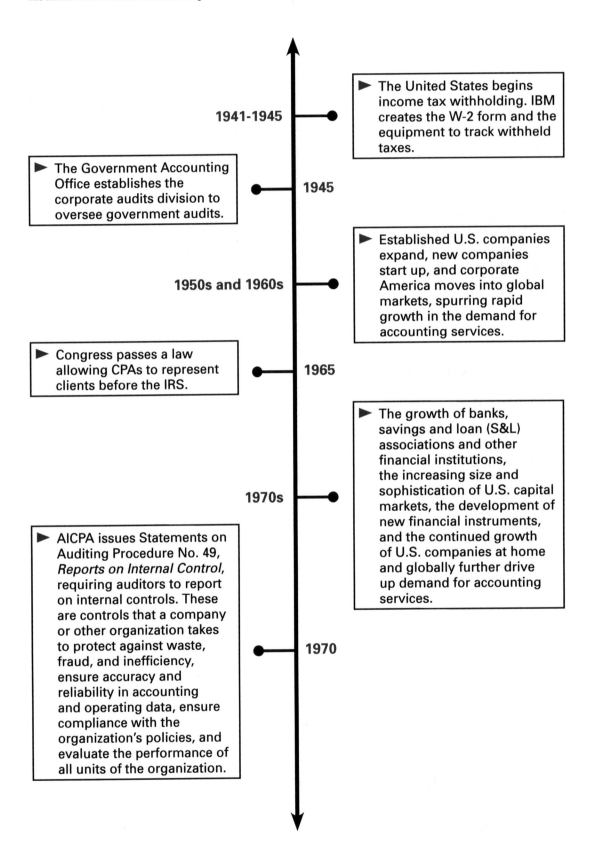

1941-1945

▶ The United States begins income tax withholding. IBM creates the W-2 form and the equipment to track withheld taxes.

▶ The Government Accounting Office establishes the corporate audits division to oversee government audits.

1945

▶ Established U.S. companies expand, new companies start up, and corporate America moves into global markets, spurring rapid growth in the demand for accounting services.

1950s and 1960s

▶ Congress passes a law allowing CPAs to represent clients before the IRS.

1965

▶ The growth of banks, savings and loan (S&L) associations and other financial institutions, the increasing size and sophistication of U.S. capital markets, the development of new financial instruments, and the continued growth of U.S. companies at home and globally further drive up demand for accounting services.

1970s

▶ AICPA issues Statements on Auditing Procedure No. 49, *Reports on Internal Control*, requiring auditors to report on internal controls. These are controls that a company or other organization takes to protect against waste, fraud, and inefficiency, ensure accuracy and reliability in accounting and operating data, ensure compliance with the organization's policies, and evaluate the performance of all units of the organization.

1970

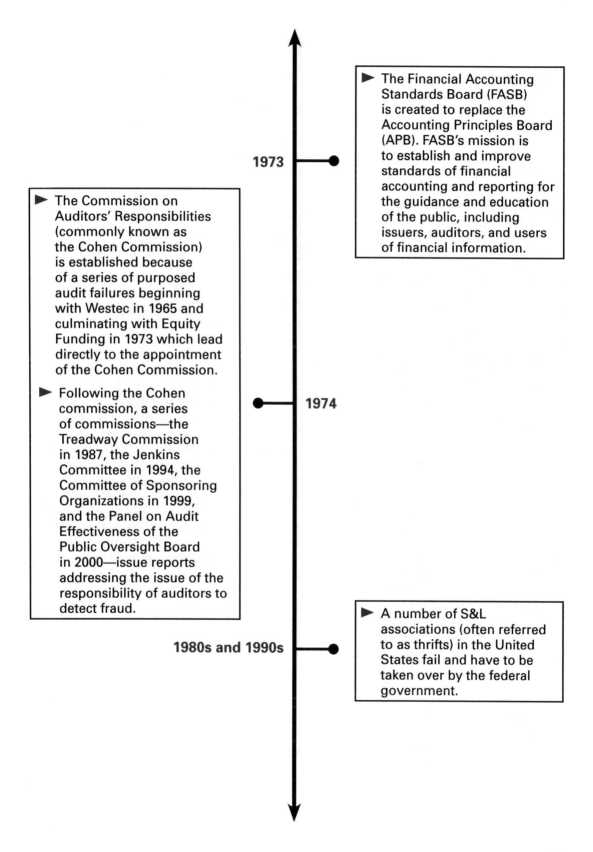

1973

▶ The Financial Accounting Standards Board (FASB) is created to replace the Accounting Principles Board (APB). FASB's mission is to establish and improve standards of financial accounting and reporting for the guidance and education of the public, including issuers, auditors, and users of financial information.

▶ The Commission on Auditors' Responsibilities (commonly known as the Cohen Commission) is established because of a series of purposed audit failures beginning with Westec in 1965 and culminating with Equity Funding in 1973 which lead directly to the appointment of the Cohen Commission.

▶ Following the Cohen commission, a series of commissions—the Treadway Commission in 1987, the Jenkins Committee in 1994, the Committee of Sponsoring Organizations in 1999, and the Panel on Audit Effectiveness of the Public Oversight Board in 2000—issue reports addressing the issue of the responsibility of auditors to detect fraud.

1974

1980s and 1990s

▶ A number of S&L associations (often referred to as thrifts) in the United States fail and have to be taken over by the federal government.

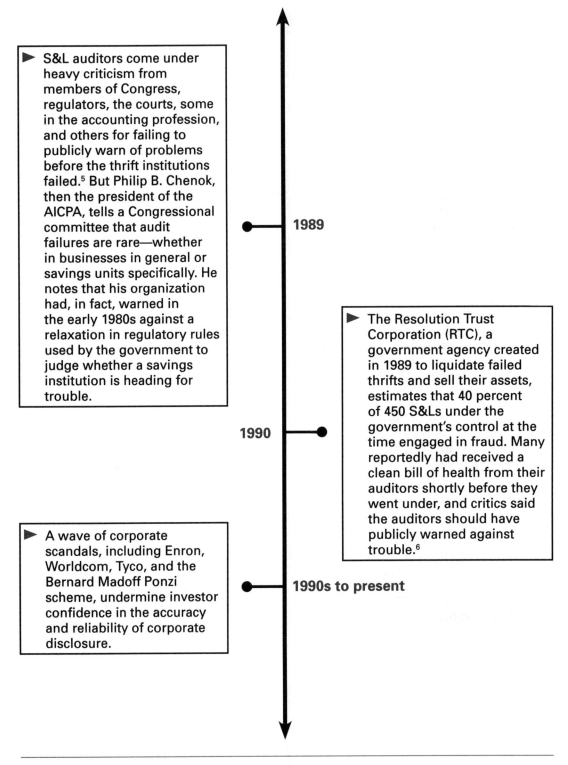

► S&L auditors come under heavy criticism from members of Congress, regulators, the courts, some in the accounting profession, and others for failing to publicly warn of problems before the thrift institutions failed.[5] But Philip B. Chenok, then the president of the AICPA, tells a Congressional committee that audit failures are rare—whether in businesses in general or savings units specifically. He notes that his organization had, in fact, warned in the early 1980s against a relaxation in regulatory rules used by the government to judge whether a savings institution is heading for trouble.

1989

The Resolution Trust Corporation (RTC), a government agency created in 1989 to liquidate failed thrifts and sell their assets, estimates that 40 percent of 450 S&Ls under the government's control at the time engaged in fraud. Many reportedly had received a clean bill of health from their auditors shortly before they went under, and critics said the auditors should have publicly warned against trouble.[6]

1990

A wave of corporate scandals, including Enron, Worldcom, Tyco, and the Bernard Madoff Ponzi scheme, undermine investor confidence in the accuracy and reliability of corporate disclosure.

1990s to present

5 "Where Were the Accountants," Leslie Wade, *New York Times*, March 12, 1989. http://query.nytimes.com/gst/fullpage.html?res=950DE7DD1F39 F931A25750C0A96F948260&sec=&spon=&pagewanted=all.

6 "Accountants Fear S&L Backlash," Alison Leigh Cowan, *The New York Times*, July 31, 1990.

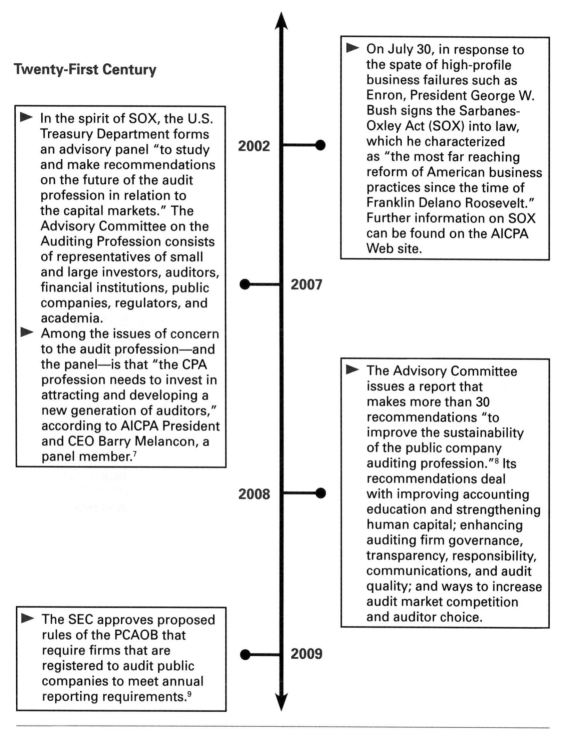

Twenty-First Century

► In the spirit of SOX, the U.S. Treasury Department forms an advisory panel "to study and make recommendations on the future of the audit profession in relation to the capital markets." The Advisory Committee on the Auditing Profession consists of representatives of small and large investors, auditors, financial institutions, public companies, regulators, and academia.

► Among the issues of concern to the audit profession—and the panel—is that "the CPA profession needs to invest in attracting and developing a new generation of auditors," according to AICPA President and CEO Barry Melancon, a panel member.[7]

2002

2007

2008

2009

► On July 30, in response to the spate of high-profile business failures such as Enron, President George W. Bush signs the Sarbanes-Oxley Act (SOX) into law, which he characterized as "the most far reaching reform of American business practices since the time of Franklin Delano Roosevelt." Further information on SOX can be found on the AICPA Web site.

► The Advisory Committee issues a report that makes more than 30 recommendations "to improve the sustainability of the public company auditing profession."[8] Its recommendations deal with improving accounting education and strengthening human capital; enhancing auditing firm governance, transparency, responsibility, communications, and audit quality; and ways to increase audit market competition and auditor choice.

► The SEC approves proposed rules of the PCAOB that require firms that are registered to audit public companies to meet annual reporting requirements.[9]

---

7 "U.S. Treasury Department Forms Panel to Look At Audit Profession," *The CPA Letter*, December 2007. AICPA.com, www.aicpa.org/Magazines+and+Newsletters/Newsletters/The+CPA+Letter/December+2007/U.S.+Treasury+Department+Forms+Panel+to+Look+at+Audit+Profession.htm.

8 "Fact Sheet: Final Report of the Advisory Committee on the Auditing Profession," Press Room, U.S. Department of the Treasury, September 26, 2008. www.treas.gov/press/releases/hp1158.htm.

9 "Audit Firms Now Fact Annual Reporting Requirement," Accounting and Auditing Update, Tammy Whitehouse, *Compliance Week*, August 18, 2009. www.complianceweek.com/blog/whitehouse/category/annual-reports/.

Chapter 1

Accounting: A Hot Career Path

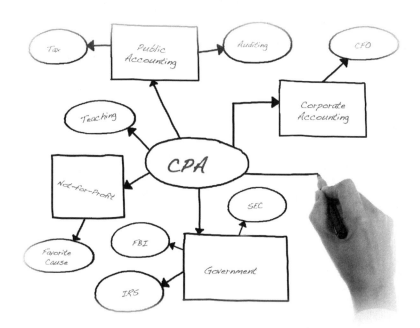

> "It's clear the accounting profession is at the forefront in enrollments, graduates and hiring."
>
> Denny Reigle, Director • Academic and Career Development, AICPA

As a Certified Public Accountant (CPA), You Can Work Just About Anywhere

What do Microsoft Corporation, the New York Yankees, the American Red Cross, the FBI, the University of Southern California, and Cleveland's Rock and Roll Hall of Fame and Museum have in common? At least this much—they all employ accountants. So do many U.S. corporations, small businesses, nonprofit organizations, government agencies, educational institutions and other organizations, in addition to accounting firms themselves. The 1.3 million accountants in the United States work in many different jobs, from auditing the world's biggest companies to preparing the financial reports of nonprofit organizations to assisting individuals with their tax returns. Some accountants even work for other accountants, such as auditing the financial statements of professional accounting firms. Some work for themselves—they have their own businesses, providing accounting services.

So, just what is accounting? What do accountants do? Why do people become accountants?

This chapter will give you the big picture, a little background to put accounting into context (but no quiz at the end), a look at the hot job market for accountants, why people go into accounting, and some of the career choices. Later chapters will look closely at the many facets of accounting, like public accounting or nonprofit accounting, at the many career opportunities in accounting,

and how you can get started on an exciting career in accounting. Exciting? Yes. As the many interviews in this book attest, accountants are at the center of the action in business, finance, and industry, in government, nonprofit organizations, and educational institutions, in sports and entertainment. These days, it seems just about everyone has need for an accountant. Who knows, the time may come when you can dial an emergency number and shout, "Send me an accountant! Fast!" An ambulance with a big "A" on the side will screech to a stop at your door and a team of accountants will come to the rescue. (O.K., maybe that's a stretch.)

About Accounting

If I were to ask my grandchildren what I do as an accountant, one grandchild would say, "You count numbers," another, "You shuffle papers," and a third, "You count money." The other nine wouldn't venture a guess. Will any of them become accountants? We'll see.

Besides my grandchildren, more formal definitions of accounting come from dictionaries and glossaries, accounting textbooks, and other sources.

Merriam-Webster's Dictionary says accounting is "the principle or practice of systematically recording, presenting and interpreting financial accounts."

The American Accounting Association has a broader definition, which states accounting is "the process of identifying, measuring and communicating economic information to permit informed judgments and decisions by users of the information."

Likewise, the American Institute of Certified Public Accountants (AICPA), a national organization of CPAs, broadly defines accounting as the art of recording, classifying and summarizing in a significant manner and in terms of money, transactions and events which are in part at least, of a financial character, and interpreting the results thereof."

The Accounting Principles Board says "accounting is a service activity. Its function is to provide quantitative information, primarily financial in nature, about economic entities that is intended to be useful in making economic decisions—in making reasoned choices among alternative courses of action."

A common thread that weaves through these and other definitions of accounting is the use of information. Note the following words associated with information:

- Identifying
- Systematically recording
- Measuring
- Summarizing
- Verifying
- Analyzing
- Interpreting
- Presenting
- Communicating

These are all steps in a process, which might look like this:

1. Identifying and recording, or deciding what information to use, and recording it in some form
2. Measuring, or quantitative analysis
3. Summarizing, or capturing the essential details in the information
4. Verifying, or providing an independent verification of the information
5. Analyzing and interpreting, or drawing meaning from the information
6. Presenting and communicating the information to users of the information
7. Delivering comprehensive, accurate, and reliable information to users

Beyond Crunching Numbers

Accountants are sometimes described as "number crunchers," and they do work with numbers, but the phrase doesn't capture the essence of accounting.

Essentially, accountants are in the information business—they provide or verify many different kinds of information. Accountants provide information in the sense that some accountants work inside organizations, producing financial statements, income statements or profit and loss statements, balance sheets, statements of cash flow, and statements of capital accounts and shareholder's equity. Accountants verify in the sense that other accountants are independent auditors who review, analyze, and verify the financial statements and other information produced by the organization. This information is used by a variety of decision-makers, such as the CEO or CFO of a Fortune 500 corporation, the owner of a small business, the head of a government agency, the board of directors of a nonprofit organization, an entrepreneur starting up a new company, the general manager of a Major League Baseball team, the audit committee of a local school district, the executive director of a pension fund, stock traders, investors, lenders, and many other people in a variety of positions with thousands of companies, businesses, government agencies, nonprofit organizations, and other organizations across the United States. Figure 1-1, "Who Uses Accounting Output?," lists the various entities that use accounting information and describes how it is used.

The value of this information depends on the competence, knowledge, skills, experience, and, most importantly, the integrity of the accountant. Whether the users of information are Chief Financial Officers (CFOs) of Fortune 500 companies or individuals preparing their tax returns, they depend on their accountants for accurate, complete, and useful information to help make decisions.

Accountants are trusted advisors who are indispensable to the management and operations of thousands of companies and businesses, government agencies, nonprofit organizations, small businesses, and other enterprises. Without accountants and accounting systems, companies would have no way of measuring their financial performance, benchmarking their performance against the competition, or communicating their financial results to shareholders and regulators. Government agencies would have no way of accounting for their revenue from taxes and other sources or how they spend taxpayer dollars. Nonprofit organizations would have no way of knowing how much money they are raising from donors or how they are spending that money.

Figure 1-1: *Who Uses Accounting Output?*

Regulators

Agencies

Nonprofits

Governmental Bodies

Taxing Authorities

Lenders

Investors

Shareholders

Management

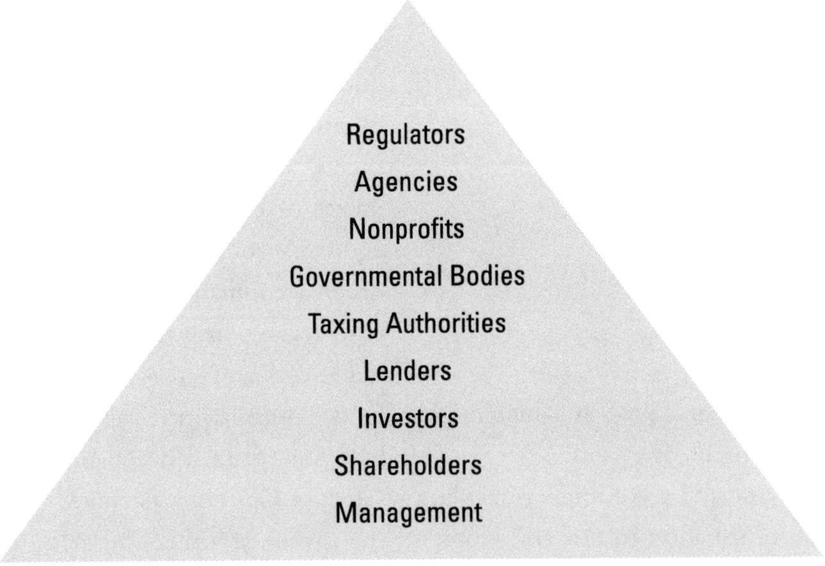

The private sector, including management of corporations and businesses, shareholders and investors, and lenders, is the largest user of accounting information. Companies are continually engaged in the process of creating, analyzing, evaluating, and disseminating accounting information for hundreds of different uses from automated tracking of inventory to recording sales or expenses to the preparation of annual financial statements. The public sector is the second-largest user. Government bodies, taxing authorities, and agencies use accounting information for many different purposes, such as preparing budgets to tracking spending. Government regulators use their own information as well as information produced by others; for example, taxing authorities use accounting software programs to analyze the tax returns of corporations and businesses. Finally, not-for-profit entities use accounting information to manage budgets, decide whether to invest in particular programs and services, track spending, and many other purposes.

To Whom are Accountants Accountable?

Accountants are accountable not only to their employers or clients, but to the public. Many people and organizations depend on the accuracy and reliability of the information that accountants produce or verify. They include investors in a company, a company's managers and workers, banks, and other lenders that provide financing to a company, consumers who buy a company's products or services, government regulators, and tax collecting authorities. Accountants for a nonprofit organization or its outside auditors produce or verify information, such as the organization's spending to alleviate poverty, create jobs, help the homeless, improve healthcare, or provide educational opportunities that is needed by the organization's directors, executives, and staff, donors, and agencies and organizations that are the recipients of the nonprofit's funding. Accountants and auditors produce or verify information produced by federal, state, or local government agencies that is needed by agency executives and staff, political leaders, and the public. A state legislature, governor's office, cities and counties, the public, and agency officials themselves, all have a need to know the budget of a state transportation agency for funding highways and roads.

Accounting: The Profession

Accountants are members of a profession like doctors, lawyers, architects, and engineers. Although the term *profession* has different meanings, it generally is an occupation that

- has formal qualifications.
- requires specialized education and knowledge.
- requires continuing education.
- has a specific, practical purpose (such as providing accounting services).
- includes membership in a professional society (such as the AICPA).
- has a system of self-regulation based on a code of ethics.
- is subject to government review and licensing.
- serves the public interest.

CPA Designation

In many states, anyone can call themselves an accountant. However, not all accountants are CPAs any more than all health care professionals are doctors or registered nurses. The CPA is a state-licensed professional who has passed what is known as the Uniform CPA Examination and has met specific education and experience requirements. Many accountants seek to become CPAs because the CPA designation opens up more career opportunities (for example, only CPAs can audit public companies); CPAs earn the recognition of peers and promote public trust. Becoming a CPA may also mean more income. One indication of the interest in the CPA designation is that the AICPA has more than 350,000 members, including CPAs in business and industry, public practice, government, nonprofit, and education. The AICPA develops standards for audit and other services provided by CPAs, provides educational guidance materials to its members, creates and grades the Uniform CPA Exam, and monitors and enforces compliance with the profession's audit, technical, and ethical standards. Table 1-1 illustrates the differences between the professional requirements for CPAs and accountants.

Table 1-1: *CPA Versus Accountant: Professional Requirements*

	CPA	Accountant
Required to pass CPA exam	X	
Required to obtain state license to practice*	X	
May be required to pass ethics exam (depends on state)	X	
Generally required to complete 150 hours of college credits	X	
Must meet continuing education requirements to keep license	X	
Required to undergo rigorous peer review (review by other CPAS of professional competency)	X	
Required to observe professional standards in all services provided to the public	X	
Provide public attestation services (including auditing)	X	
Provide tax services**	X	X
Provide bookkeeping services	X	X

* CPAs generally must have 1–2 years of professional experience to obtain license.

** Depending on the state, an accountant may have to obtain a license to provide tax services.

As professionals, many CPAs work for profit-making enterprises, including public accounting firms. Among other functions, public accounting firms audit the books of public companies and are regulated by the Securities and Exchange Commission (SEC) and other regulators. In addition, CPAs work for public companies (companies whose shares are listed and traded on stock exchanges); these companies are regulated by the SEC and other regulators. CPAs also work for private companies that are subject to various types of government regulations. They also work for the regulators—government agencies whose responsibilities include regulation of the private sector. And they work for nonprofit and other organizations. Finally, some CPAs start their own businesses, providing accounting services to clients. All of these topics will be covered later in this book.

Core Functions

Accounting has four core functions: accounting, audit, assurance, and tax. Accountants generally work in one or more of these functional areas; they may also specialize in certain areas, such as litigation accounting, and in a certain industry, such as real estate. In the past, the largest accounting firms also did consulting. (See the glossary for definitions of accounting terms and other terms used in this book.)

Accounting

Look inside most organizations today and you'll find accountants. Manufacturers, producers, and distributors, financial institutions, small businesses, professional services firms, nonprofit organizations, schools, hospitals, and other institutions, government agencies, and other organizations, all employ accountants One of the most important functions of internal accountants is to record an organization's financial activities and prepare its financial statement for a particular period: a month, a quarter, a year, or some other period. External accountants, known as independent auditors, audit their work and issue an independent report on whether the financial statement fairly represents the financial position of the organization.

In profit-making enterprises, accountants measure a business's profit or loss and communicate the determinants of its profit or loss in a financial statement known as the *income statement*, or *statement of operations*. It measures revenue inflows and expense outflows, and the difference between the two—a profit if revenues exceed expenses, and a loss if expenses exceed revenue. The following is an example of a simple income statement:

XYZ Company: Statement of Operations

Revenues		$2,000
Operating expense	$400	
Depreciation	200	
Interest expense	100	
Interest & other income	(100)	
		$ 600
Earnings before income tax		$1,400
Income tax expense		
Current	$500	
Deferred	300	$ 800
Net earnings		$ 600

Accountants prepare and present another important report known as the *statement of financial condition*, also known as the *balance sheet*. It uses the double entry bookkeeping system. One side of the balance sheet shows the assets of a business. These are the economic resources used in the business. The values of these assets are recorded on the balance sheet at historical cost, their values when they were acquired—whether two months or two decades ago. The other side of the balance sheet lists the liabilities of a business, such as loans to acquire assets, plus the owner's investment (equity) in the business and profit retained in the business. The assets equal the liabilities plus owner's equity and retained profits.

The following is an example of a balance sheet:

XYZ Company: Balance Sheet

Assets:	
Cash	$ 100
Accounts receivable	300
Inventory	500
Other assets	200
Total Assets	$1,100
Liabilities and shareholders equity	
Liabilities:	
Accounts payable & accrued expenses	$ 200
Notes payable	300
Income taxes payable	100
Total liabilities	$ 600
Shareholders Equity	
Preferred stock	$ 50
Common stock	100
Paid in capital	150
Retained earnings	200
Total shareholders equity	$ 500
Total liabilities & shareholders equity	$1,100

The following is an example of a statement of cash flow:

XYZ Company: Statement of Cash Flow

Net earnings	$1,000
Depreciation and amortization	200
Decrease in accounts payable and accrued expenses	(300)
Decrease in accounts receivable	(200)
Increase in other assets	400
Net cash provided by operations	$1,100
Cash flow from investing activities	
Capital expenditures	($ 300)
Proceeds from disposition of other investments	500
Net cash used in investment activities	$ 200
Cash flow from financing activities	
Borrowings from banks	$ 500
Increase in common stock	0
Dividends paid	(100)
Net cash provided by financing activities	$ 400
Net increase in cash	$1,700

Another key element of the financial statement is the *statement of cash flows*, which measures a business's cash inflows and outflows during a period and the net increase or decrease in cash flows. This net figure can be different from a business's profit or loss.

The financial statement—the income statement, balance sheet, and statement of cash flows—has many uses. Owners and managers use it to evaluate the performance of a business and decide whether any action should be taken to improve its performance. Investors use it to consider whether to invest in the business. If the business is in a regulated industry like banking, regulators may use it in gathering information to assess the overall performance of the banking sector. Prospective employees may use it to gauge a business's financial health before deciding whether to seek employment there.

Generally Accepted Accounting Principles

Financial statements are based on generally accepted accounting principles (GAAP), the authoritative rules for preparing and presenting financial statements, and for disclosure of financial information. Unless they say otherwise, public companies and other companies and businesses are assumed to follow GAAP in their financial reporting. (Because of differences in the reporting of financial information under GAAP and the federal tax code, many large companies maintain two sets of books: one for GAAP reporting and the other for tax reporting.) If a company is not using GAAP, it is incumbent on the company to make clear that it is using a different form of reporting that is less comprehensive than GAAP; for example, a simple cash receipts and cash disbursements form of accounting. Some companies—small businesses in particular—use a tax basis for their financial statements, based on the rules in the federal tax code for preparing and presenting financial information. As a result, companies could maintain a single set of books.

The primary private sector authority responsible for issuing and updating pronouncements on GAAP is the Financial Accounting Standards Board (FASB). On a larger scale, the SEC has broad authority over accounting and financial reporting standards for publicly

traded companies. This includes authority over FASB.

GAAP uses what is known as the cost basis of accounting. It's the original cost (also known as the historical cost) of an asset. If you bought 10 shares of stock in 2001 for $10 a share, the cost basis of that stock is still $10 a share, regardless of whether those shares are trading today at $2 or 50 cents a share. Critics of cost accounting say that its usefulness is diminished by the fact that it looks backward to when the asset was acquired, and not at the current value of the asset. This can result in severe distortions of asset value. I know of one company that is carrying land on its books at 75 cents an acre, or the cost of the land when the company acquired it more than 100 years ago under a Spanish land grant. Today, the land is worth millions of dollars an acre.

In the United States, there is a push for a fair market value system, which essentially values an asset at its current value. Thus, if your stock is trading on the New York Stock Exchange at $30 a share at the close of trading for the day, that is the stock's fair market value. FASB issued FASB Statement No. 157, Fair Value Measurements, intended to clarify the definition of fair value accounting and when it might be used. It is not intended as a substitute for GAAP, but to augment GAAP. If you study accounting in school, you will learn all about GAAP, leaving no gap in your knowledge.

The International Financial Reporting Standards (IFRSs) system used by many countries is based on a form of fair value accounting. The SEC is considering whether to require U.S. companies to use IFRSs. For updates on IFRSs, go to the AICPA's IFRS Resources at www.IFRS.com.

Other Functions

Although preparing or validating financial statements is one of the most important responsibilities of accountants, accountants also perform many other functions. They manage the internal financial operations of a business, including cash receipts and cash payments, accounts receivable and accounts payable, payroll, purchases, inventory, and property records. They determine how to measure and record the costs of products and how to allocate costs within a company. They prepare reports for the managers of a business, such as an analysis of a company's profits or its sales volume. Accountants prepare an organization's federal and state income tax returns as well as its sales, payroll, and property taxes.

Auditing

Two types of auditors—*internal auditors* and *independent auditors*—are frequently called accountants. *Internal auditing* is intended to help an organization accomplish its objectives by bringing a systematic, disciplined approach to evaluate and improve the effectiveness of risk management, control, and governance processes. *Internal auditors* are employed by companies or other organizations to provide counsel for improving controls, processes and procedures, performance, and risk management. They examine and evaluate a company's financial and information systems, management procedures, and internal controls to ensure that records are accurate and controls are adequate. They suggest ways to reduce costs, enhance revenues, and improve profits.

They review company operations, evaluating their efficiency, effectiveness, and compliance with corporate policies and government regulations. They help to provide internal training in risk management, fraud management, and other issues. And they educate management and the company's board on critical issues.

Independent auditors determine whether an organization's economic activities are fairly reflected in its financial statements. CPAs examine an organization's financial statements and its statement of operations (income statement) and express an opinion regarding whether they fairly present the financial condition of the organization. An audit requires a thorough understanding of the company's strategic goals, business plan, operations, financial structure, internal controls, and other aspects of the organization. Auditors conduct a detailed examination of an organization's internal controls, including the procedures for authorizing transactions, safeguarding assets, and ensuring the accuracy of financial records. They analyze financial documents, check bank balances, review inventory, physically inspect assets, check depreciation schedules, examine contracts and review minutes of meetings. They discuss a company's financial conditions, operations, and business plans with its directors, managers, and others. Finally, the audit work ends in the issuance of an audit report. The auditor issues an opinion on the fairness of the financial statement, a process that is known as an *attest function.*

The SEC requires the financial statements of all publicly held U.S. companies to be audited every year by an independent auditor. It also requires the annual report of every

Adventures in Inventory

One of the common functions of auditors is to verify inventory, that is, the goods or products in a retail store or raw material in a manufacturer's warehouse that hasn't been sold or used by the end of a calendar year or some other time period. Inventory has value—often substantial value. For example, 100 computers valued at $500 each have a total value of $50,000, and companies need to determine the number of computers or other goods in inventory as well as their value for financial reporting purposes. They also need to take inventory for security reasons, such as preventing theft.

The auditor's client, whether it's a company or business, a government agency, or other organization, actually does the inventory. If you ever worked in a retail store or manufacturing plant, you may have some experience doing inventory, possibly at night or on weekends when the company is closed. Whereas the company does the inventory, its auditor provides independent verification of the inventory. As part of this process, the auditor samples the inventory, that is, it counts selected inventory items.

When I was just starting out as a young accountant, I spent a lot of time traveling around the country to visit clients and verify their inventory—all kinds of inventory. A person known as a comp operator traveled with us. He operated a 10-key machine that recorded inventory. We'd shout out numbers to him and he'd plug them into the machine. Today, you can do inventory much more efficiently using computers and hand held calculators, but I kind of miss shouting out numbers to that comp operator.

One time I found myself in a manufacturing plant, dropping a dipstick into a big vat of some kind of liquid and trying to figure out how much of the stuff was left. At least I didn't fall in. I might have vanished, and with it my career in accounting. Another time I verified the shoe count on the shelves of a retailer. You have no idea how many different kinds of shoes there are until you've done shoe inventory. The ones on display in the store are only the tip of the proverbial iceberg, or "shoeberg."

My most memorable experience, one that a kid from the Bronx could especially appreciate, was spending time on a farm verifying the farmer's count of his pigs, chickens, and other livestock. One important lesson I learned was not to count chickens before they're hatched.

Just kidding.

Later in my career, I participated in an audit of a developer who was in the business of buying land, putting in roads, power lines, water systems and other improvements, and dividing the land into individual lots. The developer sold the lots to homebuilders, and titles to the lots, or proof of ownership, passed from the developer to the builders. The builders, in turn, would build houses and sell them to home buyers.

As it turned out, a bookkeeper working for the developer had concocted an elaborate scheme involving one of the developer's projects with hundreds of lots. She secretly created a shell corporation and transferred the title of every tenth lot or so from the developer to the shell. Her plan was to sell these lots to builders through the shell company and pocket the sales proceeds. If she had gotten away with this shell game, she had a lot to gain. If she didn't, she had a lot to lose, starting with her job.

Our audit uncovered the scam, which she tried to justify by saying she worked very hard for the developer and deserved a share of its profits. It was sort of a variation on the song, "this land is your land." Her version was, "your lot is my lot." Needless to say, her rationalization for her actions didn't go over very well with her employer. But the episode did demonstrate the value of conducting audits. Score one for the auditors.

That's Not the Academy Awards—That's an Assurance Service!

Probably the most famous assurance service is controlling and counting the ballots for the annual Academy Awards ceremony. Since 1933, the firm now known as PricewaterhouseCoopers has been managing the annual balloting under the Academy's direction. And how does the firm count the ballots? The old fashioned way. By hand. The firm says this provides better security than electronic tallying.

Accountants not only tabulate the votes for the Academy Awards, they also have been featured in a number of movies. A sample:

In *Dave*, a comedy about an ordinary citizen impersonating the President of the United States, Charles Grodin plays an accountant who drops by the White House to advise the "President" on budget cutting.

Grodin also plays an accountant who steals from the rich and gives to the poor in *Midnight Run*. After jumping bail, he's chased by bounty hunters, the FBI, and the mob.

In *Ghostbusters*, Rick Moranis plays an accountant possessed by evil spirits.

In *The Producers*, Zero Mostel persuades accountant Gene Wilder to collaborate in a scheme to rip off old ladies.[*]

In *Casino Royale* (2006), Eva Green played Vesper, an accountant who helped James Bond (Daniel Craig) fight the evil Le Chiffre (Mads Mikkelsen).

In the *Crimson Permanent Assurance*, a short film that precedes Monty Python's Meaning of Life, members of a staid British accountancy transform themselves into pirate accountants who rebel against their autocratic American owner.

[*] "Accountants in Movies & TV," John Schachter + Associates, www.johnschachter.com/Accountants_in_Movies.htm

publicly held corporation to contain a "Report of Independent Public Accountants." The standard audit report states that the goal of the audit is "to obtain reasonable assurance that the financial statements are free of material misstatement" and that the audit was performed "in accordance with generally accepted auditing standards." Mandatory audit requirements also extend to most pension plans, local and state governments, and certain not-for-profit organizations. Audits by CPAs also have become part of real estate and other commercial agreements, as well as many bank loan requirements. CPAs also conduct other types of audits, such as tax audits or environmental audits.

Assurance

Accountants also provide what are known as *assurance services*. These are defined as "independent professional services that improve the quality of information, or its context, for business or individual decision-makers."[1] They represent an evolution in the nature of services provided by CPAs, who provide not only accounting information but also many other types of information that people need in order to make decisions. Assurance services are generally distinct from *consulting services*, which generally involve providing advice to clients or creating internal systems such as new or upgraded computer systems. Types of assurance services include financial forecasts and projections as well as assurance

1 American Institute of Certified Public Accountants (AICPA) Special Committee on Assurance Services

on internal controls, e-commerce, system reliability, comprehensive risk assessments, business performance measurement, policy compliance (an organization is in compliance with its own policies), and mergers and acquisitions.

Tax

Tax services have been a growth area for many accounting firms. New tax laws and regulations, continuous changes in existing laws, the globalization of business, the increasing complexity of the business environment and other factors have all increased demand for tax services.

A basic service is the preparation of tax returns for corporations and other organizations as well as individuals. All taxpayers must keep records for their tax returns. Larger companies may keep two sets of books, one for tax and one for accounting. Tax accountants review those books and reconcile the differences between tax and accounting. Among other reasons, they do this to calculate an organization's provision for income taxes, which is reflected in its financial statements.

CPAs are often asked to advise a company on strategies to minimize taxes or to take advantage of tax opportunities such as new government tax incentives. For example, businesses frequently have to make economic decisions such as whether to invest in a new plant, new equipment, or to buy real estate. The implications of tax deductions, such as depreciation or interest expense could have a material effect on a company's return on investment and therefore its decision to make the investment.

A Word About Consulting

Over the last few decades, the largest accounting firms have built up highly profitable consulting services. The consulting services, for example, advise clients on mergers and acquisitions, capital market transactions, or buying, installing, and managing computer systems. When firms began to earn more money from consulting rather than from providing auditing services, critics said they faced a conflict of interest in providing consulting services to clients for whom they also served as independent auditors.[*] The firms long maintained that firewalls in their organizations clearly separated consulting and auditing and enabled them to maintain their independence. Over the last 10 years, however, they have spun off their consulting divisions. Arthur Andersen & Co. spun off its consultancy as Andersen Consulting, which later changed its name to Accenture and went public in an initial public offering. Accenture is now one of the world's largest management consulting firms. (Arthur Andersen subsequently went out of business). Ernst & Young sold its consultancy to the French group Capgemini. KPMG spun off its consultancy as KPMG Consulting Inc., a provider of management and technology services that later changed its name to BearingPoint Inc. PricewaterhouseCoopers sold its consultancy to IBM.[**] When these accounting and consulting practices were separated, some of the accountants who worked for the accounting firms moved over to the consulting firms.

[*] "PwC Consulting to go Public," CNN Money, January 31, 2002, http://money.cnn.com/2002/01/31/news/pwc/index.htm

[**] "IBM Swallows PwC Consulting," Thor Olavsrud, Internet News, July 30, 2002, www.internetnews.com/bus-news/article.php/1436271

Another area where tax is significant is in compensation. Most senior executives have some form of base compensation as well as incentives such as stock options, performance shares, stock appreciation rights or other participating agreements. The base compensation would be taxed at ordinary income tax rates. Some of the incentives might be structured to create future capital gains, which are taxed at a lower rate than ordinary income.

A CFO looks at the tax implications at almost every capital transaction that a company enters. The decision whether to raise debt or equity is driven by both financial and tax considerations.

Other Functions

In addition to working in one or more of the core functional areas, accountants also provide a variety of other specialized services. Some focus exclusively on a specialty area where they have developed a high level of knowledge and experience. These functions, to name a few, include:

- Forensics
- Information Technology
- Environmental (Green)
- Management Consulting
- Restructuring
- Entreprenurial
- Expert Witness
- Mergers and Acquisitions
- Litigation Accounting
- Personal Financial Planning
- Strategic Planning
- Business Process Outsourcing
- Transaction Services
- International
- Enterprise Risk Management
- Insolvency
- Feasibility

Chapter 4 provides a look at these specialized functions, including hot markets such as forensic accounting, environmental (green) accounting, restructuring, and more.

Industry Specialization

Some accounting firms and accountants specialize in services to a particular industry such as real estate, healthcare, information technology, or banking. Clients in these industries require accountants who are highly knowledgeable about the industry and experienced in working with companies and businesses within the industry.

Where Accountants Work

In general, accountants work in public accounting or corporate, government, or non-profit accounting. Some teach at colleges and universities.

Public Accounting

Public accounting firms provide auditing, tax, accounting, and consulting services to businesses and individuals. These firms range in size from single practitioner to large international firms with hundreds of offices worldwide and thousands of professionals. Accountants in these firms work with a variety of companies, organizations, and institutions, and, in the process, gain wide professional exposure and experience.

Corporate Accounting

Accountants work in a variety of positions for companies and businesses, ranging from the large multinational corporations to small businesses, and in every industry from aerospace to computer software to financial services to transportation. They also work for professional services firms that provide accounting, architecture, legal, educational, engineering, environmental, human resources, security, and other services to clients; for hospitals and other healthcare organizations; and for a variety of other organizations. In large organizations, they may work in specific areas such as internal audit, tax, or computer systems. In small companies, they may have responsibility for a variety of functions.

Government Accounting

More than 100,000 accountants in the United States work in federal government agencies such as the General Accounting Office, the IRS, the SEC, the Defense Contract Audit Agency, and so on. Many others work in state government agencies such as the Franchise Tax Board, the Board of Equalization, the Employment Development Department, and so on. At the local level, accountants work for various county and city agencies, special districts, and other entities.

Nonprofit Organizations

Nonprofit organizations provide goods or services considered socially desirable by and for the general public, a community, or its members. About 1.2 million tax-exempt organizations currently exist in the United States, and they cover the gamut of civic, religious, social, professional, scientific organizations, hospitals, schools, colleges, universities, and voluntary health and welfare organizations, and so on. They range in size from local agencies to large organizations of national or international scope, and most employ CPAs for a variety of positions.

Teaching

Accounting could use a few good teachers—in fact, a lot of good teachers. Rising enrollments in accounting programs, looming retirements of more faculty members, the startup of accounting programs at more schools, and the expansion of accounting curriculums are creating more demand for PhD faculty to teach and to direct accounting programs at colleges and universities across the country.

Why People Choose Accounting as a Career

People choose careers for a variety of reasons. The following paragraphs examine the reasons noted by those who choose the accounting profession.

Interesting Work

The solitary accountant, wearing a green eye shade and glasses, spends lonely hours and days cloistered in a musty room, surrounded by stacks of paperwork, toiling over reams of numbers no more. Today's accountants are likely to be found working in teams or out in the field, meeting with clients and others or, increasingly, working from home part of the time. Technology enables today's accountant to work more productively and efficiently than ever before. Not to mention, accountants work on a variety of projects, helping to audit the financial statements of a Fortune 500 corporation, assisting the founder of a startup company in preparing financial information for potential investors, providing research and analysis to a manager of a pension fund for use in making investment decisions, working with a small business in preparing its tax returns, assisting a sports star in managing their investment portfolio, or investigating a business fraud.

Develop Broad Set of Skills

Accountants today have the opportunity to develop a broad set of skills—skills that are much in demand. "While being skilled at managing and analyzing figures and facts will be important for your career path, today's companies are seeking to hire—and are paying well for—accountants who can bring something extra to the table," notes Robert Half International, an international recruiting firm specializing in finance and accounting.[2] "Wanted are professionals with strong business, technical and interpersonal skills, and the potential to become trusted advisors who can help the organization navigate through an increasingly complex business environment."

Essential to Business

Accounting is indispensable to business. Accountants prepare, analyze, present, and verify information that is used by companies and businesses to make decisions such as starting a new line of business, restructuring, opening a new manufacturing plant or office, hiring new managers or employees, investing in new technology, or improving internal audit controls. In the business world, accountants are at the center of the action.

On-the-job Learning

Ask students why they decided to study accounting, and an often-heard answer is that it's a great way to learn about business. Whether they are working for a public accounting firm with business clients, or working on the inside for a company, accountants get a close-up look at how an organization operates. That's also true of accountants who work in government, nonprofit, and other sectors. They learn not only how an organization works, but also what it takes to succeed in an organization, which is an understanding of the organization's vision and culture and one's role and responsibilities in the organization, plus discipline, focus, attention to detail, and other attributes of success.

Work with People

"Accounting is 25 percent working with numbers and 75 percent working with people," said a partner with a Big Four firm. Yes, accountants crunch the numbers to produce balance sheets, income statements, and a variety of other information, but they spend most of their time working with their colleagues, managers, and clients. Their work and professional interests often involve other people. An auditor with a large accounting firm may meet with the CEO of a major corporation; the CFO of a nonprofit organization may meet with its outside directors; the owner of a small accounting firm with a prospective client; an IRS recruiter with college students; or a new accountant with members of a professional society.

Challenging Work

People also like accounting because it is challenging work. Companies, businesses, government agencies, nonprofit organizations, and others, look to accountants for help in solving problems, addressing issues, and meeting objectives. A company may ask its accountants for assistance in preparing for

---

2 "The Modern Accountant: A Well Rounded Executive," Robert Half International

the multibillion dollar acquisition of another company, a nonprofit in balancing its budget, a regulatory agency in investigating fraud, or an entrepreneur in planning his or her estate. Such expectations require accountants to have strong critical thinking and problem solving skills. By honing these skills early in their careers, accountants will be better prepared for the day when they have to make critical decisions as a partner in an accounting firm, the head of a government agency, the CFO of a nonprofit organization, or the principal of a small accounting firm.

Faster Career Advancement

With more baby boomers reaching retirement age over the next decade, young accountants will have more opportunities to advance, and more quickly, than in the past. But that also means that they will have to be prepared to assume more responsibility quicker.

Multiple Career Paths

Accounting is the foundation for a range of career pursuits not only in the accounting profession but also in business, government, education, nonprofit, consulting, and other sectors. An accountant may spend his or her career with a public accounting firm or move from public accounting into business, industry, government, or education. Michael Roth began in public accounting; today, he's chairman and CEO of The Interpublic Group, a global advertising and marketing company. Ed Altamonte founded his own accounting firm and went on to become auditor general of the

state of Rhode Island. Marilyn Niemark started with Arthur Andersen; now, she's a professor of accountancy at Baruch College, part of the City University of New York system.

Transferable Skills

Accountants have portable skills. They can apply their critical thinking, technical, communication, and other skills not only in accounting, but in other areas of business, government, education, the nonprofit sector, and many more. They can build on their skills and experience to achieve their career goals, whether they aspire to start their own business, become a partner in a public accounting firm, teach in a university accounting program, or manage a nonprofit organization.

Opportunities for Public Service

Beyond revenue generating work, many accountants give back to their communities by providing pro bono services to nonprofit organizations such as Accountants for the Public Interest, a national nonprofit organization whose mission is to encourage accountants to volunteer their time and expertise to nonprofit, small businesses, and individuals who need but cannot afford professional accounting services.[3] CPAs often volunteer for organizations whose goals they support or with which they feel an emotional connection.[4] Services offered commonly include consulting on accounting and auditing matters and providing accounting or income tax assistance and help in preparing for audits.

---

3 Accountants for the Public Interest home page

4 "Giving Back: Pro Bono Accounting Services," William E. Shafer, L. Jane Park, and Alice A. Ketchand, *Journal of Accountancy*, http://www.journalofaccountancy.com/Issues/1999/Nov/shaferl.htm

Educational Foundation

An undergraduate degree in accounting is the foundation for graduate education and a future career. Some graduates go on to earn master's degrees in law, business, taxation, and other disciplines, and then become practicing lawyers, business executives, or tax advisors. And in some states, graduates of 4-year (120-hour) accounting programs must complete another 30 hours, usually another year of school, to meet the 150-hour educational requirement for a CPA license. (This is covered in further detail in chapter 3.) From their experience in school, some students may decide to pursue their PhD in accounting and join a college faculty, or they may be interested in teaching in a school's professional development program for working professionals.

Job Outlook for CPAs

At the time the Sarbanes-Oxley Act (SOX) passed in 2002, there was concern in the accounting profession that accounting scandals at Enron, Tyco, and other companies, would dampen interest in accounting as a career. In fact, just the opposite happened. The scandals and subsequent SOX reforms focused public attention on the importance of accountants in helping companies to maintain ethical standards, and the consequences to companies and their executives when those standards are not maintained. Students became more interested in accounting as a career just as SOX sparked a hiring boom in accounting. Public accounting firms increased staff to assist public companies in reviewing, evaluating, and strengthening their internal controls to comply with Section 404. The recession that began in 2007 has caused CPA firms, companies, and other employers to slow the hiring of CPAs, but CPAs still remain in demand, particularly in small CPA firms, and in areas such as financial analysis, budgeting and forecasting, and in advising clients and companies on reducing taxes.[5]

Employment

Although SOX sparked an increase in employment in accounting, other trends are also powering job growth, including the following:

International

Globalization of business. The globalization of business has created more demand for accounting and tax expertise and services related to international trade and investment.

Increasing complexity of business. As businesses continue to grow and expand globally, the volume and complexity of information reviewed by accountants and auditors regarding costs, expenditures, taxes, and internal controls is likewise expanding.[6]

International shortage of accountants. A worldwide shortage of experienced accounting professionals is creating opportunities for U.S. accountants to work overseas for global businesses and accounting firms. Patrick Henry, a

---

5 "Accountants Say Recession Has Changed Their Job Responsibilities," press release, Ajilon Professional Staffing, April 22, 2009, http://ajilon.com/professional/AboutUs/Pressroom/Pages/Accountantssayrecessionhaschangedtheirjobresponsibilities.aspx

6 "Occupational Outlook Handbook: 2008-2009 Edition," Bureau of Labor Statistics, U.S. Department of Labor, www.bls.gov/oco/ocos001.htm#outlook

partner with Deloitte, spent part of his career with the firm in Hong Kong, where he was the lead partner for the Asia/Pacific region. India has about 130,000 accountants versus more than 1 million in the United States.[7] China could face a shortage of as many as 100,000 accountants, and there is a need to train local accountants in Western business practices.

Adoption of IFRSs. The adoption of IFRSs by many countries is adding to worldwide demand for accountants.

United States

U.S. economic growth. Despite a cyclical slowdown in 2008, the U.S. economy will continue to grow, and the number of U.S. businesses will increase, requiring more accountants and auditors to set up books, prepare taxes, and provide management advice.

Baby boomer retirements. Employers are scrambling to hire, train, and promote a new generation of accountants to replace the growing numbers of baby boomers—those born between 1946 and 1964—who are starting to retire. Business executives surveyed in 2008 by Robert Half International, found that baby boomer retirements will have the greatest impact on the workforce over the next decade.[8]

Shortage of U.S. accountants. Despite record numbers of students graduating from accounting programs and record hiring of accountants, companies, businesses, accounting firms, government agencies, nonprofit organizations, and other employers, are having difficulty meeting their hiring goals. Competition for accounting talent is intensifying.

Consolidation of public accounting firms. A wave of consolidations and mergers of public accounting firms in the United States is expected over the next decade as smaller firms seek the advantages of size and scale in attracting employees and clients, growing their businesses, competing with larger firms, and operating in a global business environment. [9]

Advances in technology. Advances in technology have created demand for accountants with strong technical skills. Knowledge of enterprise-risk software and tools that allow for continuous audits and monitoring of internal controls are particularly valued.[10]

Fraud prevention. An increase in financial crimes such as embezzlement, bribery, and securities fraud will increase demand for forensic accountants to detect illegal financial activity by individuals, companies, and organized crime.[11]

---

7 "Have CPA, Will Travel?", *CFO* magazine, August 4, 2006, http://cfo.com/article.cfm/7240760/c_2984294

8 "Baby Boomers Stand Alone," press release, Robert Half International, January 10, 2008, http://rhfa.mediaroom.com/index.php?s=305&item=409

9 "U.S. Treasury Department Forms Panel to Look At Audit Profession," *The CPA Letter,* December 2007, AICPA.com, comments by AICPA President and CEO Barry Melancon.

10 "Wanted: Tech Savy Accountants," Alan Rappeport, CFO.com, May 1, 2008, www.cfo.com/article.cfm/11118258?f=search

11 Bureau of Labor Statistics, Occupational Outlook Handbook, 2008-09 Edition, www.bls.gov/oco/ocos001.htm#outlook

The Ghost Squad

I got my first taste in forensic accounting some years ago when I was in the U.S. Army. I was assigned to the Army Audit Agency. Among other things, we audited payrolls. Our most interesting audit turned up a ghost squad.

It all started innocently enough. Every payday, a captain routinely picked up and personally delivered paychecks to members of a squad. One day the captain was ill, and the checks were sitting in an office, waiting for his return. A clerk got permission to distribute the checks himself. Problem was, he couldn't find any of the soldiers in the squad—nobody had ever heard of them. We were called in to investigate and discovered that the squad didn't exist. The captain had invented a fictitious squad, gotten checks cut, and endorsed and deposited the checks himself. This had been going on for about a year. Needless to say, that ended the captain's career.

Demand for Accountants

Accountants are in demand. According to the 2009 Fall Salary Survey of the National Association of Colleges and Employers, jobs in public and private accounting were among those most likely to be offered graduates in the class of 2009. See Table 1-2 for a complete list of the top jobs for the class of 2009.

Separately, *Money* magazine and PayScale, a global provider of compensation data, ranked CPA among "The Best Jobs for 2009," based on work that's meaningful, job growth prospects, salary, quality of life, and other criteria.[12]

Accountants will remain in demand well into the future. During the 10-year period between 2006 and 2016, employment in accounting and auditing will increase 18 percent from 1.274 million to 1.5 million, the result of 226,000 new jobs being created, according to the U.S. Labor Department's *Occupational Outlook Handbook: 2008-2009 Edition*.[13]

Accountants are being recruited for positions from entry level to senior executive, and in every industry from computer technology to entertainment to finance to sports. Some companies have created a new position of chief accounting officer to focus on

Table 1-2: *Top Jobs for the Class of 2009*[*]

Job	Starting Salary Offer
Teaching	$35,496
Management Trainee	$41,353
Financial/Treasury Analysis	$52,043
Consulting	$56,472
Sales	$41,577
Accounting (Public)	$49,437
Accounting (Private)	$45,859
Software Design & Development	$63,798
Registered Nursing	$45,229
Project Engineering	$58,570

[*] "Top Jobs for the Class of 2009," press release, National Association of Colleges and Employers, September 25, 2009, www.naceweb.org/Press/Releases/Top_Jobs_for_the_College_Class_of_2009.aspx?referal=pressroom&menuid=273

---

12 "Best Jobs in America 2009," CNNMoney.com and PayScale.com, http://money.cnn.com/magazines/moneymag/bestjobs/2009/full_list/index.html
13 *Occupational Outlook Handbook: 2008-2009 Edition*, Bureau of Labor Statistics, U.S. Department of Labor, www.bls.gov/oco/ocos001.htm#outlook

internal financial and operating controls and SOX compliance (see "Job Outlook for CPAs" in this chapter).[14]

Other Hiring

Although many accounting graduates go to work in the private sector, a number are joining federal, state, or local government agencies, such as the IRS, the leader among government employers in hiring college graduates. The FBI, the CIA, the SEC, and many other federal agencies also are hiring. Among other areas, the CIA looks for forensic accountants and business analysts. A typical assignment involves tracking international cash flows to identify money-laundering patterns.[15] The FBI has an Accounting Entry Program for special agents. Applicants must be CPAs or have earned a business degree with a major in accounting or related business degree and meet certain other requirements.[16] Nonprofit organizations, educational institutions, and other organizations are also actively recruiting new accountants.

Enrollment is Up

Students are flocking to accounting programs. More than 203,000 students were enrolled in undergraduate and graduate degree programs in accounting in the 2006-2007 school year, according to a survey of accounting graduates published in 2008 by the AICPA.[17] More than 64,000 students graduated with bachelor's or master's degrees in accounting in 2006-2007.

This represents a 19 percent increase in both enrollments and graduates from the 2003-2004 school year, the last time the AICPA survey was conducted. The number of graduates in the 2006-2007 school year was the largest since the AICPA began its survey with the 1971-1972 school year.

The survey also noted that accounting as a career choice continues to interest women. A woman who joined a small accounting firm said "it has provided a great opportunity to learn, to work with a variety of clients, and to quickly take on more responsibility. I love it."

Women represented 53 percent of enrollments in 2006-2007; however, this was down from a peak of 57 percent in 2002. Enrollment of minority students increased in the 2006-2007 school year compared with 3 years earlier. Because overall enrollment increased, however, the percentage of minorities enrolled remained the same in 2006–2007 at 26 percent—11 percent, Black/African American; 8 percent, Asian; 6 percent, Hispanic/Latino; and 1 percent, American Indian/Alaskan Native.

"One way to look at this is that, without efforts by schools and the accounting profession to attract more minorities, the percentage might have declined," said Dennis R. Reigle, AICPA director of academic and career development. "But the fact that the percentage remained the same means the profession has more work to do."

14 "Return of the Bean Counters," Alex Stuart, *CFO* magazine, December 1, 2002, www.cfo.com/article.cfm/3007332/c_3036064

15 "Uncle Sam Wants Accountants," Kate Sullivan, *CFO* magazine, July 2005

16 "Federal Bureau of Investigation, Careers, Special Agents, FBI Agent Critical Skills," www.fbijobs.gov/1112.asp#1.

17 "2008 Trends in the Supply of Accounting Graduates And The Demand For Public Accounting .Recruits," AICPA, www.aicpa.org/aec

The Singing CPA

In their career choices, some accountants march to their own tune. Steve Zelin quit his job as a corporate accountant to pursue songwriting. (To support himself, he does tax work for some private clients.) One of his lyrics, to the tune of "Unforgettable," by Irving Gordon, starts out:

> Tax deductible
> That's what you are.
> Tax deductible
> Just like my car*

The last few years, he's shown up at a New York City post office around April 15 to serenade people mailing last-minute returns. Word of "the singing CPA**" got around, and, in 2008, he was profiled in *The Wall Street Journal*.

---

* www.stevenzilin.com

** "Why Tax Day Makes Mr. Zelin Want to Sing," Shelly Banjo, *The Wall Street Journal*, April 10, 2008.

Enrollment Outlook

Enrollment in accounting programs is expected to continue increasing. Of the 242 U.S. colleges and universities that participated in the AICPA's survey, 60 percent said enrollment in bachelor's accounting programs would increase in the 2008-2009 school year, while 63 percent expected a rise in enrollment at the master's level.

Capacity Restraints

As enrollments soar, some schools are starting to experience capacity restraints. Of the schools responding to the survey, 13 percent faced space limitations and rejected an average of approximately 65 applicants. Bachelor's programs accredited by the Association to Advance Collegiate Schools of Business were most likely to be short on space.

Hiring

The same survey found that the hiring of graduates soared in the summer of 2007, with more than 36,000 graduates hired, up 83 percent from 2003-2004. Of the new hires in 2007, 52 percent were women, which mirrored the percentage of women enrolled and graduating. Ethnicity of new hires was 13 percent, Asian; 8 percent, Black/African American; 4 percent, Hispanic/Latino; 1 percent Native American/Alaskan Native; and 2 percent, Other/Unknown. These percentages were up slightly from 2003-2004, except for the Hispanic/Latino figure, which declined. Public accounting firms remained the primary employer of graduates, hiring 34 percent of those with bachelor's degrees and 70 percent with master's degrees.

"Overall, it's clear the accounting profession is at the forefront in enrollments, graduates and hiring," Reigle commented.

Accounting Career Paths

Accountants today have more career choices than ever. Some, like Jim Turley and James Quigley, decided on public accounting and, over the course of their careers, moved from entry level positions to the top of their organizations. Today, Turley is chairman of Ernst & Young, and Quigley is CEO of Deloitte. Krista McMasters joined Clifton Gunderson 30 years ago; in 2009, she became its CEO, and the first woman to lead a top 25 public accounting firm. Bert Mitchell and a partner founded Mitchell & Titus, one of the first public accounting firms in the United States founded by African Americans. Michele Mark Levine worked in public

Do You Speak Accountant?

To outsiders, accountants may seem to speak an impenetrable language just like lawyers or doctors or commodities traders. Accountant-speak has been the subject of countless jokes—some by accountants spoofing their own profession. Here's a good one: What's the definition of an accountant? Answer: Someone who solves a problem you didn't know you had in a way you don't understand. Or how about this one: What's the difference between an accountant and an economist. Answer: The accountant didn't have the personality to become an economist.

From the outside, accountants seem to follow unusual rituals, like observing a fiscal year. For various reasons, businesses, government agencies, and other organizations and their accountants, close the organization's books not at the end of a calendar year, but at the end of what is known as a fiscal year, such as the year ended June 30. A while back, *The Onion*, a satirical newspaper, spoofed the fiscal year observance with an article headlined "Accountants Pack Times Square for Fiscal New Year," complete with a photo of accountants partying in Times Square. "Amidst a blizzard of white, yellow, and pink forms in triplicate," the article began, "a jubilant crowd of more than 800,000 accountants jammed Times Square Saturday night to ring in the fiscal new year."*

Although it's true that accountants spend some of their time in "tech talk" with other accountants, maybe discussing the latest FASB pronouncement, they also spend a lot of their time talking with other people. The leader of an audit team may present the results of an audit to a company's CEO and CFO. A government accountant may meet with the head of an agency to prepare the agency's budget for the next fiscal year. The owner of a small accounting firm may make a presentation to a prospective client. Interaction with many different people requires accountants to have not only strong technical skills but also strong communication skills—the ability to clearly explain a balance sheet, an income statement, a budget, or a cost analysis in ways that business people, government officials, and others can understand. To help future accountants, the accounting programs at many universities and colleges are focusing more resources on improving students' communication skills.

* "Accountants Pack Times Square for Fiscal New Year," *The Onion*, April 11, 2001, http://www.theonion.com/articles/accountants-pack-times-square-for-fiscal-new-year.356/

accounting for a few years, shifted to the government sector, and today is director of accounting services in New York City's Office of Management and Budget, which assists the city's mayor with developing and implementing the budget. Thomas Falk started in public accounting, then joined Kimberly-Clark as an internal auditor, and worked his way up to CEO of the global consumer products company. (Interviews with these leaders appear in this book. See the Table of Contents for page numbers.)

Wrap-up

In this chapter, you learned the following:

- As an accountant, you can get a job just about anywhere—in public accounting, business, government, the not-for-profit sector, and academia.
- Accountants are in the information business, they provide financial information that is used by CEOs and other decision-makers to manage their organizations.
- Accountants are trusted advisors who are indispensable to the management and operations of companies, businesses, and other organizations.

- Accountants generally work in one or more of these core service areas: accounting, audit, assurance, and tax. They may also specialize in an industry such as real estate, and a particular service, such as forensic accounting.
- People are drawn to careers in accounting because the work is interesting and challenging, CPAs develop multiple, portable skills, there are opportunities for public service, and many other reasons.
- The job market for CPAs is one of the strongest in the United States.
- Demand for accountants will continue to grow well into the future.

In subsequent chapters, we take a closer look at the accounting profession, its different sectors, such as public or corporate accounting, career choices, finding that first job, and getting started in a career. As in other professions, education is the foundation of a career in accounting, and in chapter 2 we'll look at the accounting programs at U.S. colleges and universities.

Interview: Manny Espinoza

Association of Latino Professionals in Finance and Accounting (ALPFA)

Since 2002, Manny Espinoza, CPA, has served as the chief executive officer of the Association of Latino Professionals in Finance and Accounting (ALPFA), the leading national professional association dedicated to enhancing opportunities for Latinos in accounting, finance, and related professions. Previously, he was the organization's president. He joined ALPFA from Pricewater-houseCoopers (PwC), where he was a partner from 1986 to 2001. During his career at PwC, he served in leadership positions in the firm's U.S. offices, including managing partner of the Tucson office. He went on to represent the firm as its Country Desk for Mexico and Central America. Based in PwC's Mexico City office, he was responsible for the U.S. subsidiaries of international companies doing business in those countries. Upon returning to the United States, he provided financial advisory services from the Houston office, where he specialized in international litigation support services. Espinoza was a member of PwC's Diversity Champion Task Group and received the prestigious Eagle Award for his dedication and commitment to leadership and diversity issues. In 2007, Diversity Edge magazine named him to its Top 20 Diversity Champions list and in 2009, Hispanic Business named him to its 100 Most Influential Hispanics list.

> *"My experience with my firm and with clients reinforced my belief that change was needed at the top levels of organizations to create opportunities for people of color."*

What excited you about becoming a CPA?

It opens the door to great career opportunities, and just as important, to make a difference in the world. I grew up in Nogales, Arizona, a border community that was almost entirely Hispanic. It was very apparent that our community leaders had names like Kissinger, Hughes, Rockland, and Smith, and not Espinoza, Garcia, or Gonzalez. It was at this point that I committed to a long range goal of identifying, building, and creating Hispanic leadership in our community and nationally.

What did you enjoy about working in public accounting with PwC?

I started with Peat Marwick Mitchell (now KPMG), moved to Touche Ross (now Deloitte Touche Tohmatsu) and then to Coopers & Lybrand, which through a merger became PwC. The training programs at all these firms were superb, and I got to work with and for some very smart people. In addition to the opportunity to practice in tax, audit, advisory services, and forensic accounting, I had great clients.

Who were they?

I actually met the Pope through my client, the Vatican Observatory Foundation, as well as the well-known Latino singer Luis Miguel, and many CEO's, CFO's, and other important executives. My assignments were challenging and interesting. One was a fraud investigation in the jungles of Ecuador, right next to the Colombian border, where the FARC, a guerilla group, operated. All the while I was also very involved with diversity and creating opportunities for minorities. My experience with my firm and with clients reinforced my belief that change was needed at the top levels of organizations to create opportunities for people of color.

If a student or young professional wanted to work internationally, as you did, how would they go about it?

You need to work in public accounting for five or more years, develop a solid understanding of all aspects of accounting, and gain experience in working with a variety of clients. Fluency in a foreign language is a plus. You should have strong interpersonal, communication, and problem solving skills and the ability to work with others, to show enthusiasm and dedication, and be adaptable. That's true wherever you work.

How did you move from public accounting to the leadership of ALPFA?

I had been active in ALPFA for a number of years, and knew a lot of people in the organization. At the suggestion of some people in the organization, I ran for national president in 1999 and won. In 2002, ALPFA named me to the newly created position of CEO. Since then, the organization has grown dramatically. We have 11,000 members and 37 local chapters for professionals and students across the United States. ALPFA offers opportunities for networking, career and professional development, and job placement as well as a variety of events and programs throughout the year. For students, we provide a variety of career resources, career counseling, scholarship, mentoring and internship programs, online resume posting and job searches, interview opportunities, career fairs, and other events. We help our members to stay informed and connected through our national newsletter.

Interview: Kimberly A. Fantaci
American Woman's Society of Certified Public Accountants (AWSCPA)

The American Woman's Society of Certified Public Accountants (AWSCPA) is a national organization dedicated to serving all women CPAs. According to its mission statement, the AWSCPA "provides a supportive environment and valuable resources for members to achieve their personal and professional goals through various opportunities including leadership, networking and education."

> "Compared with 15 or 20 years ago, there are more women partners in CPA firms today, and more women CFOs and CEOs. But women have a long way to go to achieve full equality."

The AWSCPA has four key goals: increase public awareness of the organization and the accomplishments of its members; promote member networking and mentoring through affiliates in 25 major cities nationwide; provide members with opportunities for professional growth; and work towards a professional environment that fosters equity for all CPAs. For more information about AWSCPA, visit the organization's Web site at awscpa.org.

Kimberly Fantaci is executive director of AWSCPA.

What progress have women made in advancing into leadership positions in professional accounting and business?

Compared with 15 or 20 years ago, there are more women partners in CPA firms today, and more women CFOs and CEOs. But women have a long way to go to achieve full equality.

Even though more women are going into accounting?

Although more women than men are graduating with accounting degrees, the accounting profession is still considered a male dominated field when it comes to executive level positions. In public accounting, it's often difficult for women to make partner. If they take a hiatus to start families, they find it challenging to get back on the leadership track. The same is true in the corporate world for women seeking to advance to senior management.

How is AWSCPA helping women CPAs to address the leadership issue?

We serve primarily as a support organization in promoting leadership opportunities for women. We work with our local and regional affiliates, other accounting organizations, professional groups, state CPA societies, and other organizations to encourage and support public accounting firms, corporations and businesses, and government agencies in developing and sustaining diversity and leadership programs. And we issue papers and press releases, sponsor conferences, and conduct surveys to promote equity within the accounting profession. We also assist our members to develop their leadership skills, for example, by providing opportunities in our organization to serve in leadership positions from local committees to our national board of directors. We devote a full day of our national conference, held jointly with the American Society of Women Accountants (aswa.org), to leadership development. And we have an awards program to recognize the achievements of our members as well as other women in the profession. In addition, the Educational Foundation for Women in Accounting has produced a Leadership Training Series of 14 workshops for use by our organization and others. The EWFA was established through the support of AWSCPA and the American Society of Women Accountants.

Have you started student chapters of AWSCPA?

We are starting chapters. The first was established at Saint Mary's College (saintmarys. edu) in Notre Dame, Indiana. Through our student chapters, our members discuss their experiences as CPAs with our student members and help them to prepare for the real world of accounting. Our best connections with students are through women's colleges that have accounting programs. That's our niche.

Do you provide scholarships to students?

We do through our local affiliates. At the national level, we have a scholarship program that pays the cost of a CPA review course, which generally costs $3,000-$4,000. In addition, the Educational Foundation for Women in Accounting awards scholarships to women who are pursuing accounting degrees at the undergraduate and postgraduate levels.

Interview: Gregory Johnson
National Association of Black Accountants

Gregory Johnson is executive director and chief operating officer of the National Association of Black Accountants (NABA), a membership and advocacy organization based in Greenbelt, Maryland. Its core mission is to expand the influence of minority professionals in the fields of accounting and finance. One way it fulfills its mission is by encouraging and assisting minority students in entering the accounting profession. Johnson holds a BBA in accounting degree and a master's of business administration degree from Adelphi University. He is a CPA in the state of New York.

> *"NABA was one of the first organizations to establish a college residency type program to familiarize high school students with accounting. It's called Accounting Career Awareness Program, or ACAP. That program has been hugely successful."*

How did you get interested in accounting as a career?

In my family, no one had a background in business. But I thought I might like business because I could wear a suit and tie and work in an office. When I started college, a counselor asked me what I wanted to do. I said I was interested in business. He said he was studying business, too, but he was going to make more money than me because he was going to become an accountant. That was an eye opener. I decided to study accounting. In the summer after I finished my junior year, I worked as an intern for Coopers & Lybrand (now PricewaterhouseCoopers), which had started an internship program for minority students. By the time I graduated, they had offered me a job, and I started in their New York City office as a staff accountant. I worked in audit for about four-and-a-half years, and advanced to audit supervisor. Then I joined the AICPA.

What were your responsibilities at the American Institute of Certified Public Accountants?

I worked in several areas at the AICPA. I began my career in the Peer Review Team, then moved to Academic & Career Development as the manager of minority initiatives. Among other things, I helped to increase scholarship funding, created a leadership workshop program for scholarship recipients, developed an advertising campaign to interest minority students in careers in accounting, and worked with NABA on minority recruitment. In this role, I also worked with the KPMG Foundation on its program to educate and recruit minorities into accounting PhD programs (the PhD Project). I also served as director, CPA examination (external relations and strategy), where I was responsible for the strategic positioning and launch of the computer-based CPA examination, and as staff lead to the AICPA board of examiners, which sets policy for the CPA exam.

Where did you go from the AICPA?

I joined Grant Thornton International (GTI) as director, quality control. I was responsible for creating methods to monitor GTI member firms' audit practices worldwide and administering its audit review program. I left Grant Thornton in 2007 to join NABA in my current position.

What are examples of the programs that NABA has sponsored to interest students in accounting careers?

NABA was one of the first organizations to establish a college residency type program to familiarize high school students with accounting. It's called Accounting Career Awareness Program, or ACAP. It was started in 1980. High school juniors and seniors participate in a 1-week college residency program. We acclimate them to college and talk to them about business careers, particularly in accounting. That program has been hugely successful. It has been replicated by state CPA societies. We also work with public accounting firms, corporations, and student organizations to promote careers in accounting. One example: in 2008, Microsoft agreed to provide $1 million in cash, software, and technical support for NABA programs, including ACAP. We have launched a "CPA Bound" program to help overcome barriers to certification, such as the need to finance a fifth year of college, and to inform students and young professionals about the value of CPA certification. We have a number of chapters throughout the United States, and at the grass roots level, we offer any number of training programs, events, scholarship programs, and the like.

What are among the benefits of NABA membership to students and young professionals?

One of the primary benefits is to develop professional relationships with accountants, and to have opportunities to work with mentors who can assist students and young professionals with their careers. Members have the opportunity to develop relationships through NABA memberships and events. The leaders of NABA have all benefitted from such relationships. Membership really does turn into a lifelong experience for a lot of folks.

Who are some black owned firms that are members of NABA?

Within NABA we have a Division of Firms (DOF), which are minority-owned CPA firms. It currently has more than 60 members. An example is King, King Associates, a family-owned firm started by Benjamin L. King in 1957. Another is Bert Smith & Co., founded by Bert W. Smith, Jr., in 1948. Its current managing partner, George Willie, has been one of my mentors and coaches.

How does NABA measure success in promoting careers in accounting for African Americans?

Among other things, we look at our student membership, including students who join NABA through the ACAP program. We track and monitor the success of our student members in becoming CPAs. We recognize professionals who have passed the CPA exam. In addition, I want to work with the state boards of accountancy to get demographic data on CPA exam candidates in order to measure the success of African Americans and other minorities in passing the CPA examination.

Interview: Lee Lowery
American Society of Women
Accountants (ASWA)

Founded in 1938, the American Society of Women Accountants (aswa.org) represents professional women in all fields of accounting and finance. ASWA has 100 chapters throughout the United States and nearly 4,000 members, including 1,900 CPAs. The organization represents all levels within the accounting profession, from recent graduates to senior partners in major accounting firms. Members can be found throughout the workforce from academia and government to the private and public sectors.

"Each year, the Foundation recognizes 'best in market' companies for their commitment to work/life balance as well as individuals for their positive influence on others in the profession."

ASWA's mission is to enable women in accounting and related fields to achieve their full personal, professional, and economic potential and to contribute to the future development of their profession.

Lee K. Lowery is the ASWA's executive director.

How does ASWA achieve its mission of helping women realize their full potential?

ASWA provides members with opportunities to network through online discussion forums as well as through chapter meetings, regional conferences, and our Joint National Conference, held annually in conjunction with the American Woman's Society of Certified Public Accountants. Through networking, our members can utilize practical resources that strengthen their professional growth. For example, if they need help finding solutions to complex technical issues, they can connect with accounting and finance professionals in our organization who can provide technical assistance.

We also provide low cost, quality, educational seminars on a variety of accounting and other topics such as public speaking or creating and making presentations. These seminars are presented locally through our chapters, regionally through our regional conferences, and nationally through our Joint National Conference.

With the support of our corporate sponsors, we provide members with discounts to attend CPA Review courses. Members can earn CPE credit by participating in our various course offerings and activities such as monthly meetings of our local chapter. Members who attend our Joint National Conference can earn up to 24 CPE credits. To develop their leadership skills, members can serve as committee chairs or officers at the local, regional and national levels of our organization. In addition to these various services, we have a number of initiatives designed to benefit our members and the profession.

What are examples of these initiatives?

Our National Corporate Partnership program provides public accounting firms, corporations, and other organizations with the opportunity to become ASWA sponsors, providing additional benefits to our members while achieving a high level of visibility in our organization. Another initiative is the ASWA Educational Foundation. Its primary programs include scholarships for qualified community college and undergraduate students as well as scholarships that cover the exam fees of ASWA members studying for the CPA or certain other designations. Each year, the Foundation recognizes "best in market" companies for their commitment to work/life balance as well as individuals for their positive influence on others in the profession. The foundation also supports and encourages our chapters and members to provide financial literacy within their communities by recommending curriculum that is published by the FDIC.* We provide "train the trainer" type education at the Joint National Conference that gives our members and chapters the tools they need to initiate the programs locally. We also recognize members and chapters that provide financial literacy through our annual "Financial Literacy" awards.

Do you offer career guidance and job placement services?

Yes. We have a career center on our Website. Among other features, it provides information on current job opportunities for prospective employees, and a job listing service for employers. It also provides advice on job hunting and career management, and various resources to assist with career planning. Accountemps and Robert Half Finance & Accounting are national corporate partners of ASWA. They provide a plethora of career guidance and job placement resources to our members, including, but certainly not limited to, the career center's content. With nearly 100 memberships, they have employees in most ASWA chapters who are ready and willing to assist our members in need of career guidance and job placement services.

---

* "Money Smart—A Financial Education Program," Federal Deposit Insurance Corporation.

Interview: Misean Reed
American Institute of Certified Public Accountants

Misean Reed is the manager of Diversity, Work/Life, and Women's Initiatives with the AICPA. Before joining the AICPA in 2007, she was the public relations specialist with the North Carolina Association of CPAs.

For more information on the AICPA's Women's Initiatives, go to the AICPA home page at aicpa.org.

"Alternative ownership arrangements would be a huge step for women, and some firms are adopting these business models with great success, but it remains to be seen how widespread these models become."

What's the purpose of the AICPA's Women's Initiatives?

Its purpose is to attract women into the accounting profession and provide the opportunities for them to remain in the profession and advance in their careers.

How do the women's initiatives aim to achieve these objectives?

One way is to promote the advancement of women to leadership positions in the profession. For example, in 1988, 45 percent of new public accounting recruits were female. In 2008, only 23 percent of partners in public accounting firms were female. After 20 years of rough parity with men, women should make up more of the leadership in public accounting.

Another of our initiatives is to help women achieve work/life balance—the successful integration of personal and professional lives.

Who provides the direction for the women's initiatives?

The AICPA's Women's Initiatives Executive Committee. Members include professionals in public accounting, industry, consulting, and academia. A representative of a state CPA society is also on the committee. I'm the AICPA staff liaison.

Helping women to remain in the accounting profession—retention—is a core purpose of the women's initiatives. Why is retention an issue for public accounting firms?

One reason is that women leave public accounting firms to start families, take care of aged parents, or for other personal reasons. Many return to the workforce after a couple of years, but they don't necessarily rejoin their firms. They may find career opportunities elsewhere—with another firm, for example, in industry or outside of accounting altogether.

How can organizations retain these women?

We assist organizations to develop programs that enable these women to stay connected with their firms in simple but important ways, for example, by continuing to have access to the firm's internet, or being invited to firm functions, or having access to clients. As an additional resource, we have published an "Off Ramping Guide" to help organizations set up such programs.

Advancing women to positions of leadership is a goal of the women's initiatives. Why the focus on leadership?

Women represent more than 50 percent of the talent pool in the accounting profession. However, as I noted, they constitute just 23 percent of shareholders/partners at public accounting firms, and they are not proportionately represented at all levels.

How can firms help women to reach the partner level?

Our committee members recently have begun to hear more discussion in firms about alternative pathways to ownership. For example, a lot of women have flexible work arrangements, but in some cases that could lessen their opportunities to make partner. If firms want women in ownership, they have to create different ownership structures, for example, partners who work part time. Alternative ownership arrangements would be a huge step for women, and some firms are adopting these business models with great success, but it remains to be seen how widespread these models become.

Are there firms that have a particular need to develop or enhance programs to recruit, retain and advance women?

The top 20 or so public accounting firms have programs in place and the resources to support them. We are starting to reach out to firms in the next tier—some 50 to 400 firms below the top 20. These firms often are looking for help in developing programs or improving existing programs. We have developed a workshop that specifically targets these firms, and to date we have held two workshops for some of them.

Interview: Ostine Swan
American Institute of Certified Public Accountants

In 1969, the AICPA Council passed a resolution to integrate the accounting profession in response to the lack of awareness of or employment in the accounting profession of minorities. The resolution included:

• Encouraging minority men and women of high potential to attend college and major in accounting.
• Providing educational opportunities for minority men and women to prepare them to enter the accounting profession.
• Encouraging hiring of minority men and women in order to integrate the accounting profession in fact as well as ideal.

> "The AICPA Accounting Scholars Leadership Workshop, first launched in 1995, is an annual invitational program for minority accounting students who plan to pursue the CPA designation. Its purpose is to strengthen students' professional skills and increase the awareness of the benefits of earning the CPA credential."

The Minority Recruitment and Equal Opportunity Committee, now called the AICPA Minority Initiatives Committee, was formed to carry out the resolution.

Today the committee is made up of 14 members from public accounting, business and industry, the not-for-profit sector, professional associations, state CPA societies, and academia.* The committee develops comprehensive programs that encourage students from underrepresented ethnic groups to become accounting majors and obtain the CPA designation.

In honor of the AICPA Minority Initiative Committee 40th anniversary, an eBook, entitled "CPAs of Color: Celebrating 40 Years," was launched in August 2009. Forty-one accomplished professionals who work in fascinating fields and occupations are featured. Their challenges, goals, dreams and words of advice for CPAs who will follow in their footsteps are shared by the CPAs profiled.

For information on the AICPA's minority initiatives programs, including academic scholarships, visit aicpa.org/diversity.

---

* The current list of committee members can be found on the AICPA's web site at http://www.aicpa.org/members/div/career/mini/mic_roster.htm

Ostine Swan, CPA, AICPA's Senior Manager of Diversity Programs and Relationships, is Staff Liaison to the Minority Initiatives Committee. Swan graduated from North Carolina A&T State University with a bachelor's degree in accounting and earned her Master of Arts in Liberal Studies from Duke University. She started her career in the corporate sector as an accounting intern for Mobil Oil Company. She subsequently worked for Deloitte in their Bermuda office and rose to the position of senior audit manager. From Deloitte, she joined the Bermuda government as Inspector of Companies in the Ministry of Finance. She then returned to the corporate sector as director of internal audit for an insurance company. She joined the AICPA in 2007.

How did you get interested in accounting as a career?

Mathematics was one of my favorite classes in high school and I was enrolled in advanced math. During a discussion about different professions, my high school math teacher said that accounting was an excellent career choice. At the time I had no idea what a general ledger was! However, encouraged by my high school teacher and family, I decided to major in accounting at university.

And you started your career in the corporate sector?

Yes. After I graduated with my bachelor's of science in accounting, I worked for Mobil. After joining the Deloitte office in Bermuda, I set and passed the CPA exam.

When did you get your CPA certification?

In 1979, when approximately one percent of CPAs were African American. The number of African American CPAs has increased since then, but it's somewhat disturbing that today they still constitute only about three percent of CPAs.

What is the AICPA doing to interest minority students in careers in accounting?

One initiative is the AICPA Scholarship for Minority Accounting Students.** Scholarships are awarded to outstanding minority students to encourage their selection of accounting as a major and their ultimate entry into the CPA Profession. Funding is provided by the AICPA Foundation, with contributions from the New Jersey Society of CPAs and Robert Half International. Some state CPA societies also award minority scholarships.

How many scholarships have been awarded?

Since the program's inception in 1969 we have awarded more than $14 million in scholarships to approximately 8,500 accounting scholars. For the 2009-2010 school year, we awarded 95 accounting students with scholarships ranging from $1,500–$5,000 each.

** AICPA, Scholarship for Minority Accounting Students. http://www.aicpa.org/members/div/career/mini/smas.htm

What are the other AICPA programs for minorities?

The AICPA Accounting Scholars Leadership Workshop, first launched in 1995, is an annual invitational program for minority accounting students who plan to pursue the CPA designation. Its purpose is to strengthen students' professional skills and increase the awareness of the benefits of earning the CPA credential. Through speaker presentations, panel discussions and interactive programs, students attending the two-and-half day workshop gain a better understanding of the many career paths in the accounting profession. We also cover a variety of other topics, such as preparing for the CPA exam and community service.

And the other AICPA program for minorities?

Our other program is the AICPA Fellowship for Minority Doctoral Students, which began in 1975.[†] Its purpose is to ensure that CPAs of diverse backgrounds are visible in college and university classrooms to serve as role models and mentors to young people in planning their education and careers. Competitive, renewable fellowships of up to $12,000 are awarded annually to full-time minority accounting scholars who demonstrate significant potential to become accounting educators. For the 2009-2010 academic year, 21 accounting PhDs were selected for fellowships.

Do you have programs for high school students?

We are starting to reach out to high schools with accounting programs. Some of the state CPA societies already have high school programs in place. For example, the Michigan Association of CPAs (MACPA) hosts the MACPA High School Leaders Conference. It's a one-day program modeled after the AICPA's Accounting Scholars Leadership Workshop. MACPA has created a tool kit that other state CPA societies can use to create similar programs. In addition, the AICPA provides presentation materials that CPA firms and individual CPAs can use for classroom presentations.

---

† AICPA, "Fellowship for Minority Doctoral Students" http://www.aicpa.org/MEMBERS/DIV/CAREER/MINI/FMDS.HTM

Chapter 2

Education: Foundation of a Career

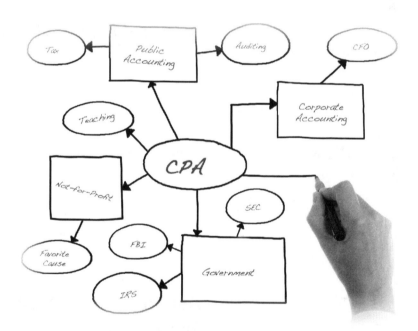

"The world has seen what happens when we do our job well—and when we don't. We are relevant—what we do matters."

James Turley, Chairman and CEO • Ernst & Young

Many Choices of Schools and Accounting Programs

You're a high school senior who learned about accounting from your mother, a CPA. You want to attend a university to study accounting. What schools offer accounting programs?

You're a college senior studying for a bachelor's degree in political science. You initially plan a career in government after you graduate, but you've decided on a career in accounting instead. Is there a program available for you to study for a master's degree in accounting, even though you did not study accounting as an undergraduate?

You're a freshman studying accounting at a community college, and you plan to transfer to a university in your junior year to earn a bachelor's degree in accounting. Can you transfer credits for the accounting and other courses you take in community college?

This chapter provides a look at educational programs in accounting and what to consider in planning your education, including meeting the educational requirements to take the CPA exam. The next chapter covers the specifics of preparing for and taking the exam and earning a CPA certificate.

Interest Grows in Accounting Programs

Today, accounting programs are a magnet for students. "More students are studying accounting today than at any time in the past 30 years," said Ira Solomon, head of the department of accounting at the University of Illinois at Urbana-Champaign. "Accounting is seen as relevant and important." (An interview with Solomon is on page 72 of this book.)

"Because of the condition of the financial markets today and the corporate scandals of recent years, we are under intense public scrutiny," said James Turley, chairman and CEO of Ernst & Young, a global accounting and professional services firm. "The world has seen what happens when we do our job well—and when we don't. We are relevant—what we do matters." (An interview with Turley appears on page 145 of this book.)

Demand for Graduates

Graduates with accounting degrees are much in demand in public accounting, business, government, not-for-profit, and other organizations that employ accountants.

One indication of this demand: firms offering accounting services headed the list of top employers for the class of 2009 (table 2-1), based on the number of job offers reported, according to the National Association of Colleges and Employers.

Accounting Degree Programs

To meet the growing demand for accountants, hundreds of U.S. schools from small private colleges to large state universities offer undergraduate and graduate degree programs in accounting. The American Institute of Certified Public Accountants (AICPA) has an online list of these schools by state, and

Table 2-1: *Top Employers of 2009 College Graduates*

Employer Type	Average Salary Offer
1. Accounting Services	$50,362
2. Engineering Services	$57,524
3. Educational Services	$35,240
4. Consulting Services	$54,143
5. Aerospace	$58,495
6. Financial Services	$51,190
7. Government (Federal)	$45,497
8. Retail/Wholesale Trade	$41,318
9. Petroleum & Coal Products	$73,768
10. Healthcare Services (For Profit)	$67,175

Source: Summer 2009 Salary Survey, National Association of Colleges and Employers. Data is for bachelor's degree graduates only.

links to the schools themselves. See "Colleges and Universities Offering Accounting Degree Programs" on the AICPA's Web site (www.aicpa.org/collegelist/index-text.htm). Later in this chapter, we look at community college programs designed for students who plan to transfer to four-year colleges or universities in their junior year to study accounting.

Choosing a School

With a choice of a number of schools offering accounting programs, how do you select the school and program that's right for you? The following topics provide some considerations.

Accreditation

A good place to start is with the accreditation of schools. The goal of accreditation is to ensure that education provided by institutions of higher education meets acceptable levels of quality. Accrediting agencies, which are private educational associations of regional or national scope, develop evaluation criteria and conduct peer evaluations to assess whether or not those criteria are met. Institutions and programs that request an agency's evaluation and that meet an agency's criteria are then accredited by that agency.[1]

The Association to Advance Collegiate Schools of Business

The Association to Advance Collegiate Schools of Business (AACSB) is an international association of educational institutions, businesses, and other organizations devoted to the advancement of higher education in management education. It describes itself as "the premier accrediting agency of collegiate business schools and accounting programs worldwide." AACSB International was founded in 1916 and adopted its first accreditation standards in 1919. Additional standards for programs in accountancy were adopted in 1980. In 2003, members approved a revised set of standards that apply to business programs globally and support and encourage excellence in management education worldwide. You can find a list of schools that are AACSB accredited in accounting on its Web

---

1 U.S. Department of Education, "Accreditation in the United States," www.ed.gov/admins/finaid/accred/index.html

Increase in Accounting Enrollment

In 2008, the American Institute of Certified Public Accountants (AICPA) published a report on the supply of accounting graduates. The report, based on a survey of U.S. schools offering under-graduate and graduate degrees in accounting, looked at trends for the 2006-2007 school year in the enrollment of students, graduation rates, and employment of graduates. The AICPA's previous trends report was in 2005, based on survey findings for the 2003-2004 school year.

Among the findings of the 2008 report:

- In the 2006-2007 school year, enrollments in bachelor's and master's accounting degree programs totaled more than 203,000 students, up nearly 19 percent from the 2003-2004 school year. The following table compares accounting enrollment statistics from the 2003-2004 class to the 2006-2007 class.

Accounting Enrollment by Program

Degree	2006-2007	2003-2004
Bachelor of Accounting	173,299	143,735
MA Accounting	21,253	18,795
MBA Accounting	4,482	4,030
MA Taxation	3,239	3,595
PhD	1,095	955
Total	203,368	171,110

- Of the 203,000 students enrolled in 2006-2007, 52 percent were women and 48 percent were men.
- Minorities comprised 26 percent of bachelor's enrollments in 2006-2007: 11 percent, Black/African American; 8 percent Asian; 6 percent, Hispanic/Latino; and 1 percent, American Indian/Alaskan Native.
- Graduates in bachelor's and master's degree programs totaled 64,221 in 2006-2007, up 19 percent from 2003-2004.
- About 60 percent of the schools that responded to the survey anticipated a continuing rise in enrollments at the bachelor's level, while 63 percent expected increases at the master's level.

To see the 2008 trends report, visit the AICPA's Web site or Google search "AICPA trends report."

site at www.aacsb.edu. Click on "Accreditation" and "Accredited Institutions."

The AACSB has another Web site, www.bestbizschools.com, designed to help students select schools, including those with accounting programs. You can search for schools by degree (undergraduate, master's, or doctorate), by programs, including accounting, and by state. This site notes, by the way, that the accounting, audit, and tax fields are among the "highest demanded fields in business."

The Association of Collegiate Business Schools and Programs

Founded in 1988, The Association of Collegiate Business Schools and Programs (ACBSP) "is the leading specialized accreditation association for business education supporting, celebrating, and rewarding teaching excellence."[2] In 2007, the ACBSP approved standards for separate accreditation in accounting. As of August 2008, ACBSP membership included 585 educational institutions as members, 413 that have successfully achieved accreditation.[3] A list of the organization's members can be found on the ACBSP Web site at www.acbsp.org. Click on "About ACBSP" and "ACBSP Member Institutions."

U.S. Department of Education

One of the reasons that institutions seek accreditation is so their students are eligible to receive federal student aid or other federal benefits. The U.S. Department of Education maintains a database of accredited postsecondary institutions and programs on the U.S. Department of Education home page (www.ed.gov) under "How do I find . . .," click on "Accreditation." Each of the programs in the database is accredited by an accrediting agency or state approval agency. These agencies are recognized by the U.S. Secretary of Education as a "reliable authority as to the quality of postsecondary education" within the meaning of the Higher Education Act of 1965, as amended. The department itself does not accredit institutions.

You can search the department's database by the institution or the accrediting agency. For example, you can enter "University of Texas" and "Austin" and "Texas" and the database provides a link to "University of Texas." Click on "University of Texas" and a page comes up that shows the university is accredited by the Southern Commission on Colleges and Schools, Commission on Colleges. There is a link to the Southern Commission's Web page at www.sacscoc.org. The commission is the regional body for the accreditation of degree-granting higher education institutions in the Southern states. You can also search the database by accrediting agency to see which institutions are accredited by that agency. Another way to search is on the Web sites of the schools themselves. The accounting department of the University of Texas McCombs School of Business notes on its home page that it is accredited by the Southern Commigssion as well as AACSB.[4]

> **! NOTE:**
> Something to keep in mind is that some employers, institutions, and licensing boards only recognize degrees earned from institutions accredited by an accrediting agency recognized by the Department of Education. That does not necessarily mean you should limit your search only to these institutions. As the Department of Education notes of its database: "The database does not include a number of postsecondary educational institutions and programs that elect not to seek accreditation but nevertheless may provide a quality postsecondary education." If you are interested in an unaccredited institution, you could do further research to assess the quality of its program, for example, by talking to school alumni or students.

---

2 The Association of Business Schools and Programs, "About ACBSP," www.acbsp.org/p/st/ld/&sid=s1_025about
3 Ibid.
4 University of Texas, McCombs School of Business, Department of Accounting. www.mccombs.utexas.edu/dept/accounting/index.asp

Location

If you are willing to go to school anywhere in the United States, then location is not an issue. But if you want to go to school in the city or town where you live, or in the region or state where your community is located, you can narrow your search to the location that interests you. For example, on the previously mentioned AICPA Web site that has a list of all the accounting programs in the United States, you can do a search by state (www.aicpa.org/collegelist/index-text.htm). If you click on "Illinois," for example, you will find a list of more than 30 schools from small private colleges to large public universities. Some of these schools offer bachelor's degree programs, while others offer both bachelor's and master's programs. A PhD program is offered by 3 of these institutions: Northwestern University, the University of Chicago, and the University of Illinois at Urbana-Champaign.

Cost

With college costs continuing to rise, and many people on tight budgets, cost is a major consideration for students and their families in selecting a college. But a college education also is an investment, one that will be repaid in more job choices, better pay, greater career opportunities, and personal and professional fulfillment.

Public Versus Private

Students attending public institutions, particularly in their home states, may have lower tuition and other costs than those attending private college, which usually cost more, sometimes a lot more. But many private schools, because of their substantial endowments, are often able to offer financial aid packages, such as loans, grants, and scholarships, that make them relatively affordable compared with public institutions.

Large Versus Small

The number of students at a school will make a difference in your experience of the institution.[5] Large institutions may have a wider choice of majors, programs, classes, and activities. They also may have larger size class sizes, which raises the question of how much personal attention you could expect from teachers. Smaller schools tend to be more conducive to quiet contemplation and inner reflection and enable more interaction among faculty and students. Some large schools have established honor colleges or other programs to try and create a similar atmosphere within a big campus.

Campus Life

Just like your hometown, the college you attend is a community. To decide which college community is the right fit, you can start by visiting a school's Web site to learn not only about academic programs but also about school activities, student and academic organizations, programs that serve the community, and other information. If you visit the school, plan to sit in on a few classes (with the school's permission), visit the cafeteria and other places where students hang out, and talk to students about why they chose the school, and what they think of the institution. Explore the town or city where the campus is located

---

5 "Tips for Finding Your College Match," College Board, Apply to College, www.collegeboard.com/student/apply/the-application/52.html

Rankings

Various organizations, researchers, and others, publish rankings of schools and programs. *U.S. News and World Report* produces an annual ranking of business school graduate programs, including rankings by specialties such as accounting. (From the U.S. News home page [www.usnews.com]: Education → Best Graduate Schools → Best Business Schools → Business Specialties → Accounting.[6]) *Public Accounting Report*, a subscription newsletter published by CCH, which provides leading tax and business law information and software solutions, publishes an annual professor's survey that ranks undergraduate and graduate accounting programs.

Deciding on a School

What matters most in deciding on a school is not whether you attend a public or private institution, a large or small school, but the people you will meet and get to know and your experience of college life.[7] If you do diligent research on schools and visit campuses, you will know whether a school is the right fit for you.

College Selection Resources

A wealth of information is available in print and online to help you with the college selection process, deciding whether to attend a public or private institution, or a large or small school, financing your education, and other questions. Sources of information include the following:

- U.S. Department of Education home page (www.ed.gov): At the top of the page in search, type in "students" for a link to other links on such topics as planning for college, finding a college, paying for college, a federal student aid gateway, and more.
- CollegeNavigator (http://nces.ed.gov/collegenavigator): A Department of Education tool to help you through the process of selecting a college based on state, programs and major, level of degree (for example, bachelor's, institution type, and other criteria).
- National Center for Education Statistics (NCES) (www.nces.ed.gov/IPEDS): The NCES, part of the Department of Education, has a data center where you can look up information about schools such as an institution's graduation rate which is one measure of a school's performance.
- College.gov: Provides advice on planning for college, finding schools, taking admission tests, applying for college, paying for college, preparing to attend school, and more. It also looks at the benefits of attending college, such as more earning power. For example, a college graduate can afford to buy a large, flat-screen TV in 1–2 months, whereas a noncollege graduate might have to work for 3–4 months to buy the same TV. No wonder your inner couch potato is telling you to attend college!
- students.gov: Official U.S. government Web site designed for students and their families. Includes information on planning for college, student financial aid, scholarships and grants, and federal internships and jobs for students.
- Collegeboard.com: Among other features, this site has a "College MatchMaker" to help you select among more than 3,800 schools based on size (number of students), public or private, program, setting (urban, suburban, rural), location, distance from home, and other criteria.
- FinAid! (www.finaid.org): This financial aid site includes calculators to help you figure out how much school will cost, how much you need to save, and how much aid you'll need.

---

6 http://grad-schools.usnews.rankingsandreviews.com/best-graduate-schools/top-business-schools
7 "How to Choose a College That's Right for You," Martha O'Connell, NPR, February 21, 2007

- FastWeb (www.fastweb.com): Fill out an online questionnaire and get customized information about colleges, scholarships, internships, jobs, and more.
- "A Pocket Guide to Choosing a College: Are You Asking the Right Questions on a Campus College Visit?" National Survey of Student Engagement.[8]

See appendix 1 for other sources of information on attending college.

Why Become a CPA?

In planning for college and your career in accounting, you should give consideration to becoming a CPA for the following reasons:

- *Career opportunities.* As a CPA, you have a wider choice of career options in public accounting, corporations and businesses, government, and the not-for-profit sector.
- *Commitment.* The CPA designation demonstrates your commitment to the profession by completing educational and other requirements.
- *Prestige.* It validates that you have the knowledge, skills, and experience to serve as a trusted advisor to employers, clients, and others.
- *Competitive edge.* CPA certification could give you an edge in competing for a job. "It enhances your credibility with prospective employers, and prepares you for a career in many industries, including the nonprofit sector," said Amy Coleman, vice president and treasurer of the Kresge Foundation, a $2.8 billion private, national foundation. (An interview with Coleman is on page 266 of this book.)
- *Employer requirement.* If you work for a public accounting firm, you must be a CPA to conduct audits of public companies that are registered with the SEC. If you work for a corporation, you may be required to be a CPA to move up to senior financial positions in the organization, such as CFO.
- *Networking opportunities.* As a CPA, you can join professional organizations such as the AICPA or your state CPA society and enjoy the benefits of membership. Such organizations provide opportunities to network and develop professional relationships with other CPAs who could be sources of business, provide career advice, or help you to address professional questions or issues.
- *Higher income.* As a CPA, you may have the opportunity to earn more income over the course of your career. According to one estimate, CPAs earn at least 10 percent more than non-CPA accountants in similar positions. However, factors such as geographic location, years of experience, level of education, and the size and revenue of an employer, all play a role in determining the salary of a CPA.[9]

Table 2-2 outlines a typical salary comparison for CPAs at different career levels and their non–CPA counterparts.

For more information, see "Becoming a CPA" on the AICPA's Web site (www.aicpa.org/Becoming+a+CPA), and "Start Here, Go Places," (startheregoplaces.com), a Web site on CPA careers hosted by the AICPA. Also, check out the career sections of the Web sites of state CPA societies. For example, the California society has a guide to becoming a CPA that begins: "One day you're sitting in history class learning about the wives of Henry VIII when suddenly you see a flash—the curtains fly open, light pours through the window, a voice booms from above—and deep in your heart you realize your calling: You were meant to be a CPA!"[10]

---

8 http://nsse.iub.edu/html/pocket_guide_intro.cfm

9 "What CPAs Earn," Becker Professional Education, www.becker.com/accounting/cpaexamreview/become-a-cpa/what-cpas-earn.cfm

10 "What It Takes: A Guide to Becoming a CPA," CalCPA Education Foundation, www.calcpa.org/Content/licensure/requirements.aspx

Table 2-2: *Non-CPA Versus CPA Salaries: An Example*

2009 Projected Accountant Salaries (Large Firms)	Non-CPA Salaries Up To	CPA Salaries** Up To
Senior Manager/Director	$159,500	$175,450
Manager	111,750	122,925
Senior	86,750	95,425
1-3 Years	69,250	76,175
Up to 1 Year	60,000	66,000

Source: "What CPAs Earn," Becker Professional Education; derived from 2009 Robert Half Salary Guide.

* Large public accounting firms = $250 million + in sales. Salary does not reflect overtime or bonuses, which are significant portions of compensation for these positions.

** CPAs earn up to 10 percent more than peers without professional designations.

Finally, talk to CPAs about why they became CPAs. You may already know some CPAs, or you may meet them through family, friends, teachers, classmates, or other connections. If you're still having trouble finding a CPA, you could shout in a crowded room: "Are there any CPAs in here?" But only as a last resort.

To be sure, not every accountant is a CPA, and you can find a meaningful career as an accountant. But the CPA designation does, as noted, provide attractive career benefits.

Check out the interviews in this book to learn more about why people became CPAs, and how the CPA designation has helped them in their careers. Interviews are listed in the Table of Contents.

CPA Requirements

To become a CPA, you must meet three criteria, sometimes known as the "three e's"—education, examination, and experience.

Education

Students enrolled in college accounting programs must meet specific educational requirements to become CPAs. Those requirements are set by the states. In 1989, the AICPA membership voted to recommend that states require candidates to complete 150 credit hours to sit for the CPA exam, and today most states have the 150-hour requirement. Depending on the state, candidates may, as part of the 150-hour requirement, have to earn a bachelor's degree and complete a minimum number of hours in accounting and business subjects. (Check the AICPA's Web site for a list of states that have the 150-hour requirement.[11])

According to the AICPA, the purpose of the 150-hour requirement is to improve the overall quality of the work performed by CPAs confronted with advances in technology, an increasingly complex business environment, and society's continuing demand for accounting and assurance services. James J. Benjamin, head of the accounting department in the Mays Business School at Texas A&M University said: "We strongly embrace the 150-hour requirement because it provides students with exposure not only to accounting but also to other subjects including financial markets, information systems, public policy, the marketing of professional services, and the impact of

11 AICPA: "Jurisdictions That Have Passed the 150-Hour Education Requirement," www.aicpa.org/download/states/150_Hour_Education_Requirement.pdf

technology on accounting and business." (An interview with Benjamin is on page 58 of this book.)

For more on the 150-hour requirement, including Frequently Asked Questions, go to the AICPA's home page.[12]

Uniform CPA Examination

In addition to meeting the educational requirements, CPA candidates must take the Uniform CPA Examination, which is developed and administered by the AICPA. (Some states allow candidates to take the exam after completing 120 semester hours of college education, but still require 150 hours for licensing as a CPA.) The CPA exam is discussed in chapter 3.

Professional Experience

In addition to obtaining a CPA certificate, you must also obtain a license to practice as a CPA. CPAs are licensed by states, and requirements for professional experience depend on the state. State boards of accountancy regulate licensing, and many require that you complete 1–2 years of professional work under a CPA's supervision. Some states will accept other accounting experience (for example, industry and government), although the number of years required is typically higher than for public accounting. Most states have what are known as CPA practice mobility laws, which allow CPAs and CPA firms to serve clients across state lines with minimal licensing barriers.[13] (For a link to state boards of accountancy, and state licensing requirements, go to

the home page of the National Association of State Boards of Accountancy (www.nasba. org). Click on "State Board Listing."

CPE Requirements

After you graduate and receive your CPA credential and license to practice as a CPA, you must satisfy continuing professional education (CPE) requirements throughout your career. Among other requirements, the AICPA requires its members to complete 120 CPE hours over a 3-year period (minimum of 20 hours a year) if they are in public practice, and 90 hours over 3 years (minimum of 15 hours a year) if they are in private practice. CPAs also must satisfy the CPE requirements of the states where they practice. For information on state CPE requirements, check the Web sites of state boards of accountancy and state CPA societies as well as the AICPA.

Course of Study: It's Not Just Accounting

What does it mean to be a CPA? It's an essential question to consider in planning a course of study.

This is how the AICPA addresses it:[14]

> CPAs must be broadly educated professionals who are technically competent and who possess the analytical abilities, communication, and interpersonal skills, and cultural awareness that will enable them to serve the public in a complex and changing environment. To obtain

---

12 www.aicpa.org/Becoming+a+CPA/CPA+Candidates+and+Students/150+Hour+Requirement.htm#why

13 "With 45 States Enacting CPA Practice Mobility Laws, AICPA Turns to Nationwide Implementation," *Reuters,* July 27, 2009, www.reuters.com/article/pressRelease/idUS197766+27-Jul-2009+PRN20090727

14 The AICPA, "Schools and Courses: The Basics, " www.aicpa.org/Becoming+a+CPA/CPA+Candidates+and+Students/Schools+and+Courses.htm

these skills and abilities, students should have a good balance of accounting, business administration, and general (i.e., liberal arts) education.

Three core areas of study for CPA candidates include the following:

- *Accounting.* Students should have an understanding of the functions of accounting, the underlying body of concepts that constitute accounting theory, and the application of those concepts to accounting problems and situations.
- *Business administration.* Education in business administration enables students to understand the concepts, processes, and institutions involved in the production and marketing of goods and services, as well as in the financing of a business and other forms of organization.
- *General education.* A strong general education forms the foundation for lifelong learning, development, and growth. CPA candidates should have a general understanding of history, philosophy and languages as well as the arts and sciences.

What to Study?

The AICPA suggests a course of study that includes the following areas.

- *Financial Accounting.* Students should be knowledgeable about real world financial problems and how to apply accounting principles and practices to their solutions.
- *Managerial Accounting.* Students should understand accounting and control issues and approaches from a management perspective.
- *Auditing.* Students should have a solid grounding in auditing, both theory and practice. *Auditing theory* covers the concepts of gathering and evaluating financial information, the purposes and contexts of auditing, the responsibilities and risks in auditing, and communication. An *auditing practice* course, including audit problems and case studies, provides a practical understanding of how the audit itself is

---

The Well-rounded Professional

Our students have a high degree of interest and enthusiasm, and a real desire to learn. While they are technically proficient, they sometimes don't fully appreciate what it means to be a well rounded professional— they need to give more value to development of communication, teamwork, leadership and other skills. More than that, they must be well rounded human beings, with an appreciation of history, the arts and culture, and be open to all that life has to offer. One of our jobs is to help students understand that.

—John Elliott, dean, Zicklin School of Business; professor of accounting, Baruch College, City University of New York. (An interview with Elliott can be found on page 69 of this book.)

---

administered. "Audit courses are valuable, among other reasons, because many companies and public agencies have strengthened their internal audit capability post-Enron," said Douglas R. Carmichael, professor of accountancy at New York's Baruch College. (An interview with Carmichael appears on page 64 of this book.)

- *Taxation.* Students should have adequate knowledge of taxes and their impact on decision making. In addition, they should have a hands-on understanding of tax so they can apply tax principles and perform tax research in solving complex problems.
- *Behavioral sciences.* The behavioral sciences are important in understanding individual, group, and organizational behavior as well as management practices in business organizations.
- *Business law.* Students must be aware of the meaning of constitutionality and jurisdiction, the relationships between federal and state laws, and the roles of common law and equity, statutory law, and administrative regulation.
- *Communication.* Effective communication, whether listening, speaking, or writing, is an indispensable

skill for any professional. It is particularly important to CPAs because accounting is not only the identification, accumulation, and analysis of information, but also the communication of that information to others.

- *Economics.* CPAs should understand both macroeconomics and microeconomics. By studying macroeconomics, they can acquire an overview of how the economy operates. By studying microeconomics, they can learn about the effects of economic forces on organizations.
- *Ethics.* Fundamental to any profession is the obligation of its members to maintain the highest standard of ethical conduct. CPAs must be acutely aware of the underlying ethical concerns when analyzing business and accounting situations. They must have an in-depth understanding of the codes of ethical conduct of the state accountancy boards, the AICPA, and other accounting organizations, in order to appreciate their legal and ethical responsibilities.
- *Finance.* CPAs need to understand the concepts and tools used in financial analysis because one of the primary applications of accounting information, whether internal or external, is in finance.
- *Globalization.* CPAs should have an understanding of the international aspects of finance, economics, marketing, and accounting itself.
- *Information Systems.* The widespread use of computer and telecommunications technology makes an understanding of these technologies and their applications and limitations essential.
- *Legal and Social Environment.* CPAs must understand the regulatory and legal framework that government and the private sector provide to protect the public interest.
- *Marketing.* CPAs need to have a general familiarity regarding how marketing functions, and a more specific knowledge of operations that require accounting information in the making of business decisions and the solution of problems.
- *Quantitative Applications.* Quantitative methods are essential to the understanding and analysis of a wide range of business and accounting issues. CPAs should be familiar with the quantitative techniques

that apply to the solution of business and accounting problems, including the study of mathematics and statistics.

At many schools with accounting programs, you can take courses that cover these different areas. Depending on your interests, you may decide to take additional courses in a particular area, such as finance or information systems.

Master's Programs

Students are not required to have a master's degree to be eligible to take the CPA exam, but more students are enrolling in master's programs and earning degrees. According to the AICPA's 2008 *Trends in the Supply of Accounting Graduates* report, master's degrees in accounting were awarded to 16,599 graduates of the 2006–2007 class, a 24 percent increase from the 2003–2004 year. Graduate study helps students develop a level of technical competence and professional skill that will better prepare them for successful careers. Graduates with master's degrees may have an edge in competing for some jobs. For that matter, some employers may require that graduates have a master's degree to fill certain jobs or to advance to senior positions in an organization. Finally, master's graduates may earn higher incomes over the course of their careers.

Some schools have structured their accounting programs so that students planning to become CPAs can choose among different combinations of bachelor's and master's degrees. New York's Baruch College has a five-year bachelor's/master's CPA program.

Depending on the undergraduate major, students pursue one of the following degree combinations:

- BBA in Accounting, plus MS in Taxation or Accountancy
- BBA in a major other than accounting, plus MS in Accountancy
- BA or BS in any major, plus MS in Accountancy

Thus, if you were to study for the BBA degree, you could major in accounting or another subject. And if you were to study for a BS or BA degree, you could earn an undergraduate degree in, say, economics and a master's degree in accountancy.

Schools offer other graduate programs for accounting students. The University of Texas' McCombs School of Business, for example, offers an MBA with a concentration in accounting.[15] And should you have an interest in teaching and research, some schools such as the University of Southern California (through its Marshall School of Business) offer PhD programs in accounting. "It's not just standing in front of a class and talking that I enjoy," said Randolph Beatty, dean of the USC Leventhal School of Accounting, part of the Marshall School. "It's helping students on projects, getting to know them, learning about their career aspirations and what they want out of life. I love working with students." (Teaching as a career, and PhD programs in accounting, are discussed in chapter 9.)

For more information on the accounting programs of individual colleges and universities, visit their Web sites.[16]

Bringing the Real World into the Classroom

To better prepare students for careers in accounting, schools have increased their efforts to bring the real world of business and accounting into the classroom. Some examples follow.

Trading Centers

Accounting and other students in Baruch College's Zicklin School of Business can trade stocks, bonds, and commodities in a trading room that's real in every way but one—the trades. The Wasserman Trading Floor, under the direction of Richard Holowczak, associate professor of computer information systems, is a fully equipped, simulated trading environment with financial news terminals displaying currency trading, economic reports, and running stock quotes. Using the same technology as in "live" markets, students can learn about markets and financial services. And they can play the roles of hedgers, traders, portfolio managers or speculators—valuable experience for graduates seeking positions in finance, banking, or accounting. Only a handful of trading centers existed 10 years ago in schools worldwide. Now there are more than 60, including centers at some U.S. schools.[17]

---

15 University of Texas at Austin, McCombs School of Business, "Texas MBA with a Concentration," http://mba.mccombs.utexas.edu/students/academics/special.asp#Concentration

16 For a link to these sites, see "Colleges and Universities Offering Accounting Degree Programs" on the AICPA's Web site (www.aicpa.org/collegelist/index.htm)

17 "Technology: Virtual Trading Floors Useful in Real Life," *Financial Times*, June 16, 2008

Adoption of International Financial Reporting Standards

International Financial Reporting Standards (IFRSs) currently are used or coming into use in many countries around the world. The United States uses a different set of standards known as generally accepted accounting principles. U.S. adoption of IFRSs would have such benefits as facilitating worldwide investment—investors could more easily compare the financial statements of U.S. companies with those of companies in other countries. Although it's uncertain when the United States might adopt IFRSs, schools are working with accounting firms and the AICPA to introduce IFRSs into business and accounting curriculums. Because of the time it takes to train, and resources required to prepare students, schools cannot wait for a certain date to start this process. And with the increasing globalization of business, more U.S. accounting graduates could, at some point in their careers, find themselves working in other countries where knowledge of IFRSs is essential.

"We have made a major change in our program to integrate IFRSs across three classes, and we can ramp up our program as IFRSs become required and incorporated into the CPA exam," Texas A&M's Benjamin said.

For more on IFRSs, visit the "IFRS Resources" section on the AICPA's Web site (www.ifrs.com).

Emphasis on Communication and Other Skills

Consistent with the notion that CPAs must be well rounded professionals, schools such as the University of Illinois Urbana-Champaign have restructured their programs to give more emphasis to enabling accounting students to develop communication, critical thinking, analytical and other skills. The university's restructured program "still provides the technical knowledge that is necessary to a practitioner, but that alone is not sufficient," Solomon said. "Practitioners need a set of skills and attitudes that help them to succeed. We have brought in to our learning objectives a heavy emphasis on these skills and attitudes such as communicating, negotiating, and the ability to adapt."

At the University of Southern California, all undergraduate accounting majors are required to take business communication for accountants. "This experiential class covers theory, practices, and techniques essential to external and organizational communication; interpersonal communication; and development of skills in presenting oral and written reports," said Shirley Maxey, professor of clinical accounting and management communication. Undergraduate accounting students also take advanced writing for business, which helps them learn how to write about technical subjects for varied audiences. Graduate students in accounting and business taxation programs are required to take a communication course as part of their degree. (An interview with Maxey is on the CD included with this book.)

Emphasis on Ethics

In the wake of well-publicized business and accounting scandals earlier in this decade, schools are emphasizing ethics in their curriculums. "We stress ethical behavior—it's the backbone of our school," said John Elliott, dean of the Zicklin School of Business and professor of accounting, Baruch College, City University of New York. "We focus on preparing students to deal with ethical issues—with the Enrons of this world," he said. "And we try to inculcate a healthy skepticism in our students, to encourage independent thinking, and to help them appreciate that their reputation is one of their most important assets."

Community Colleges

U.S. community colleges have 2 major purposes.[18] The first is to serve as a bridge from high school to college by providing courses for transfer toward a bachelor's degree. In fact, 4 out of 10 college-bound high school graduates start their college education this way. The second purpose is to prepare students for the job market by offering entry-level career training, as well as courses for adult students who want to upgrade their skills for workforce re-entry or advancement.

"The mission of community colleges has evolved over time," said Susan V. Crosson, professor and coordinator of accounting at Santa Fe College, a community college in Gainesville, Florida. "Originally they offered vocational and job training, then they added programs for students to transfer to four year colleges in their junior year, and now some have started to offer four year programs and degrees in certain disciplines." (An interview with Crosson can be found on page xx of this book.) A snapshot of community college facts can be found in box 2-1.

Box 2-1: *U.S. Community College Fast Facts**

Number: 1,195

Enrollment: 11.5 million

% of all U.S. undergraduates enrolled in college: 46%

Average age: 29

21 or younger: 43%

22 to 39: 42%

40 or older: 16%

Women: 60%

Men: 40%

Minorities: 35%

First generation to attend college: 39%

* "Community College Fast Facts," American Association of Community Colleges, www2.aacc.nche.edu/research/index.htm

Community colleges are primarily two-year institutions. Consistent with their purpose, many have two-track degree programs.

In one track, students earn an associate's degree in two years and then go into jobs that require some college education but not a four-year degree from a college or university; for example, a student might take accounting, business, and other courses, and get a job as a bookkeeper or office assistant.

In another track, students complete a core curriculum of courses in accounting or other subjects that can be transferred to the state's four-year colleges or universities. These students earn an associate's degree and transfer to a four-year school in their junior year and complete the studies required to earn a bachelor's degree in accounting or other disciplines.

18 "Six Benefits of Community Colleges," College Board, www.collegeboard.com/student/csearch/where-to-start/8169.html.

Figure 2-1: *Six Steps to Becoming a CPA*

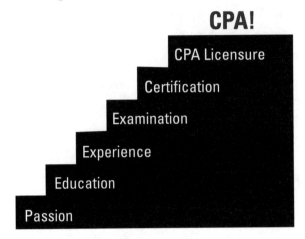

Community colleges usually cost much less (particularly for state residents) than state or private colleges and universities. By living at home and going to your local community college, you can save money to help pay for your last two years at a four-year college or university. One thing to find out from a college's career advisor or other source is whether or not you will be able to transfer the courses you take to a four-year college or university where you plan to finish your college studies.

Wrap-up

In this chapter, you learned the following:

- Accounting is one of today's hottest careers.
- More schools are offering accounting programs, and more students are studying for degrees.
- As a student, you should have a good balance of accounting, business administration, and liberal arts education.

- To become a CPA, you must meet educational, certification, and licensing requirements. The key steps are illustrated in Figure 2-1.
- As a CPA, you could earn more income, have an edge in competing for a job, and realize many other benefits.

In the next chapter, we look at preparing for and taking the CPA exam. In subsequent chapters, we look at career opportunities for CPA in public accounting, corporations and businesses, government, the not-for-profit sector, and as sole practitioners. Once you have learned about the educational programs in accounting, the CPA certification and licensing requirements, and the different career paths, you will be ready to make an informed decision about whether you want to pursue a career in accounting, and which accounting career path to take.

Interview: Randolph Beatty
University of Southern California

Accounting education has been an integral part of the School of Business at the University of Southern California (USC) since the business school's inception in 1920. At that time, the department of accounting offered a bachelor of science degree in business. In the early 1970s, the American Institute of Certified Public Accountants (AICPA) Committee on Accounting Education strongly endorsed the idea of establishing schools of accounting. In 1979, the USC Board of Trustees approved the establishment of a School of Accounting at USC. In 1996, USC renamed its School of Accounting the Elaine and Kenneth Leventhal School of Accounting in recognition of the support of Kenneth Leventhal and his wife Elaine to the school and to the university. The Leventhals founded the CPA firm of Kenneth Leventhal & Co. in 1949 in Los Angeles. The Leventhal firm became the largest CPA firm in the United States specializing in real estate, and, all-in-all, one of the largest U.S. accounting firms. It merged with Ernst & Young in 1995.

> "I'm most concerned that students master the subject matter—that they 'get it.' To accomplish that goal, I take a simple approach: I tell students what I am going to teach them, I teach them, and then I tell them what I've taught them."

The USC Leventhal School of Accounting offers the BS in Accounting degree that provides a general background in business necessary for entry into the accounting profession and prepares students for entry into the professional program leading to a master's of accounting degree. There are three undergraduate tracks which students can choose: the accounting track, the accounting information systems track or the graduate track. The Leventhal School of Accounting offers two graduate degrees: the Master of Accounting (MAcc) and the Master of Business Taxation (MBT). The MAcc program provides an integrated curriculum to prepare graduates for careers in professional accounting, public accounting, industry and government. The MBT program provides in-depth specialization in taxation to prepare students for careers as tax professionals. In addition, the school offers the MBT-Working Professionals program, a part time, evening program designed specifically for students who wish to remain fully employed while pursuing their graduate studies. Finally, the Leventhal School offers the PhD program in accounting, a five-year program of courses, examinations, teaching, research, and a dissertation leading to the doctorate degree.

Randolph Beatty was appointed dean and holder of the Alan Casden Dean's Chair at the USC Leventhal School of Accounting in August 2001. Prior to joining USC, Beatty was The Distinguished Professor of Accounting at Southern Methodist University (1992-2001). He also has held faculty positions at the Graduate School of Business at the University of Chicago (1987-91) and the Wharton School of the University of Pennsylvania (1981-87). Beatty has won numerous teaching awards throughout his career. In 1994, Business Week named him 1 of 12 Masters of the Classroom. At the USC Leventhal School, he teaches an innovative financial statement analysis class to both undergraduate and graduate students. Beatty has widely published work in management, law, finance, and accounting journals. His research addresses contemporary management concerns from an applied economics perspective, spanning a wide range of issues relating to initial public offerings, private firm valuation, and corporate control. His research on "Investment Banking, Reputation and the Undertaking of Initial Public Offerings" was a Journal of Financial Economics All Star Paper. Beatty earned his PhD at the University of Illinois at Urbana-Champaign in 1982. He holds a master of accounting science and a bachelor of science in mathematics from the University of Illinois at Urbana-Champaign.

How did you get interested in accounting?

In high school, I enjoyed studying math. When I enrolled at the University of Illinois, the shortest lines seemed to be for math, so I signed up. I subsequently decided to major in math. As part of my math studies, I took some accounting courses, which I also enjoyed.

How did you get into teaching?

To help pay off my student loans, I did some part-time teaching while I was in school. I found that I enjoyed teaching and ultimately decided on a career in the field. I had toyed with the idea of being a football coach, like my father, but decided that teaching was a more practical choice. My only coaching these days is as an armchair quarterback, pretending to call in plays when I'm watching USC on television or from the stands.

How's your play calling?

Not bad, but I haven't been invited to join the USC coaching staff.

After you earned your undergraduate degree, what did you do?

When I graduated in 1974, the job market was weak, and not many companies were hiring. So I enrolled in graduate school. After I earned my master's, I went on to study for a PhD. It took me about 6 years to earn my degree because I was teaching over 200 students a year at Illinois.

From your years of experience, what have you found is the best approach to teaching?

I'm most concerned that students master the subject matter—that they "get it." To accomplish that goal, I take a simple approach: I tell students what I am going to teach them, I teach them, and then I tell them what I've taught them. It's an approach that I have found works the best, regardless of the subject matter. But it's not just standing in front of a class and talking that I enjoy, it's helping students on projects, getting to know them, learning about their careers aspirations and what they want out of life. I love working with students.

What does it take to succeed in accounting?

You must, of course, have a mastery of accounting. Beyond that, the requirements for success are much the same as in other fields including drive, ambition, critical thinking skills, the ability to work well with others, and, most important, strong communication skills. These are the skills of the complete professional.

Where do you suggest that graduates start in accounting?

I would start in public accounting, and it doesn't necessarily have to be with a Big 4 firm. You could begin with a large national firm or a regional or local firm. Regardless, public accounting provides the foundation for a career not only in the accounting profession, but also in business, government, and many other fields. We try to communicate this to our students, to help them think in broad terms about the career opportunities available to accountants.

During your time in teaching, have you ever thought of giving it up for something else?

I thought about investment banking, but decided against it. At one time I did some litigation support for a public accounting firm, but never was interested in it full time. Teaching is my first love. You really can make a difference in the lives of students.

Interview: James Benjamin
Texas A&M University

James J. Benjamin is the Deloitte Leadership professor and head of the Accounting Department in the Mays Business School at Texas A&M University. He joined the faculty at Texas A&M in 1974, and has served as department head since 1982. Dr. Benjamin received his BS degree from the University of Maryland and his MBA and DBA degrees from Indiana University. He is a certified public accountant. He previously served as the PhD coordinator for the Mays School and the director of the College Honors Program.

> *"We strongly embrace the 150-hour requirement because it provides students with exposure not only to accounting, but also to other subjects including financial markets, information systems, public policy, the marketing of professional services, and the impact of technology on accounting and business."*

Dr. Benjamin is the co-author of two textbooks and he has written more than 70 articles for academic and professional journals. Dr. Benjamin has received awards for both outstanding research and service in the Mays Business School and he received the University Distinguished Achievement Award for Administration from Texas A&M University in 2004. He also was named an Outstanding Educator by the Texas Society of CPAs in 1999 and he received the Faculty Merit Award from the Federation of Schools of Accountancy in 2009. He is a member of a number of professional and academic organizations and he has served as the chair of the AACSB Accounting Standards Committee, a trustee of the Accounting Education Foundation of the Texas Society of CPA's, and president of the Federation of Schools of Accountancy.

Through the Mays Business School, Texas A&M offers a bachelor's of business administration in accounting, a master's of science in accounting, and a doctoral program in accounting. In addition, it offers the Professional Program, a two-and-a-half year program that students enter in the spring semester of their junior year. Upon completion of the program, they earn both a BBA degree in accounting and a master of science degree in accounting, finance, management information systems, marketing, or entrepreneurship.

Where does the accounting program fit in a large university like Texas A&M?

About 95 percent of the university's 38,500 undergraduate students are from Texas—Texas is such a large state that they could live 800 miles from here and still be from Texas. Accounting is one of the more popular majors in spite of Texas A&M's being an enrollment controlled college. The business school is limited to about 1,200 students each year and about a fourth major in accounting. Texas A&M is by far the largest provider of CPAs in the state of Texas each year. Texas A&M started offering accounting courses in the 1920s, and began offering an undergraduate degree in accounting in 1927. The business school was accredited in 1972, the accounting programs in 1982, and we started the Professional Program in 1992. The Professional Program is very visible and highly thought of throughout campus.

What's the focus of the accounting program?

The accounting program focuses on developing the skills important to success in the profession and other financial related jobs. Texas requires students to complete 150 hours of course work, including 30 hours of accounting courses beyond principles of accounting, to sit for the CPA exam. We strongly embrace the 150-hour requirement because it provides students with exposure not only to accounting, but also to other subjects including financial markets, information systems, public policy, the marketing of professional services, and the impact of technology on accounting and business. While the 150 hour requirement initially got some pushback from students, it appears that most students, their parents, and employers, now see the value of the additional education requirement.

Why do students enroll in the Professional Program?

I believe that the Professional Program has been very attractive to students because it helps develop the skills necessary for success in business. Moreover, it is well recognized that almost all students in the program have a paid professional internship and accept a permanent job prior to graduation. Other positive factors include the opportunity to get a master's degree in an integrated program and to select from interesting track choices including assurance services/information management, financial management, management information systems, tax planning, marketing, and entrepreneurial leadership. Graduates are well prepared to achieve their career goals, whether their aspirations are to become a partner in an international public accounting firm, an executive in a major corporation or financial institution, or managing their own business.

What does it take to succeed in accounting?

People skills, communication skills, the ability to adapt to change, the ability to work with others, and, of course, analytical ability. From the very beginning of the Professional Program, students start developing and refining these skills.

What are examples of how you help students to develop these skills?

Our introductory courses in accounting help students to address problems and find solutions. But there seldom is one right answer, or one solution. In our intermediate courses, we introduce students to uncertainty. By the end of these courses, they learn how to frame a problem, consider alternatives, and decide on the best answer among several choices. Another example is a sophomore course that focuses on teamwork, communications, and ethics. We train students in how to form teams and work on real projects. Virtually all of our accounting courses have individual and team projects.

When did you start the PhD program in accounting?

In 1968. Since then we've graduated 3–4 PhDs a year. While this likely sounds like a small number, Texas A&M has been one of the largest producers of PhDs in accounting over the past 25 years. When I started teaching in the 1970s, about 70 business schools in the United States were turning out about 200 accounting PhDs a year. In the late 90's that number dropped to under 100 a year. While it has increased somewhat in recent years, there continues to be an incredible PhD shortage in accounting. We are almost in a crisis situation for audit and tax professors. A number of business schools are struggling to have enough PhDs to prevent a loss of accreditation.

What can schools do to attract more PhD candidates?

While compensation for educators is certainly less than accounting positions in the private sector, the PhD is attractive to some because they have the opportunity to do research and to teach, to work with students and to help them to prepare for careers in accounting or related fields. One key to attracting more candidates is to better inform qualified individuals about the benefits of an academic career and to provide better financial support for PhD students. I believe that the Accounting Doctoral Scholars Program, which was recently funded by a number of major accounting firms, will have an impact on both counts.

How do you cope with the PhD shortage in the Mays School?

A key strategy has been to utilize highly qualified professionals who do not hold a PhD. Indeed, we currently have 11 full-time faculty members in accounting who have master's degrees and relevant work experience. One recently left a large accounting firm after years as a senior partner. He spoke to classes prior to his retirement and it was obvious that he was very good with students. All of these people enjoy teaching and they are typically not in it for the money.

What are your challenges in planning the accounting program?

A big concern is changing and adapting the program as the world changes. An example is International Financial Reporting Standards (IFRSs). We have made a major change in our program to integrate IFRSs across three intermediate classes, and we can ramp up our program as IFRSs becomes required and incorporated into the CPA exam. In planning our program, we are advised by employers, faculty, alumni, and others. Since we don't have the time to cover everything important, we constantly have to make hard choices regarding the details of the program.

Interview: Douglas Carmichael
Baruch College, City University of New York

Douglas R. Carmichael is the Claire and Eli Mason Distinguished Professor of Accountancy in the Stan Ross Department of Accountancy, Baruch College, Zicklin School of Business, City University of New York. He has been a professor at Baruch since 1983. Carmichael is the founding director of the Robert Zicklin Center for Corporate Integrity, a discussion forum for a broad range of contemporary issues confronting U.S. corporations and capital markets. In April 2003, he was appointed to a three-year term as chief auditor and director of professional standards of the Public Company Accounting Oversight Board (PCAOB). He has also served as a consultant for the Securities and Exchange Commission and as an expert witness on forensic accounting and independence issues. Carmichael is the co-author of The CPA's Guide to Professional Ethics *(John Wiley, 2000). Before joining the PCAOB, he was vice president auditing, for the AICPA. In 2007, Carmichael was named one of the Top 100 Most Influential People by* Accounting Today, *which described him as "one of the country's foremost authorities on auditing standards and financial integrity." He holds a BS in economics and MAS and PhD degrees in accounting from the University of Illinois. He is a certified fraud examiner as well as a CPA.*

> ## "We have never had sufficient numbers of well qualified people in accounting because the profession is so demanding. You must have a solid knowledge of accounting, your clients, and their industries. You must be dedicated to your work, and enjoy what you do."

What got you interested in accounting as a career?

I was inspired by a professor, Art Wyatt. I was an undergrad majoring in economics when I took his audit course. I became a teaching assistant for Wyatt, worked for Wyatt's accounting practice, and passed the CPA exam along the way. I was fascinated by auditing because there are so many diverse areas under the audit umbrella such as ethics, evidence, and statistical sampling. Another mentor at Illinois was Robert Mautz, who wrote a monograph on the philosophy of auditing. It established that auditing is a very serious discipline.

Did you work in public accounting?

Just briefly—long enough to get my CPA certification. I wanted to be a professor. I started teaching undergrad classes at the University of Texas. I also worked summers at Haskins and

Sells. I later interviewed at the University of Iowa, whose head of the accounting department had left to work as the right hand man for Len Savoy, head of AICPA. The AICPA under Savoy created the position of audit research consultant, whose purpose was to provide support for audit standard setting. I was hired as the AICPA's first auditing researcher. We produced the first research report on audit reporting. A lot of people used it. There was nothing else like it at the time. After 14 years at the AICPA, I left to return to teaching. I subsequently got a call from the chairman of Coopers & Lybrand, who asked me to serve as an expert witness in a trial. I went on to serve as an expert witness in a number of cases, including some high profile trials.

From your experience with the SEC, what are the benefits of CPAs working for government agencies sometime during their careers?

In government, there is the personal satisfaction of working for the good guys. What impressed me most about the PCAOB was how dedicated everyone was to serving the public interest.

How interested are CPAs in serving in government?

Lawyers understand the value of government service, accountants less so. Not surprisingly, then, lawyers are more proactive about seeking government jobs than accountants. Working for a government agency provides an opportunity to learn how it works. That knowledge benefits you and your clients when you return to the private sector. And from their initial experience in government, some CPAs decide that they want to spend their careers in government.

When is an opportune time for CPAs to work in government?

I suggest that graduates spend a few years working for a government agency before they join the private sector. It is easier to go into government at the start of your career because the salary disparity between government and the private sector is not as great as at the more senior levels. If you go into government later in your career, you sacrifice a lot in salary— unless you already have accumulated money and the salary disparity is not as important.

What's the value to students of taking audit courses?

Audit courses are valuable, among other reasons, because a lot of companies and public agencies have strengthened their internal audit capability post Enron. At Baruch, one course in independent auditing is offered at undergrad level. It includes technology as an audit tool. There is also a graduate audit course that is more advanced. It covers ethics, legal liability, computerized audit systems, and other topics.

What's your advice to students planning careers in accounting?

We have never had sufficient numbers of well qualified people in accounting because the profession is so demanding. You must have a solid knowledge of accounting, your clients, and their industries. You must be dedicated to your work, and enjoy what you do. Interpersonal skills are very important. Auditors are seen as interlopers—they are not universally loved. They have to be able to interview people, to get information from them. I am the first to admit that I'm not a good interviewer—I tend to intimidate people. That's why I appreciate auditors who are skilled interviewers.

Interview: Susan Crosson
Santa Fe College

Susan V. Crosson is professor and coordinator of accounting at Santa Fe College, a community college in Gainesville, Florida, where she has been a faculty member since 1989. In her academic career, she has been an adjunct lecturer at the University of Florida, a lecturer at Washington University and the University of Oklahoma, and a faculty member at Johnson County Community College, Overland Park, Kansas, and Kansas City Kansas Community College. Among other awards, she received the 2008 McGuffey Longevity Award (Accounting/Business/Economics/Management) as a co-author of Principles of Accounting.* The award is given by the Text and Academic Authors Association in recognition of textbooks and learning materials whose excellence has been demonstrated over time. In 2007, she received The Lifetime Achievement in Accounting Education Award of the Two-Year Section of the American Accounting Association. The award recognizes full-time college accounting educators who have distinguished themselves for excellence in teaching and for involvement in the accounting profession. She has co-authored books on managerial accounting, computer accounting essentials, and the use of software programs in accounting. Crosson received a BBA in accounting and economics from Southern Methodist University and an MS in accounting from Texas Tech University.

> "People want to learn about accounting—they see it as a ticket to business and a better life."

How did you decide to go into teaching?

Two of my uncles were accountants, and when I was in college, I took a course in accounting, liked it, and decided to minor in accounting. I worked in the private sector for a time, as an internal auditor for the Federal Reserve Bank, as a credit analyst for a bank, and as an internal auditor and assistant to the vice president of finance at Texas Tech University. When my husband, who is a psychologist, began to study for his PhD, I enrolled in the master's program at Texas Tech while I worked full time and earned my CPA certificate. Upon graduation with my MS in Accounting, I went to work in public accounting. When it was time to start a family, I thought teaching might be a good fit, so I joined the faculty of a community college. We moved from time to time, and I taught at different colleges.

---

* *Principles of Accounting*, 10th ed., by Belverd E. Needles, Jr., Marian Powers, and Susan V. Crosson, published by Houghton Mifflin Company College Edition.

What's the role of community colleges like Santa Fe in educating and preparing students for jobs and careers?

The mission of community colleges has evolved over time. Originally, they offered vocational and job training, then they added programs for students to transfer to four-year colleges in their junior year, and now some have started to offer four-year programs and degrees in certain disciplines. For example, Santa Fe began offering the bachelor of applied science degree in the fall of 2009.

What programs do you offer students planning to go into accounting?

We offer an associate of arts (AA) degree for students who plan to transfer to 4-year colleges and universities in the Florida state university system, including students who plan to earn a BS in accounting. Students must satisfactorily complete 60 credit hours to earn the AA degree, and the credits are transferable to a 4-year school, assuming students meet the admission requirements. Many of our students are enrolled in the AA program.

What accounting programs do you offer for students who have other job or career interests?

We have a certificate program, including a business operations—accounting certificate that provides students with a general introduction to business management and operations. Students must satisfactorily complete 18 hours of study including courses in financial and management accounting. Students in this program may get jobs as bookkeepers or office managers, or work for the IRS, for example, or enroll in other certificate programs in business administration or business management.

How do you interest students in accounting?

It's not so much selling students on accounting as offering courses that attract their interest. Our courses in financial accounting and management accounting are designed to help students learn how to read a financial statement, learn about the role of independent auditors, understand the work of management accountants, and other topics. Some students decide that they are interested in accounting, and that they can be good at it.

What are the backgrounds of your students?

Many of our students are the first in their families to attend college, and about a third are from Latin America. They ask themselves whether they belong here, and whether they can succeed. We provide guidance, support and encouragement to help them develop self-confidence, to trust themselves, and, for those going on to 4-year schools, to prepare for the challenges of being students in larger institutions.

What courses do you teach?

Besides the financial and management accounting courses, I teach courses on the use of computer programs in accounting. All of these courses are designed not just for accounting students but for students planning to go into business, where they will be expected to have a basic understanding of accounting and know how to use accounting systems their first day on the job.

Besides teaching, you've reached a larger audience through the accounting books you've co-authored. How else do you reach the world beyond the classroom?

I've done about 200 YouTube videos based on my courses. They're very popular—they get about 3,000 hits a day. I receive comments and e-mails from people all over the world with questions about accounting. If you put anything on the Internet about accounting, the world will come to you. People want to learn about accounting—they see it as a ticket to business and a better life.

Interview: Dan Deines
Kansas State University

Dan Deines is the Ralph Crouch KPMG professor of accounting, College of Business Administration, Kansas State University. His main research interests are student recruitment and retention. He has developed and implemented a recruitment program aimed at counteracting the negative stereotypes of accounting among high school students. Deines also was involved in designing and implementing a nationally recognized revision in the college accounting curriculum, work that was supported with a grant from the Accounting Education Change Commission. The commission was formed in 1989 to create innovative accounting curricula that would better prepare students to become professional accountants.

> *"It's not simply a matter of attracting more students to accounting, but of attracting the best and brightest students. For that to happen, there has to be a change in attitudes."*

In 2007, Deines received the American Institute of Certified Public Accountants' (AICPA's) Distinguished Achievement in Accounting Education Award, which honors, among other accomplishments, excellence in teaching and innovation in curriculum development. The first academic to serve as president of the Kansas Society of Certified Public Accountants, he also has received the society's Outstanding Educator Award. Deines is a recipient of the Kansas State College of Business Administration's Outstanding Teaching and Advising awards. He has chaired the AICPA's Accounting Career Subcommittee and served on its Accounting Education Executive Committee. Deines is the co-author of the textbook, Introduction to Accounting: An Integrated Approach. *He earned his bachelor's degree in history in 1970 from Fort Hays State University, Hays, Kansas. In 1974, he completed a master's degree in business with an emphasis in accounting at Emporia State University, Emporia, Kansas. He went on to complete his doctorate in financial accounting at the University of Nebraska in 1985.*

How did you get interested in accounting?

When I was in high school, you wouldn't dare take a business class, which included accounting. It was seen as something for students who wanted to be secretaries. In college, I thought about going to law school, and I asked my dad what courses I should take to prepare. He said business and accounting. I took an accounting class, taught by a gifted teacher named Terry Cummins, who made accounting interesting. I was so fascinated by accounting that I continued to take classes in the field. After I earned my MS, I received job offers from some smaller CPA firms and from Conoco, but I decided I wanted to teach. I started as a teacher at Doane College, a small liberal arts college in Nebraska, and studied part time in the PhD program at the University of Nebraska. I came to Kansas State in1982.

How did you get interested in student recruitment and retention?

I got to thinking about my negative attitude towards accounting when I was in high school, and wondered if students then in high school had the same attitude. In 1985, I did a survey in Kansas City of high school juniors and seniors who were enrolled in college prep programs. I asked them to rank ten professions based on their interest in the profession and other criteria. CPA ranked dead last after teaching, law enforcement, and other careers. These were bright, talented, personable kids who participated in the survey, and they stereotyped accounting as boring, unappealing, and not for them.

What was the reaction of the accounting profession to the survey findings?

Indifference, at first. Then enrollment in college accounting programs began to fall in the late 1980s, and continued to fall in the 1990s, and my research began to get the attention of the profession. I was invited to serve on the AICPA's Accounting Careers Subcommittee whose mission was to interest students in careers in accounting. In 2000, the AICPA did a study, conducted by the Taylor Research and Consulting Group, and known as the Taylor Report, to examine the causes of the downturn in accounting majors in college and new CPAs and determine what could be done to reverse the trend.[*] Among other findings, the report said most students were ignorant of the basics of an accounting career, much of the student information regarding accounting was limited or faulty, and high school accounting courses were a systemic barrier to student interest in accounting.

What did you do about the resistance of high school students towards accounting careers?

For students to be interested, teachers have to be interested in accounting, so I set up a program to educate high school teachers about the profession. We asked accounting majors at Kansas State to nominate the best teachers in their high schools, regardless of the classes they taught. We brought these teachers to the Kansas State campus to meet with practicing accountants and our students to learn about the profession. The program was very successful in that it sparked the interest of teachers in accounting as a profession. I also established a program to bring high school students from around the state who were nominated by these teachers to campus to meet with our accounting students and young CPAs. We also revised the introduction to accounting course.

---

* "Taylor Report on Student and Academic Research Study," American Institute of Certified Public Accountants, July 2000.

Did you propose any changes to the high school accounting curriculum?

While we had programs to inform teachers and students about accounting careers, we still came up against the high school accounting curriculum. It was very vocational oriented—like a bookkeeping class—and it is the same course that has been taught in high schools for decades. I talked to the AICPA about creating a new curriculum based on a college prep model. To build a bridge from high school to college, the new high school accounting should be an AP** course with college credit. But it has been a hard sell, this concept. Today, most high schools in the U.S. still teach accounting as a vocational course, and most college bound kids aren't interested in taking it because it is not college prep and they don't get college credit. Their first exposure to accounting usually is in an introductory course in their freshman or sophomore year, but too many bright students won't consider taking these courses as a result of the stereotype created by a high school course.

What are the prospects for interesting more high school students in accounting careers?

It's not simply a matter of attracting more students to accounting, but of attracting the best and brightest students. For that to happen, there has to be a change in attitudes. High school administrators and teachers have to be receptive to introducing college level accounting classes in addition to the traditional, vocational accounting curriculum. Colleges and universities have to work with high schools in giving college credit for high school accounting courses, and in advising and assisting students in preparing for careers in accounting. And the profession itself has to work with high schools and colleges and universities in encouraging and assisting students to pursue accounting careers. The profession needs to attract the very best people. It is my belief that using the existing educational infrastructure is the most effective and efficient long-term solution to this challenge.

** College level courses and exams offered in high schools. According to the College Board, AP courses are recognized by more than 90 percent of U.S. colleges. www.collegeboard.com/student/testing/ap/about.html

Interview: John Elliott
Baruch College, City University of New York

Baruch College dates to the founding, in 1847, of the Free Academy, the very first free public institution of higher education in the nation. (Baruch's landmark building at 23rd Street and Lexington Avenue occupies the site of the Free Academy). Established in 1919 as City College's School of Business and Civic Administration, the school was renamed in 1953 in honor of Bernard M. Baruch—statesman, financier, and distinguished alumnus. In 1968, the school became an independent senior college in The City University of New York (CUNY) system.

> *"Although I did not realize it at the time, when I was a junior and senior in college I was really interviewing for a teaching position years later at Maryland. Many students will have an experience like mine when an unsolicited and unexpected opportunity creates a fundamental shift in their career path."*

Baruch offers undergraduate and graduate programs through its 3 schools: the Zicklin School of Business, the largest business school in the nation; the Mildred and George Weissman School of Arts and Sciences; and the School of Public Affairs. Baruch also offers nondegree and certificate programs through its division of continuing and professional studies. The BBA in accountancy is offered by the Stan Ross Department of Accountancy within the Zicklin School of Business. The undergraduate accounting program is intended to provide students with a general liberal arts and sciences background as well as a foundation in general business practices and an understanding of accounting concepts and theory. In the 2008-09 school year, 597 students graduated from the program.

Undergraduate students who apply to take the New York State CPA exam after August 1, 2009, will be required to have completed at least 150 credits of college coursework. The school offers various bachelor's and master's degree programs that meet the 150 hour requirement; for example, a BBA in accounting and an MS in Taxation or Accounting. Undergraduate students who meet the eligibility requirements graduate with their bachelor's degree and then enroll in the MS program.

John Elliott has been dean of the Zicklin School of Business and a professor of accounting at Baruch since 2002. He came to Baruch from Cornell University, where he was associate dean in the Johnson Graduate School of Management. He earned a bachelor's degree in economics and an MBA at the University of Maryland and—after working in public accounting and business—a PhD in accountancy at Cornell. He describes accounting as "the lens through which you understand business."

How did you get interested in accounting as a field of study?

When I was an undergraduate at the University of Maryland, I took some courses in accounting, which I enjoyed. I particularly remember an extraordinary professor named Howard Wright who brought the real world of accounting into the classroom. When APB 9 (Accounting Principles Board [APB] Opinion No. 9, *Earnings Per Share*) came out, he gave us copies. We had to read it and be prepared to talk about it. We really dug into APB 9; we learned about it, analyzed it, and discussed what it was trying to accomplish. It was a great intellectual experience.

Where did you work after you earned your bachelors?

I interviewed with Arthur Andersen and also with GE and Westinghouse. I decided to join Andersen and started in the firm's Washington, DC, office.

Why did you choose public accounting?

It was a hard choice. GE had an excellent financial training program for new employees. Westinghouse also had its benefits. Both companies and Andersen were very professional. Wherever I went, I would join a high functioning meritocracy. But I felt a stronger affinity for public accounting, and the career path seemed clearer.

What did you do at Andersen?

I joined the audit staff initially. But Andersen was just beginning a consultancy practice for government agencies and private companies doing business with the government. I was reassigned to help with systems design work during the less busy part of each year. I rotated through clients and acquired a lot of experience in the process. After three years, I joined Westinghouse, mainly for personal reasons. I wasn't there long before I got a call from Howard Wright.

What did he want?

A candidate for the University of Maryland accounting faculty had changed his mind and turned down a job offer. Howard asked if I could fill in by teaching some classes. It was an exciting opportunity. By the time I completed my MBA, I knew I wanted a career in teaching. I really loved teaching financial accounting, cost accounting, and other classes. I went on to earn a PhD at Cornell, joined the faculty, and remained there for about 25 years. Along the way, I served as dean of academic affairs and as associate dean in the graduate school of management. Later on, I had the opportunity to become dean of the Zicklin School. Although I did not realize it at the time, when I was a junior and senior in college I was really interviewing for a teaching position years later at Maryland. Many students will have an experience like mine when an unsolicited and unexpected opportunity creates a fundamental shift in their career path.

How would you characterize the students who enroll in the accounting program at Baruch?

Many of our students are first generation college and/or first generation American, and they plan careers in accounting—they don't see it as a stepping stone to something else. They and their families see accounting as a true professional opportunity not just a job. To be sure, we have had graduates who have gone into business, government and other fields, and have been highly successful. But for many of our students, accounting is their chosen profession. Our students have a high degree of interest and enthusiasm, and a real desire to learn. While they are technically proficient, they sometimes don't fully appreciate what it means to be a well rounded professional—they need to give more value to development of communication, teamwork, leadership and other skills. More than that, they must be well rounded human beings, with an appreciation of history, the arts and culture, and be open to all that life has to offer. Public accounting firms in New York City and elsewhere who hire our graduates know how important these skills and attributes are to advancement in the profession. One of our jobs is to help students understand that.

How do you help students to prepare for their careers as accountants in a fast changing business and professional environment?

We try to follow the example of my mentor Howard Wright, which is to bring the real world of accounting into the classroom, for example, through discussion and debate about the move towards adoption in the United States of International Financial Reporting Standards. We stress ethical behavior—it's the backbone of our school. We focus on preparing students to deal with ethical issues—with the Enrons of this world. And we try to inculcate a healthy skepticism in our students, to encourage independent thinking, and to help them appreciate that their reputation is one of their most important assets.

What can the academic community do to encourage more students to pursue careers in accounting?

The AICPA and the state societies have a number of programs and initiatives to increase student awareness of career opportunities in accounting. To the extent that we in the academic world do our jobs well, we can help to attract more talent. That begins with the first accounting course that undergraduates take, usually in their sophomore year. If an energetic, passionate professor teaches the course, and provides interesting, engaging material, that teacher can plant the idea that accounting is an interesting profession, and a possible career choice.

Why does a career in teaching accounting interest students or working professionals thinking of making a career change?

Above all, a love of teaching. Teachers are passionate about what they do. They won't earn as much money as in industry, although they will earn more today than in the past. But they get great satisfaction from teaching.

What does it take to succeed as a teacher?

To teach at the college level, you must earn a PhD, and you must have the ability not only to teach well but also to produce scholarship and research. To a considerable degree, teaching is a solitary profession—you design the course, deliver it, and evaluate the students. So you have to be a self-starter, and know how to allocate time. Most important, you must know how to motivate your students, to get them excited about learning. It's very challenging, but for the best of teachers, very rewarding.

Interview: Ira Solomon
University of Illinois at Urbana-Champaign

Ira Solomon, CPA, PhD, heads the department of accountancy and holds the R.C. Evans Endowed Chair in Business at the University of Illinois at Urbana-Champaign. His research and teaching focuses on external auditing. Previously, he was an audit research fellow in KPMG's executive office. He has served the American Accounting Association Auditing Section as research director, vice president (academic), president (1994–95), and past president (1995–96). And, he presently is a vice president of the American Accounting Association.

> "Industry specialists have greater insight into what key business processes are in an organization. In turn, they are able to translate what they learn about how effective and efficient a company is with its business processes into a risk assessment. They see not an isolated piece of information, but a pattern of information."

Solomon is the 2009 recipient of the Distinguished Achievement in Accounting Education Award from the American Institute of Certified Public Accountants (AICPA). In announcing the award, the AICPA noted, "Solomon has made significant contributions to the development of the accountancy program at the University of Illinois at Urbana-Champaign and elsewhere via his leadership with respect to innovative accounting curricula, especially Project Discovery. Project Discovery requires students to apply accounting principles to real-world problems through discovery learning, role-playing, case studies and other activities."

Solomon holds a BBA in Accounting, an MPA in accounting, and a PhD in accounting from the University of Texas at Austin.

How did you decide on accounting as a career?

I started out as a political science major, but found polysci too limiting. So I went to business school, and took various courses including accounting. I found that accounting was interesting, and that I was good at it. I decided to study for a master's in accounting. I also applied to law school, and was accepted. I was trying to decide whether to go into accounting after I earned my master's or go to law school. I was working for Peak

Marwick while I was in graduate school, and I decided to forego law school and work for them full time after I graduated in 1976. But I knew that at some point I wanted to return to the academic world.

What was the value of your experience in public accounting?

It gave some tacit knowledge of how companies work, and how audits are done. On one engagement we were using what I would call a judgment sampling of S&L loans. I said to the senior on job that it could be done more efficiently and accurately using a statistical technique. So I was asked to design it. Peat Marwick thought it was good enough that we starting using it to improve our analysis.

Where did you go from Peat?

I got a PhD in accounting from the University of Texas in 1977, and took a teaching position at the University of Arizona. I taught introductory and graduate level auditing. In 1981, I happened to attend a conference at Urbana-Champaign. I found the campus interesting. I called my wife and talked to her about joining the faculty, and I did in 1982. I had no clue at the time that I would stay here for so many years.

What interests you about academic life?

Part of it is the research. I always want to figure out not only how but why things work. One of the attractions here is understanding why things are as they are in the world of accounting.

What's an example?

Today, most large public accounting firms are organized around industry specialization. What do auditors who are industry specialists know that others don't? How does this knowledge help them to perform better audits? What are the gains versus the losses? It is not uncommon in the medical field to have specialists. You wouldn't go to a general practitioner to do brain surgery. I've written a couple of papers on this. Industry specialists have greater insight into what key business processes are in an organization. In turn, they are able to translate what they learn about how effective and efficient a company is with its business processes into a risk assessment. They see not an isolated piece of information, but a pattern of information. Nonindustry specialists might see the same pattern but not draw as much meaning from it. The industry specialist can apply risk assessment to provide value to the company, for example, in the risk assessment of a financial statement to ensure regulatory compliance or to prevent fraud.

Another interesting thing about research is how to bring it into the classroom. Fifteen years ago we had an accounting program that ranked with those of other top schools. But we decided it needed improvement. It wasn't as dynamic as we wanted. We embarked on a 5-year restructuring. We threw out our existing program and replaced it with a very complex program with probably 50 or 60 dimensions.

How is the new program different?

It still provides the technical knowledge that is necessary to a practitioner, but that alone is not sufficient. Practitioners need a set of skills and attitudes that help them to succeed. We have brought in to our learning objectives a heavy emphasis on these skills and attitudes such as communicating, negotiating, and the ability to adapt. On the communication front, we have divided this into both oral and written communication. In every accountancy course, we have a communications specialist team. They sit in the back of the room and provide feedback on how well students are communicating. We count this as part of their grades. Even students with good skills can move up to a better level. The feedback we get from employers is that this enhances the skills of graduates they hire. We have also learned how to intertwine skills and attitudes.

What do you mean by "attitude"?

What is attitude? It's partly an attitude of professional skepticism. If you read SEC sanctions of auditors, the No. 1 complaint is inadequate professional skepticism. So we build the development of professional skepticism into our program. Another point is that we use different teaching methods. We have educational philosophy known as constructivism. It's a contrast with traditional lecture modes, or what is known as "sage on the stage" in which students are passive recipients of learning. Constructivism encourages active learning. You have to take information and do things with it. You have to construct a mental model of how the world works. This is not inconsistent with the Harvard model of experiential learning. The idea is that you get powerful learning outcomes when students engage in activities related to the how and why of the world of accounting and taxation—how this world works.

So no "sage on the stage"?

If you walked into our classrooms, you would see chaos. There is a "guide on the side," not a sage on the stage. The student is responsible for learning—we can facilitate but not teach. The guide on the side is a facilitator along with students in the classroom. Our students often work in teams. There is lots of learning outside the classroom. If you were to debrief students as I do in spring with focus groups, the students would say the team thing seems weird but they learn from faculty and fellow students. It is more interesting and powerful than traditional classes. Plus, it helps to prepare students for the working world, where teams are commonly used.

Chapter 3

Certification

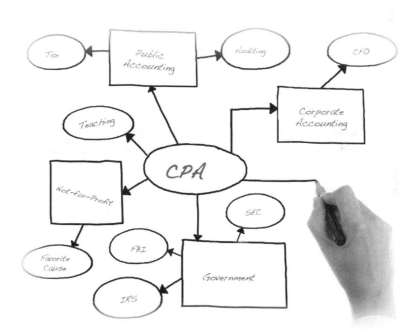

"Your advancement will be limited if you are solely a technician."

Ted Phillips, CEO • Chicago Bears

Three "E's" Add Up to CPA Certification and Licensing

To become a CPA, you have to meet the requirements sometimes known as "the three E's" (see box 3-1).

The educational requirements—the first "E"—were discussed in chapter 2. This chapter covers the other two "E's"—examination and experience.

How the Exam Got Started

To be licensed as a CPA in any of the 50 states and 5 jurisdictions[1], you must pass an examination. The CPA exam goes back—way back. In 1896, New York became the first state to enact legislation for the certification of accountants. Upon passing a CPA exam, accountants could legally use the title "certified public accountant." The first CPA certificate was issued to Frank Broaker, a New York City accountant who had lobbied for certification and was instrumental in the creation of the CPA exam.[2] It all started when Broaker got into a dispute with a client. Broaker had billed the client $3 an hour to straighten out its books, but the company was only willing to pay $1 an hour. Broaker went to court, and a jury found on his behalf. Although he won, Broaker believed such problems would continue until the state formally recognized accountants as professionals through the certification process. He went on to serve on the country's first CPA

Box 3-1: *The Three "E's": Requirements for CPA Certification and Licensing*

Education	Examination	Experience
Most states require 150 hours of college credits and a bachelor's degree. Check with the board of accountancy in the state where you plan to apply for a license.*	You must pass the Uniform CPA Examination. Generally you must satisfy the 150-hour credit requirement before you can take the exam. **NOTE:** Some states allow you take the exam after you've earned 120 hours of credits, but you still must complete 150 hours to apply for a license. Check with the board of accountancy in the state where you plan to apply for a license.	Most states require applicants for a license to have at least two years of experience in public accounting. Many states and jurisdictions also accept nonpublic accounting experience (for example, industry and government), although the number of years deemed acceptable are typically higher than for public accounting.** You may be required to pass an ethics course. Again, check with the board of accountancy in the state where you plan to apply for a license.

* For links to state boards, go to the home page of the National Association of State Boards of Accountancy at nasba.org. Click on "State Board Listing."

** The American Institute of Certified Public Accountants (AICPA): "Becoming a CPA/Academic and Career Resources; Students and CPA Candidates; Education and Experience Requirements." www.aicpa.org/Becoming+a+CPA/CPA+Candidates+and+Students/Education+Experience+Requirements.htm

1 District of Columbia, Puerto Rico, U.S. Virgin Islands, Guam, and the Commonwealth of Northern Mariana Islands.

2 "Institute Receives papers from First CPA," The *Journal of Accountancy*, May 1998, www.journalofaccountancy.com/Issues/1998/May/inaicpa.htm

examination board and as president of the American Association of Public Accountants, a predecessor of the American Institute of Certified Public Accountants (AICPA).

If Broaker somehow were able to visit our time, he would be astonished at what he started with the first CPA exam. (He would be even more astonished to be here, but that's another story.) In 2008, 85,000 candidates took what is now known as the Uniform CPA Examination. By comparison, 44,500 candidates took the exam in 2004.[3] The growing number of candidates is indicative of the strong interest in accounting as a career. (The benefits of CPA designation were discussed in chapter 2 under "Why Become a CPA?")

Purpose of Exam

According to the AICPA, the purpose of the Uniform CPA Exam is "to admit individuals into the accounting profession only after they have demonstrated the entry-level knowledge and skills necessary to protect the public interest in a rapidly changing business and financial environment." (For information on the exam, visit the Uniform CPA Examination Web site at www.cpa-exam.org).

Same Exam in Every State

The exam is called "uniform" because the same exam is given at authorized test centers in the 50 states and 4 of the 5 jurisdictions.[4,5]

So forget about jumping in your car and driving from state to state, looking for the easiest exam to take. It's the same exam wherever you take it.

Exam Sponsors

Three organizations jointly offer the exam. They are the AICPA, the National Association of State Boards of Accountancy (NASBA), and Prometric, a provider of testing and assessment services. The AICPA is responsible for developing and scoring the examination, NASBA for maintaining a national database of candidates, and Prometric for operating authorized testing centers where the exam is given. The exam is given on behalf of state boards of accountancy, which have the ultimate authority for licensing CPAs in their respective states.[6]

Exam Content

The Uniform CPA Exam is a computer-based exam consisting of four sections. The main content covered in each section includes:

- Auditing and Attestation (AUD)
  — Planning the engagement
  — Internal controls
  — Obtain and document information
  — Review engagement and evaluate information
  — Prepare communications

---

3 "The CPA Examination 2004–2009," The Uniform CPA Examination Alert—Fall 2009, www.cpa-exam.org/alerts/download/cpaalertfall09.pdf

4 The exam is not yet available in the Commonwealth of Northern Mariana Islands.

5 Candidates take different but equivalent examinations at each test center. The questions presented to candidates are drawn from a pool of test questions according to defined specifications. Although candidates take different tests, the specifications ensure that the results are comparable.

6 "The Uniform CPA Exam: FAQs," www.cpa-exam.org/

My Experience with the CPA Exam

If you're studying for the CPA exam, it's an endeavor best undertaken at a relatively quiet time in your life—if there is such a thing—so you can focus on the exam with a minimum of outside distractions.

But life has a way of surprising you. I know from my own experience with the exam.

When I studied for the exam a long time ago, my colleagues and I could choose to study on our own, meet in study groups with other students, sign up for a CPA study course, or hire a private tutor. I elected to study on my own, partly because that was the way I had studied most of the time in college and also because I couldn't afford the cost of a study course. I reviewed questions from old exams, reviewed accounting principles and auditing standards that might be covered in the exam, and otherwise burned the midnight oil. Although I didn't attend a CPA study course, I did the next best thing—I talked to students who attended the course about what they were studying. That helped me to make sure I was covering all the topics that might be included in the exam.

I informed my wife Marilyn that my goal was to take the exam only once in my life. I wasn't going to let anything interfere with my taking the exam. Marilyn was pregnant at the time, so you can imagine how my pronouncement went over. Anyway, we reached a compromise about my study routine, and I took breaks from time to time to help Marilyn as best I could.

Only a week before the exam, Marilyn was ready to deliver, and we went to the hospital. I sat in the waiting room, spread out my study papers, and continued studying right up until the time our son was born. Some of the doctors and nurses gently chided me about making a mess, with my study papers all over the place, but I kept right out on studying. I thought about taking my study materials into the delivery room, but that would have been too much.

Between a new baby in the house and studying for the exam, I wasn't getting much sleep. I studied almost nonstop, trying to remember everything, talking to colleagues about last minute preparations, getting more nervous as exam day approached.

At long last, exam day finally arrived.

Marilyn and I were living in New York at the time and, as I recall, the exam was held at what was then the New York Armory, which was filled with hundreds of exam takers. It was very organized. We were told to go to a certain area and sign in. There were proctors and monitors to direct us. Some of the kids came prepared for what was an all-day affair. They brought candy bars, which were allowed. During the exam you could hear wrappers opening and people chewing. It was annoying, but you couldn't do much about it. I forgot to fortify myself, and I did get hungry during the exam.

I had thought about how I was going to approach the exam. If I had a clear-cut understanding of the question and felt confident in the answer, I answered immediately. I rolled through these questions rather quickly. If I had a question that was extremely challenging, I decided to leave it for later. That strategy worked very effectively. I breezed through probably 80 percent of the exam, and the other 20 percent kept me busy until the end. I did complete the entire exam—a little early, in fact. I was concerned that maybe I hadn't given it enough time. So I reviewed my answers again before turning in my exam.

I left the exam feeling relatively good about my results, but still nervous. To complicate matters, I had committed to take a position with the CPA firm of Kenneth Leventhal & Company in Los Angeles. We had a new child, we were relocating to California, and I still didn't know if I had passed the exam. I did not get the results until we had arrived in California several weeks later. I had passed! I was awarded a New York State CPA certificate. Fortunately, the state of California accepted my New York State certificate because I met all of California's educational and experience requirements. I was a CPA!

It was an extremely proud moment in my life. I didn't think anyone else, even a medical doctor, could have felt any better than I did at this achievement.

- Business Environment and Concepts (BEC)
  — Business structure
  — Economic concepts
  — Financial management
  — Information technology
  — Planning and measurement[7]
- Financial Accounting and Reporting (FAR)
  — Concepts and standards for financial statements
  — Typical items in financial statements
  — Specific types of transactions and events
  — Accounting and reporting for governmental entities
  — Accounting and reporting for nongovernmental and not-for-profit organizations
- Regulation (REG)
  — Ethics and professional responsibility
  — Business law
  — Federal tax procedures and accounting issues
  — Federal taxation of property transactions
  — Federal taxation—individuals
  — Federal taxation—entities

For more details on the content of the exam (in effect until December 31, 2010), go to the Uniform CPA Examination home page at cpa-exam.org. Click on "Frequently Asked Questions" and "Examination Content, Structure and Delivery." Scroll down to "Access the Content Specifications Outline"(in effect until December 31, 2010), which provides more detailed examination content information."[8]

Exam Changes in 2011

The AICPA has announced that, beginning January 1, 2011, the Uniform CPA Examination will have a new structure, format and content, supported by enhanced technology known as Computer-Based Testing evolution.[9,10] The exam content updates will include, for the first time, testing on International Financial Reporting Standards. They will also include a new research task format and a new release of authoritative literature—the Financial Accounting Standards Board *Accounting Standards Codification*™, the single source of authoritative U.S. generally accepted accounting principles.[11]

For more details on the exam changes, go to cpa-exam.org, "Frequently Asked Questions," and "Examination Content, Structure and Delivery." Scroll down to "The new Content and Skill Specification Outlines (CSOs/SSOs) are available here (effective date January 1, 2011)."[12]

The Exam Process

The steps in the exam process include:
1. *Apply to take the examination* (request, complete, and submit an application). Contact the state board of accountancy or its designated agent in the state where you want to be licensed. For

---

7 *Measurement* refers here to organizational performance measures, such as various financial or nonfinancial scorecards for measuring an organization's performance; or to benchmarking, including quality control and best practices.

8 www.cpa-exam.org/cpa/computer_faqs_2.html.

9 "CBT-e Launch Date Announcement," AICPA, September 25, 2009. www.cpa-exam.org/download/CBT-e-Launch-Announcement-9-25-09.pdf

10 "CBT-e Launch is Scheduled for January 1, 2011," AICPA, The Uniform CPA Examination Alert, Fall 2009. www.cpa-exam.org/alerts/download/cpaalertfall09.pdf

11 "FASB Standards Codification Launches Today," Financial Accounting Standards Board (FASB) News Release, July 1, 2009, www.fasb.org/cs/ContentServer?c=FASBContent_C&pagename=FASB/FASBContent_C/NewsPage&cid=1176156318458

12 Or www.cpa-exam.org/download/CSOs-SSOs-Final-Release-Version-effective-01-01-2011.pdf.

links to state boards, go to the home page of NASBA at WWW.nasba. org. Click on "State Board Listing."[13] You can also access the state boards through the AICPA's Web site.[14]

If you haven't decided where you want to take the exam and want to get an idea of the application process in different states, you can to go the NASBA "Tools for Accountancy Compliance" home page at nasba-tools.com. Under "I Want to be a CPA," click on "Download Forms for the CPA Exam," and an interactive map of the United States (and the four jurisdictions that offer the exam) will appear.[15] Click on the state or jurisdiction that interests you, then click on "How to Apply."

2. *Pay the examination fees.* The two fees are the following:
   - The application fee is established by and paid to the board of accountancy of the state where you plan to apply for a license.
   - The examination fee depends on which section of the exam you take. You pay it to your board of accountancy (or its designated agent) or NASBA.

3. *Review the Uniform CPA Examination Tutorial and Sample Tests* (required). Go to the Examination's home page at cpa-exam.org. Click on "Tutorial and Sample Tests."

CPA Exam Sources

Here's a summary of the information sources about the Uniform CPA Examination cited in this chapter:

- The Uniform CPA Examination Web site: cpa-exam.org
- *CPA Examination Alert:* Quarterly newsletter about the exam. Go to cpa-exam.org. Click on "Press Room" for the latest issue.
- National Association of State Boards of Accountancy (NASBA): nasba.org.
- *The Uniform CPA Examination Candidate Bulletin,* which NASBA recommends you read before applying to take the exam. On the NASBA home page, click on "Exams and Publications," and "Candidate Bulletin."
- AICPA: aicpa.org.
- Prometric: prometric.com/cpa. Operates test centers for the exam.

4. *Receive your Notice to Schedule.* Once your state board (or designated agent) has processed your exam, determined you are eligible, and you've paid your fees, you will receive a Notice to Schedule (NTS) from NASBA listing the sections of the exam you are approved to take. The NTS is valid for a certain period of time set by your state board, and you must schedule and take the exam within this period, which generally is six months. If you have not taken the exam after six months, you will hear the soundtrack from *Mission Impossible* and your NTS will self-destruct. Just kidding. But the

---

13 www.nasba.org/nasbaweb.nsf/exam

14 AICPA *USA Map,* www.aicpa.org/Legislative+Activities+and+State+Licensing+Issues/State+News+and+Info/States/stmap.htm

15 You can pull up the map directly by typing www.nasba.org/nasbaweb/NASBAWeb.nsf/WPECUSM in your browser.

NTS will no longer be valid, and you will have to start the application process all over—and pay the fees. Again.

5. *Schedule your examination.* Contact Prometric to begin the scheduling process (prometric.com/cpa). You must schedule your exam at least 5 days before the test date, but it is recommended that you schedule it at least 45 days in advance to increase the likelihood that you will get your preferred date and location. You can take the exam at any authorized Prometric center—you don't necessarily have to take it in the state where you plan to apply for a license.

6. *Take your examination.* See the *Candidate Bulletin* about check-in procedures and taking the exam.

7. *Receive your score reports.* After you take your exam, your exam and those of other candidates are sent to the AICPA for scoring. Each test is identified only by an examination section ID. The AICPA transmits the exam scores to the NASBA, which matches the scores to individual candidates. NASBA then sends the scores to state boards of accountancy for approval and release to candidates.

Exam Schedule

The exam is offered five, sometimes six, days a week in the first two months of every quarter. A sample schedule can be found in box 3-2.

Generally, you can take the exam in any testing window and in any order you wish; for

Box 3-2: *Uniform CPA Exam: Schedule*

Exam Given (5 or 6 days a week)	Exam Not Given
January	March
February	June
April	September
May	December
July	
August	
October	
November	

example, you could take the BEC section in the April/May window. Once you pass 1 section, you usually are allowed up to 18 months to pass the other 3, but check with your state board. If you do not pass a section, you can take the exam for that section again. Check with your state board for details.

Incidentally, candidates have a lot more flexibility to schedule the exam today than before the computer-based exam was introduced in April 2004. Previously, a pencil-and-paper exam was administered. It was held only twice a year and candidates had to complete all four parts in two days.[16]

Exam Structure

The examination is composed of testlets (groups of 24 or 30 multiple-choice questions) and simulations (condensed case studies). Each section—AUD, FAR, and REG—includes 3 testlets and 2 simulations. BEC consists of 3 multiple-choice testlets only. Table 3-1 outlines the structure of a typical Uniform CPA Exam.

---

16 "Milestone: One Million Sections of CPA Exam Administered," AICPA *CPA Letter*, August 2009, www.aicpa.org/pubs/cpaltr/aug2009/articles.htm#9

Examination Time

The examination time allocated for each section is as follows:

Auditing and Attestation:	4.5 hours
Financial Accounting and Reporting:	4.0 hours
Regulation:	3.0 hours
Business Environment & Concepts:	2.5 hours
Total	**14.0 hours**

Examination Scoring

See the Uniform CPA Examination Web site for information on how the exam is scored. On the home page (cpe-exam.net), click on "Frequently Asked Questions" and "Scoring."[17]

Examination Pass Rate

No question about it, the CPA exam is a challenge, just like the bar exam is for future attorneys. Table 3-2 shows that in the first 3 quarters of 2009, about 50 percent of candidates passed the CPA exam. As with any exam, the better you prepare, the greater your chances of passing.

AICPA Award for Top Performers On Exam

The American Institute of Certified Public Accountants (AICPA) annually presents Elijah Watt Sells Awards to the 10 candidates who earn the highest cumulative scores on the 4 sections of the Uniform CPA Examination. These candidates must have completed testing during the previous calendar year and passed each exam section on their first attempt. The AICPA created the award in 1923 to honor Sells, one of the country's first CPAs (under the 1896 New York State law establishing CPA licensing) and a leader in advancing professional education. He was active in the establishment of the AICPA and a founder of New York University's School of Commerce, Accounts, and Finance. He died in 1924.

Table 3-1: *Uniform CPA Exam: Structure*

	Testlets (groups of 24 or 30 multiple-choice questions)	Simulations (case studies)
Auditing and Attestation (AUD)	3	2
Financial Accounting & Reporting (FAR)	3	2
Regulation (REG)	3	2
Business Environment and Concepts (BEC)	3	none

---

17 www.cpa-exam.org/cpa/computer_faqs_3.html

Table 3-2: *2009 Examination Pass Rate*

Section	1st Quarter	2nd Quarter	3rd Quarter	Cumulative
AUD	47.61%	51.79%	51.52%	50.47%
BEC	46.23%	48.62%	52.27%	49.39%
FAR	45.54%	50.58%	51.18%	49.38%
REG	47.96%	52.25%	52.41%	51.09%

Source: Uniform CPA Examination Web site: www.cpa-exam.net. Click on "Press Room."

Key:
AUD: Auditing and Attestation
BEC: Business environment & concepts
FAR: Financial Accounting and Reporting
REG: Regulation

CPA Exam Resources

Many resources are available to help you prepare for the exam.

You can talk to people who have recently passed different sections of the exam—or passed the entire exam. Ask them about their strategies for preparing for and taking the exam. You might pick up some ideas on how to approach the exam. Unless an idea is really out there, like, "Go to a cemetery at midnight and study under the full moon. Worked for me." Or, "If you want to know how you're going to do on the CPA exam, visit a palm reader." Yeah, right.

You can utilize your school's resources. If you are currently studying accounting, exam preparation may be part of your coursework. And you can talk to your professors and classmates about studying for the exam.

Take a CPA test preparation course. Companies offering such courses include:

- Becker Professional Education (becker.com)
- Bisk Education (bisk.com)
- Gleim Publications (gleim.com)
- Kaplan (Kaplan.com)
- Lambers Review Courses (lambers.com)
- Rigos Professional Education Programs (rigos.net)
- John Wiley and Sons (wiley.com)[18]

Take a test preparation course at a local college. Community colleges, private colleges, and other schools in your area may offer prep courses that cover the entire exam or focus on particular sections.

Planning for the Exam

Preparing for and taking the exam requires focus, self-discipline, persistence, careful planning, and lots of coffee. Well, the coffee is optional, but if you plan well, you will be ready for the day when you walk into an exam center, sit down, and take the exam. Some considerations to keep in mind follow.

---

18 "Best Bets to Prep for the CPA Exam," Dona DeZube, Monster Finance Careers Expert, http://career-advice.monster.com/career-development/education-training/best-bets-to-prep-for-the-cpa-exam/article.aspx

Write out a plan for taking the exam and stick to it. Decide when you will take the test for each section of the exam, in what sequence, and how you will study for the exam. Do you plan to study mainly on your own, or maybe with some other candidates? Or will you sign up with a test preparation service? Take a class at a local college? How do you study best? Reading books, study guides, and other printed material? Viewing CDs, videos, online study guides, and other online resources? Taking a class? Or maybe you'll benefit from a combination of approaches to studying.

Thoroughly review the CPA Examination tutorial and sample tests on cpa-exam. org. The tutorial is basically a guided tour of the CPA Examination. You learn what types of questions to expect, how to use the tools and resources for taking the exam, and how to navigate through the various parts of the examination. The sample tests are a preview of the examination. They help you to become familiar with the exam format and content and how the exam functions. You can download and answer a set of multiple-choice questions for all sections. You can also download a simulation for one of the three sections that have simulations—AUD, FAR, and REG.

Do not apply to take a section or sections of the exam until you are ready. You do not want to put off taking the exam indefinitely, but you only have six months to take it once you receive the NTS, so be ready.

You have 18 months from the date you take and successfully pass the first section to pass the other 3. That may seem like a long time and give you reason to procrastinate, but before you know it, 18 months has collapsed into 9 months, and then 3, and procrastination

may give way to panic as your time to finish the exam runs out. Instead of 18 months, you might consider trying to complete the exam in a shorter time period, say 9 months. That could help you to stay focused.

Be prepared to put in the many hours required to study and prepare for the exam. Be disciplined. Avoid frequent distractions, but do take a break from time to time to recharge. As part of your overall plan, work out a study schedule: What are you going to study, and when, and for how long? You can change your schedule as you proceed and become more familiar with the exam topics. But keep on track.

The day will come when you are notified that you have passed the final section of the exam and are certified as a CPA. But you're not done yet. You also have to be licensed as a CPA. And that means you have to get a license from the state where you plan to practice as a CPA.

Licensing

The practice of accounting is regulated at the state, not the federal, level—there is no U.S. Board of Accountancy. There's no Intergalactic Board of Accountancy, either. But there will be: in the year 3010. You heard it here first.

In most states, the accounting regulatory agency is known as the board of accountancy. Among other responsibilities, boards of accountancy are responsible for the licensing of CPAs. You apply for a license to the board of accountancy of the state or jurisdiction where you plan to practice accounting.

As noted at the beginning of this chapter, you usually must have two years of experience in public accounting to obtain a license from the state where you plan to practice accounting. You may also get credit for experience in other sectors, such as corporate accounting, but you may have to have more experience than in public accounting. The experience requirements vary by state, and, as always, you should check with the board of accountancy of the state where you are applying (or plan to apply) for a license.

One other note on experience: you usually must acquire the necessary experience under the supervision of a CPA licensed in the state where you are seeking a license. Thus, you could work under the supervision of a manager at a large CPA firm, the owner of a small CPA firm, an accounting manager at a corporation, or any other licensed CPA in the state of your choice.

An important consideration when applying for a license is whether you plan to conduct attest engagements, for example, as a member of a public accounting firm that audits public (Securities and Exchange Commission–registered) companies. In California, you can choose to obtain a license that allows you to practice, but you are not allowed to do attest work. Alternatively, you can choose to obtain a license that permits you to do attest work (as well as other types of accounting work), but you must have acquired at least 500 hours of attest experience under the supervision of a licensed CPA or "comparable authority to

provide attest services."[19] As in all matters of licensing, check with your state board about attest requirements.

Most states have what are known as *CPA practice mobility laws*, which allow CPAs and CPA firms to serve clients across state lines with minimal licensing barriers. As of July 27, 2009, 45 states had enacted such laws.[20] For more on the practice mobility laws, go to the AICPA Web site at aicpa.org and click on "Legislative Activities and State Licensing Issues" and "Mobility and State Licensing Issues."[21]

As an example, the following are two pathways to licensing as a CPA by the California Board of Accountancy.

Pathway 1[22]

This pathway is designed for CPAs who will practice only in California. It requires the following:

- A bachelor's degree;
- 24 semester units in accounting-related subjects;
- 24 semester units in business-related subjects (accounting courses beyond the 24 required units may apply toward the business units);
- Passing the Uniform CPA Exam;
- A total of 2 years of general accounting experience supervised by a CPA with an active license; and
- Passing an ethics course.

Pathway 2

If you are licensed under this pathway, the majority of other states will recognize your license. If you think that someday you might want to practice in another state, Pathway

19 State of California, Department of Consumer Affairs, "CPA Licensee Handbook," www.dca.ca.gov/cba/publications/handbook.pdf

20 "With 45 States Enacting CPA Practice Mobility Laws, AICPA Turns to Nationwide Implementation," AICPA press release, July 29, 2009, www.aicpa.org/download/news/2009/WITH-45-STATES-ENACTING-CPA-PRACTICE-MOBILITY-LAWS.pdf

21 www.aicpa.org/Legislative+Activities+and+State+Licensing+Issues/Mobility+and+State+Licensing+Issues

22 "What It Takes—A Guide to Becoming a CPA," CalCPA Education Foundation. http://www.calcpa.org

2 may provide you the professional mobility you desire. Requirements include the following:

- A bachelor's degree;
- 24 semester units in accounting-related subjects;
- 24 semester units in business-related subjects;
- 150 semester units (or 225 quarter units) of education;
- Passing the Uniform CPA Exam;
- A year of general accounting experience supervised by a CPA with an active license; and
- Passing an ethics course.

There are 3 differences between Pathway 1 and 2, including the following:

- Education: Bachelor's degree, Pathway 1 versus bachelor's degree and 150 semester units, Pathway 2
- Experience: 2 years, Pathway 1 versus 1 year, Pathway 2
- License recognition: California only, Pathway 1 versus majority other states, Pathway 2

As the California example suggests, applying for a license is not simply a matter of deciding in which state you want to apply. You may have to address other questions as well, such as whether you expect to practice only in that state or in other states as well. For example, if you are a member of a CPA firm with a national practice, you might be based in California but travel to other states to assist the firm in providing services to clients, and at some point the firm might relocate you to another state, and you might have to obtain a license from that state as well. I had licenses to practice in New York, California, Louisiana, and Ohio, which were among the states where our firm had offices.

Just as you planned for the CPA exam, you need a plan for getting your license, beginning with the state where you want to practice. You may decide on a particular state because you have a job opportunity there or because you want to work in that state, or for other professional or personal reasons. Regardless, once you know where you want to apply for a license, get a clear understanding of what's required for licensing and be prepared to take the steps necessary to get your license as soon as possible. Figure 3-1 illustrates the typical process for obtaining a CPA license.

Figure 3-1: *Lift Off to a CPA License*

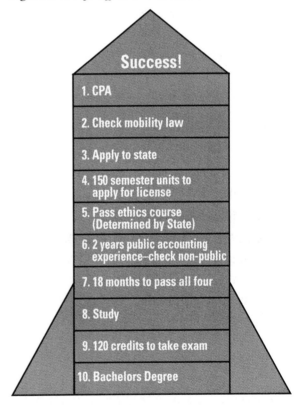

Success!

1. CPA
2. Check mobility law
3. Apply to state
4. 150 semester units to apply for license
5. Pass ethics course (Determined by State)
6. 2 years public accounting experience–check non-public
7. 18 months to pass all four
8. Study
9. 120 credits to take exam
10. Bachelors Degree

> **! NOTE:**
> CPAs who are AICPA members must meet the organization's continuing professional education (CPE) requirements. For more information, go to the AICPA's home page at aicpa.org. Click on "Conferences, Publications, CPE and the AICPA Library." Then click on "CPE Requirements...."[23] Likewise, states generally require CPAs to meet CPE requirements in order to keep their licenses current. Check the Web site of the state where you plan to be licensed.

Other AICPA Certification Programs

As you advance in your career, you may develop interests and skills in forensic accounting, business valuations, or other specialized practices in accounting. You may want to consider earning a credential that demonstrates to current or prospective employers, clients, and your peers, that you have a specific level of skill and experience in your specialty.

The AICPA has four credential programs as outlined in the following sections.

Certified in Financial Forensics (CFF) Credential

Forensic means "suitable for use in a court of law," and forensic accounting is one of the fastest growing practices in accounting. Forensic accountants use accounting, auditing, and investigative skills to conduct investigations for clients in connection with disputes or litigation. They are often called on to present evidence and provide expert witness testimony in court, which requires an ability to communicate information clearly and concisely in a courtroom setting.

In 2008, the AICPA launched its Certified in Financial Forensics (CFF) credential.[24] In announcing the new credential, the AICPA said "the demand for forensic accounting services is growing and the trend is expected to continue as businesses increasingly seek out experts to help them with a broad range of issues, such as economic damages, family law, fraud investigations and litigation."

The CFF credential encompasses fundamental and specialized forensic accounting skills that CPA practitioners apply in a variety of service areas including:

- Bankruptcy and insolvency
- Computer forensics
- Economic damages
- Family law
- Fraud prevention
- Detection and deterrence
- Financial statement misrepresentation
- Valuations

To qualify for the CFF credential, a CPA must be an AICPA member in good standing, have at least five years of experience in practicing accounting, and meet minimum requirements in relevant business experience and CPE.

For more information, go to the AICPA's online Forensic and Valuation Service Center.

---

23 www.aicpa.org/Conferences+and+Publications+and+CPE+and+the+AICPA+Library/CPE/

24 "AICPA to Launch Certified in Financial Forensics Credential," *CPA Letter*, July 2008, www.aicpa.org/Magazines+and+Newsletters/Newsletters/ The+CPA+Letter/July+2008/AICPA+to+Launch+Certified+in+Financial+Forensics+Credential.htm

87

Accredited in Business Valuation (ABV) Credential

Among other services, CPAs may be asked by clients to perform *business valuations*, estimates of the value of assets or liabilities using different valuation methods. Business valuations usually are done in connection with transactions such as acquisitions, mergers, initial public offerings, and many other engagements; litigation such as bankruptcy, breach of contract, economic damages computations, divorce, and other litigation; and tax reasons including gift and estate taxes, estate planning, family limited partnerships, and other tax-related reasons.

The AICPA established the Accredited in Business Valuation (ABV) credential program, among other reasons, to increase public awareness of the CPA as the preferred business valuation professional, to increase exposure for CPAs who have obtained the ABV credential, and to enhance the quality of business valuation services that its members provide.

To be eligible for the ABV credential, CPAs must be members of the AICPA, pass a comprehensive Business Valuation Examination, satisfy business experience requirements, and meet educational requirements. For more information, go to the AICPA's online Forensic and Valuation Service Center.

Personal Financial Specialist (PFS) Certification

Personal financial planners provide a variety of services, including the following:

- Personal financial planning, such as helping clients establish financial goals, making recommendations for money management and budgeting, assisting with estate planning, and other services.

- Income tax planning, including analyzing the tax consequences of financial decisions, tax structuring of partnerships and other investments, and other services.
- Insurance planning, such as analyzing client exposure to risks and recommending methods for managing risk, advising clients on various types and uses of life insurance, and other planning.
- Investment planning, including reviewing clients' investment preferences and risk tolerance to help them develop appropriate investment strategies, discussing available investment options with clients, monitoring the performance of invested assets, and other services.
- Retirement planning, including helping clients develop or refine retirement planning goals and determining cash requirements to realize those goals and other services.
- Estate planning, including estimating liabilities for federal estate tax, state death taxes, and other obligations; reviewing tax and probate considerations of various forms of property ownership; developing strategies for minimizing estate and death taxes, and achieving other estate-planning goals.

AICPA initiated the Personal Financial Specialist (PFS) certification program to enhance the quality of personal financial planning services provided by CPA and PFS professionals, increase career and practice development opportunities for PFS credential holders, and help credential holders promote their practices. The AICPA also is working to increase public awareness of the value of the PFS credential.

To qualify for the PFS credential, a CPA must be a member of AICPA, pass an examination, and meet education and experience requirements. For more information, go to the AICPA's home page and search for "Personal Financial Specialist."

Certified Information Technology Professional (CITP)

The Certified Information Technology Professional (CITP) credential is predicated on the fact that in today's complex business environment, technology plays an ever increasing role in how organizations meet their business obligations, and that no single professional has a more comprehensive understanding of those obligations than a CPA. The CITP program encourages and recognizes CPAs' unique ability to provide business insight by leveraging knowledge of information relationships and supporting technologies. The CITP credential is granted exclusively to CPAs who specialize and demonstrate specific skills, expertise and experience in information management, assurance and analysis, and reporting.

To be eligible for CITP certification, a CPA must be a member of the AICPA, have at least 5 years of experience in practicing accounting, complete the CITP application, including the 100-point requirement, and pay the application fee. For more information, go to the AICPA's home page and search for "Certified Information Technology Professional."

Other Certifications

As a CPA, you may also obtain certification from other organizations. Some examples include the following:

- *Certified Fraud Examiner* (CFE). Issued by the Association of Certified Fraud Examiners (ACFE), a professional organization, the CFE "denotes proven expertise in fraud prevention, detection, deterrence and investigation." A candidate for CFE certification must be an associate member of the ACFE, meet education, experience and character-based criteria, abide by the ACSE code of professional ethics, and pass the CFE exam. Incidentally, the CPA credential may count toward the professional experience requirement for the CFE. For more information on qualifying for CFE certification, go to the ACFE's Web site at acfe. org. Click on "Membership and Certification."

- *Certified Internal Auditor* (CIA®). Internal auditors work for corporations, businesses and other organizations. (See chapter 5.) CIA® certification is awarded by The Institute of Internal Auditors (IIA), an international organization whose mission "is to provide dynamic leadership for the global profession of internal auditing."[25] Candidates for CIA® certification must meet educational and experience requirements and pass the CIA® exam. According to the IIA, certification provides members with "educational experience, information, and business tools that can be applied immediately in any organization or business environment." For more information, visit the IIA's Web site at theiia.org. (An interview with David Richards, president of the IIA, is on page 189 of this book.)

- *Certified Management Accountant* (CMA®). Management accountants work for corporations, businesses, and other organizations. (See chapter 5.) CMA® certification is awarded by The Institute of Management Accountants (IMA).[26] Members include CPAs and other professionals as well as people in business, finance, not-for-profit organizations, academic institutions, and other sectors of the economy. To qualify for CMA® certification, candidates must be members of the IMA, meet educational and experience requirements, pass the CMA® examination, and comply with the IMA Statement of Ethical Professional Practice. According to the IMA, "professional certification is the most effective way for IMA members and management accounting and finance professionals to

25 Institute of Internal Auditors web page. www.theiia.org

26 Institute of Management Accountants Web site, "IMA Frequently Asked Questions," www.imanet.org/about_faqs.asp#5

demonstrate and maintain the highest standard of relevant knowledge and skills."

- *Certified Government Financial Manager* (CGFM). If you are a CPA working in government, you might consider whether to obtain certification as a CGFM. The Association of Government Accountants (AGA), a professional organization, offers CGFM certification to government financial managers (federal, state, or local) who meet the CGFM education and experience requirements and pass an examination. According to the AGA, the CGFM certification is a mark of professional excellence—it enhances a manager's professional reputation with executives, supervisors, and peers, and with constituencies served by government. It also helps a manager to develop the broad professional knowledge necessary to perform effectively and stand out in an organization. It also enhances a professional's opportunities for career development and advancement. Candidates for CGFM certification must meet education and experience requirements and pass an examination. For more information, see "CGFM Certification" on the AGA's Web site (www.agacgfm.org). To learn about careers for CPAs in government, go to chapter 6.
- *Certified Financial Planner* (CFP®)[27] As a CPA, you may provide financial planning services to individuals either as a sole practitioner or as a member of a CPA firm. The Certified Financial Planner Board of Standards, Inc., an independent certification body, awards the CFP® designation to candidates who meet educational and experience requirements, comply with the board's code of ethics and fitness standards, pass a background check, and pass an exam. Your CPA certification may satisfy the experience requirement. For more information, visit the board's Web site at cfp.net.

- *Not-for-profit certification.* If you decide to work in the not-for-profit sector, various colleges and organizations offer certification programs in not-for-profit management. See chapter 7.

Wrap-up

In this chapter, you learned the following:

- To be licensed as a CPA, you have to meet three requirements, known as the three "e's"—educational, examination, and experience.
- First "e": Generally, you must have 150 credit hours and a bachelor's degree to obtain a license. (This subject was discussed in chapter 2.)
- Second "e": You have to pass the Uniform CPA Examination to obtain a license.
- Third "e": You usually must have two years of general accounting experience to be issued a license.
- Have a plan for taking the exam and stick to it. The better you plan and the more diligent you are in executing your plan, the greater your chances of success.
- Be ready to put in the many hours necessary to prepare for the exam. Use your time well—don't procrastinate.
- Have a clear understanding of the requirements to obtain a license in the state of your choice. You will then be prepared to take the steps to get your license as quickly as possible.
- Finally, that CPA license is worth the effort in better career and employment opportunities, greater credibility with clients, potential for higher earnings, peer recognition, and qualifying for membership in the AICPA and state societies with all the attendant benefits.

---

27 *Financial planning* is the process of meeting life goals through the proper management of personal finances. Life goals can include buying a home, saving for a child's education, or planning for retirement. Source: Board of Certified Financial Planners.

Chapter 4

Careers in Public Accounting

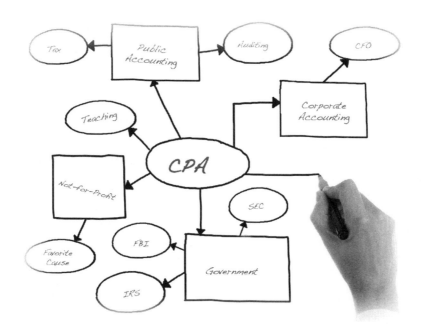

> "Success is measured not only in personal success, but in the success of those on your team, and everyone in [your] organization."
>
> Krista McMasters, CEO • Clifton Gunderson

Public Accounting as a Launch Point

As the name suggests, *public accounting* is the providing of accounting services to the public. The "public" includes companies and businesses, government agencies, not-for-profit organizations, individuals, and other clients of public accounting firms or individual accountants. This chapter covers public accounting, including:

- Types of public accounting firms
- Services
- Structure
- Industry specialization
- Value to clients
- Thought leadership
- Need for talent
- Recruiting college graduates
- Career ladder
- Advancement
- Benefits
- Women's initiatives
- Diversity
- Starting at a firm
- Career decisions
- Career lattice
- Moving on
- Generational change

Today, there are about 43,000 public accounting firms in the United States.[1] They generally fall into the following 3 categories:

1. The four largest public accounting firms with worldwide clients, offices, and employees (Big 4)
2. Major firms that generally have national or regional practices in the United States and are members of international networks
3. Thousands of other firms that operate in communities across the United States

The Big 4

College football has the Big 10 and the Big 12. Public accounting has the Big 4! But no "Accounting Bowl." Table 4-1 shows 2008 Big 4 firm statistics at a glance.

Although the firms that constitute the Big 4 trace their roots back to the 19th century, (see the "Big 4 Timeline" in appendix 3), it is only in recent decades that they have actually become the Big 4 through a series of mergers.

- In 1987, there was the Big 8: Arthur Andersen, Arthur Young & Co., Coopers & Lybrand, Deloitte Haskins & Sells, Ernst & Whinney, Peat Marwick & Mitchell, Price Waterhouse, and Touche Ross.
- In 1987, KPMG was formed with the merger of Peat Marwick International (PMI) and Klynveld Main Goerdeler (KMG) and their individual member firms.
- In 1989, Ernst & Whinney and Arthur Young merged to form Ernst & Young.
- In 1990, Deloitte Haskins & Sells merged with Touche Ross to create Deloitte & Touche. (In 1993, the name of the international firm was changed to Deloitte Touche Tohmatsu.)
- In 1998, Price Waterhouse and Coopers & Lybrand merged to form PricewaterhouseCoopers.
- In 2002, Arthur Andersen stopped practicing as a consequence of the Enron scandal and many of its clients and employees went to other firms.

---

1 American Institute of Certified Public Accountants (AICPA) Web site (aicpa.org); Becoming a CPA/Academic Resources; Career Paths; Public Accounting, www.aicpa.org/Becoming+a+CPA/CPA+Candidates+and+Students/Career+Paths.htm#public

Table 4-1: *Big 4 Snapshot**

	Deloitte (deloitte.com)	Ernst & Young (ey.com)	KPMG (kpmg.com)	PricewaterhouseCoopers (pricewaterhousecoopers.com)
Fiscal 2008 international revenue (billions)	$27.4	$24.5	$22.7	$28.2
Employees in worldwide network	165,000	136,000	137,000	155,000
Global headquarters	New York	London	Amsterdam	London
U.S. headquarters	New York	New York	New York	New York
Chairman/CEO	James H. Quigley	James S. Turley	Timothy P. Flynn	Samuel A. DiPiazza, Jr.

Source: Company Web sites

* As of December 31, 2008

Since then, there has been the Big 4, sometimes referred to as "The Final Four."

Of the 1,500 largest public companies—those with annual revenue of more than $1 billion—almost all are audited by the Big 4.[2] Among other reasons, the largest public companies chose the Big 4 for their global network of professionals, technical capability, industry expertise, and bench strength—they have CPAs and other professionals who are highly knowledgeable and experienced in audit and tax as well as in many other areas, such as finance. The Big 4 provide audit and other services not only to the biggest companies, but also to some midsize and smaller companies. They are not only the largest public accounting firms in the world, but also rank among the largest private companies in the nation.

Major Firms Group

The difference between the Big 4 and the Major Firms Group is a matter of scale. The major firms have highly qualified CPAs and other professionals and provide many of the same services as the Big 4. The major firms have annual revenue of about $1 billion annually, mainly from the U.S. market; the Big 4 have revenue of more than $20 billion each from worldwide markets, including the United States. But the major firms, which

2 "Audits of Public Companies: Continued Concentration in Audit Market for Large Public Companies Does Not Call for Immediate Action," United States Government Accountability Office, Report to Congressional Addresses, January 2008.

Table 4-2: *Major Firms: A Selection**

Firm	Fiscal 2008 Revenue	U.S. employees	Headquarters	CEO
BDO Seidman	$659 million	3,020	Chicago	Jack Weisbaum
BKD LLP	$353 million	2,000	Springfield, MO	Neal Spencer
Clifton Gunderson	$247 million	2,000	Milwaukee	Krista McMasters
Crowe Horwath	$492 million	2,500	Oak Brook, IL	Charles Allen
Eisner	$123 million	450	New York	Charles Weinstein
Grant Thornton	$1.2 billion	3,900	Chicago	Stephen Chipman
Plante & Moran	$286 million	1,600	Southfield, MI	Gordon Krater
Moss Adams	$340 million	1,800	Seattle	Rick Andersen
Reznick Group	$275 million	1,500	Bethesda, MD	Kenneth E. Baggett
RSM McGladrey/ McGladrey Pullen	$1.5 billion	8,000	Minneapolis	Steven Tait/ David Scudder

Sources: Firm Web sites; Inside Public Accounting, *August 2008.*

* This is merely a sampling of the major firms. It is not intended as a ranking or as a comprehensive list. Appendix 1 provides information for researching firms including publications, Web sites, and other resources.

generate hundreds of millions, or even a billion dollars, a year in revenue, are substantial organizations in their own right, and they got there through strong and sustained growth. They typically started out as small partnerships in a single city and grew by winning new clients, selling more business to existing clients, opening offices in other cities, and hiring more professionals. They have expanded into regional or national firms in the nation and have joined international networks of accounting firms. Table 4-2 summarizes some of the firms that are considered in the Major Firms Group.

(Growth has long been the story of accounting firms in the United States. Kenneth Leventhal & Company, a firm founded by Kenneth Leventhal in the mid-1940s, grew from a single entrepreneur, Leventhal, to 65 partners and a total of about 1,000 people at the time it merged with Ernst & Young in 1995.[3] I was managing partner of the Leventhal firm at the time of the merger.)

Other Firms

In addition to the Big 4 and the major firms, there are thousands of other public accounting firms in the largest metropolitan areas, other cities, small towns and other communities across the nation. (You can search for these firms on Yahoo!, Google, or other general search engine sites, or on specialized sites like cpadirectory.com.) The largest of these firms has dozens of partners and hun-

dreds of employees, offices in multiple cities, and generate millions of dollars in annual revenue. The smallest are firms owned by a single CPA (sole proprietorships), with small staffs, and perhaps a few hundred thousand dollars in revenue. Clients of these firms include large corporations (that are not serviced by the Big 4 or major firms), other companies, small businesses, government agencies, not-for-profit organizations, educational, healthcare and other institutions, individuals, and other clients. Many of these firms have a core service (or services) such as tax preparation and advisory, and many also offer other services such as personal financing planning or forensic accounting.

As might be expected, there are pros and cons in working for a Big 4 or major firm versus other firms. The largest firms have a variety of excellent in-class and on-the-job orientation and training programs, and mentors and advisors to help you get started in a firm and guide and assist you as you advance in the organization. There are defined career paths in audit, tax, or perhaps advisory, and you may be able to select a path depending on the firm's needs and your interests. You may develop an industry specialization in healthcare or other industries. And you will work on a variety of client engagements. But larger firms tend to be more structured and formal, and you may not have the same flexibility to pursue your career interests as in a smaller firm. By contrast, a smaller firm may not have the depth of training and other career resources as a larger

3 "Ernst & Young and Kenneth Leventhal to Merge," Business Wire, April 14, 1995, http://findarticles.com/p/articles/mi_m0EIN/is_1995_April_24/ai_16857214/

Best Accounting Firms to Work For Awards

In January 2008, *Accounting Today*, a news publication for tax and accounting professions, and Best Companies Group, a firm that researches excellence in the workplace, announced the winners of a "Best Accounting Firms to Work For," an inaugural program created by the 2 firms. Awards were presented to 60 public accounting firms in the following 3 categories:

- 5 small-sized firms (15-24 employees)
- 40 medium-sized firms (25-249 employees)
- 15 large-sized firms (more than 250 employees)

The awards were based on an evaluation of a firm's workplace policies, practices, philosophy, systems, and demographics, and a survey of employees to evaluate their experience in working for the firm.

The five small firms to receive awards were:

- Mark Bailey & Company Ltd. (markbaileyco.com)
- Swindoll, Janzen, Hawk & Loyd LLC (sjhl.com)
- Garcia, Espinosa, Miyares & Company LLP (gemco-cpa.com)
- Kreinces Rollins & Shanker LLC (krscpas.com)
- Bartolomei Pucciarelli LLC (bp-cpas.com)

Of the 40 medium firms to receive awards, the top 5 were:

- Frazier & Deeter LLC (frazierdeeter.com)
- Porter Keadle Moore, LLP (pkm.com)
- DiCicco, Gulman & Company LLP (dgccpa.com)
- Berlin, Ramos & Company, P.A. (berlinramos.com)
- Cowan, Gunteski & Co., P.A. (cowangunteski.com)

Of the 15 large firms to receive the award, the top 5 were:

- Kaufman, Rossin & Co. (kaufmanrossin.com)
- Friedman LLP (friedmanllp.com)
- BKD LLP (bkd.com)
- WithumSmith+Brown, P.C. (withum.com)
- Citrin Cooperman & Co. (citrincooperman.com)

For more on the awards, go to bestaccountingfirmstoworkfor.com.

company, and training may be more on-the-job than in the classroom. But you would have the opportunity to work in tax, audit, and other areas early on, to assume more responsibility more quickly, to work with senior management, and to get to know many of the people in an organization.

Services of Public Accounting Firms

Public accounting firms generally provide clients with audit and assurance, tax, and advisory services—these are the firms' core services. (For various reasons, many small firms do not

The Case of the Phantom Sales

In *CSI*, a popular television show, a little thing can have big consequences.

So, too, with an audit. I once worked on an audit that I called "The Case of the Phantom Sales."

When I first started in accounting, I was assigned to a company's accounts receivable, or money that customers owe companies for goods or services. Companies typically give customers a certain period of time, such as 90 days, to pay their bills. Meanwhile, companies carry the money owed them on their books as accounts receivable.

I helped to go through the company's books and records and get a listing of all the accounts receivable. We would then send a confirmation letter to each of the customers at the address shown on our records. Among other information, the letter asked the customer to confirm the amount due.

When we received a confirmation from the customer, we would check whether it was signed. We would also check whether there was any difference between the amount the customer said it owed the company and the amount of the account receivable on the company's books. It was a very simple, repetitive process that was rather boring.

Then, things got interesting. We received an envelope with a return address that had a completely different city and state than where we had sent our confirmation request. Hello! We tried calling the customer, and found there was no such company at that address.

Our audit manager told us to investigate further. We determined the customer didn't exist—anywhere. Through a ruse, the owner had received our letter requesting confirmation, signed it with a fictitious name on letterhead of the fictitious customer, and sent it back to us. It turned out the owner was inflating his revenue by booking phony sales to nonexistent customers and recording them as accounts receivable.

The problem with this scam was that the amount of accounts receivables kept increasing as the owner booked more phony sales. The ballooning of accounts receivable was a red flag to the company's investors and lenders that it might be taking on too much risk. The owner tried to cover this up by crediting cash received from real sales to paying customers against some of the phony accounts receivable. It was a sort of Ponzi scheme. Named after Charles Ponzi, one of the most famous swindlers of all time, this is a common description of any scam that pays early investors returns from the investments of later investors. The owner subsequently was convicted of fraud.

The Case of the Phantom Sales was my first exposure to accounts receivable, and accounting got more exciting after that.

provide audits of Securities and Exchange Commission [SEC]-registered companies; for example, the firm does not want the liability risk of an audit or to commit time and resources to performing audits.) Some firms emphasize particular service lines such as tax.

Audit and assurance services include the following:

- *Financial statement audit.* Conduct audits of companies that are required to file audited financial statements; assist in preparing and filing statements.
- *Internal audit.* Advise and assist with internal audit risk management; support internal audit with technology and training; provide resources such as outsourcing.
- *Financial accounting.* Advise on U.S. and international accounting issues, laws, and regulations.

- *Corporate reporting improvement.* Assist with the quality of the reporting of nonfinancial information such as a company's brand, market share, customer retention levels, and intellectual capital that are of interest to investors and company managers.
- *Independent controls and systems process assurance.* Control reviews, risk assessment, operational efficiency.
- *Regulatory compliance.* Provide advice and support to companies in managing compliance with a variety of regulations issued by different regulators.
- *Sarbanes-Oxley compliance.* Advise on compliance with the internal control, reporting, and other requirements of The Sarbanes-Oxley Act (SOX).
- *International Financial Reporting Standards (IFRSs) reporting.* Assist companies to prepare for conversion to IFRSs reporting, to compare IFRSs and generally accepted accounting principles (GAAP) reporting.
- *Assistance on capital market transactions.* Assist companies to raise debt or equity capital in the capital markets.

Tax services include the following:

- *Federal, state, and local tax compliance.* Assist with managing the complexities and risks of state and local tax reporting and compliance; minimize the tax and other costs of compliance.

- *Indirect taxes.* Advise and assist with tax issues and planning related to indirect taxes such as value added tax, sales taxes, energy taxes, customs taxes, and other taxes.
- *International tax.* Advise international companies on tax preparation, integration of financial and tax reporting, addressing legislative and regulatory issues, and managing tax risk.
- *Mergers & acquisitions.* Assist with tax planning, managing tax risks, and achieving tax efficient mergers.
- *Transfer pricing.* Advise on tax issues; assist with tax planning related to inter-company pricing arrangements between related business entities.
- *Tax efficiency.* Assist companies to manage their tax departments, functions, and operations more efficiently.
- *Worldwide management services.* Advise companies engaged in international trade on compliance with export and import regulations; develop strategies to minimize duties, fees, and other costs.
- *Economic consulting.* Analyze legislative and regulatory proposals, evaluate the tax consequences.

According to a survey of accounting professors by *Public Accounting Report* (box 4-1), most of the professors' students plan to start their careers in public accounting.

Box 4-1: *Public Accounting Report's 27th Annual Professor's Survey—2008*

Most of my students hope to work for:	% Responses
Big Four firm	84.5%
Non-Big Four national firm or large regional firm	10.4%
Smaller accounting firm	3.3%
Fortune 500 company	6.8%
Sub-Fortune 500 corporation	2.2%
Smaller company	1.2%
Government	1.1%
Plan to start own firm or business immediately after graduation	0.5%

Editor's Note: Percentages based on the answers of 1,497 respondents

Structure of Firms

In contrast with public corporations, which are owned by shareholders, public accounting firms are owned by their partners, who invest their capital in the firm and share in its profits. In the United States, most states allow CPAs to form limited liability partnerships (LLPs). Although the particulars in each state differ, the most significant feature of LLPs is that their partners have some form of limited liability—in general, they are not individually liable for the negligence or other misconduct of other partners or employees unless the partner participated in or supervised the wrongdoing.* It used to be that only CPAs could have ownership interests in public accounting firms; however, most states now allow non-CPAs to own up to 49 percent of a firm.** Among other reasons, firms need to attract and retain professionals who are not CPAs. If non-CPAs did not have an opportunity to become owners at some point, they might not stick around. Also, modern audits require not only CPAs, but also professionals with other skills.

Big 4 International Networks

Traditionally, the Big 4 firms have marketed their services globally under individual brand names, but they are not single firms. Rather, they are networks of partnerships, each a separate legal entity that is owned and managed independently. The intent is to try and limit the liability of individual partnerships—if a partnership in one country is sued, partnerships in other countries do not want to share the liability, especially because the potential liability could far exceed the fee from a client engagement. Depending on the country, only auditors can be partners in the local partnership. Although they are individual partnerships, members of Big 4 networks share a common name, brand, and quality standards. Deloitte member firms are linked through Deloitte Touche Tohmatsu; Ernst & Young members through Ernst & Young Global Limited; KPMG members through KPMG International; and PricewaterhouseCoopers member firms through PricewaterhouseCoopers International Limited.

Commenting on the network structure, the *Financial Times* noted that "the Big Four networks face a perennial struggle between the desire to meet clients' worldwide needs, the strict national regulations governing audit firms and the desire to limit the risk of a catastrophic lawsuit against one partnership bringing down the entire network."† As a matter of law or practice, local partnerships in a network raise capital only from local partners. The intent is to maintain auditor independence, but this has limited the ability of firms to raise capital in their home markets or globally, and the question has been raised whether local rules need to be changed to allow firms to raise capital from a variety of sources, for example, by incorporating and selling stock to the public.‡ Another question is whether firms could more easily raise capital if they were a single global partnership.

In 2008, Ernst & Young took a step towards creating a global partnership when its partners in 87 countries—in Western and Eastern Europe, the Middle East, India, and Africa (EMEIA)—approved the integration of country practices into a single EMEIA area. The firms in the EMEIA already worked closely, but this marked a new step by integrating them financially with a single profit-sharing scheme and region-wide investment decisions.§

---

* "The CPA Profession: Opportunities, Responsibility, Services," Harry T. Magill, Gary John Previts, Thomas R. Robinson, Prentice Hall Inc., 1997.
** "Should Non-CPAs Be Allowed to Own CPA Firms?" CPA Journal, May 2007, www.nysscpa.org/cpajournal/2007/507/perspectives/p7.htm
† "Ernst & Young to Form Single Business," Jennifer Hughes, Financial Times, 20 April 2008.
‡ "Global or Local? For Accounting Firms, It All Depends," Floyd Norris, New York Times, 14 March 2008.
§ "Ernst & Young to Form Single Business," Jennifer Hughes, Financial Times, 20 April 2008.

Advisory Services

Public accounting firms also offer what are known as advisory services, subject to the restrictions of the SOX. SOX prohibits public accounting firms from providing nonaudit services (other than tax) to SEC-registered audit clients—if a firm audits a client, it cannot provide advisory services to that client. Within this restriction, public accounting firms have found substantial room for growth in providing advisory services to clients that they don't audit.

Advisory services include the following:

- *Business planning.* Advise businesses on entering new markets or launching new products or business lines.
- *Corporate finance.* Advise companies on equity and debt capital raising, securitization, and restructuring.
- *Corporate governance.* Board advisory (to improve effectiveness of boards), ethics and compliance, executive compensation, risk oversight, and management.
- *Crisis management.* Advise companies on how to handle business crises. These can range from internal fraud to a risk of a downgrade in a credit rating to a class action lawsuit to a theft of intellectual property.
- *Deal structuring.* Advise on balancing the accounting, tax, regulatory, financial, legal, and other considerations in structuring a transaction.
- *Due diligence.* Assist with preparing and ensuring accuracy of financial information required for acquisition, merger, sale, or other transaction.
- *Expert opinion.* Provide companies, shareholders, attorneys, courts, regulators, and others with independent, expert opinion for the valuation of an asset or business in order to resolve commercial or shareholder disputes, verify values in an acquisition or disposition, or for other purposes.
- *Forensic.* Includes forensic and fraud investigations to identify vulnerabilities and manage risks and support companies and their attorneys in investigations, mediation lawsuits, and other work.
- *Human capital.* Advising on recruiting, training, and retaining talent; complying with national and international employment laws and regulations; structuring compensation and benefits; and other employer issues.
- *Restructuring.* Assist companies to restructure their business operations and balance sheets to mitigate the adverse impact of such problems as cash flow shortages, falling share prices or diminished margins, or underperforming operations.
- *Transaction.* Advise companies on acquisitions, divestitures, alliances and joint ventures, raising capital, and other transactions.
- *Valuation.* Advise on the accounting treatment for valuing assets (such as assets acquired in the acquisition of a company) based on GAAP or IFRSs.

Industry Specialties

Many CPA firms have developed industry specialties, for example, providing audit and assurance, tax, and advisory services as well as others to firms in a range of industries. Clients want firms whose professionals are knowledgeable and experienced in their industries and have an understanding of the issues and challenges facing companies in these industries.

Among the industries and markets served by CPA firms are the following:

- Aerospace
- Agribusiness
- Automotive
- Banking
- Biotechnology
- Consumer products
- Education
- Food
- Financial services
- Government: Federal, State, Local

Why Industry Expertise Matters

Many of the accounts and components of the financial statements of corporations and business-es are generic—they have common attributes. For example, cash is cash, and receivables are receivables. However, there are also many significant differences in the auditing of companies in different industries, differences that can have substantial impact on a company's financial position and results. So, it is extremely important that a CPA has industry expertise in auditing clients or in doing tax, advisory, or other work for clients.

In auditing, perhaps the single largest area where industry expertise is critical is in inventory. Having a good understanding of the company's product line, its manufacturing process, materials used, stages of product development, and common industry practices in supply chain management and inventory are essential in performing the audit procedures.

As I think of my work for clients in the real estate industry, I can't imagine being able to come up with the right analysis and conclusions without having the necessary background and experience. For example, a company that I audited did large scale land development and verti-cal building. I had to understand how to properly allocate costs to the stages of development including land acquisition, site planning and development, building design, labor and materials, and construction. Imagine a multimillion dollar subdivision development that includes hundreds of for-sale single family homes, townhouses, multifamily rental units, and commercial proper-ties, including shopping centers, warehouses and other industrial space; roads, water and sewer lines, electric power lines, and other infrastructure; a city hall and other public buildings; parks, lakes, and other recreational areas; and other development. As an auditor preparing a financial statement for this huge development, you have to think through all the complexities of allocat-ing the costs and decide which cost allocation method to use, such as a percentage of comple-tion method or completed contract method for reporting development. If you don't know what you're doing, the result could be an overstatement of inventory on the balance sheet, an under-statement of costs on the income statement, and a corresponding overstatement of income, and a distortion of actual economic results between various product lines. Likewise, if you are a tax specialist, you have to have a deep understanding of the tax reporting for the development and know how to advise your client on minimizing the tax costs.

Obviously, you cannot become an expert in every industry. It is important early in your career, to get exposure to as many industries as possible, talk to people in your firm who are industry specialists, decide on an industry that interests you, and begin to develop experience and expertise in that industry. In the process, you will become more valuable to your firm—and your firm's clients. Plus, working in an industry can be fun. Over the years I've advised a number of developers and other clients in real estate. I've enjoyed the chance to talk with them about their vision for projects, about how they work with architects, planners, environmental consul-tants, construction managers, lenders and investors, and others, to design, plan, finance, and build projects, and to watch their developments go from vacant land to finished office buildings, shopping centers, hotels, or entire subdivisions.

- Health care providers
- Hospitality and leisure
- Insurance
- Law
- Life sciences
- Manufacturing and distribution
- Media and entertainment
- Mining and metals
- Not-for-profit
- Oil and gas
- Pharmaceutical
- Power and utilities
- Private equity
- Real estate and construction
- Technology
- Telecommunications

Creating Value

The many services that firms provide to clients in different industries have a common denominator: they are designed to help clients address issues, solve problems, and capitalize on opportunities. In other words, they have value. Thus, a firm might advise a manufacturing company on managing its supply chain more efficiently to reduce transportation and other costs, a health care provider on the efficient management of its business in an increasingly complex regulatory environment, or a real estate company on restructuring its balance sheet in order to improve its credit rating and attract new financing. Of course, the services offered by firms are not static. Firms introduce new services or adapt existing services to meet changing market conditions, changing client needs, or for other reasons. Some examples include the following:

- **Forensic services**
  Well-publicized cases of fraud have rocked the business world and investment community in recent years. Fraud has cost companies billions of dollars in lost revenue and triggered investor and shareholder lawsuits as well as civil and criminal investigations and prosecution by regulatory agencies. To protect against or investigate fraud, corporations as well as governments, nonprofit organizations, and other clients are employing public accounting firms to develop computer systems to detect fraud, using the firm's forensic specialists to examine internal documents for forgery, electronic tampering, or other instances of fraud, to investigate possible money laundering and other illegal acts, or to advise companies on regulatory issues such as compliance with the Foreign Corrupt Practices Act. Large public accounting firms have put together teams of CPAs, lawyers, systems experts, former investigators for government agencies, and others to provide fraud services in the United States or globally. But fraud services are not exclusive to the biggest firms. Other firms have developed niche practices within the forensic market, for example, in providing expert witness testimony in connection with fraud investigations.

- **Cleantech**
  Venture capital funds have been investing billions of dollars in clean technology or cleantech companies that are developing new or improved technologies to reduce energy consumption, waste or pollution, increase efficiency, improve performance, and cut costs. Demand for cleantech solutions is increasing due to higher energy and resource costs, regulatory requirements, and the desire for corporations to pursue climate change related market opportunities. CPA firms are advising cleantech companies in the design, testing, and development of a range of solutions in energy, such as electricity generation (tidal/wave, hydrogen, geothermal, solar, wind, hydro); energy storage (batteries, fuel cells, flywheels); energy efficiency (energy efficiency products, power and efficiency management services, industrial products); water (treatment processes, conservation & monitoring) environment (air, recycling, waste); and industry focused products and services (agriculture, construction, transportation, materials, and consumer products.)

- **Green buildings**

  The problem-solving talents of accounting professionals are in demand in the real estate and construction industry, where green standards for buildings are coming into wider use. Buildings are among the leaders in electricity consumption and energy use in the United States; they also are a major source of carbon dioxide (CO_2) emissions.[4] To help conserve resources and protect the environment, many cities and states have adopted green guidelines for the design, construction, and operation of new buildings; some jurisdictions have enacted mandatory standards. Pressure for green buildings is coming from another direction: major corporations and other tenants prefer to locate to them. In response, architects and developers are designing and building a new generation of buildings that are more energy efficient, consume less water and other resources, and leave less of a carbon imprint, Owners of existing buildings are looking for cost-effective ways to green their buildings, such as through the installation of solar panels, on-site power generation, or recycling of waste water. CPA firms are advising clients on a range of green building issues, such as planning development of green buildings, regulatory compliance, measuring the costs of green technologies and practices in buildings versus the benefits, valuing existing green buildings, or using tax and other financial incentives in green building construction or retrofitting.

- **Environmental accounting**

  Environmental accounting is one of the hot growth areas in public accounting. Firms are assisting businesses to identify environmental costs that may be hidden in overhead accounts or otherwise overlooked. Firms are assisting companies to significantly reduce or eliminate such costs, for example, through investment in greener process and technology, the redesign of processes or prod-

ucts, or to generate revenue to offset such costs, for example, through sales of waste materials. Environmental accounting is an important component of overall corporate environmental management, quality management, and cost management. (To learn more about environmental accounting, see "An Introduction to Environmental Accounting As A Business Management Tool: Key Concepts and Terms," June 1995. It's a report of the U.S. Environmental Protection Agency.[5]

- **Environmental impact statements**

  Another growing area for public accounting firms is assisting companies or other clients in preparing an environmental impact statement or environmental impact report (EIR). Companies may be required by government laws or regulations to file an EIR that assesses the impact that a proposed project will have on the environment. If a company must take action to correct an environmental problem, such as removing hazardous waste from the site of a proposed manufacturing plant, the public accounting firm may assist the company in estimating the cost of the cleanup, preparing a budget for the cleanup, and ensuring that the cleanup is completed within budget. The firm may also assist the company to prepare and file a report with a government agency that documents that the cleanup has been completed.

- **Personal financial planning**

  As personal financial planners, CPAs assist individuals and companies in identifying financial objectives and counseling on the risk, liquidity, management, and tax characteristics of investments. Personal financial planning services include helping clients to better manage their money through debt reduction and expense control, developing investment strategies and asset allocation plans, tax consulting, insurance analysis and planning, retirement planning, and minimizing estate and gift taxes.

---

4 U.S. Green Building Council, www.leedbuilding.org/DisplayPage.aspx?CMSPageID=1718

5 United States Environmental Protection Agency, Office of Pollution Prevention and Toxics, "An Introduction to Environmental Accounting As A Business Management Tool: Key Concepts and Terms," June 1995, www.epa.gov/oppt/library/pubs/archive/acct-archive/pubs/busmgt.pdf

- **Analysis of government legislation and regulation**

  Companies, businesses, investors, and other clients often call upon public accounting firms to prepare analyses of proposed federal, state, or local legislation, laws or regulations, or proposed changes to existing laws or regulations. Companies want to know the economic effects of proposed laws on their businesses or on the businesses of their clients, customers, and even their competitors. A common example is proposed tax legislation or changes in existing tax law that could expose companies and businesses to new or higher taxes, or, conversely, present them with opportunities to reduce taxes. Public accounting firms also advise clients on the effects of proposed healthcare or other legislation. And companies may ask for an analysis of reports

> **NOTE:**
> For more on forensic accounting, environmental accounting, and other service lines, examples of jobs in these areas, and other career information, go to the AICPA-sponsored Web site "Start Here Go Places" at www.startheregoplaces.com. Click on "Why Accounting?" and "Career Options."[6]

or studies of a congressional committee or a committee of a state legislature to try and anticipate the possible economic effects if such studies were to lead to enactment of new legislation, such as new laws to regulate greenhouse gas emissions.

- **Restructuring**

  Public accounting firms may assist companies and businesses in restructuring their organizations as part of bankruptcy proceedings or restructuring outside of bankruptcy through what are commonly known as workouts. Through restructuring, companies may renegotiate terms of loans with their banks, sell off businesses or assets to pay off lenders and creditors, dispose of unprofitable operations, and otherwise try to strengthen their companies and position them for future growth.

Thought Leadership

The Big 4 and other CPA firms are continually developing written reports, studies, surveys, issue papers, newsletters, and press releases, as well as webcasts, videos, and other online communications on a variety of issues of concern not only to clients but also to larger audiences such as businesses (generally) or government policymakers or public interest groups. Through such efforts, firms aim to position themselves as informed, experienced commentators, or thought leaders, on a range of issues such as managing companies through difficult economic times, improving corporate governance and sustainability practices, or evaluating corporate business performance—how well is a company executing in achieving its goals? The expectation of firms is that they will be seen as the "go to" firms in their markets—prospective clients will select them for assistance and advice to address issues and solve problems, and current clients will continue to seek their assistance.

Career Implications

So what does all this—the many services and industry specialties of CPA firms, their efforts to create value for clients, their initiatives in thought leadership—mean to students planning careers in accounting or young professionals just starting their careers?

If firms are going to hold themselves out as thought leaders and technical experts and deliver services across a range of industries,

---

6 www.startheregoplaces.com/why-accounting/career-options/

then they will require the necessary professional expertise. They will need talented professionals in audit and assurance, tax, and advisory services with industry expertise, and with the skills to work with a variety of clients in addressing all sorts of challenges. That means more opportunities for CPAs and other professionals who are joining firms out of college.

Of course, you won't become an expert just by walking in the door of a CPA firm, but firms see you for your potential. With the right skill sets, training, and work experience, you could become a skilled and experienced auditor, or a tax expert; manage an office; serve as partner-in-charge of a major client account, head a firm's biotech practice, become a forensic accountant, or lead a group working on green building projects. There are multiple career paths and many career choices. What path you take depends on your interests and the firm's needs.

Finding Talent

Although hiring by public accounting firms has slowed in the 2008-2009 recession, the long-term outlook is for continued strong hiring, not only by the Big 4, but also by other firms. Firms will need to recruit more talent to replace the increasing number of baby boomers in their organizations who will be retiring—about 73 percent of AICPA members will reach or approach retirement age in the next 15 years.[7] Firms also need to recruit to fill vacancies created by normal turnover, to provide the staff and develop the leadership to support continued growth, and, as noted, to provide technical expertise and industry experience. In addition, regulatory changes and increased oversight will require more CPAs in both the private and governmental sectors.

College Recruiting

Colleges are the farm system for accounting firms. Every year, the Big 4 and other public accounting firms recruit thousands of graduating students at hundreds of four-year U.S. colleges that offer undergraduate or graduate degrees in business or accounting. (Firms also recruit graduates with degrees in law, economics, computer science, and other disciplines to fill specific needs in their organizations.) The Big 4 have the largest recruiting presence on campus, which is not surprising because they recruit more graduates than other firms and even many corporations.[8]

During the school year, firms send teams of partners or senior managers along with recent hires to targeted schools to participate in career days and other events, meet with students, and build relationships. Firms also employ a variety of other approaches to recruitment, for example, individual partners may visit their alma maters to meet with students. Students themselves reach out to the firms by contacting them through the firms' Web sites or by calling or writing directly to a firm.

---

7 "Mentoring Part of Recruiting and Retaining, Too," Linda J. Zucca and Donald W. McFall, Jr., Journal of Accountancy, August 2008, www.journalofaccountancy.com/Issues/2008/Apr/RecruitingandRetainingtheNextGenerationAccountantOneUniversitysExperience.htm

8 "The Long Arm of the Big 4," David McCann, CFO.com/U.S., March 21, 2008, www.cfo.com/article.cfm/10903973?f=search

Internships

Internships are a leading source of talent for CPA firms. Every year, each of the Big 4 offers thousands of paid internships to students at hundreds of U.S. colleges. Many other firms also have internship programs. Many interns work for 8-10 weeks during summer vacation, typically between their junior and senior years. Others work during the school year, for example, in assisting firms during tax season from January 1 to April 15. Interns work in the firms U.S. offices; however, some firms have programs for selected interns to work overseas.

Internships enable students to learn about a firm, its culture, and career opportunities in the organization, to actively participate with teams of professionals on client engagements, to work with mentors, to network with the firm's leaders, other professionals and other interns, to develop analytical, problem solving, communication and other skills, and to decide whether they want to join the firm. For their part, firms use internships to identify and evaluate potential hires. Successful interns are offered jobs in their senior year or while in graduate school, and if they accept, as most do, they join the firm after earning their degree.

More Outreach to Students

To meet their need for talent, CPA firms have been expanding their outreach to community colleges and even high schools. Firms aim to develop relationships with students early in their academic careers, educate them about the accounting profession, and generally interest them in careers in accounting and their organizations, in particular. In these efforts, the firms have been supported by the AICPA, state CPA societies, and other accounting organizations. The AICPA, for example, has broadened its educational outreach to include not only college but also high school students.[9] The National Association of Black Accountants has a high school outreach program known as Accounting Career Awareness. Some firms sponsor scholarships for undergraduate or graduate students who plan to go into accounting.

Building a Web Presence

To connect with prospective employees, CPA firms are using a variety of print and online media to provide information about careers in public accounting and the firms themselves. Many firms have invested in building a stronger presence both on company Web sites, on such popular social networking sites as Facebook, YouTube, MySpace, and Twitter, and on Second Life, a virtual world created and used by millions of people worldwide and by companies to recruit employees. On their company Web sites, CPA firms are using videos, podcasts, online newsletters, examples of work for clients, questionnaires about career

---

9 "CPA Recruitment Campaign Expands to Attract High School Students Earlier, Keep Them Longer, AICPA Web site, www.aicpa.org/ Magazines+and+Newsletters/Newsletters/The+CPA+Letter/May+2008/CPA+Student+Recruitment+Campaign+Shifts+to+Attract+High+School+ Students+Earlier+Keep+Them+Longer.htm

interests, postings of jobs available, and other tools to inform students and other prospective employees about career opportunities and different career paths in their organizations. Some examples include the following:

- Deloitte sponsored a first-ever "Deloitte Film Festival" based on the theme, "What is Deloitte?" People in Deloitte's U.S. firm were invited to submit films about their experiences in the organization. Among those deemed the best from nearly 400 submissions was "Food for Thought," a parody of the benefits of working for the firm. The story line: "This organization really is about one thing: food."
- Ernst & Young's online "Interview Insider" offers tips on job interviewing and its "Inside Scoop" provides questions that Ernst & Young interviewers might ask. Sample question: "Describe a situation in which you initially thought you could easily handle alone, and soon realized you were in over your head. What did you do?"
- KPMG held an online World Jobs Fair for students and college graduates and others interested in employment with the firm. KPMG recruiters from about 40 countries convened in a virtual "exhibition hall" to present information about job opportunities.
- An article in the "Feed Your Future" online magazine of PricewaterhouseCoopers followed three associates and a senior associate through their work day.
- Moss Adams has a series of photos of people who joined the firm in the careers section of its Web site. A viewer clicks on the photo to learn about this person and why they joined Moss Adams.

Advancement in Firms

When you join a large public accounting firm after graduating from college, you usually start in an entry level position in audit, tax, or perhaps advisory services. Some firms have programs to rotate you through these service areas; for example, assisting with an audit or helping to prepare the tax returns of a large corporation, or helping a team in advisory services evaluate a potential acquisition for a client.

In other firms, there may not be a formal rotation program, but you could find yourself working in the different service lines. Regardless, try to get some exposure to all three service lines early in your career. This will give you a broad perspective on how the firm provides different types of services to clients and how it structures services to address particular client needs. And, as you work in different service lines, you can think about which one most interests you.

After one or two years, you will normally start to focus on one service line, depending on the firm's needs and your interests. Whatever service area you specialize in, you will continue to work with professionals from other service lines; for example, you might team up on one client engagement with professionals in audit and tax, and on another engagement with professionals in advisory services.

From the moment you start with the firm, try to learn as much as you can in your current position, and learn from your supervisors, the people you work with, and others in the firm. Ask questions not just about your

Public Accounting Career Ladder

Title	Years with Firm
Partner	12+
Senior Manager	9-12
Manager	6-9
Senior	3-6
Semi-Staff Assistant	1-3
Staff	0-1

Note: This is a general guide of the time spent at each career level in public accounting. Actual times may vary with individual firms.

current position or work assignments, but about the larger firm, its organization, its services, and its people. Take the initiative to volunteer for assignments or assist others with projects.

After as little as one year with the firm, you will be eligible for promotion and you will begin to take on some supervisory responsibilities. This will give you the opportunity to not only work on a project, but to begin to direct and assist others with projects. As you gain more supervisory experience, you will be given more responsibility and more authority. Firms have an urgent need to train the next generation of leaders in their organizations, and if you do exceptionally well as a supervisor, you could be on a fast track for advancement.

Now, here's a look at the core service lines in a large firm, the positions in each service line, and the progression of advancement.

Audit

Working as an auditor gives you an introduction early in your career to companies in a variety of industries—it's an opportunity to study business, not in a classroom, but in the real world. You learn about a company's management and its system, clients or customers, balance sheet, financial structure, financing methods, operations, human resources, administration, regulatory compliance, plant and equipment, and other aspects of its business. You also get experience in auditing U.S. corporations, partnerships, not-for-profit organizations, benefit plans or other entities, as well as international companies with U.S. subsidiaries or international not-for-profit, or other organizations headquartered in the United States.

The positions in audit and the progression of advancement are as follows:

* *Junior staff auditor.* This is an entry level position. Auditors work in teams on client engagements, with the scope and procedures determined by their supervisors. The size of the team varies from a few professionals on the audit of a small public company to a number of professionals on the audit of a multinational corporation. You assist with auditing cash, accounts receivable, inventories and costing methods, payrolls and fixed assets, as well as accounts payable, notes payable, and bonds payable. You validate the accuracy and completeness of a company's financial records, and you may be assigned to investigate specific accounts and identify, resolve and document any material issues.

    A staff auditor usually is eligible for promotion after one year with the firm.

* *Semi-staff assistant auditor.* You supervise staff accountants and assume more in-charge responsibilities. You direct the day-to-day execution of engagements.

An assistant auditor usually is eligible for promotion after three years with a firm.

- *Senior auditor.* As a senior auditor, you plan, organize, and supervise the work of staff auditors and review their work product to ensure the audit is thorough and properly documented. You establish that scope and procedures have been performed. You review conclusions and resolve any accounting issues and identify and document audit risks. You help to develop and maintain relationships and communicate with the client and ensure the supervising manager and partner on the account are properly informed.

A senior auditor usually is eligible for promotion after six years with a firm.

- *Audit manager.* You plan and set the scope and procedures and manage multiple projects concurrently, identify risks, solve problems, and ensure that audits are accurate and completed on time. You supervise, train and evaluate supervisors, seniors, and staff. You evaluate work performed and conclusions reached. You oversee personnel scheduling, audit working paper review, financial statement

Public Accounting Salaries: Audit & Assurance

Title/Experience	2008	2009	% Change
Audit/Assurance Services—Large Firms			
Senior Manager/Director	$98,750–$151,500	$102,000–$159,500	4.5%
Manager	$80,000–$106,250	$ 82,750–$111,750	4.4%
Senior	$64,000–$ 83,000	$ 66,250–$ 85,500	3.2%
1 to 3 years	$54,500–$ 66,250	$ 55,500–$ 69,250	3.3%
Up to 1 Year	$47,500–$ 57,500	$ 49,000–$ 59,250	3.1%
Audit/Assurance Services—Midsize Firms			
Senior Manager/Director	$88,250–$129,250	$ 91,750–$135,250	4.4%
Manager	$74,250–$ 93,500	$ 76,750–$ 98,000	4.2%
Senior	$57,500–$ 76,250	$ 59,250–$ 78,750	3.2%
1 to 3 years	$48,750–$ 59,500	$ 50,500–$ 62,250	4.2%
Up to 1 Year	$41,500–$ 51,000	$ 42,500–$ 53,000	3.2%
Audit/Assurance Services—Small Firms			
Senior Manager/Director	$80,750–$105,500	$ 83,750–$110,750	4.4%
Manager	$66,500–$ 82,000	$ 69,000–$ 86,250	4.5%
Senior	$52,000–$ 66,500	$ 53,750–$ 69,750	4.2%
1 to 3 years	$44,750–$ 53,250	$ 46,000–$ 56,000	4.1%
Up to 1 Year	$40,000–$ 47,250	$ 41,000–$ 49,000	3.2%

Source: Robert Half 2009 Salary Guide: Accounting & Finance

disclosure, budgets, and final determination of the billing for the engagement. You maintain client relationships and ensure proper communication with the audit partner. You help to develop new clients.

An audit manager is generally eligible for promotion after nine years with a firm.

- *Senior manager.* You are highly experienced in managing multiple audit engagements and often are the client's primary contact. You are able to make sound decisions, solve problems, efficiently manage simultaneous engagements, coordinate multiple services for the same client, and supervise staff and develop new business.

  A senior manager generally is eligible for promotion after 12 years with a firm.

- *Audit partner.* As an owner, you are responsible for providing the best possible service to clients, maintaining client relationships, and overseeing the administration of audits. You participate in front-end meetings and planning, and you solve problems for clients and your firm, and assist the profession to address issues of common concern. You are responsible for new business development and client retention.

Tax

Just like in audit, working in tax can be an on-the-job education. By preparing and reviewing income tax returns, you learn how the tax code and tax laws and regulations apply to companies, small businesses, and other clients. You learn how to assist companies to calculate provisions for income taxes or the money they reserve for quarterly or annual tax payments. You learn about different tax strategies that clients legitimately can use to avoid (not evade) income taxes. You learn about state and local taxes, and different types of taxes, such as property taxes on land or buildings owned by companies. You learn about taxes that are specific to industries like real estate, and about various types of tax credits such as housing tax credits, energy credits, and empowerment zone credits.

The tax positions and progressions of advancement are:

- *Tax staff.* This is an entry level position. You may prepare federal tax returns or portions for corporations, partnerships, trusts, estates, individuals, and other clients. You might also work on state or city tax returns. You may research tax issues, prepare tax projections under different income and deduction variables, assist in research for IRS examinations and gather detail to support client position, draft responses to federal, state, and city notices from taxing authorities.

  A staff person usually is eligible for promotion after a year with the firm.

- *Tax semi-staff assistant.* You supervise tax staff and assume more in-charge responsibilities, research tax issues, and begin to review returns.

  A tax assistant usually is eligible for promotion after three years with a firm.

- *Tax Senior.* You manage tax staff, oversee research, review returns, and help to plan tax engagements. You discuss tax issues with the client and help to find solutions.

  A tax senior usually is eligible for promotion after six years with a firm.

- *Tax manager.* Your responsibilities are similar to those of an audit manager. You plan and manage multiple engagements concurrently, train and supervise tax staff, identify and then review research, approve returns, and advise clients on tax planning. You may work with auditors in reviewing tax items in clients' financial statements. You are responsible for maintaining relationships with existing clients and helping to develop new business.

  A tax manager usually is eligible for promotion after nine years with the firm.

- *Senior tax manager.* You are highly experienced in planning and managing tax engagements. You exercise sound judgment, solve problems, coordinate multiple engagements, and supervise managers, supervisors, and staff. You maintain client relationships and develop new business. You will identify critical issues and research that present solutions or options.

  A senior tax manager usually is eligible for promotion after 12 years with a firm.

Public Accounting Salaries: Tax

Title/Experience	2008	2009	% Change
Tax Services—Large Firms			
Senior Manager/Director	$98,750–$151,500	$101,750–$159,250	4.3%
Manager	$80,000–$106,250	$ 82,500–$111,750	4.3%
Senior	$64,000–$ 83,000	$ 66,750–$ 86,000	3.9%
1 to 3 years	$54,500–$ 66,250	$ 55,500–$ 69,250	3.3%
Up to 1 Year	$47,500–$ 57,500	$ 48,750–$ 59,500	3.1%
Tax Services—Midsize Firms			
Senior Manager/Director	$88,250–$129,250	$ 91,250–$135,750	4.4%
Manager	$74,250–$ 93,500	$ 76,500–$ 98,500	4.3%
Senior	$57,500–$ 76,250	$ 59,500–$ 78,500	3.2%
1 to 3 years	$48,750–$ 59,500	$ 50,000–$ 62,500	3.9%
Up to 1 Year	$41,500–$ 51,000	$ 42,750–$ 52,750	3.2%
Tax Services—Small Firms			
Senior Manager/Director	$80,750–$105,500	$ 83,250–$111,250	4.4%
Manager	$66,500–$ 82,000	$ 68,500–$ 86,250	4.2%
Senior	$52,000–$ 66,500	$ 54,000–$ 69,250	4.0%
1 to 3 years	$44,750–$ 53,250	$ 45,750–$ 56,000	3.8%
Up to 1 Year	$40,000–$ 47,250	$ 41,000–$ 49,000	3.2%

Source: Robert Half 2009 Salary Guide: Accounting & Finance

- *Tax partner.* Like your peers in audit, you are an owner responsible for providing superior service to clients, maintaining client relationships, and developing new business. You oversee the planning and administration of tax engagements and help clients to address tax issues and solve problems. You may become an expert in a tax area such as estate taxes, or in an industry such as financial services. You will review all major issues and conclusions and discuss with the client.

Advisory Services

Just as with audit and tax, working in advisory services (known as *consulting* in some firms) provides you with insight into a company— but from a different perspective, that of an advisor. You will be on a team that advises companies in different areas, including corporate strategy, mergers and acquisitions, financial management, information systems, enterprise business applications, operations, human capital, or extended business services, also known as *outsourcing*. Your team may assist a company to launch an initial public offering, or sale of stock to the public, enter new markets, test and launch new products, restructure its balance sheet, or structure transactions such as mergers or acquisitions or accessing new capital. Advisory work covers a broad area, and to prepare you, your firm may put you through in-house learning programs before sending you into the field. You also may be rotated through audit, tax, and advisory engagements to give you broad exposure to a company.

The advisory positions in a firm and progression of advancement are:

- *Staff advisor (consultant).* You develop the necessary technical skills to complete major components of engagements. You demonstrate completeness and thoroughness in completing work assignments. A staff advisor generally is eligible for promotion after a year.
- *Senior advisor (consultant).* You show an understanding of client issues, prepare work plans and budgets, follow through on assignments, identify client problems and solutions, and supervise staff. A senior advisor usually is eligible for promotion after three years.
- *Supervising advisor (consultant).* You manage multiple and concurrent engagements, develop in-depth technical expertise, and participate in developing new business. A supervising advisor generally is eligible for promotion after six years.
- *Managing advisor (consultant).* You do final reviews of consulting engagements; manage the budget, billing and collection; apply firm resources in an efficient and effective manner to engagements; develop referral sources; and coordinate employee performance reviews. Usually eligible for promotion after nine years.

- *Senior managing advisor (consultant).* You demonstrate technical competence; show you are a team leader; consistently develop new business. Usually eligible for promotion after 12 years.
- *Managing partner/principal.* As an owner, you are responsible for providing superior service to clients, the general administration of engagements, and developing solutions to problems affecting clients and the firm. You are creative and develop new ideas and concepts for the client. You are responsible for developing new clients and retaining existing ones.

Benefits

Many U.S. companies offer work-life programs, flexible schedules, and other benefits, but CPA firms, led by the Big 4, have taken them to a whole new level. So, it's not surprising the Big 4 and other large CPA firms have been recognized by publications such as

Stamping to the Beat

Early in my career, I worked on cash accounts and reconciliation of bank checks. I was closely monitored by the CPA firm I was working for. I was given an audit stamp with a number on it, which I remember to this day—number 233. Every time I reviewed a check, I stamped it on the front and back. Look at the front. Stamp it. Bam! Look at the back. Stamp it. Bam! If you happened to work in a room with other check reviewers, there was a cacophony of stamping. Bam! Bam-bam! Bam-bam-bam! But there was a certain rhythm to it. Sort of like conga drummers getting together. Today manual stamping is long gone—stamped out, so to speak, by the automation of accounting processes. For old time's sake, maybe some of my longtime colleagues and I should dig out our old audit stamps and get together for a stamping session. Bam! Bam-bam! And who knows? If we got really good, maybe we could get booked into a local club as The Stampers. Dream on.

Public Accounting Salaries: Management (Advisory)

Title/Experience	2008	2009	% Change
Management Services—Large Firms			
Senior Manager/Director	$98,750–$151,500	$102,250–$159,250	4.5%
Manager	$80,000–$106,250	$ 82,750–$111,500	4.3%
Senior	$64,000–$ 83,000	$ 66,250–$ 86,750	4.1%
1 to 3 years	$54,500–$ 66,250	$ 56,500–$ 69,000	3.9%
Up to 1 Year	$47,500–$ 57,500	$ 49,000–$ 60,000	3.8%
Management Services—Midsize Firms			
Senior Manager/Director	$88,250–$129,250	$ 91,000–$135,500	4.1%
Manager	$74,250–$ 93,500	$ 76,500–$ 98,500	4.3%
Senior	$57,500–$ 76,250	$ 59,500–$ 79,750	4.1%
1 to 3 years	$48,750–$ 59,500	$ 50,250–$ 62,000	3.7%
Up to 1 Year	$41,500–$ 51,000	$ 43,000–$ 53,000	3.8%
Management Services—Small Firms			
Senior Manager/Director	$80,750–$105,500	$ 83,000–$111,250	4.3%
Manager	$66,500–$ 82,000	$ 69,000–$ 86,000	4.4%
Senior	$52,000–$ 66,500	$ 54,250–$ 69,000	4.0%
1 to 3 years	$44,750–$ 53,250	$ 46,000–$ 55,750	3.8%
Up to 1 Year	$40,000–$ 47,250	$ 41,500–$ 49,000	3.7%

Source: Robert Half 2009 Salary Guide: Accounting & Finance

BusinessWeek,[10] *Fortune*, and *Working Mother*[11] as the best places to work among companies in a range of industries. But it's not only the large firms that are considered desirable places to work; so, too, are other accounting firms. For a report titled "Best Firms to Work For," *Accounting Today* and Best Companies Group looked at 3 categories of firms: small (15-24 employees), mid-sized (25-249), and large (more than 250). Based on a number of criteria concerning employee benefits and employee satisfaction, the best in the small firm

---

10 "The Best Places to Launch a Career," BusinessWeek, 15 September 2008.
11 "2008 100 Best Places," Working Mother (not dated).

category were 5 firms led by Mark Bailey & Co. of Reno, Nevada; in the mid-sized category, 40 firms led by Frazier & Deeter LLC of Atlanta; and in the large category, 15 firms led by Kaufman, Rossin & Co., Miami.[12]

Although benefits vary by firm, they generally include the following:

- Signing bonuses: Percent of new hires receiving bonuses and amounts vary.
- Performance bonuses: Awarded to employees based on performance criteria.
- Promotion bonuses: Amounts vary with firm and individual.
- Paid time off: For vacation, holidays, personal days off, additional days off, illness.
- Paid medical & dental: Full or partial reimbursement.
- Pension: Eligibility for new hires depends on firm.
- Group insurance plans: Life, accident, disability, other.
- Group legal plan: Access to local attorneys.
- 401K matching: Amount of company matching varies.
- Charitable contributions: Company matching.
- Employee discounts: Available on car rental, gym, cultural events, publications, and so on.
- Education expenses: Employees are reimbursed. Some firms have a ceiling.

BusinessWeek 2008 Ranking: Best Places to Launch a Career

Of 119 companies, the Big 4 were in the top echelon:

1. Ernst & Young
2. Deloitte
3. PricewaterhouseCoopers
4. Goldman Sachs
5. KPMG

Other large firms also made the rankings:

76. Grant Thornton
104. McGladrey Pullen

- CPA exam: Applicants receive time off to prepare for the exam and are reimbursed for exam expenses.
- Fast advancement: Most entry level staffers are promoted to supervisory positions within one to two years of their hire date.
- Working parents: Family medical leave, parental leave, and other programs for working parents.
- Life management: Services vary with firm but may include personal financial planning, college coaching (for students and their parents), child and adult care services, commuter benefits, home mortgage referral programs.
- Memberships: Paid memberships in business, civic, and other organizations.

Flexible Careers

Among the many benefits desired by prospective and current employees, flexible careers are high on the list. Professionals want the right balance in their personal and professional lives. They want to be able to have time to raise families or care for aging parents, or take a year and travel, or go back to school, but without jeopardizing their career opportunities in a firm.

Accounting firms have numerous programs and initiatives to accommodate the life and work needs of their professionals and other employees, beginning with flexible work hours and locations. A professional might work four days a week and take Fridays off to have more time with his or her family. Another might average 40-45 hour work weeks during the year; however, the hours vary from 70-80 hours a week during busy season to 20 hours a week at other times. Still another might come in at 7 a.m. and leave at 3 p.m. to get home earlier in the day.

---

12 "Best Firms to Work For," Accounting Today, 2008.

Depending on the firm, professionals who work outside the office much of the time might use a firm's hoteling system when they need to come into the office. They log on to the firm's Web site or call the firm to book office space. The purpose of such flexible programs and schedules is not only to recruit people but, equally important, to keep them with the firm. Or as one partner said, "I would rather have someone averaging 40-45 hours a week who stays with us than someone who continually works 80 hour weeks, inevitably burns out, and leaves."

Workplace flexibility not only contributes to talent retention but also to an organization's profitability and productivity and strengthens employee commitment to the organization.

Women's Initiatives

With women accounting for more than half the graduates of accounting programs and half the new hires at CPA firms, the firms have developed a variety of programs and initiatives to recruit, retain, and promote women professionals. These are collaborative efforts in which a firm's leadership, partners, professionals, and employees actively participate.

Ernst & Young has "Offices for Flexibility and Gender Equity Strategy," that support local and national teams in developing women leaders and also advise senior leadership on strategies related to gender. Leadership teams in each business unit ensure that women and minorities are given opportunities to work with top clients in sales opportunities and other high visibility roles.

To help women realize their full potential, KPMG has established a Women's Advisory

Where Are You?

Having a flexible schedule doesn't mean you can disappear at two o'clock in the afternoon without a trace. You have to let your supervisor and others in the firm know where you are. Professionals today can easily stay in touch by e-mail and cell phone and other ways. Even so, firms probably have heard some whoppers from people about why they were incommunicado. Like: "My dog went crazy! He ate my cell phone, trashed my computer, knocked out my electricity and phone service, and kept me prisoner in my own house!" Sure, blame it on your five pound Chihuahua. Arf!

Board. It is working to create a more compelling work environment and enhance career opportunities for women across the firm by driving national and local initiatives that support, advance, retain, and reward them.

PricewaterhouseCoopers has a Full Circle program that allows people who decide to separate from the firm for an extended period of time, such as women who want to stay home to raise families, to stay connected to the firm for up to five years. Participants in the program can stay in touch with colleagues at the firm, use numerous firm resources (such as the firm's paying them to retain their professional credentials), participate in firm training, networking, and other events, and consult with a senior coach in the firm. The firm's goal is to do everything possible to help women return, should they decide to do so.

In 1993, Deloitte launched the Women's Initiative (WIN) aimed at retaining and advancing women.

Grant Thornton has a Women @ Grant Thornton program to enhance the recruitment, retention, and advancement of women in the firm. Such initiatives are yielding results in increasing the number of women joining CPA firms, and in the number moving into the leadership ranks of firms.

About 22 percent of Deloitte's partners are women, the most of any Big 4 firm. Although much progress has been made, much remains to be done, as firms themselves are well aware. They are continuing to work to train and prepare women for leadership positions and to advance them in their organizations.

Diversity

In coming years, the U.S. population will become more ethnically diverse because the number of Asian Americans and Hispanic Americans will grow faster than the population as a whole. Many industries and professions, including accounting, could face severe talent shortages, and competition among CPA firms to recruit talent is expected to increase. Not surprisingly, CPA firms are stepping up efforts to recruit Asian American, Hispanic American and African American college graduates, and to reach out to colleges and high schools to inform students, including minority students, about accounting careers. Many firms have started initiatives and programs to train and promote minority professionals in their organizations and to create a culture of diversity in their organizations. Deloitte has an eight-month professional development program for high performance minority managers and senior managers to prepare them for the next stage in their careers. As with their efforts to recruit and advance women, firms are making progress in recruiting, training, and promoting minority professionals, but more remains to be done to further diversify the workplace.

Community Service

CPA firms have strong ties to the communities they serve. For professionals who are interested in community service, firms provide a variety of opportunities to participate in volunteer projects sponsored by the firms or others. Deloitte has a program in which new employees defer starting with the firm in order to first work for Teach for America, a nonprofit organization dedicated to increasing the quality of education in public schools. Ernst & Young sends selected, high-performing managers or directors to Central or South America for three months at their current salaries (and with their current benefits) to assist entrepreneurs in starting up, financing, or operating their businesses. KPMG is a sponsor of Major League Baseball's (MLB) Inner Cities program, with the firm's professionals volunteering to help organize and coach games. Deloitte has a program for its professionals to provide pro bono services to selected not-for-profit organizations.

In many firms, much of the volunteer work is done through local office initiatives. BKD LLP has a foundation that has given millions of dollars to charitable causes, and people in its local offices work as volunteers for local community, educational, religious, and charitable organizations. By volunteering, CPAs can not only give to their communities, but they may also have opportunities to develop their leadership skills, for example, by serving on boards of directors of not-for-profit organizations.

Starting at a Firm

Particularly if you join a Big 4 or other large firm with thousands or tens of thousands of people, getting started on your career can seem pretty daunting. But firms provide a lot of resources, support, and training. Soon after you join, you will participate in an orientation program of a few days to a few weeks that typically includes computer training, guest speakers, diversity exercises, team building activities, facilities tour, benefits overview, technical training for business functions, overview of firm and its culture, people, and policies. Depending on the firm, you'll get to meet the senior leadership and get to know other people in the firm, form relationships, and develop your network. And do fun stuff. Maybe a game of pickup basketball, or bowling, or whitewater rafting, or testing your talents at a karaoke bar. You will hook up with a coach, usually a manager or partner, who will answer questions, provide feedback on your performance, offer career guidance, and act as a mentor as you progress in the firm. You will also be assigned a buddy, usually someone who has been with the firm for a year or two, to help you learn about the firm, its culture, and its people, offer encouragement and support, and share their experiences with the firm. You may join others in the firm in community service activities that interest you, or help to welcome new employees to the firm. On the job, you typically will rotate through a variety of audit and tax engagements, and possibly some advisory (consulting) engagements. You might get some exposure to an industry specialty.

Your learning doesn't end with orientation. During your first year, and every year thereafter, you will participate in a variety of learning programs in the firm to help you develop your technical expertise in audit, tax, and advisory, and build communication, leadership, and other personal skills. Learning will include classroom and Web-based learning programs using a variety of technology tools and knowledge resources as well as on-the-job training and development. If you haven't passed the CPA exam when you join a firm, it will give you time off (paid or unpaid, depending on the firm) to prepare. Firms pay your expenses to take the exam.

As you gain experience and hone your skills, you will take on new assignments and responsibilities. You may move from one practice area to another, work in different offices and, depending on the firm, have a chance to work overseas. You will be given regular feedback from superiors, coaches, mentors, and others in the organization, and regular performance reviews.

In return for providing resources, advice, support, and guidance, your firm will expect you to take full advantage of the opportunities offered to you, to take ownership of your career, and to learn, grow, and advance in the organization. So don't be lulled into a false sense of security because you are working in a very supportive environment. You are expected to perform, and you are in competition with other talented people for promotions, raises, and opportunities to advance in the organization.

Career Decisions

After your first year or two with a firm, you will reach a point where you will have to start addressing career questions and making career choices. Key questions are addressed in this section.

Do you want to specialize in audit, tax, or advisory services? Professionals specialize in a single discipline because of the high level of learning, knowledge, and experience required to develop expertise, because of the complex questions and issues involved in each discipline—for example, in conducting a modern audit of a large corporation—and because firms expect it. Your decision to specialize in audit, for example, doesn't preclude you from developing some knowledge of tax or advisory; indeed, such knowledge will be very useful in working with your peers in tax or advisory on client engagements or addressing issues that cut across disciplines. But your expertise will be in a single discipline.

What industry expertise do you want to develop? Clients increasingly expect their CPAs to have deep knowledge and experience in their industries, and firms are developing strong industry practices—the largest firms in multiple industries, other firms in selected industries. So it's not a question of whether you should develop such expertise. It's in which industry? Take every opportunity to work in different industry specialties in your firm, to learn about different industries, and to talk to those in your firm who are industry specialists. Then you will be in a position to make an informed decision. And, over the course of a career, you may change industry specialties, depending on the demands of your firm and your professional interests.

How can you refine your skills? Every professional, even those in senior management, can find ways to improve their skills. How can you improve yours? Many CPAs, for example, have a high degree of technical skill, but they could improve their communication skills. Through your firm's training programs, outside classes, speech or writing clinics, online courses, and other resources, you can develop and polish your skills in making presentations to colleagues or clients, making speeches to business groups or professional organizations, writing proposal letters, writing reports, or contributing articles for firm newsletters or outside publications.

How can you help your firm develop business? Public accounting firms are in the business of selling services to clients, and as you advance in the organization, you will be expected to bring in a book of business. You can learn from other partners and managers in the firm how they develop business, learn from clients what they look for in a firm and in its professionals, and learn from people in other professions and industries how they develop business. You can take classes in marketing and sales, or earn a graduate degree in business or marketing. You can attend meetings of business, professional and industry organizations, participate in panels or make presentations at industry events, write articles and reports for posting on your firm's Web site or in industry publications, and otherwise market your firm's services.

Making Partner

After you've advanced to the manager level in a firm, typically after about 7–9 years, you have a key decision to make. Do you remain with the firm and see if you make partner, which could take another 5 years or more, or do you consider other options? Not every professional in a firm will make partner, of course, any more than every lawyer in a law firm will make partner, or every professional in a corporation will make it to the ranks of the top executives. Although promotion rates vary, about 15 percent to 20 percent of the professionals in large CPA firms are partners. The typical career path at most firms is illustrated in figure 4-1.

What do firms look for in promoting people to partners? Although the requirements may vary among firms, the following are their key expectations:

- You excel at bringing in business and maintaining excellent client relations. Although the amount varies by firm, a young partner might be expected to bring in, for example, $1 million of new busi-

Figure 4-1: *Career Advancement*

| Partner |
| Senior Manager |
| Manager |
| Senior |
| Semi-Senior |
| Staff Associate |

Stage Fright

When I was managing partner of Kenneth Leventhal & Company, a CPA firm founded by Kenneth Leventhal (and merged with Ernst & Young in the 1990s), Ken and I and some other partners went to a meeting with a client—a large and prestigious company. We walked into a big, ornate room and sat at a large conference table with the stern looking senior executives of the company. One of our young partners was scheduled to make a presentation, but he was obviously nervous about it. Shortly after the meeting got underway, the jittery partner slipped a note to Ken. "I can't do this." He said later that "I felt like a rookie starting his first Major League game." With the partner suffering from stage fright, Ken turned to me and whispered, "You're on." That was a surprise, but I managed to make it through the presentation. I had the benefit of experience: I had made presentations to major clients before. But that taught me one thing: in making presentations, or in any other endeavor, always have a plan B in case plan A falls through. And maybe even a plan C. You never know when you might get the call.

ness annually, and more experienced partners some multiple of that.
- You have exceptionally high technical skill in tax, audit, or advisory services.
- You have specialized expertise in one or two industries; you are actively involved in those industries (for example, serving in a leadership position in industry organizations); and you might even be generally recognized as an expert in an industry.
- You are extremely articulate and you have excellent communication skills, both verbal and written.
- You are very people oriented.
- You have strong leadership skills.
- You have demonstrated a high level of management skills by managing multiple projects, working with many different people, and supervising large teams, and by realizing high profit margins and keeping your billings, accounts receivable, and client payments current.

- You have received strong support for the promotion to partner from senior people, supervisors, mentors, and others in your firm.
- You are actively involved in community activities, charitable institutions, civic organizations, educational institutions, public policy forums, and professional organizations, both inside and outside of accounting.
- You have been very active in the speaking circuit; you are frequently called upon to be a major speaker at high level events such as national conferences of professional or industry organizations.
- You frequently write articles for professional publications, trade journals, and other publications; you are sought out by the media and are quoted frequently on a range of issues.
- You are energetic and creative. You take the initiative in proposing and implementing new thoughts and ideas.

Career Lattice

In the rigid career ladder of the CPA firms of the past, you moved up or out. At the manager or senior manager level, if you weren't expected to make partner, you left of your own volition, or you were quietly shown the door. Today, the career ladder has given way to what Cathy Benko, Deloitte's chief talent officer, describes as a "lattice world."[14] Professionals who don't make partner may go down a different path. They may become directors or principals in their firms or remain senior managers or managers. They have many of the same benefits as partners, which, depending on the firm, may include an ownership interest. These "partner equivalents" are valued for their knowledge, skills, and experience, the service they provide to clients, and their expertise. A tax manager, who knows the intricacies and complexities of the U.S. tax code

and myriad tax laws and regulations, particularly as they apply to banks, can be invaluable in providing tax services to bank clients. Furthermore, their work may be somewhat less stressful and less pressurized than if they were a partner. They may have somewhat more flexible work schedules and better work and life balance. If they do not have an ownership interest, they do not have the liability that comes with being an owner.

Moving On

However, the time may come when you decide that you want to leave public accounting to work as a CPA in the corporate world, in government, for a not-for-profit organization, or start your own CPA firm or start another business. From your experience in public accounting, you have highly portable skills, and you can work in many different jobs and for many different organizations, where you will also have opportunities for advancement.

Generational Change

When I started out in public accounting, I worked for a large firm where I was required to wear a dark suit, white button-down shirt, hat and, in the winter, a dark overcoat. My black shoes had to be properly laced and my tie, conservative. I had a lot of blue suits, white button-down shirts, black shoes, and red ties in my closet. The people at the stores where I bought my clothes, and at the cleaners where I dropped off my dry cleaning and laundry, were always glad to see me.

---

14 "Up the Ladder? How Dated. How Linear," Cathy Benko, New York Times, 9 November 2008.

Back then, junior auditors had only limited contact with people in a firm. You worked mostly with the senior who was supervising you. You didn't talk to partners and you never got to meet with the firm's leadership. If you went to a client meeting, you were under strict rules regarding whom you talked with and what you talked about. You never interacted with anyone whose job title began with "C"—like CFO, CEO, or COO. You were also under strict rules for conducting audits of clients. You followed very detailed audit procedures and used checklists that showed what work was to be performed and by whom. You had to sign off on a work paper or quality control procedures before you could move forward to the next procedure. If you accidentally dripped coffee on a work paper—yikes!—you had to circle the paper, date it, and state there was nothing intentionally eliminated or erased. You also had an excruciatingly uncomfortable moment telling your supervisor you spilled the coffee. On an engagement, there was very little discussion, dialogue, or debate among auditors and supervisors. You did what you were told. There was little opportunity to show initiative or creativity, for example, in offering suggestions on how to improve the audit.

The generation of CPAs who came into the profession in those days is now in senior positions in public accounting firms. And it is not surprising that there is a certain tension between this senior generation used to old ways of doing things and young people coming into the profession today—Generation Y—who have a very different way of doing things. Some senior people may see this younger generation as too casual, too disorga-nized, too lacking in focus, and too unwilling to put in long hours grinding out work, or to spend years climbing up the corporate ladder. Some young people may see the senior generation as too authoritarian, too inflexible, and too unwilling to adapt to change.

But the fact is each generation brings something to the table. The older generation brings the experience in working with many different clients, the judgment honed from assisting clients with all sorts of problems, and the technical knowledge and skills from years in audit, tax, and other disciplines. The younger generation brings an energy, inquisitiveness, and an eagerness—indeed, a certain impatience—to grow and try new experiences, and an easy familiarity with collaboration and teamwork and the use of modern technology. I know from my experience in meeting with, advising, and mentoring students, that young professionals are ready, willing, and indeed, eager, to learn from their seniors, provided that it's the right learning. In firms today, the authoritarian "this is the way we do things" has given way to "this is how we're doing things now—what are your ideas on how we might do better?" Learning is not didactic; it's collaborative.

It's important that this learning process is going on. Senior professionals—the baby boomers—will be retiring from the profession in increasing numbers, while the younger generation will advance in CPA firms much faster than in the past. In the process, public accounting will continue to change, with firms becoming more collaborative, open, and diverse, offering more career opportunities, and being more supportive of their professionals and employees. Public accounting will be more exciting, interesting, challenging, and professionally rewarding than when I started out. And that is all to the good.

Wrap-up

In this chapter, you learned that the following:

- Public accounting has many career and job opportunities.
- You can work for one of the Big 4 firms, a major firm, or one of the thousands of other firms in the United States.

- You can work in audit, tax, or advisory services.
- You can work in different services lines like forensic accounting or environmental accounting.
- You can develop a specialty in one or more industries.
- You can work for a variety of companies, businesses, and other clients.
- You can advance to partner of a firm or other senior position such as director of tax services.
- If you decide to leave public accounting, your skills and experience will provide a solid foundation for work in the corporate, government, or not-for-profit sectors, or in teaching.

Interview: Rick Anderson
Chairman, Moss Adams

Headquartered in Seattle, Moss Adams is one of the largest accounting firms in the United States, and the largest firm in the western United States, with offices in Arizona, California, New Mexico, Oregon, and Washington. Rick Anderson has been with Moss Adams since 1973, spending his career in the firm's Seattle and Yakima, Washington, offices and providing audit and consulting services to manufacturing, agricultural, and food processing entities. Named chairman of Moss Adams in June 2004, he has remained actively involved in strategic planning activities with clients and specializes in acquisition, expansion, and divestiture analysis.

> *"In a large firm such as ours, we are able to match up a person's interests with our needs."*

Anderson believes that professionals should find time in their busy lives to give back to their communities, and in doing so, "they should focus on things they have a passion for and truly believe in." He has served on several not-for-profit boards, and one of his current interests is related to multiple sclerosis. "Our son-in-law has the disease, but fortunately it has not progressed in recent years," he said. When his son and daughter were growing up, he spent time with them on a variety of outdoor activities. "Now that we are empty nesters, I continue to spend a lot of time outside on our 20-acre 'gentlemen's farm' or occasionally playing golf, hiking and the like."

Why did you decide on accounting as a career?

In college, I started out studying engineering. In my sophomore year, I switched to business. I took some introductory accounting courses, which came easily to me. At some point, I asked myself what I was going to do in the real world. I took some auditing courses, which I really enjoyed. I decided to major in accounting and to go into public accounting. After graduation, I joined Moss Adams as an auditor.

Why Moss Adams?

I grew up in a rural environment in Washington state, and, rather than attending the University of Washington, I decided to enroll in a smaller school, Western Washington University, in Bellingham. When I graduated, I wanted to work for an accounting firm that was smaller than the Big 8 but still had a significant presence in the market. Moss Adams was a leading firm on the West Coast, with offices in smaller towns as well as the largest cities. That appealed to me.

What is the firm's business philosophy?

Our focus is to have significant, sustained internal growth based on exceptional service to a targeted segment of the market. We have a very strong industry focus. For example, we have people whose primary responsibilities revolve around the health care community. They are very good at health care and they can add clients because of their high level of skill in a narrow area. The same is true of other industries we serve. The market demands expertise.

Should students specialize in an area like tax while they are in school, or after they join a firm?

That depends on what you're interested in, and excited about. If you are an undergraduate who develops an interest in tax, you may go on to earn a master's degree in taxation. Once you join a firm, you may decide after a year or two, or five years, that health care interests you, and you develop an expertise in healthcare. What's important is to have a passion for what you do, and to excel at it.

How do you match up a person's interests with the work they do for your firm?

We give our new people broad exposure to the firm to help them decide what interests them. We don't say, "Here comes this year's staff hire No. 23 and they're going to work in tax." In a large firm such as ours, we are able to match up a person's interests with our needs.

How has accounting changed since you started?

One of the biggest differences is that young people entering the profession today expect—indeed, they almost demand—new challenges and new opportunities to learn and grow. When I started, these were expressed more as a hope or a wish. Today, more than ever, we as a firm have to understand what motivates people, and learn how to meet their expectations, for example, for more flexible work schedules. In the past, the work schedule was the employee's problem. Now, it's also our problem because we want to help employees figure out how to make their careers work. We're much more adaptable than before.

How do you determine whether a graduate will be a good fit with your firm?

We look at demonstrated aptitude, and college grades are a factor. We look for a high level of energy. We also look at a person's experience. For instance, have they worked in jobs where they had real responsibility as opposed to just doing task oriented activities?

What do you look for in future leaders at Moss Adams?

We look for people who have been in an extremely valuable and important role like client service partner, and who have demonstrated success in prior roles. For example, the person who comes up through our organization as an auditor first of all, has to be an effective auditor, and then has to be an effective leader in the audit department. We look at whether people have invested time and energy in training others. We look for strong communication skills. We look at whether a person has the vision, the moral character, and the talents and skills to lead others. If you walk into a room, do you immediately recognize that person as a leader? Is that a person you would choose to follow?

Interview: Kenneth E. Baggett

Managing Principal and CEO,
Reznick Group, P.C.

Kenneth E. Baggett initially majored in architecture at Auburn University. "I realized early on that I didn't have the artistic ability to be an architect," he said. "I wandered down to the business school, took an accounting class, and said to myself, 'This is something I really want to do.' So I majored in accounting." He graduated from Auburn in 1977, and, after working the required 2 years, passed the CPA exam in 1979. Today, he's managing principal and CEO of Reznick Group, P.C., one of the top 20 public accounting firms in the United States, with headquarters in Bethesda, Maryland, and 10 offices nationwide.

> "*Whatever black eyes we may have taken, the accounting profession is known for its integrity. And young people look for that. They want to know that you mean what you say, and to back up your words with substance.*"

What was your first job after you graduated?

I worked for a small tax firm before moving to Atlanta to take a job with Habif, Arogeti & Wynne, a large accounting firm, in late 1977. I was hired as a staff accountant and worked primarily on audits.

How did you progress from there?

In my second year with the firm, I evolved into real estate, a practice area for which the firm was known in the Atlanta market. I made partner in 1981, and later served as managing partner for a couple of years. I remained with the firm until 1995.

You became a partner only four years after you graduated. How did you accomplish that?

I helped the firm to find clients beyond the Atlanta area and to grow from a local to a regional organization. In one case, a friend of mine had moved to a firm that needed assistance organizing 4 small partnerships. I did that work, and within 2 years, that client was generating $300,000 a year of business for our firm. All told, I helped to bring in about $500,000 a year of new business for our firm, which at the time was generating about $3 million a year in revenue. So they made me a partner in 1981.

Why did you focus on real estate?

Real estate was exciting because most of our clients were developers, and I was able to be at the front end of a deal that was being put together. I could make an impact early in the planning process, whether with financing or anything else. In addition, we also got the annuity work—the recurring business.

When did you join Reznick?

I left Habif, Arogeti, in 1995 to open an Atlanta office for Reznick, which did not have a presence in Atlanta at the time. We started with 15 people, and today that office has about 275 people.

How did you get a job with Reznick?

I knew David Reznick, the founder, and I had a high regard for his firm's real estate practice. It happened that he was hosting a real estate seminar in Atlanta, and he asked me to speak on a panel. We got to talking, and he asked me if I thought there was any possibility of our firms merging. I really didn't think that was a fit, but I was intrigued with the idea of joining Reznick. They had a strong reputation in the marketplace, and a bigger footprint. At the time I was 40 years old, and I had been with Habif, Arogeti, for almost my entire career, or about 18 years. I thought that if I were going to make a change, now was the time. So I joined Reznick.

After you joined, did Reznick diversify into new geographic markets or service lines?

At the time we had 4 offices on the eastern seaboard, but in real estate, we were practicing all over the country. We also had expanded a little into new areas such as nonprofit services, but even these had a real estate focus, for example, in helping nonprofits to facilitate development projects. In 2001, we had planned to participate with 8 other accounting firms in a public company rollout, but for various reasons that didn't go through. At that point, we decided to regroup and to refocus our talents and resources on our core real estate services. I took over as CEO in 2003, when the firm had 4 offices and about $65 million in revenue. Today, we have 10 offices and about $240 million in revenue, of which only about $20 million has been through mergers with other firms. The rest has been organic growth, mainly from expanding into other parts of the United States.

Considering your growth, you must be doing a lot of hiring

Yes. Prior to my joining, there were very few lateral partner movements into our firm. We have 109 partners today, and in the last 3 years we have laterally hired 32. What that does is help us to find opportunities for new growth. We are very passionate about what we do, and I think that comes across when we are recruiting partners or others to join our firm. If you are excited about what you are doing, it's contagious. Others feel that, too.

What do you look for in hiring college graduates?

One is demonstrated intelligence, whether through an academic record, or accomplishments through after school or summer jobs, internships while in school, or achievements with student organizations. Another is a demonstrated work ethic. Did they just coast through college or work hard? Work doesn't necessarily mean having seven part time jobs, but that they were involved in the community, and the community could be the university itself. The last piece is that they have a desire to win, to establish something successful out of a career.

How has accounting changed today compared with when you started out in the late 1970s?

When I started, the economy was in a recession. Work was a grind. You went to work, you ground it out, you went home, and you didn't complain. Today, the next generation, the students who have come out of school in the last five years, and who will be graduating now and long into the future, want work that is meaningful, and that has purpose. And purpose is not just revenue growth and bottom line profit but being part of a community in the sense of giving back, of doing the right thing. Whatever black eyes we may have taken, the accounting profession is known for its integrity. And young people look for that. They want to know that you mean what you say, and to back up your words with substance. There is also concern with quality of life, with life work balance—much more so than when I started out. When I graduated, I went to a city where I could get a job. Young people today decide where they want to live, and then look for a job there. And they have much more international exposure.

Do graduates joining your firm have a choice of career tracks?

Yes. In the past we used to only hire traditional CPAs. Today, we are hiring more people who were finance majors, marketing majors, and other different types of talent. We are a more diverse organization—about 25 percent of our partners are women, a higher percentage than comparable firms. We've reached that level even though we don't have any special initiatives to recruit women. We attribute that to our willingness to understand the career expectations of women in our organization, depending on where they are in their careers.

What does it take to advance to a senior management position with Reznick?

Part of your responsibility is developing people around you and below you. There is so much opportunity in our organization, and we need great people to move up. For example, to make principal in our firm, to be a nonvoting principal, you have to show who you have helped to develop in senior manager roles. To move from nonvoting to voting principal, you have to show that you helped someone who recently made partner or is about to make partner.

What qualities does it take to become a CEO?

The CEO position is a five-year term, and a maximum of two terms. We set the similar term limits with other senior positions. The intent is to keep bringing fresh talent into leadership positions. You have to be able to build a consensus. Unlike a stockholder owned corporation, in a partnership our partners and principals are owners, and they all have a say to varying degrees. And you have to know how to motivate people, so they have a clear sense of purpose, feel that they are part of the decision-making process, and are inspired to achieve common goals.

Interview: Bill Hermann
Former Managing Partner, Plante & Moran

While in college, Bill Hermann worked part time as a proofreader for Plante & Moran. That experience sparked his interest in the accounting profession, and he went on to earn a degree in accounting from the University of Detroit. He considered going to law school, but decided to join Plante & Moran full time.

"The Wheel of Progress states, 'Good work attracts good clients who are willing to pay good fees, which allows us to pay good wages which attracts good staff who do good work.'"

"I wanted a career that was a natural fit, and accounting was it," Hermann said.

He was the managing partner of Plante & Moran, one of the largest U.S. accounting firms, headquartered in Southfield, Michigan. It has more than 1,600 professionals in offices throughout Michigan, Ohio, and Illinois, as well in Monterrey, Mexico, and Shanghai, China. After concluding his second 4-year term as managing partner on July 1, 2009, Hermann was succeeded by Gordon Krater, the former group managing partner. He stayed on at Plante & Moran in an active leadership role after stepping down as managing partner.

What is your firm's business philosophy?

We subscribe to what we call the "Wheel of Progress," created about 50 years ago by Frank Moran, one of our founders. The Wheel of Progress states, "Good work attracts good clients who are willing to pay good fees, which allows us to pay good wages which attracts good staff who do good work."

What are the firm's focus areas?

We provide core accounting and audit, tax, and consulting services, and we specialize in seven industries: construction and real estate, financial institutions, government and nonprofit, health care, manufacturing, private equity groups, and service companies such as automobile dealers. Despite the weak Midwest economy, there are opportunities to expand into other industries, but we expect to continue to focus on those seven.

How do you staff your offices in China and Mexico?

Those offices are staffed by nationals in those countries. Partners and staff from our U.S. offices rotate through our international offices for a few weeks on a planned basis throughout the year. In addition, we bring people from our international offices to the United States to work for a time.

What does it take to succeed in the accounting profession generally, and your firm in particular?

We have identified a progression of attributes and skills that are needed to serve clients, build a practice, and to coach and mentor staff in these skills. The model is built in the shape of a pyramid. From the bottom up, the skills and attributes are technical skills, a high level of technical proficiency; communication, ability to articulate your ideas and thoughts, and, equally important, to listen to and understand others; relationships, ability to develop and maintain relationships with your peers, clients, and everyone else with whom you deal professionally; insight, ability to see ways to solve problems or to identify new opportunities; problem solving (solutions), once you are able to help clients find solutions, they will start turning to you for advice; advisor and trusted advisor, over time, as you continue to build relationships with clients, solve their problems, and gain their confidence, they will see you as a trusted advisor, your ultimate achievement.

What have you learned from working with clients?

One is don't be afraid to ask questions of a client. If you need information, ask for it. Another is knowing when to speak up and when to be silent. I once made the mistake of speaking out of turn during negotiations a client was conducting. The client educated me on when silence can be golden. I learned my lesson.

What has been the most significant change in accounting in your years in the profession?

Possibly the greatest change has been in technology. When I started, there was a lot of busy work—mundane tasks that had to be done. Now thanks to technology, much of the work is automated, enabling us to manage work more efficiently. That's essential in a fast moving business like accounting. Plus, it frees up time for us to be consultants and advisors to our clients.

Interview: Deborah Holmes
Ernst & Young Global Director of Corporate Responsibility

When she was a student at Harvard Law School, Deborah K. Holmes wrote a dissertation on the structural causes of unhappiness in the law profession. Essentially, lawyers were spending too much time at work and not enough away from it.* After earning her JD, Holmes joined a law firm. It didn't take long for her to decide that a career in law was not for her—she didn't want to become one of those unhappy lawyers she had written about. She took a position as senior research director with a small nonprofit organization, Families and Work Institute, which assists corporations and government to support employees in balancing their careers and their lives outside work. She went on to become research director of Catalyst, a nonprofit organization that works globally with businesses and the professions to build inclusive workplaces and expand opportunities for women and business.

> "We provide our people with the tools and resources to apply their talents and skills in volunteer service to their communities and to give back in ways that are personally fulfilling, for example, by mentoring students or assisting entrepreneurial businesses."

In the fall of 1996, Holmes met with Phil Laskawy, chairman of Ernst & Young, to present the results of a Catalyst study for the firm on turnover among its women employees and partners. The study found that half of the firm's new hires were women; however, the firm was slow to promote them—only about 8 percent were partners.** Just 27 percent of Ernst & Young's women told Catalyst that becoming partner was "a realistic goal," compared with 59 percent of their male peers. The firm was losing 22 percent of its women professionals annually. To reverse this trend, Laskawy created a new Office of Retention and hired Holmes as its director. She went on to create a corporate responsibility function at Ernst & Young. Today, she is the firm's global director of corporate responsibility.

---

* "Holmes Make Professional Jobs Mother-Friendly," Julie Leupold, *WomensNews*, December 16, 2002.

** "Can Ernst & Young Retain Women by Rethinking Work," *BusinessWeek*, Keith H. Hammonds with Gabrielle Saveri, Business Week, February 12, 1998.

When the Office of Retention was created, what were its goals?

There were four goals: One, create a work environment that is inclusive of life outside work; two, ensure that women have equal access to mentors; three, encourage an internal support network—it can be lonely for women in a largely male firm; and four, support women in networking in the business community.

How did you communicate these goals within Ernst & Young?

At the time I joined Ernst & Young, the firm's U.S. practice was organized into 19 regions. Phil Laskawy and I went on a road trip, visiting all 19 regions. His message was that the firm's culture had to change to provide equal opportunities for women. He recalled that when he was in high school, all the smart kids in math were girls. He wondered what happened to the girls after they grew up—he didn't see enough of them at Ernst & Young. We talked to people about the Office of Retention, its goals, and how to achieve them.

What was the firm's plan for achieving these goals?

We selected four offices as pilots, and each office was asked to address one of the four goals. For example, one office addressed the challenge of creating a work environment that was inclusive of life outside work. At the time, flexible work arrangements were in the shadows—the firm's employees and their supervisors quietly agreed to flex schedules without any fanfare. We brought flex work into the sunshine. Under the pilot program, employees had more flexibility to work adaptable schedules, subject to approval of their supervisors.

What were the results of the flexible work program?

It worked so well that it was rolled out nationally. We set up a huge data base to support and manage the program. It was a herculean effort, but worth it. I would rather have 40 hours of someone on a flex schedule who remains with the firm than 80 hours of someone who ends up leaving. The firm also initiated programs to achieve the other 3 goals.

Why did the firm create the corporate responsibility function?

The accounting scandals of the late 1990s and the early part of this decade got the leadership of Ernst & Young thinking about how the accounting profession, generally, and the firm, in particular, were perceived by the business community, government regulators and other constituencies. As a result, the firm initiated a number of changes, for example, we substantially strengthened our independence practice. We also reexamined our societal impact.

Why the concern with societal impact?

While we had made great progress in improving our work environment and we provided excellent service to our clients, we hadn't thought through the strategic impact of our business on the communities we serve and how we could improve our community service. So I was appointed Americas director of corporate responsibility in 2003. I also continued to work with the firm on its gender equity initiatives until 2004, when someone else assumed these responsibilities. In 2008, I took on the additional role of global director of corporate responsibility. In my global role, I am responsible for creating a global strategy and facilitating the sharing of best practices and programs that ally with our global strategy. In the Americas, I am responsible for developing and implementing programming that aligns with our global strategy.

How has this emphasis on corporate responsibility been received within the firm?

At first, there was push-back. So I initiated friendly conversations with leaders and others in the firm and over time, people began to see the value of this initiative, for several reasons. First, the accounting profession has a long tradition of service to the community. Accountants are the white hats—they like to do good. Second, our clients are concerned with corporate responsibility, for example, in measuring and reducing their carbon imprint. Third, there are market opportunities for Ernst & Young in advising and assisting our clients to imbed socially responsible thinking in their organizations. And if we are going to advise our clients on this, we have to lead by example.

What are the opportunities for people who join Ernst & Young to participate in community service?

We provide our people with the tools and resources to apply their talents and skills in volunteer service to their communities and to give back in ways that are personally fulfilling, for example, by mentoring students or assisting entrepreneurial businesses. People new to the firm can join a community engagement network of their peers who are participating in a variety of volunteer activities and use an internal volunteer website to learn about and sign up for volunteer work in their communities based on their interests, time commitment and other criteria. As they become more experienced, they may want to assume more responsibility, for example, by serving on a not-for-profit board, and we provide training and assistance to help them in such leadership roles. High performing professionals may be able to participate in our Corporate Responsibility Fellows Program, which gives them the opportunity to spend three months on paid sabbatical advising and assisting entrepreneurs in Central and South America. Through these various programs, our people not only can serve their communities but also develop their professional skills. Everyone benefits—the communities we serve, our professionals, and the firm.

Interview: Aaron Maguire
Partner, KPMG

KPMG partner Aaron Maguire says clients value accountants with industry experience.

College graduates who join large public accounting firms usually start in either audit or tax, two core service lines of most firms. Over time, they work with different teams on different projects that give them broad exposure to a variety of clients, including corporations and small businesses. In the process, they become generalists; they develop a broad knowledge of the firm and its clients.

> "It's advantageous to specialize. You have more marketable skills and experience than if you are only a generalist."

Today, however, clients typically want partners and managers who also have deep knowledge and experience of a client's industry. Thus, a tax partner working with clients in the insurance industry will not only be well versed in tax laws and regulations generally, but also in tax issues that particularly concern that industry.

"The Big 4 and other large firms and their clients want people who are industry specialists," said Maguire, a tax partner with KPMG LLP, and an insurance industry specialist.

Maguire majored in accounting at Miami University (Ohio). "In freshman orientation, an advisor asked us to pick a major from a list of choices, and accounting was near the top," he said.

Actually, his decision was based on a very practical consideration: accounting graduates almost always find work in their field. "That's not necessarily true of some other majors," he noted. "History majors may not necessarily do something related to their degree." Furthermore, public accountants are almost always in demand regardless of economic conditions. "In good times, top investment bankers may receive million dollar bonuses, but as soon as there's a market downturn, they could be out on the street," Maguire noted. "I'll never get a million dollar bonus but I'm in a stable profession," he said. "Even in a down economy, public accounting firms tend to hold on to their professional staffs, and they still give decent raises."

Between his junior and senior years, Maguire worked as an intern in the New York office of another Big 4 firm, where he learned about the firm's tax practice. After graduation, he joined the firm and continued in tax and advanced to manager. Seven years later, he moved to KPMG when an opportunity to advance to senior manager opened up. During his time in public accounting, he worked with insurance clients and developed a specialty in the industry. "It's advantageous to specialize," he noted. "You have more marketable skills and experience than if you are only a generalist."

Another advantage of specialization is that generalists tend to move from team to team and project to project, and do not always have the same opportunity as specialists to develop long-term professional relationships with managers who can act as mentors. "People who are constantly moving within a firm may not find managers who have a vested interest in their careers," Maguire said. "Managers know you'll be gone as soon as a project is finished."

Among young professionals, industries such as entertainment or sports attract a lot of interest. But, as Maguire observed, "Even if you specialize in those industries, you aren't hobnobbing with the rich and famous, you're doing accounting work—just as in every other industry." He advises young professionals to find industries that may not seem as glamorous but where there is less competition and where demand for accountants with industry knowledge is strong.

For young professionals, developing an industry specialty enhances their chances of advancement in public accounting. "Because of the turnover in large firms today, young professionals may be able to move up the ladder faster, and in-depth knowledge and experience in an industry can help put them on the fast track for promotion," Maguire commented.

As they advance, young professionals will find themselves working with different managers and peers, and they should try to learn from others. "Learn not just how your immediate boss works, but how others do their jobs—study their management styles and skill sets," Maguire said. Professionals can put their observations and insights to use when they themselves become managers, typically after five or seven years. "If you stay with the firm long enough to make manager, you are very marketable," Maguire noted. "You can continue to remain with the firm and work to become a partner, or you could go into industry at a senior management level."

As for his own career plans, Maguire expects to remain with KPMG, but "I could be in a different role" in the future. And public accounting itself will change. "Our focus changes with the times," he said. "Over the last 10 years, for example, financial reporting has become even more important," he said. "You have to learn to adapt to what the real world dictates."

Interview: Krista McMasters
CEO, Clifton Gunderson

On June 1, 2009, Krista McMasters became CEO of Clifton Gunderson, the first woman to lead a top 25 CPA firm in the United States. Clifton Gunderson provides assurance, accounting, tax, and consulting services to clients in a variety of industries. Founded in 1960 and headquartered in Milwaukee, the firm has a staff of more than 2,000 professionals serving clients from 45 offices across the country. McMasters joined Clifton Gunderson as an associate accountant in 1978 after graduating from the University of Illinois, Urban-Champaign, with a bachelor's degree in accounting. She was admitted as a partner in 1985, became director of assurance services in 1989, and currently serves as chief practice officer. McMasters succeeded Carl George, who was the firm's CEO since 1993 and continues to play a strategic role until his retirement in 2012.

"Success is measured not only in personal success, but in the success of those on your team, and everyone in our organization."

A health and fitness devotee, McMasters makes time in a busy schedule to work out daily. In quiet moments outside the office, she likes to read. "I love reading, especially biographies," she said. "I really enjoy presidential biographies— Doris Kearns Goodwin is one of my favorite authors." She and her husband, a commercial airline pilot, own a small plane. "We spend much of our free time flying, exploring, and seeking new adventures."

Why did you choose Clifton Gunderson?

After I graduated, I wanted to remain in the central Illinois area for personal reasons. I received offers from all of the firms in the area, and I chose Clifton Gunderson. I had a very engaging interview with Carl George, who at the time was in charge of the Danville office, and has been my mentor during my 30 years with the firm. He talked about the opportunities with the firm, the chance to learn and grow, and the variety of its clients. Clifton Gunderson was, and remains today, a very progressive, forward looking firm. Shortly after I started, a couple of women were promoted to partner, and women continue to play key leadership roles in our firm.

Where did you start?

I started in the Danville office, and I knew from day one that I had made the right choice in Clifton Gunderson.

Why?

I had the chance to lead assignments early on, to work on different engagements, and to interact directly with clients. Over time, I assumed more responsibility, and I got increased exposure to the profession, for example, by serving on national committees of our profession. All of these experiences contributed to my professional development and put me in a position to assume a leadership role.

What does it take to succeed in public accounting today?

People skills are more important than ever. Especially in public accounting, you have to invest not only in your own career, but in the careers of your colleagues and peers. You have to work well with others, and help them to succeed. Success is measured not only in personal success, but in the success of those on your team, and everyone in our organization.

How do you recruit people in what is a highly competitive market for accounting talent?

It's a challenge to recruit and retain people today. Our ability to retain people begins with our recruiting process. We want to make sure we clearly define ourselves to prospective recruits. We want people who understand our culture, who will succeed in our organization, and who will remain with us.

How do you retain people?

We have tremendous people programs, for example, an internal university provides training above and beyond the basic requirements for a job. We have a strong mentor program—all of our mentors are strongly invested in the success of the people they are mentoring. As a middle market firm, we offer people opportunities to quickly start working directly with clients, and to begin performing high level work early on. And we offer flexible work schedules, which has been particularly important to our ability to retain and promote women.

What kinds of questions do you get from people who are thinking about accounting as a career?

There's a lingering impression that accounting is sitting in an office and doing the same thing over and over. Especially if you are an auditor, you are out of the office much of the time, meeting with clients. You have the opportunity to work on a variety of interesting assignments, and to learn and grow professionally, and to advance in your career.

What are your plans for the firm as the future CEO?

I want to build on our mission: growth of our people and growth of our clients. That means doing even more to hire, retain and promote the best talent, to provide first class service to clients, and to grow strategically.

What does your reaching the top position in a leading CPA firm mean to other women in the accounting profession?

I'm hoping that other firms will see that women are capable of assuming CEO level responsibilities and this will open up more opportunities for women in their organizations. I'm humbled and grateful I can help women see that they can be champions of their own careers, and accomplish their career goals.

Interview: Bert N. Mitchell
Former CEO, Mitchell & Titus

Bert N. Mitchell is the former CEO of Mitchell & Titus LLP, the largest minority-owned account-ing firm in the United States. On January 1, 2009, he retired as CEO; he remained chairman until 2010. He was succeeded as CEO by Anthony E. Kendall, vice chairman of client services, and a member of the firm's executive committee.

"There is a great demand for talent, and we need to demonstrate to minority students that there are opportunities for them in the field of accounting."

With more than 150 people, Mitchell & Titus provides auditing, tax, and advi-sory services for Fortune 1000 companies, entrepreneurial enterprises, not-for-profit organizations, government entities, and high net worth individuals. The firm has offices in New York, Philadelphia, Baltimore, Rutherford, N.J., and Wash-ington, DC. In 2006, Mitchell & Titus became a member firm of Ernst & Young Global Ltd., operating under the Mitchell & Titus brand. The global Ernst & Young organization consists of separate member firms in 140 countries, including Ernst & Young LLP in the United States.

During his 45-year career, Mitchell has written extensively on accounting and business issues, particularly the need to attract more blacks into accounting. He earned his bachelor of business administration and master of business administration from Baruch College of the City University of New York. He has served on the boards of numerous not-for-profit organizations involved in community and economic development as well as various educational institutions, both in the United States and abroad.

"I have a 45-year relationship with significant financial commitment to my elementary school in Jamaica, West Indies," Mitchell said. "I maintained direct contact with my third and fourth grade teachers until the last one died only 3 years ago. I think we all have 1 or 2 special persons, outside of our parents, to whom we give the credit for our success."

An avid golfer, Mitchell said that while he's not a great player, "I hold my own. At one point my handicap was 8, but now that age has caught up with me, I play with a 12 handicap."

How did you get started in accounting?

When I was 20 years old, I moved to New York from the West Indies. I went to the City University of New York to enroll in the engineering program. By mistake, I wound up at the wrong location, and found myself at Baruch College. So I decided to see what Baruch had to offer. After learning about Baruch's accounting program, I decided to enroll. I studied for my accounting degree at night while working full time. I worked for a number of smaller accounting firms, so that by the time I graduated in 1963, I already had 2 years of accredited experience for CPA accreditation.

Where did you work after you graduated?

I was interested in working for one of the Big 8 firms, but I didn't have any success in getting a job. At the time, there were almost no black accountants working for the Big 8. So I went to work for a small firm for a couple of years, and then joined another firm, J. K. Lasser & Co., one of the largest accounting firms, just below the Big 8. The firm's clients included leading publishing companies as well as some insurance companies. While working at Lasser, I studied at night for a master's degree in business, with a focus on taxation. After 3 years at Lasser, I joined the Ford Foundation as assistant controller in the international division, a very large division with 25 offices worldwide.

Where did you go from the Ford Foundation?

I wanted to help advance minorities in public accounting, so I became a partner at Lucas Tucker & Co., the oldest black CPA firm in the United States. It was founded in 1938 by Wilmer Lucas and Alfred Tucker. Lucas was only the third black CPA in the United States. His firm provided the opportunity for blacks to get the necessary experience in accounting that wasn't available through white firms at the time.

How did you come to found Mitchell & Titus?

In 1973, I decided to start a firm with another partner, who left after about nine months. In 1974, I formed a partnership with Bob Titus, who retired in 1995. Just as at Lucas & Tucker, a core mission of our firm is to provide more opportunities for minorities. Now, as a member of Ernst & Young Global, we are working side by side with Ernst & Young on the same mission.

What can the accounting profession do to interest young people, and especially young people of color, in careers in accounting?

The profession has to attract its share of the best minds from diverse parts of the community. To accomplish that goal, individual firms must offer upward mobility—people have to be convinced that there is a real opportunity to rise in the ranks. Firms have to support this with demonstrable evidence, for example, more firms are promoting people of color to partner. Our own firm is highly integrated. We call ourselves a minority firm but we've had white partners ever since we've had more than 2 partners. Currently, 20 percent of our partners are white. That model works for us, and it could work for other firms the same way.

How can the profession work with schools to interest students in accounting?

Many of the issues relating to a lack of minority professionals in accounting are deeply rooted at the middle school and high school levels. We have to reach out to those students to give them exposure to the profession. There is a great demand for talent, and we need to demonstrate to minority students that there are opportunities for them in the field of accounting.

Where should students start in accounting?

It's important for students to get experience in auditing, so they could start with a public accounting firm. But students and young professionals have more choices today, and more career flexibility; for example, an accounting graduate could start in the corporate world, and then move into public accounting.

If students plan to go into public accounting, should they start with a large or small firm?

It's more a question of a firm's culture, and its attitudes towards diversity. Today, we work in an international world, with diverse cultures, colors, and races. That is the kind of look that accounting firms need to model for themselves if they hope to attract the best talent.

What does it take to succeed in accounting today?

Accounting and business are so complex that a very high level of technical knowledge is required. But that alone isn't enough. Accountants need to develop strong communication and interpersonal skills, an ability to work with people of diverse backgrounds and cultures, marketing skills, managerial skills, sound judgment, and, equally important, the drive to succeed. To advance in their careers, accounting professionals should consider getting an advanced degree in business, accounting, or another discipline.

Interview: Ed Nusbaum
CEO, Grant Thornton International Ltd.

On Jan. 1, 2010, Edward E. Nusbaum became the Chief Executive Officer of Grant Thornton International Ltd, one of the leading global accounting organizations, with member firms including more than 30,000 employees in 100 countries. In this role, Ed is responsible for the leadership and management of the global organization, including the implementation and execution of the global strategy. Prior to assuming his new global role, Ed was chief executive officer and executive partner of Grant Thornton LLP, the U.S. member firm of Grant Thornton International Ltd. Under Ed's eight-year leadership, Grant Thornton LLP tripled revenues to approximately $1.2 billion.

> "You have to be open to learning, regardless of how much experience or education you have. People who fail assume they know everything."

In his nearly 30-year career with the firm, Nusbaum has served as national managing partner of professional services, managing partner of the Philadelphia office, and national director of assurance services based in New York.

Outside of the office, "my favorite way to relax is to spend time with my friends and family," Nusbaum said. "I have three daughters, and each is unique. For example, I went to a Bon Jovi concert with one daughter and discussed accounting with another. I took all three on their first trip to Paris this summer. We had a great time. I also love to travel and enjoy watching movies."

Among philanthropic endeavors, Grant Thornton as a firm, and Nusbaum personally, are very involved in supporting the Breast Cancer Network of Strength, an organization that provides information and support to anyone touched by breast cancer.

Whenever possible, Nusbaum speaks to students about careers in accounting, and why accounting matters. "Accounting is a vehicle for making a difference," he said. "It is vital to the health of the capital markets."

Why did you decide on accounting as a career?

When I was growing up in a Cleveland suburb, I was always interested in anything analytical and math-oriented. I decided early on that I wanted to be an accountant. My high school didn't offer an accounting course, so I took a class at John Carroll University. The teacher, a Jesuit priest, got us excited about learning the science of accounting. He showed us how it could be used to analyze and solve problems. In college, I studied for a bachelor of science degree in business administration at Ohio State University. I took accounting classes, and the professors were excellent—they gave us a solid grounding in both theoretical and real world accounting.

What was your first job in accounting?

While at Ohio State, I did a summer internship in the Houston office of Alexander Grant (a predecessor to Grant Thornton). Accounting firm internships weren't as common then as they are today, and I was the first intern in the Houston office. They didn't quite know what to do with me, but everybody talked to me and made the work interesting. They even gave me the chance to help audit companies in offshore drilling, retail, and real estate. I took time to go to grad school and earn an MS in management from Purdue University. After graduation, I joined the firm's audit staff in the Chicago office, and although I have moved around, I've been with Grant Thornton ever since. This year marks my 30th anniversary with the firm.

What does it take to move from entry level auditor to senior management in an organization like Grant Thornton?

You have to be open to learning, regardless of how much experience or education you have. People who fail assume they know everything. They think they have all the answers. You need to have a burning desire to learn continually and grow as a professional. You also have to be eager to take on new roles and responsibilities.

How can people be open to learning, as you suggested?

One way, of course, is through formal education. I'm grateful I got a master's in management because I can apply what I learned about finance, psychology and other disciplines in managing this organization. Regardless of whether you have an advanced degree, however, you can learn in a variety of other ways—for example, by attending seminars, taking online courses, and so on. Above all, you can learn from other people. I study leaders not only in accounting, but also in a variety of industries and professions to see how they lead their organizations.

What else is required to advance in an organization?

Learn everything about the organization, not just your particular area. Talk to everyone in the organization. Get to know them, and what they do. Hone your skills—keep challenging yourself to improve. Work not only for personal success, but, more importantly, for the success of others—people on your team, your colleagues, people in your community.

In your position, you meet with and work with a variety of people inside and outside of the firm. How do you connect with them?

I listen—really listen. I encourage our people to learn to listen, to pay close attention to what their clients, their fellow partners, other people in our organization are saying, what's on their minds, how they go about solving problems, addressing issues, or capitalizing on opportunities. I also advise thinking carefully about what you want to say before you say it. People do not have endless attention spans, so learn to communicate simply and clearly.

Final question. What's your advice to someone considering a career in accounting?

My youngest daughter is in college. She asked me if she should major in accounting. I told her that's her decision. I added, however, that if you do decide on accounting, the hardest part can be the first few years. Some of what you will do is not that intellectually challenging, but some is. I've advised her that if she hangs in there for a few years, she will get into more interesting and challenging work. I hope I have been a role model for her in that if you are passionate about what you do, you will find a rewarding career. In my case, that happens to be in accounting.

Interview: James Quigley
CEO, Deloitte Touche Tohmatsu

When he was an undergraduate student at Utah State University, James Quigley initially studied general business. He decided to switch majors to accounting, and graduated with a bachelor's of science degree. Today, he is CEO of Deloitte Touche Tohmatsu (Deloitte). Deloitte is the brand under which 165,000 professionals in independent firms throughout the world offer audit, tax and other consulting and advisory services to clients. Quigley previously was CEO of Deloitte United States.

> *"You need to develop market relevant skills that clients value and appreciate. Then you will have a career with some real leverage and momentum."*

Quigley says that in his life, "my family is No. 1. I try to integrate family and work so I don't have to choose one over the other. So far it seems to be a strategy that works." For recreation, he likes to bike ride, golf, hike and ski. "As a boy from Utah, I thoroughly enjoy skiing." He has a passion for education and creating opportunities for the next generation. "I always enjoy being on campus and having the opportunity to learn and exchange views with students." Quigley is actively engaged in a number of international business organizations and committees. He is co-chairman of the Transatlantic Business Dialogue (TABD), an organization of European and U.S. business leaders that, in the words of the TABD, "offers an effective framework for enhanced cooperation between the transatlantic business community and the governments of the European Union and the United States." Quigley said he is involved in and supports international organizations such as the TABD because "I like to know that I am making a positive contribution to our interconnected world whether through facilitating cross border trade, investment, or community development." He added, "Organizations like TABD are committed to such outcomes and provide an opportunity for businesses like Deloitte who share such goals to positively contribute to the sustainable development of our world."

Why did you decide on accounting as a career?

I'm a pragmatist. I saw that the top students in my classes were accounting majors, and they were finding good jobs through the school placement office.

Why did you go into public accounting?

In school, I kept hearing the buzz among students about the career opportunities with what were then the Big 8 accounting firms. In the summer between my junior and senior years, I worked for the Utah state auditor's office, and I had a chance to talk with some auditors about their experiences in previously working for public accounting firms. They pushed me to go into public accounting, saying it was a great foundation for a career. Our school was very good at helping us to prepare for the CPA exam and careers in public accounting. In my senior year, I received offers from all of the Big 8 firms, and I decided to join Deloitte not only because it had a great reputation, but also because of the connection I felt with those I met while interviewing. That was 34 years ago, and I've been with Deloitte ever since.

What does it take for a young person to advance in their career in a large public accounting firm like Deloitte?

You have to show that you have the ability to work on teams—that you're a team player. Imagine that some managers in your firm are talking at lunch about wanting you on their teams. They say you have great people skills and you are good at developing client relationships. You are highly productive, low maintenance, and add strength to each team you join. That's what you want people to say about you. Then you'll be highly sought after, and have the opportunity to work on some great projects and to build your reputation.

What does someone do when they feel they're not growing anymore in their current job?

The beauty of working for a large, diverse public accounting firm like Deloitte is that you can find many interesting career paths, and multiple learning opportunities. If you get to the point where you feel like you're not learning anymore in your current position, you can talk to your manager, mentors and others about new assignments. When I looked at opportunities in the firm, I always considered them in the context of where I could learn the most over the next two to three years. That's how I made my first move in the firm, from Salt Lake City to New York in 1979. It meant having to relocate my family, but that was what was required to pursue a new opportunity, and my family supported me.

After you made partner, where did you work in the organization?

I had the opportunity to work with Mike Cook (J. Michael Cook, retired chairman and CEO of Deloitte & Touche). While working with Mike, I helped him develop, implement, and communicate our business strategy. It provided me with a tremendous opportunity to help manage the business and further develop my leadership skills. After a time in the leadership and management seat, I decided to repurpose my career into client service, and I became the lead partner for our client Monsanto, and later returned to New York as the regional managing partner in our New York practice. From there I went on to lead Deloitte United States and now the global organization.

What is the value to an audit or tax professional of having a specialty, such as an industry specialization?

Specialization is essential. The question is when in your career to develop a specialty—beginning with day one or later on? I believe that by the time you become a manager, your ability to progress only as a generalist is limited, and you must learn to specialize. You need to develop market relevant skills that clients value and appreciate. Then you will have a career with some real leverage and momentum.

Interview: James Turley

CEO, Ernst & Young

While studying for an undergraduate degree in economics and management studies at Rice University, James Turley took some accounting courses. He found that he enjoyed accounting. "I liked working with numbers, and I had an analytical bent," he said. He went on to earn a master's degree in accounting at Rice. Today, he's chairman and CEO of Ernst & Young, a global professional services firm of 135,000 people worldwide.

> *"To be successful, you have to understand the importance of teaming—everybody is on the same team, and working towards common goals."*

Did you initially plan on a career in accounting?

I wanted to go into business in some way, following the example of my father, who was the leader of a major St. Louis-based real estate company. When I was growing up, he would take me to conventions of real estate trade organizations, and introduce me to people in real estate and the business world. My dad wasn't an accountant, but he always talked about accounting being the language of business. He realized its importance to the management of a business.

Did you go into public accounting right out of school?

At the suggestion of one of my professors, I joined Ernst & Ernst (a predecessor to Ernst & Young) as an audit intern in Houston, and subsequently was hired as an auditor. After Houston, I worked all over the Midwest for the firm. Along the way, I took a year off to earn my master's degree.

What does it take to succeed in a large public accounting firm like Ernst & Young?

To be successful, you have to understand the importance of teaming—everybody is on the same team, and working towards common goals. You won't always get the most glamorous assignments—I did my share of tough jobs that had to be done. But I saw them as a learning opportunity, a chance to show I was a team player, and to develop the skills to advance in the organization. Another essential for success is that you have to be a really good listener. And, as you move up in the organization, you have to be comfortable working with people at all levels. I deal with presidents and prime ministers, but I also spend a lot of time with students and new recruits. Finally, having a good mentor is critical. I had the opportunity to work with many mentors, including Doug Phillips (a former vice chairman of Ernst & Young), who was probably as responsible as anybody for my becoming chairman.

How does someone decide on a career path in a large organization like Ernst & Young?

To be successful in a career, you have to find something that you really enjoy and have a passion about. So we try to give young people broad exposure to our firm, our clients, and our profession, to offer them a wide variety of career choices and options, and to offer them a high degree of mobility—young professionals don't want to be doing the same thing for very long. In my career at Ernst & Young, I've been able to do a lot of different things while drawing a paycheck from the same company. I've worked for clients in the oil and gas industry, for family businesses and public companies, and as the lead audit partner on our accounts with some of the largest U.S. companies. That's the beauty of a large organization—you have a lot of flexibility.

Do you need to develop a specialty as you advance in the organization?

You can start out as a generalist, and get a solid grounding in our core services such as tax and audit, and learn about other areas such as technology. But over time you have to develop a specialty, such as providing audit or tax services to companies in real estate. Clients expect you to have a high level of knowledge and experience in their industry. As you move into management, you may become a generalist again, and learn to develop your management skills.

What are the opportunities for Ernst & Young professionals in the United States to work internationally?

International opportunities will only continue to increase. For example, we are hiring Mandarin speakers from campuses across the country to work in China, where there is 1 CPA for every 10,000 people, compared with 1 for every 1,000 people in the United States. And, we are trying to make overseas opportunities available to all of our people who want them as a way to advance in our organization.

How do you convince college graduates that Ernst & Young is the best place for them?

To most students, all large accounting firms can look alike, at first blush. In part, that's because almost everything in our profession can be replicated: our methodologies, technologies, etc. The one thing at Ernst & Young that cannot be copied is our culture of putting people first. It's a primary reason why, for the past 10 years, we've been on the Fortune 100 list of best companies to work for.

Interview: Charles Weinstein
Managing Partner, Eisner LLP

Charles Weinstein said, "I have wanted to be an accountant for as long as I can remember." He earned a BS degree in accounting at the State University of New York at Binghamton, and started with a small accounting firm in New York City. Today, he is the managing partner of Eisner, LLP.

"It was a big change to move from a relatively small shop to a larger firm, and to work on more complex accounting issues. But the firms did have some things in common. Their cultures were similar, and people cared about one another."

Could you provide a snapshot of your firm?

We're among the top 25 CPA firms in the country, headquartered in New York City, with 80 partners and a total of about 550 people. Our 2 founders retired in 2008. We have not done a merger in 18 years. Instead, we've grown organically. We are a member of an international group, Baker Tilly International. One of our areas of focus is public company audits. We currently audit about 80 public companies. We also focus on the financial services industry, which we define as hedge funds, private equity funds, broker dealers, and venture capital.

When did you decide you wanted to become an accountant?

As far back as I can remember. My sister, who is three years older, and I were the first in our immediate family to go to college. No one in my family had ever worn a suit to work.

Where did you work after graduation?

When I graduated, it was a tough time in the profession. I sent out 200 hand-typed cover letters to all the accounting firms in New York City. I didn't get a single interview, even though I graduated magnum cum laude. I finally found a position as a junior accountant with Maxwell Shmerler & Co. It was a small firm with some very large clients, and a good place for a new accountant to start. While I was working for them, I got on an airplane for the first time in my life. I flew to Pittsburgh to meet with a client, an oil company that was based there.

How long were you at Maxwell Shmerler?

About a year. Then I went to a midmarket firm, Mann Judd Landau. It was a big change to move from a relatively small shop to a larger firm, and to work on more complex accounting issues. But the firms did have some things in common. Their cultures were similar, and people cared about one another. I received tremendous on-the-job training at both firms, and I had a lot of mentors, or career rabbis. At Mann Judd Landau, my work assignments grew every year, and I moved up to senior accountant. I led a team that took a company called Syms, a discount clothing chain, public in a $50,000,000 offering. After that engagement, I moved up to manager.

How long were you at Mann Judd Landau?

After I had been with Mann Judd Landau for about 10 years, the firm offered me a partnership. Shortly after that, the firm announced that it was merging with Deloitte & Touche, which also offered me a partnership. Instead, I decided to join Eisner as a partner. I had considered seeking a position with one of the largest firms, but I knew that a midmarket firm like Eisner was the right choice for me.

What types of client engagements did you work on?

When I joined, one of Eisner's largest clients, an entertainment company, was being sold for more than $300 million, a tremendous amount of money. I worked under a senior partner in helping to prepare audited financial statements. At that time, it was the biggest engagement in the history of firm. At one point, we had 19 partners working on different aspects of the engagement. I worked 7 days week to 11 at night. It was a terrific project, and a great way to start with the firm. You can make your reputation on a project like that.

In seeking their first job, should students work for a small, midsized, or large firm?

It depends on what you are looking for. I like the middle market, where Eisner is positioned. We have a collaborative and collegial culture that our founding partners created, and that hasn't changed. In a very large firm you may not necessarily find the same work environment—the clients are bigger, and the demands are greater. But you cannot replicate the training and exposure at the largest firms, which have resources far beyond those of other firms. At a small firm, you are able to be hands on, and to participate directly with clients in meaningful way. So there are pluses and minuses at every level.

Interview: Billie Williamson
Americas Inclusiveness Officer, Ernst & Young

As Ernst & Young's (EY's) Americas inclusiveness officer, Billie Williamson works to foster and maintain a diverse and inclusive culture where all EY people can achieve their potential. She is a senior partner and serves some of the firm's largest global accounts. She has also served as a member EY's Americas Executive Board and currently serves on the U.S. Executive Board. Prior to being named to her current role, she was the Americas director for flexibility and gender equity strategy.

"We have been able to show women that they can fulfill their responsibilities to their spouses and children and have dynamic careers."

Williamson began her career at EY in 1974 in the audit practice, and in 1984, she became 1 of only 7 female partners in the firm. She left after 20 years with the firm to become CFO of AMX Corp., a manufacturer of control systems. She subsequently joined Marriott International, Inc., as senior vice president, finance. She rejoined EY in 1998 in the corporate finance practice and has worked with CEOs of major companies to structure acquisitions and determine financial strategy. She has also served major clients in aerospace and defense, technology, and other industries. Williamson attended Southern Methodist University, where she earned a degree in business administration, with an emphasis in accounting.

Why did you study accounting in college?

I liked the logical thought processes, the mathematics of accounting, and I wasn't drawn to other professions such as law or medicine.

Why did you decide to join Ernst & Young after you graduated?

I graduated at the top of my class in business school, and I received offers from all of what were then the Big 8 firms. I liked Ernst & Young—the people, the culture, the commitment to quality, and the professionalism of the firm. I started in the firm's Dallas office and worked on a variety of client engagements. I rose through the ranks fairly quickly, and made partner after 10 years. Then I joined AMX and later Marriott.

Why did you decide to move from public accounting to the corporate world?

I saw it as an opportunity to broaden my skills. At AMX, I assisted the company in its initial public offering. At Marriott, I was part of a strong, growing company in an interesting line of business. Marriott taught me a great deal about financial transactions and acquisitions.

What brought you back to Ernst & Young?

I had the opportunity to again work with interesting clients and to help the firm with its initiatives and programs to advance women to leadership positions in the organization. In 2004, I became Americas director of flexibility and gender equity strategy, and in 2008, Americas inclusiveness officer, a new position in the firm, responsible for all of its diversity and inclusiveness initiatives in the Americas. In addition, I continue to serve clients as a global coordinating partner.

How does Ernst & Young succeed in creating and fostering a diverse and inclusive workplace?

Success begins at the top. Our chairman and senior leaders are committed to building and sustaining an inclusive environment, engaging our partners and managers in the firm's many initiatives and programs to promote inclusiveness and diversity, and holding them accountable.

What are examples of the firm's programs to promote the career development of women and minorities?

We have a number of such programs. Career Watch is designed to ensure that women and minority managers are on the right path to become partners—that they get the professional experiences they need and have people who coach them along. We have an intensive course for female senior managers and new partners and principals to help them improve their communication, presentation, and sales skills as they prepare to transition from senior manager to partner or principal. Our "Working Moms Network" provides support, resources, networking, and mentoring opportunities for new, expectant, and veteran mothers. We periodically hold an Inclusiveness Leadership Conference that brings together Ernst & Young's top women and minority executives with the entire Americas Executive Board as well as with selected senior male leaders and line partners. The conference provides an opportunity for our women and ethnically diverse professionals to network and to have a candid discussion with leadership about their progress in the firm. We also reach out to women in the business and the professional community to recognize and celebrate their accomplishments. In 2008, we initiated our Winning Women program, which is designed to foster informative relationships, build networks and provide growth opportunities and support to women-owned businesses and women in business. Five female entrepreneurs were honored as emerging Winning Women and received complimentary registration to the Ernst & Young's 2008 Strategic Growth Forum.

What progress have women and minorities made in the firm?

Women have accounted for about 50 percent of accounting graduates for many years, and about half our hires have been women. Our key accomplishment is the increase in the number of women in key leadership roles in the firm. Women have come to represent 17 percent of the firm's partnership, the number of women in titled leadership positions has grown to nearly 20 percent, and women comprise 43 percent of our client-service professionals. We have been able to show women that they can fulfill their responsibilities to their spouses and children and have dynamic careers. Public accounting is an interesting, dynamic profession that enables women to be involved with outstanding clients, to help companies grow, and to work with clients on issues and find great solutions. Our representation of ethnically diverse professionals has also increased. About $1/3$ of our hires each year are minorities, and 30 percent of our population and 8 percent of our partners today are ethnically diverse.

What do you want to accomplish during the remainder of your career?

I would like to see Ernst & Young continue to build and sustain an inclusive culture. I want to continue to serve my clients and bring strong value during different economic times. When the time comes for me to retire from the firm, I would like to be involved in helping women, people of different ethnicities, and people with disabilities to build businesses and be successful. I would also welcome the opportunity to serve on boards of directors.

Chapter 5

Careers in Corporate Accounting

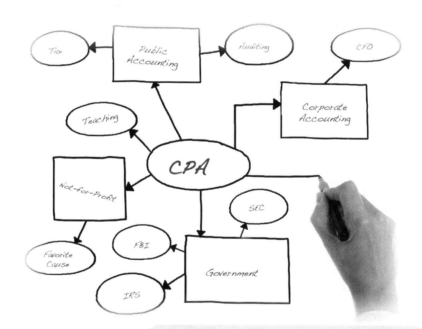

"CFOs should be accountants first and financial executives second."

Joseph Macnow, executive vice president–
finance and administration, CFO, CAO
• Vornado Realty Trust

Introduction

Under the big tent that is accounting, corporate accounting has a prominent place. CPAs are employed by thousands of U.S. companies, both public and private, ranging from the Fortune 500 to small companies or partnerships. CPAs are indispensable to the management and operation of companies. They provide, analyze, monitor, interpret, and verify financial information used by people inside and outside the company to make business and investment decisions. They participate in or lead every aspect of a company's business, including strategic planning, operations, finance, financial reporting, tax, information systems, human capital, and marketing. They are found at every level of the organization from staff accountant to CFO and CEO. They work in every department and operating unit.

Today, companies increasingly turn to CPAs for assistance, advice, and leadership in addressing the challenges of doing business in a complex global business environment. The structural upheaval in global economies—precipitated by the deepest global recession since the Great Depression—increased competition for markets, customers, and talent worldwide. Tighter regulation, stricter credit requirements, rapid advances in information technology, increased focus on fraud prevention, and other issues, are driving increased demand for CPAs. What this means for accounting graduates going into corporate accounting—or experienced CPAs joining companies from public accounting or other sectors—is that they will have opportunities to apply their knowledge and skills in innovative ways that have financial, as well as strategic, value for companies. Advances in information technology and the automation of routine accounting functions have freed CPAs to play a larger role in their organizations. But they will also have to meet the higher expectations of corporate management; for example, by not simply collecting financial data, but analyzing it, or by not merely preparing financial statements, but interpreting their implications for the organization.

Corporate Employers

The companies that employ CPAs are in every business line. Generally, these can be divided into the following:

- *Manufacturing*—The research and development, manufacturing, sales and distribution of many different products to businesses or consumers; or
- *Services*—Providing accounting, architectural, construction, consulting, entertainment, financial, health care, information systems, legal, professional sports, and a variety of other services, to businesses, consumers and other clients, or customers.

Not every accountant working for a company is a CPA; however, the company may expect accountants to be CPAs or to obtain certification as CPAs in order to advance to senior positions in the organization, such as CFO.

After public accounting, corporate accounting is where graduates with bachelor's degrees in accounting choose to start their careers, according to a 2008 American Institute of Certified Public Accountants

(AICPA) study.[1] During their careers, some experienced CPAs elect to move into corporate accounting from public accounting. For example, a senior partner of a public accounting firm might become the CFO or CEO of a company. Such a transition is possible because the skills and experience that CPAs acquire are readily transferable. From having worked with clients in a particular industry, the partner of a public accounting firm brings industry knowledge and experience to a position as CFO or CEO of a company in that industry. In recruiting for some positions, companies prefer or require that CPAs have experience in public accounting. Some CPAs advance to CFOs or CEOs of companies.

Where CPAs Work in a Company

Although CPAs have many different functions and responsibilities in a company, they generally work in one of five areas. (In some large companies, CPAs may rotate through different areas to get broad exposure to the organization.) The five areas are the following:

1. *Management accounting*

   For many years, management accounting was largely a reporting function: accountants compiled, reviewed, analyzed, and reported historical financial information about a company. Although management accountants still carry out these tasks, their scope of work and responsibilities have evolved to meet the needs of the modern corporation. Management accountants today are business partners in an organization, providing senior executives and company managers with the information and guidance to develop strategic plans, set business goals, and carry out other management functions and responsibilities. They participate in value-creating activities such as evaluating potential investments, developing strategies to increase productivity, or developing capital market plans to fund new programs. Management accountants have a higher profile in organizations than in the past—they belong to or lead executive teams that address strategic and business issues such as forecasting a company's future financial performance.

   A key responsibility of management accountants is *cost accounting*. Management accountants develop and manage information and reporting systems to track a company's costs, such as the costs of labor and materials, or the costs of product manufacturing or providing services. They assist the company with *budgeting* including:

   a. An *operating budget* that forecasts a company's operating revenue, expenses, and net income, as well as revenues and expenses by product or service line.

---

1 "2008 Trends in the Supply of Accounting Graduates And the Demand for Public Accounting Recruits; chart: Placement of Graduates by Degree Level: 2006-2007," American Institute of Certified Public Accountants (AICPA), http://ceae.aicpa.org/NR/rdonlyres/C1E23302-17D3-4ED5-AE81-B274D9CD7812/0/AICPA_Trends_Reports_2008.pdf

b. A *capital budget* that forecasts a company's long-range capital expenditures, such as starting a new product or service line, or expanding into a new market. It considers alternative strategies for financing expenditures such as lines of credit, long-term debt financing or equity options.

c. A *cash budget* that forecasts a company's cash flows (incoming and outgoing) on a daily, weekly, monthly, or other short-term basis (in contrast with the capital budget's long-term forecasts). The cash budget helps companies determine whether they have sufficient cash to meet short-term expenses, or whether they may need to borrow cash short term, or whether they have a surplus of cash that can be parked in short-term investments.

Management accountants also are responsible for a company's *general accounting*, or maintaining the books and records. This includes the following:

a. Journalizing: Entries of daily, routine transactions.

b. Payroll: Maintaining payroll records and cutting paychecks.

c. Accounts payable: Authorizing and disbursing payments to vendors, suppliers and others.

d. Billing: Sending out billing statements.

e. General ledger: Maintaining income statement and balance sheet accounts.

2. *Internal auditing*

Since the enactment of the Sarbanes Oxley Act (SOX) in 2002, many companies have made substantial investments in designing, building, or upgrading internal control systems to ensure compliance with SOX's stringent financial reporting requirements and to protect organizations from mismanagement and fraud. Many have formed separate risk management groups, which encompass SOX compliance as well as enterprise risk management,[2] including business continuity, disaster recovery planning, and regulatory compliance. But how do companies know that their controls are working according to plan? That is where internal auditors come in. Internal auditors help companies to protect the integrity of financial data. They examine and evaluate their companies' financial and information systems, management procedures, operational processes, and internal controls, to ensure that records are accurate and controls are adequate. They review company operations, evaluating their efficiency, effectiveness, and compliance with corporate policies and government laws and regulations. (Not often). Internal auditors assist companies to manage risks, reduce costs,

---

2 Methods and processes used by organizations to assess and mitigate risks.

operate more efficiently, and achieve other strategic goals.[3] In the process, internal auditors have increased their value to companies, and in recognition of this, more companies have created positions of chief auditor, or vice president, auditing and reporting, or similar titles, reporting directly to the CFO or CEO, and to a board of directors or to its audit committee.[4]

3. *Financial accounting*

Where management accountants and internal auditors work with company executives and managers, and provide information for internal use, financial accountants deal with stakeholders outside a company. Financial accountants prepare the company's balance sheet, income statement, statement of retained earnings, statement of cash flows, and other information for use by investors, creditors, stock analysts, government agencies, labor unions, consumer groups, the media, and others. Financial accounting provides a look at a company's financial performance on an annual, quarterly, or other basis. In the wake of Enron and other corporate scandals and enactment of SOX, company financial reports have come under closer public scrutiny and financial accountants are playing a larger role in providing financial information that meets the expectations of investors, regulators, and other stakeholders. More than ever, companies are measured by the quality of their financial reporting.

4. *Tax accounting*

For companies and businesses, filing tax returns is often a complicated process. The Internal Revenue Code (IRC) is thousands of pages, and each of the 50 states has its own tax codes. Cities, counties, special districts, and other jurisdictions weigh in with their own tax systems. If U.S. companies operate in other countries, they must also address a welter of foreign tax laws. To further complicate matters, government legislators and regulators are continually enacting new tax laws and regulations or revising existing ones. Not surprisingly, then, companies have need for tax accountants who can assist them with preparation and filing of federal, state, and local tax returns, filing of foreign tax returns, and other filings. Tax accountants also advise companies on tax compliance, preparing for audits by tax authorities and other tax matters. They assist with tax planning, such as evaluating the tax effects of selling company assets, buying another company, buying back company stock, or issuing debt. Tax accountants are highly valued for their skill and experience in assisting companies to address tax obligations and identify opportunities to defer or reduce taxes.

---

3 "The changing face of internal audit," Michael Hill, *Risk Manager* magazine, May 17, 2009, www.riskmanagementmagazine.com.au/articles/c5/0c051bc5.asp

4 Committee of a public company's board of directors. It is responsible for overseeing a company's financial reporting and disclosure.

Corporate CPAs Have Bigger Role in Forecasting

A key change in corporate accounting in recent times is the increased use of forecasting. CPAs at every level of the organization work closely with department managers, the CFO, and other top executives, in periodically reevaluating a company's strategic plan and preparing budget forecasts based on the revised plan and *sensitivity analysis*, an examination of how projected performance varies with changes in the assumptions on which projections are based. CPAs are called upon to come up with realistic assumptions of a company's revenue growth, expense charges, profit margins, and running excel models (a commonly used financial modeling tool) to support the planning and budgeting process.

Forecasting is critical to companies in evaluating and implementing strategic initiatives. For example, a company considering an acquisition would prepare a forecast of the revenue and expenses of the combined companies assuming the acquisition took place under key different economic assumptions (for example, interest rates, inflation, consumer confidence). The forecasted returns would then be compared to the cost of the acquisition to evaluate and measure the expected return to see if it meets the company's risk adjusted yield goals. Other uses of forecasting follow.

Forecast of Cash Flows

This is one of the most important tools in the forecasting arsenal. Companies need accurate forecasts of cash flows to ensure that they can cover operating expenses, cover their debt obligations, build cash reserves, meet profits expectations, and otherwise use cash. Such forecasting is especially critical during recessions or at times when lenders and creditors may be concerned whether a company can meet its current and long-term debt obligations. In some cases, companies may negotiate with lenders for moratoriums, extensions, modifications, or additional funding. The accountant's analysis of asset values, cash flow, and debt service and maturities, is critical to the company's negotiations with creditors to achieve its objectives such as an extension of the repayment period.

Product Analysis

CPAs are sometimes asked to analyze the cost of introducing a new product or producing an existing product, and to measure such costs against the estimated or current revenues from manufacturing new or current products. Based on this analysis, the company can forecast the profit margins of new products and determine the margins of current products, and make strategic decisions about whether to expand, maintain, scale back, or discontinue product lines.

Overhead Management

Companies are constantly looking for ways to reduce overhead costs, especially during difficult times, such as a recession or profit slump. CPAs are often called upon to work with human resources and operating divisions in forecasting the cost savings of plans to cut staff, reduce benefits, consolidate operating units, or otherwise reduce overhead.

Asset Valuation

Valuation is important in evaluating the carrying value of assets both held for sale or long term. It may require the company to set up impairment reserves or write off some assets that have declined in value. Companies sell assets for different reasons, for example, to dispose of assets that are no longer needed, or to raise capital, or move assets off their books as part of debt restructuring plans negotiated with creditors. They also refinance assets for such purposes as raising capital. (Assuming the asset has appreciated in value, the company can take out a bigger loan against the asset and use the loan proceeds for various corporate purposes). CPAs work with company executives and managers to prepare estimates of the value that assets would command and the cash that a company could realize from such sales or refinancings. Valuing assets is a complex process, requiring CPAs who are experienced and skilled in the valuation process. This is especially true in a recession when asset values generally are depressed, few asset sales are occurring in the marketplace, and it is difficult to estimate the market value of assets.

How Green is Your Accounting?

Some corporate CPAs have developed specialties in areas such as information technology, compliance, and engineering; and in specific industries such as banking and health care. A growing field is green or environmental management accounting, which addresses how companies can be both environmentally responsible and profitable. According to the U.S. Environmental Protection Agency, *green accounting* is "the identification, prioritization, quantification or qualification, and incorporation of environmental costs into business decisions."[*] Green accounting is intended to bring transparency to the environmental costs of corporate activities. Companies traditionally have failed to determine the environmental costs of manufacturing operations, construction of new facilities or other activities; or they have hidden these costs in conventional (nonenvironmental) business accounts.[**] However, increased public concerns about the environment, regulatory pressures, and enlightened self-interest have caused companies to focus on accounting for environmental costs. As a result, company managers are able to make better informed decisions about the environmental costs of developing new products, use of manufacturing plants, warehouses, office buildings and other facilities, use of materials, consumption of water and energy, and other activities; and to identify opportunities to reduce costs, for example, through water conservation, and to protect the environment, for example, by reducing pollution. Separately, CPAs are assisting companies to study the effects on their businesses of possible cap and trade legislation under consideration by Congress and some states such as California or various proposals for an international treaty to cut greenhouse gases.

Emerging Career Opportunity

As green accounting has come into wider use, more sophisticated reporting and accounting systems have been developed to give companies more accurate and complete information about environmental costs and help them to better manage such costs. In the process, green accounting is emerging as a career opportunity for CPAs. Large companies have environmental management accountants on staff—these are CPAs who have been trained in green accounting. Public accounting firms have environmental accountants who provide services to companies and other clients that do not have an internal capability in environmental accounting. As with corporations, public accounting firms usually train CPAs in environmental accounting. Some organizations offer certification programs in environmental management accounting; for example, the Board of Environmental, Health & Safety Auditor Certifications, a nonprofit corporation originally created as a joint venture of the Institute of Internal Auditors and the Accounting Roundtable, offers the Certified Professional Environmental Auditor certification.[†] As an alternative to working as an environmental accountant in a corporation, some CPAs join consulting firms that specialize in environmental services and some start their own firms.[‡] (See Appendix 1 for further reading.

[*] "Green Accounting: Environmental Accounting," Erik Johnson, articlesbase.com, Feb. 4, 2009, www.articlesbase.com/education-articles/green-accounting-environmental-accounting-755857.html

[**] "Green ledgers: Case studies in corporate environmental accounting," World Resources Institute, May 1995, www.wri.org/publication/green-ledgers-case-studies-corporate-environmental-accounting

[†] "Certification," BEAC web page, www.beac.org/certification.html

[‡] "Environmental Accountants Do It for the Green," John Rossheim, "Today's CPA: CPA Specialties," www.startheregoplaces.com/todayscpas/careeroptions/cpaspecialties/environmental/

5. *Information technology*

Some graduates develop a specialty in accounting information technology, the result of taking courses or earning undergraduate or graduate degrees in the field (such as an MS in accounting information technology). These graduates may work in the information technology department of a company, or in other departments, drawing on their advanced knowledge and skills to assist the organization with information security, fraud detection, business intelligence, regulatory reporting or the design and development of enterprise resource management (ERP) systems. But every accounting graduate joining a company is expected to have a high level of computer skills—not at the advanced level of the information technology specialists—but sufficient to enable them to use these skills on the job in management accounting, internal audit, or other areas of the company.

Certified Information Technology Professional (CITP)

To recognize CPAs for their information technology skills, the AICPA offers the Certified Information Technology Professional (CITP) certification to CPAs who are AICPA members The CITP credential program encourages and recognizes excellence in the delivery of technology related services by CPA professionals, and provides tools, training, and support to help CPAs expand their IT-related services and provide greater benefits to business, academic, and other organizations. Applicants apply to the AICPA for certification. To be awarded the CITP credential, a CPA must earn 100 points, which will be awarded based on business experience and lifelong learning relevant to the CITP body of knowledge. More information on the CITP program can be found on the AICPA's Web site at "Overview of the Certified Information Technology Professional."

Forms of Practice

Of course, people who decide to start businesses base their decision on more than a coin flip, although in the annals of business there probably are those who went into business on not much more than a dare. Regardless of how they got started, or why, every business has a structure. The most common structures follow.

And Now, a Word About Corporate Structure

Is the C Corp. right for you?

Or will an S Corp. have to do?

What about an LLC?

Is that the right place to be?

Or should you try a partnership?

Or maybe a sole proprietorship?

Here's how to decide: give a coin a flip

That's all there is to it: just follow this tip

C Corporation

Most large companies as well as many smaller companies are C corporations. A *C corporation* is a legal entity completely separate and distinct from its owners. It is created by a group of shareholders who own the corporation through their ownership of the company's shares. Corporations have most of the same rights and responsibilities as individuals, such as, to enter into contracts, to hire employees, to sue and be sued, to own assets, to pay taxes, and so on. One of the most important features of a corporation is its limited liability; for example, its shareholders are not personally liable for the company's debts and actions.

Partnership

A *partnership* is a business entity in which the partners (owners) share the profits and losses of the business in which they have invested. Depending on the laws of the jurisdiction where the partnership is formed and the partnership structure, the partners may be exposed to greater personal liability than if they were shareholders of a corporation. A limited partnership could provide greater liability protection to the limited partners.

Limited Liability Partnership

A *limited liability partnership* is a pass-through entity similar to a limited liability company (LLC) (defined in a subsequent paragraph); however, while the partners are entitled to limited liability for the acts of the partnership, they are liable for their own acts or omissions. CPA's and lawyers frequently practice in this structure.

S Corporation

An *S corporation* is a corporation of 100 shareholders or less that has the same benefits of incorporation as a C corporation; however, it is taxed as a partnership under subchapter S of the IRC. Thus, it passes income directly to its shareholders without being subject to the double taxation of C corporations.

Limited Liability Company (LLC)

An LLC is a relatively new business structure. As with a C corporation, owners of an LLC (who are called "members") have limited personal liability for its debts and actions, but LLCs also have the features of partnerships, providing management flexibility and pass through income. Many public accounting, consulting, law, architectural, and other professional services firms are structured as LLCs.

Sole Proprietorship

Finally, *sole proprietorships* are a type of business entity that has no legal separation from its owner. The owner of a sole proprietorship is personally liable for the debts and actions of the proprietorship. Some small businesses in the United States, including home-based businesses, are sole proprietorships.

A number of business, legal, tax, and other considerations go into decisions to form these types of business entities, and owners and investors typically confer with their accounting, legal, tax, and other advisors to decide what form to use when setting up and operating the business. Of course, if you're having trouble deciding what structure to use, you could flip a coin. (See the following section, "Corporate Structure" to learn more about working for these different organizations.)

Size of Companies: Many Goliaths, Many More Davids

Accounting graduates who go into corporate accounting can work for companies ranging from the largest in the world to small businesses. ExxonMobil, ranked No. 1 on the 2009 Fortune 500 list of the world's largest companies, had revenues of nearly $443 billion in 2008.[5] Career Education, a global provider of postsecondary educational servic-es, ranked number 1,000 on the list and had revenue of $1.7 billion in 2008.

In 2007, more than 31 million U.S. businesses filed federal returns and reported revenue of approximately $26 trillion (see table 5-1).[6] Of the 31 million businesses, about 4 million were S corporations, and about 2 million were "other" corporations, including C corporations, for a total of about 6 million. Corporations represented only about 19 percent of total businesses; however, they had revenue of about $22 trillion, or 84 percent of total revenue of all businesses. Based on revenue, corporations are clearly the Goliaths of the business world. But the number of sole proprietorships and other types of businesses far exceeded the number of corporations.

Table 5-1: *Number of U.S. Business Entities 2007*

Type of Business	Number (in millions)	% of Total Businesses	Revenue ($ in trillions)	% of Total Revenue
Sole Proprietorships	22.7	71%	$ 1.2	5%
Corporations*	6.0	19%	21.6	84%
Partnerships	1.2	4%	1.4	5%
Limited Liability Companies	1.8	6%	1.8	6%
Total	31.7	100%	$26.0	100%

* Consisting of approximately 4 million S corporations and 2 million "other" corporations, including C corporations.

5 "Fortune 500: Our Ranking of the World's Largest Corporations," *Fortune*, http://money.cnn.com/magazines/fortune/fortune500/2009/

6 "Total Number of U.S. Businesses 2007," University of Central Florida, College of Business Administration Web site, www.bus.ucf.edu/ckelliher/tax_6845/beginning_a_business/number_businesses_2007.pdf; and BizStats.com www.bizstats.com/businesses.htm

Go Public! No, Stay Private! Public! Private!

Many companies started as small enterprises and grew into large corporations. Along the way, the owners may have decided to take the company public in an initial public offering of the company's shares. Among other reasons, companies go public to raise equity capital to finance investments, such as new product startups or acquisitions, to use company stock in structuring executive compensation and employee benefit programs, or to repay corporate debt. Public companies must register with the Securities and Exchange Commission (SEC) and state securities regulators and meet various reporting requirements and compliance standards. Many—but not all—of the largest U.S. corporations are public. The remaining companies are private, including some of the world's largest, led by Cargill, a farm products company, and the No. 1 company (based on revenue) on the 2008 Forbes list of America's Largest Private Companies (table 5-2).[7] Cargill had estimated revenue of $100 billion in 2008, or about a quarter of the revenue of Exxon-Mobil, a publicly traded company, and No.1 on the Fortune 1000. If Cargill was a public company, it would have ranked in the top 20 on the Fortune 500.

Table 5-2: *Forbes: America's Largest Private Companies 2008 Top Ten (of which 2 are CPA firms)*

Rank	Company	Business	Number of Employees (worldwide)	Revenue ($ billions)
1.	Cargill	Farm products	152,600	$110.6*
2.	Koch Industries	Diversified (chemicals, energy, technology)	80,000	98.0*
3.	Chrysler**	Auto manufacturing	66,409	59.7*
4.	GMAC Financial Services	Financial services	26,700	31.5
5.	PricewaterhouseCoopers	Business services	154,000	28.1
6.	Mars	Confectioners	64,400	27.4
7.	Bechtel	Heavy construction	42,500	27.0
8.	HCA	Hospitals	180,000	26.86
9.	Ernst & Young	Business services	135,730	24.52
10.	Publix Super Markets	Grocery stores	145,000	23.19

* Forbes estimate.

** Reorganized in bankruptcy in 2009.

7 "Special Report: America's Largest Private Companies," Forbes, November 3, 2008, http://www.forbes.com/lists/2008/21/privates08_Americas-Largest-Private-Companies_Rank.html

Among other reasons, some companies are private because they do not want to have to meet the reporting and other regulatory requirements of the SEC and other regulators, or deal with the pressures of meeting earnings expectations of shareholders and securities analysts. Private companies see themselves as better able to focus on long-term earnings growth rather than on short-term stock performance; however, they do not have access to the public capital markets, the liquidity (shares of a public company can readily be bought and sold on public stock exchanges), and other benefits of a public company.

Career Paths in Companies: Where Does Yours Lead?

College graduates who plan careers in accounting and who join large companies after earning a bachelor's degree, generally start as staff accountants or similar entry-level positions. (Graduates with master's degrees in business administration, accounting, tax, or other disciplines may start higher up the corporate ladder, or in a specialty such as tax accounting.) Entry level CPAs may work in a particular department such as cost accounting or finance, or in an operating division. They usually participate in on-the-job training programs intended to educate them about the company and to give them some exposure to management accounting, internal auditing, financial accounting, and tax accounting. Depending on the company's needs and their interests, they may, at some point, specialize in a particular function such as internal au-

diting. Figure 5-1 depicts a typical corporate career ladder structure in a large company or firm.

The following are typical positions for CPAs in a large corporation. This list is not intended to be comprehensive, but to provide a sense of the career paths for CPAs. Beginning at entry level, these positions include:

- *Staff accountant*, who assists supervisors and managers with managing
  — accounts payable;
  — accounts receivable;
  — payroll;
  — general ledger;
  — financial statements;
  — account analysis and reconciliations;
  — cash and cash balance sheet accounts;
  — auditing cash and cash transactions;
  — sales tax returns; and
  — other work as needed.

  After a year or so, a staff accountant usually is eligible for promotion to senior accountant.

- *Senior accountant*, who supervises staff accountants and assists with
  — reconciling various general ledger accounts;
  — reviewing financial statements and trial balances for conformity to generally accepted accounting principles (GAAP);
  — coordinating quarterly reviews and year-end audit;
  — performs various account analysis and bank and other account reconciliations; and
  — manages various projects as needed.

  After two or three years with the company, senior accountants usually are eligible for promotion. Their next step depends on the company's requirements and their skills and interests. They may advance to supervising financial analyst, a position that reports up the chain of command to the treasurer, who manages the company's cash. Alternatively, they may move up to accounting supervisor, a position that reports up to the controller or chief accountant, who is responsible for financial and managerial accounting and reporting.

Figure 5-1: *Corporate Career Ladder*

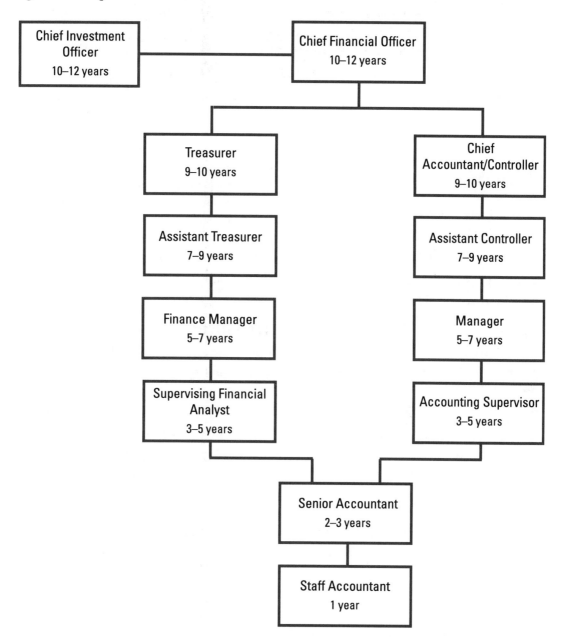

The following sections introduce key positions under the treasurer or controller. It is not intended as a comprehensive list of the responsibilities at each level or of all the positions for corporate CPAs in an organization, but simply as an illustration of the work they do.

Financial/Cash Management

A supervising financial analyst:

- supervises senior and staff accountants;
- assists with short- and long-term planning, budgeting and forecasting processes;
- assists with monthly close process; support project, service line or product line management;

- provides analytical decision support services or technical expertise for financial and operational issues; and
- conducts project planning and product profitability analyses.

A supervising financial analyst is eligible for promotion after three to five years with the company.

A finance manager:

- supervises assigned financial analysts;
- manages monthly accounting close cycle;
- prepares monthly financial statements and various detailed analyses;
- ensures all journal entries are properly recorded in accordance with GAAP;
- ensures the accuracy of monthly reconciliation schedules;
- coordinates various audits;
- responsible for the preparation and coordination of various ad hoc projects and reports;
- responsible for installing, modifying, documenting, and coordinating the implementation of accounting system changes and accounting control procedures; and
- assists in coordination and preparation of corporate budgets and forecasts.

A finance manager is eligible for promotion after five to seven years with the company.

An assistant treasurer:

- supervises assigned managers and staff;
- assist treasurers and the CFO in managing banking relationships;
- reviews documents pertaining to lines of credits and loans;
- assists with financial oversight of capital project spending;

- assesses foreign exchange risk and implement hedge programs;
- oversees interest rate risk management;
- provides detailed consolidated cash flow projections;
- manages and facilitates general insurance policies;
- monitors adherence to corporate credit and cash management policies;
- manages the corporate accounts payable and accounts receivable functions;
- supports investor relations; and
- ensures appropriate compliance with SOX requirements related to cash, debt and equity management.

An assistant treasurer is eligible for promotion after seven to nine years with the company.

Treasurer

At one time treasurers were mainly concerned with transactional activities like short-term borrowing. Now they are taking on a more strategic role in organizations, and working more closely with business units, for example, in consulting with operations on the right type of financing, or in assisting with structuring payment options to better meet the needs of customers.[8] Functions and duties of the treasurer include the following:

- Responsible for assessment, systems design, implementation and maintenance of effective investment strategy, cash forecasting, and debt management programs;
- Provide expert treasury management, analysis, and advice to maximize growth and profit;
- Provide analysis on optimal capital structure and financing strategies;
- Participate in working capital financing decisions, including forms of financing;

---

8 "Treasuring the Treasurer," Lisa Yoon, CFO.com, May 6, 2005. www.cfo.com/article.cfm/3955607?f=search

- Lead debt financing efforts;
- Build and maintain relationships with banks;
- Manage company insurance programs;
- Support the activities of pension, investment and finance committees;
- Manage investor relations;
- Manage foreign exchange risk; and
- Assist with special projects as required.

A treasurer is eligible for promotion after 9-10 years with the company.

Accounting/Reporting

An accounting supervisor:

- supervises accounts payable, payroll, and accounts receivable;
- monitors general ledger accounts to ensure accuracy and integrity;
- supervises monthly and year-end closing process;
- ensures accounting and closing routines are in compliance with corporate policies;
- oversees timely and accurate processing of information within general accounting;
- completes various projects as directed by management; and
- supervises and trains staff to ensure adherence to company policies and procedures.

An accounting supervisor is eligible for promotion after three to five years with the company.

An account manager manages general accounting staff and also is responsible for

- general ledger;
- purchasing;
- payroll;
- cash management;
- accounts payable;
- fixed assets;
- month-end close and expense reporting function;

- ERP production environment, including systems integration and enhancements that streamline processing;
- budget reports and forecasts—develop projections and provide analysis with recommendations and conclusions;
- providing U.S. GAAP accounting guidance and support to management;
- reviewing and updating SOX controls for responsible functions, support testing efforts and remediation as needed;
- working with IT team to automate and streamline process as necessary and to implement and improve internal controls; and
- focusing on system and process changes designed to improve the efficiency, accuracy, and completeness of accounting.

An account manager is eligible for promotion after five to seven years with the company.

An assistant controller:

- assists controller with accounting, financial analysis, and reporting;
- supervises accounting staff;
- coordinates internal and SEC reporting, ensuring compliance with regulatory requirements;
- prepares, controls and verifies financial and operational management reporting;
- valuates and controls inventories;
- prepares budgets, financial plans, and forecasts;
- performs a high level analysis of variances from financial plans, forecasts, budgets, and other business related duties as assigned by the controller; and
- supervises accounting research and new and updated corporate accounting and reporting policies.

An assistant controller is eligible for promotion after seven to nine years with the company.

Controller

Like the treasurer, the controller has evolved from reporting and accounting to more strategic responsibilities, such as directing all company financial planning and budget management functions. The controller also

- designs, establishes and maintains an organizational structure and staffing to effectively accomplish department of controller goals and objectives;
- establishes and implements financial best practices;
- recruits, trains, supervises, and evaluates department staff;
- prepares financial reports required by banks and investors;
- prepares cash management reports and working capital analysis;
- prepares annual operating plans and forecasts;
- serves as interface with external auditors, bankers, insurance providers, and so on;
- monitors and manages the company's line of credit;
- reviews financial data with senior management monthly;
- prepares financial analysis for contract negotiations; and
- maintains customer and vendor relationships.

A controller is eligible for promotion after 9–10 years with the company.

Chief Financial Officer (CFO)

Companies today have to adapt to fast changing conditions, and their expectations of a CFO can change just as quickly. The company that wanted a CFO with expertise in raising capital may, because of a turn of events, now need a CFO with restructuring experience.[9] The company that wanted a CFO experienced in mergers and acquisitions may now want one experienced in asset sales. So

it goes for CFOs, and they have to be flexible and adaptable to meet the demands of CEOs and boards of directors. Functions and duties of the CFO include the following:

- Provide direction, management, and leadership in the administrative, business planning, accounting, budgeting, and automation efforts of the corporation;
- Systematically and comprehensively assess the financial opportunities, challenges, and risks facing the company;
- Drive development of a sound, comprehensive financial plan that promotes growth and financial stability;
- Partner with leadership to ensure finance capabilities will enable the organization's near-term performance and support its overarching, long-term business strategy;
- Oversee all aspects of financial management within the organization, including the development of information and analysis on key financial and operational data as well as performance management;
- Communicate to a variety of internal and external audiences about the company's financial performance, risks, opportunities, and plans;
- Direct the fiscal functions of the corporation in accordance with GAAP;
- Ensure the effectiveness of all regulatory compliance and SOX programs; and
- Build and maintain a responsive, high quality finance organization within the company.

Chief Information Officer (CIO)

The role of the CIO has become even more important since SOX. SOX requires that the IT systems used to generate, amend, store, and transport data must be governed by controls that help assure external auditors the financial statements are accurate and reliable. Beyond compliance, IT is playing a larger strategic role

---

9 "Crisis Demands New CFO Skills," October 17, 2008. CFO.com www.cfo.com/article.cfm/12448582

in companies, helping them to better control costs, measure and monitor the organization's financial performance, and develop plans to increase revenue and return on investment. Functions and duties of the CIO include the following:

- Support key business goals and objectives by recommending actionable technical and process strategies;
- Formulate and execute the technical vision for the company including technologies used, plans for implementation and development of technology;
- Lead a team of professionals in corporate IT department;
- Ensure adequate security of company websites and other critical systems;
- Ensure high server and network availability for key systems;
- Develop contingency plans for continuity of critical systems;
- Collaborate with business unit IT leaders to develop current and long-range plans, processes and policies;
- Analyze and recommend new technologies, architectures, processes, approaches, and methodologies; and
- Develop IT budgets, project plans, allocate resources, and determine schedule of system implementations and project deadlines.

Lateral Career Growth

Just as not everyone in a public accounting firm will make partner, neither will everyone make treasurer, controller, CFO, or CEO in a company; however, there are opportunities for lateral career growth, such as transferring to another department or operating unit, taking on special assignments, moving to another location, or perhaps working overseas. But if you get to the point that you feel you are stagnating, you can look for work at another company or in another sector of accounting such as public accounting, or perhaps go back to school to earn a graduate degree. If you keep your skills sharp and continue to learn and grow professionally, your talents will be in demand.

A Career in Corporate Accounting

A career in corporate accounting is one career path for accounting graduates. To decide whether it's the right career for you, you need to consider the question in context. How does corporate accounting compare as a career possibility with public accounting or nonprofit or government accounting or other alternatives? Before you can answer that question, you need to have a solid understanding of the business and corporate world, only then can you make a well informed career decision. (Chapter 11, "Finding That First Job," addresses the questions you need to answer when deciding on a career in each sector of accounting.) In fact, knowledge of business is essential regardless of whether you go into corporate accounting or some other sector. In public accounting, you will work with business clients; in nonprofit accounting, with businesses that provide financial support and business advice; in government accounting, with businesses that are regulated by government agencies.

So how can you learn about business?

Take classes. You might consider taking classes beyond your normal course of study, maybe an elective course, or an online course, to help you increase your business knowledge.

Talk to people. Talk to your teachers, your campus recruiting office, representatives of companies that visit campus, business people who come to your school to make a presentation or teach a class, school alumni who are working for companies as CPAs, friends or acquaintances who work in business, and anybody else who might provide insight into the business world.

Work as an intern. Many companies hire student interns to work during summer vacation or during the school year. Find out about internships through your school placement office, teachers, company recruiters on campus, contacting companies directly, or searching the Internet. (Appendix 1 suggests some sources of information on internships.)

Read about business. Read business magazines, newspapers, newsletters, books, and articles, and other print publications. (Appendix 1 offers some suggestions.) You could start in your school's library or other libraries.

Search the Web. The Internet is a vast and rich resource of business information. Visit industry and company Web sites, peruse articles, read reports. (Appendix 1 offers some suggestions for online research.)

Stay current. Your information gathering and learning is a continuing process, not a one-time endeavor. You need to stay well informed on business issues regardless of where you decide to start your career.

Join business organizations. You may belong to your school's accounting student association or have a student affiliate membership in the AICPA. In addition, you might consider joining an association of business students at your school, or an organization of businesspeople

that offers student memberships. Belonging to such organizations provides opportunities to learn about business and to build professional and business relationships.

Work for a business. Consider getting a part-time job with a local business in the city where you attend school or your hometown. You can gain on-the-job experience in business, and the experience will look good on your resume.

Start early. Start learning about business early in your college career, when you are a freshman or sophomore. The more time you have, the better informed you will be—assuming, of course, that you make use of your time.

Industry Perspective

If, in learning about business, you decide that working for a company might interest you, the next step is to consider some prospective companies. The business world is so large, with so many companies, that you may wonder where to start researching companies. (Figure 5-2 illustrates one approach to narrowing your search.) You could begin by considering industries that interest you. A few examples:

- Aerospace: Aerospace companies are developing the next generation of commercial and military aircraft, and commercial satellite companies are developing the next generation of satellites.
- Banking: Banks are restructuring and recapitalizing their businesses to move bad loans off their balance sheets, raise capital for new lending and investment, increase their profit margins, capitalize on new business opportunities, and improve their competitive position.

Figure 5-2: *Finding Prospective Employers: One Approach*

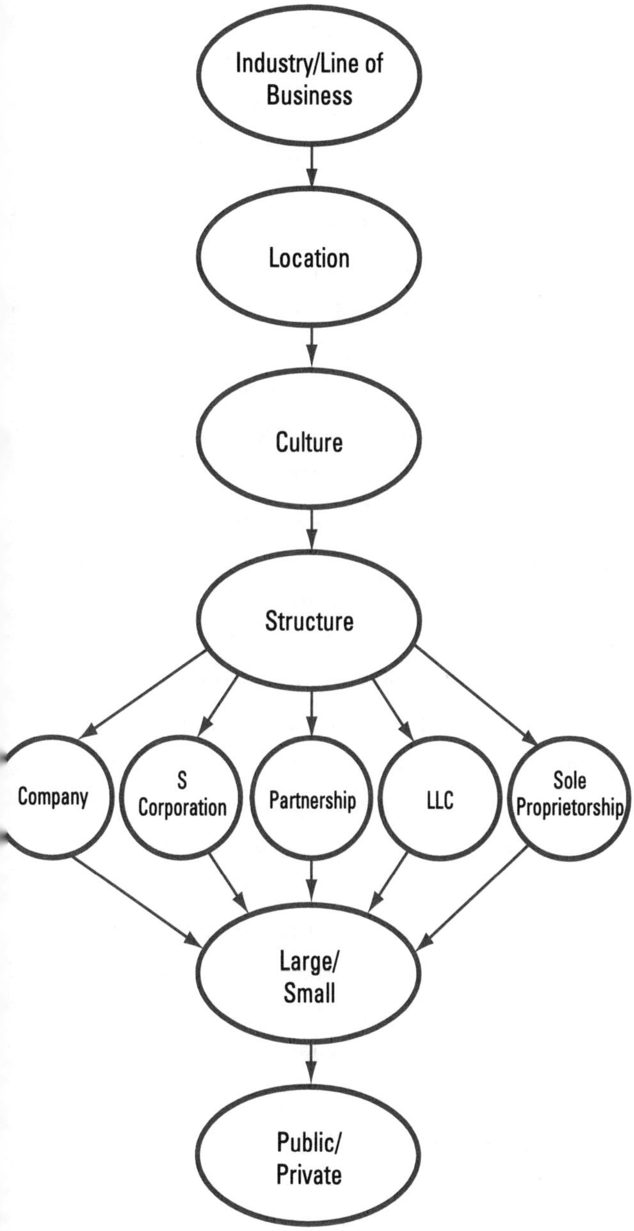

- Bioscience: Companies are developing new drugs for the treatment of disease.
- Construction: Contractors are finding new work in replacing, rebuilding, and upgrading the country's aging infrastructure.
- Energy: Oil companies, utilities, and other companies in the energy business are continuing to

invest in research and development of solar power, wind power, biofuels, and other alternative energy sources.

- Entertainment: The entertainment industry encompasses movies, television, the Internet, DVDs, professional sports, concerts, and more. The entertainment industry continues to grow.
- Health care: Health care companies face a continuing challenge in controlling costs while providing high quality care.
- Information services: Companies continue to research, design, develop, and bring to market new products and services for businesses, consumers and others.
- Real estate: Long-term U.S. economic and population growth will increase demand for homes, apartments, office buildings, industrial facilities, and other products.

Company Business Line

Once you find a few industries that may be of interest (and no more than a few, otherwise your research could start to seem overwhelming), you can do more in-depth research on these industries: their structure, markets, issues, challenges, opportunities, and so on. As with your general business research, you can learn about industries from many of the same sources: people who are knowledgeable about business and particular industries, or books, articles, reports, and so on in print or online. In addition, industry trade associations and professional societies produce reports, analyses, commentary, and other information about an industry, as do government agencies, think tanks, investment banks, securities firms, consulting firms, and others. The American Bankers Association, for example, has a "what's news" section on its Web site. You also can read about what's happening in banking on the Web site of the *American Banker*, a trade newspaper, and you can read Federal Chairman Ben Bernanke's comments on economic, financial, and other issues in the "News and Events" section of the Fed's Web site.

In the course of your industry research, you can learn about companies in an industry, and consider which companies you might want to work for. One of your first considerations is a company's business line. Does it interest you? In most industries, companies are in many different lines of business. In aerospace, for example, a company might be in manufacturing, another in supplying parts to manufacturers, and another, such as an airline company, in buying airplanes from the manufacturer. In real estate, a company might be a developer (the equivalent of a manufacturer), acquiring land and building office buildings or shopping centers, or an investor, buying and selling properties, or a property manager, managing properties owned by developers and investors; and some companies are in all these business lines. Would you want to work for a developer or investor or a company in multiple business lines? (Appendix 1 suggests some sources of information for learning about industries and companies in those industries.)

Company Characteristics

Another consideration when deciding where to work are the characteristics of a company, including the following:

Large C corporations, public or private: In general, these are U.S.-based multinational or large domestic corporations that employ the largest number of people, including CPAs. They usually have formal orientation programs for new hires, and in-house training programs to educate and train new employees in their jobs, and they may have programs to rotate employees through different jobs to give them broad exposure to the organization. They typically have structured, defined career paths. These companies are meritocracies—employees are regularly evaluated and considered for promotion based on their performance. Performance criteria and promotion policies are transparent, they are communicated to all employees. Many companies have policies and programs that provide career support, advice, and professional development for women, African American, Hispanic, Asian, and lesbian, gay, bisexual, and transgender employees.

Small C corporations: public or private: These are corporations that are smaller than those on the Fortune 1000 or the Forbes List of the largest private companies or similar lists. Although individual companies may hire fewer CPAs and other employees than their larger counterparts, collectively they are major employers in their own right, and you should not overlook opportunities to work for a smaller company. These companies may have the same structured orientation, training, and advancement policies and programs of larger companies, or they may not have formal programs. A smaller company may rotate you whenever the need arises, and not on the rotation schedule of a formal program. In a smaller company, the lines separating some job functions might be less defined, for example, you might function both as a management accountant and an internal auditor.

As might be expected, there are pros and cons in working for a large versus a small company. Larger companies may offer more formal, defined career paths, but their more formalized structures may put limits on your freedom to try your own professional and career pursuits within the organization. In a smaller company, you may have more flexibility, but you may not have the same support structure—the formal training, the defined career paths, the career guidance—as in a larger company. But you could take on more responsibility faster, and advance more quickly, than in a larger organization.

Public Versus Private

For CPAs, working for a public versus a private company may be a matter of emphasis. Public companies that are registered with the SEC must file financial reports on a regular basis, and CPAs who work for these companies could spend part of their time assisting companies to prepare these reports for the SEC and other regulators and for investors and other stakeholders. Since the enactment of SOX, public companies are subject to strict accounting and reporting requirements that affect not only CPAs but also everyone else in the company. By contrast, private companies are not as structured, and they are not subject to the same reporting requirements as public companies. However, many private companies have chosen to adhere to the same SOX internal control standards and reporting procedures as public companies, among other reasons because it makes good business sense, such as protecting against fraud, improving the efficiency of operations, managing costs, or meeting the expectations of investors and lenders. In working for a private company, then, you may still have some degree of exposure to working on SOX reporting, but the

reports could be structured to different stakeholders. Instead of thousands of shareholders of a public company, for example, the report might be designed for a smaller audience: the company's owners and investors.

S Corporations, partnerships, LLCs. These entities offer alternative career paths to the traditional C corporation. Just as many public accounting firms are structured as partnerships or LLCs, so, too, are many architectural, construction, engineering, executive recruiting, investment banking, and other professional services firms. Some real estate companies and other entities are S corporations. These enterprises generally are smaller than C corporations, but they are still important employers. CPAs starting with these firms might have positions that are a mix of management accounting, internal auditing, financial accounting and other functions. Just as in a smaller company, you may have more flexibility in your work, more responsibility, and a chance to advance faster, but you may not have the same career support as in large companies.

Sole proprietorships: Small businesses are often operated as sole proprietorships, owned and managed by the founder with the assistance of family and perhaps a few employees. Sole proprietorships may outsource for accounting services, or have only one full time CPA, so the opportunities for employment may be limited. But if you can get a job with a small proprietorship, you will get an inside look at how a small business operates. Your job would involve all types of accounting work including keeping the company's books, preparing its tax returns, providing financial information to the company's lenders, and so on. Working for a sole proprietorship could be a good education experience, especially if you decide at some point in your career to start your own business.

Location

One of the most important questions in finding prospective employers is a company's location. Is the company in a city or town where you want to live and work? Large multinational companies have operations all over the world, and you may be able to find a job for a company department or unit in a location you like. Smaller companies may only be in one or two locations, so your choices are limited. Another thing to consider is not only where you will be working now but in the future. In a multinational company, you may be rotated to other locations from time to time, and you may have an opportunity to work in another country. With a small company in a single market, you will work in the same location for as long as you are with the company—unless it decides to expand into a new market or is acquired by another company that operates in multiple locations or other reason.

Culture

A more important question than the size of the company, or whether it is a C corporation or some other structure, or whether it is public or private is simply this: what's it like to work there? Again, articles, Web sites, blogs, and other sources may give you insight into a company. So will talking to people who know about the company. Other sources are the lists of best companies to work for, or best places to launch a career, published by *Fortune, BusinessWeek*, and others. Table 5-3 outlines one such list for 2009 best companies to work for.

Table 5-3: *Fortune 100 Best Companies to Work For 2009* Top 10

	Company	Line of Business	U.S. Employees
1.	NetApp	Data storage & management	5,014
2.	Edward Jones	Stock brokerage	34,496
3.	Boston Consulting Group	Management consultant	1,680
4.	Google	Search technology	12,580
5.	Wegmans Food Markets	Supermarket chain	37,195
6.	Cisco Systems	Internet networking	37,123
7.	Genentech	Biotech	10,969
8.	Methodist Hospital System	Hospital	10,535
9.	Goldman Sachs	Investment banking	14,088
10.	Nugget Market	Supermarket chain	1,536

* "Fortune 100 Best Companies to Work For 2009," http://money.cnn.com/magazines/fortune/bestcompanies/2009/full_list/

Matching Employers to Your Interests

Let's assume that, through your research, you have identified some prospective employers. What are your expectations in working for a company? This is something to start thinking about early in school, so by graduation day you have a clear idea of your career aspirations, and the type of employer you want to work for. Here are some key questions to consider:

What are my career aspirations? Where do you see yourself in five or ten years—and how do you plan to get there from where you are now?

What are my career priorities? What's most important to you in your career—and in life? To have a satisfying and rewarding career? Accumulate wealth? Advance to a top position in a big company? Start your own business? Become a teacher in an accounting program? Serve the community? Other? Make a list; it helps you to focus on what matters most to you.

What industries interest you?

Which companies in an industry interest you?

Where might you be interested in working in a company? Management accounting? Internal audit? Financial accounting? Or perhaps IT accounting? Or tax accounting?

Corporate Culture: Will You Fit?

Like families or tribes, organizations are defined by their culture: their predominant assumptions, values and beliefs. A company's mission, business strategy, organization, operations, and relationships with employees is shaped by its culture.[*] Based on its culture, every organization has a common way of thinking, acting, and speaking. This informs every day decisions such as how to dress for work, how to talk to their managers and co-workers, what to say in meetings, or when to speak up and when not. It is evident in the organization's perquisites, from who gets preferred parking to who gets stock options.

For newcomers, one of the most difficult things about joining an organization is to understand its culture. What are the right ways of speaking and acting? Which behaviors are rewarded, which are punished? For example, how do new employees know how they are performing? Will their boss tell them, or not? Or will they learn in more subtle ways, such as being included in or excluded from an important meeting?

Because of such challenges, company executives try to determine through interviews and meetings and informal conversations whether job candidates will be able to adapt to an organization's culture. Candidates may have the requisite skills and talents, but can they become part of the corporate family?

You can learn about a company's culture in the course of your research on industries and companies. On the basis of this "cultural" research, you can decide if you are right for the company, and if it is right for you.

[*] "The Corporate Culture Survival Guide," Edgar H. Schein, Jossey-Bass publishers, 1999.

Compensation

In a corporation, as in a public accounting firm, entry level employees are paid a base salary and, usually, a performance-based bonus. In public companies, the bonus may be paid in cash, in restricted stock (trading is subject to company restrictions), or in stock options. Depending upon the success of the company, its stock price, economic conditions and other factors, stock bonuses could prove extremely valuable and create an opportunity for employees and managers to build wealth over time. Public accounting does not offer comparable wealth creation opportunities through stock ownership, but firms do offer very consistent, predictable and significant compensation packages. And, of course, there is the risk of owning stocks, In the U.S. recession that began in late 2007, share prices of many companies plunged, and stock options lost most or all of their value, much to the distress of corporate executives and employees who had substantial holdings of a company's stock or stock options.

Questions for Prospective Employers

What do you want to ask a prospective employer? Some questions to consider:

- How would you describe the company's culture?
- What is the exact nature of the work I will do.?
- Who will I report to?
- Who will I be working with?
- What support will I have: orientation, training, job rotation, mentoring, etc. For studying for the CPA exam? What is the company's continuing education policy?
- How will my performance be evaluated? By whom?
- What are my opportunities for advancement?
- When will I be eligible for advancement?
- Why should I work for you versus your competitors?

- What is your compensation package? (See Table 5-4 for examples of entry level salaries for corporate accountants.)
- What benefits do you offer?

Benefits

Like public accounting firms, corporations and other entities offer benefit programs. Consider whether a prospective employer offers these benefits, and, if not, does it compensate in some way, for example, by paying higher compensation, or providing more vacation time?

- *Promotion bonuses:* Amounts vary with firm and individual.
- *Flexible schedules:* To balance personal life and work
- *Paid time off:* For vacation, holidays, personal days off, additional days off, illness
- *Paid medical & dental:* Full or partial reimbursement
- *Pension:* Eligibility for new hires depends on firm.
- *Group insurance plans:* Life, accident, disability, other
- *Group legal plan:* Access to local attorneys
- *401K matching:* Amount of company matching varies
- *Charitable contributions:* Company matching
- *Employee discounts:* Available on car rental, gym, cultural events, publications, etc.
- *Education expenses:* Employees are reimbursed. Some firms have a ceiling.
- *CPA exam:* Applicants receive time off to prepare for the exam and are reimbursed for exam expenses.
- *Fast advancement:* Most entry level staffers are promoted to supervisory positions within one to two years of their hire date.
- *Working parents:* Family medical leave, parental leave and other programs for working parents.
- *Community service:* Does company sponsor community service programs? How does it support the community service (volunteer) work of employees?

Table 5-4: *Corporate Accounting 2009 Salaries: A Sample*

The following are examples of entry level salaries for corporate accountants:

Title	Experience	Large companies*	Midsize companies**	Small companies†
Cost analyst	Up to 1 year	$39,750-$49,000	$37,750-$45,500	$35,500-$42,250
Financial analyst	Up to 1 year	$39,500-$49,500	$38,000-$45,500	$35,000-$42,750
Internal auditor	Up to 1 year	$43,250-$52,750	$41,500-$51,500	n/a
General accountant‡	Up to 1 year	$38,000-$46,250	$35,750-$43,000	$33,500-$40,000
Budget analyst	Up to 1 year	$39,500-$49,000	$38,000-$45,500	$35,500-$42,000

Source: Robert Half International 2009 Salary Guide: Accounting & Finance

* Large companies $250+ million in sales

** Midsize companies: $25 million – $250 million in sales

† Small companies: up to $25 million in sales

‡ A function of management accounting

What Employers Look For

No matter their size and resources, companies are trying to find and hire the best people. So who are they looking for? Essentially, they are looking for people who can add value to the organization. Can a prospective employee help the company to increase its revenue and profits, reduce costs, operate more efficiently, win new business, increase its market share or achieve other business goals? Companies make substantial investments in finding, recruiting, hiring, training, mentoring, promoting and managing people, and they want to know whether they will get a return on their investment. Can you learn and grow on the job? Will you be able to move up to positions of more authority and responsibility, perform at a higher level, and increase your value?

A key question is whether your have the core skills for a job. These include:

Analytical: Understands the whole through an analysis of its components and how they fit together; finds relationships in apparently unrelated data; interprets complex information.

Communication: Uses words effectively to impart information or ideas; listens carefully to understand others; understands how she is being perceived.

Financial: Understands money and finance; relationship of finance and real estate; financial structure of an organization.

Interpersonal: Has genuine interest in other people; gets along with people of diverse backgrounds; able to work effectively with others at every level of an organization.

Leadership: Self-aware; understands interests of others; influences others; provides clear direction; motivates others to follow a course of action; takes risks; acts decisively; solves problems.

Learning: Inquisitive; eager to learn; acquires and applies knowledge; learns from experience; learns from others.

Teaming: Works well in teams; sensitive to interests of others; understands role and responsibilities; shares credit; puts group's priorities before own; knows when to lead and when to follow.

Job Specific Skills

Core skills are needed for any position—not just in accounting, but in any other profession or industry. In addition to these core skills, you need the technical skills specific to the job, for example, internal auditors must have a high degree of computer proficiency to manage internal control systems for corporations. CPAs must be able to integrate these job specific skills with their core skills. Internal auditing projects require an internal auditor to acquire data, process data, evaluate internal systems and produce complex solutions. These solutions need to be communicated to management, and the auditor will need to have strong presentation skills to present complex concepts.

It is the combination of core and technical skills that are essential for advancement in a company. "People skills and communication skills are the most important," said Ted Phillips, president and CEO of the Chicago Bears professional football team. "You can be a good technician and have a satisfying career in certain roles, but your advancement will be limited if you are solely a technician." (An interview with Phillips appears on page 184 of this book.)

Personal Ethics

Because of past corporate scandals and SOX, corporations are especially concerned with ethical actions that maintain a company's reputation and its relationships with investors, lenders, clients and customers, suppliers, regulators and the markets where they do business. Companies from Fortune 500 corporations to small companies have adopted corporate governance policies and promulgated them inside and outside of their organizations. More than ever, companies are concerned with hiring people who not only are the best qualified but who also subscribe to the company's code of ethics and governance standards.

Big Picture

Don't get so compartmentalized in your job that you fail to see the larger organization around you. Develop an understanding of the company as a whole—its strategic vision, how it operates, how the component parts are synthesized into an organization. This is an incremental process—it will take time to learn the company. But by making the effort to learn, and having an active interest in the larger company beyond your niche, you will begin to see the big picture.

Corporate Accounting: Is It For You?

Thousands of CPAs work for U.S. companies and businesses, and more will be needed as the economy starts to grow again, businesses expand, and new businesses are formed. CPAs will have greater opportunities for advancement in companies as the Baby Boomer generation continues to retire. So do your research, learn about the business and corporate world, stay current on the news about industries and companies that interest you, and learn about corporate accounting. Keep track of accounting rule and tax law changes, and changes in SEC rules and other government regulation, that affected the corporate world generally and your target industries and companies in particular. You will be well informed, and, most importantly, well prepared when it comes time for job interviews that will test your general business knowledge and your knowledge of prospective employers. Go through the same process in researching career opportunities in other sectors of accounting. Think about where you might want to start your career. "There is no single 'best' career path," said Thomas J. Falk, chairman and CEO of Kimberly-Clark Corporation, who started his career in public accounting. "Public accounting firms offer one set of opportunities and corporations another. It depends on what each individual wants and needs to achieve his or her career goals." (An interview with Falk appears on page 180 of this book.)

Wrap-up

In this chapter, you learned the following:

- Thousands of CPAs are employed by companies and businesses from Fortune 500 corporations to small businesses.
- CPAs participate in or lead every aspect of a company's business.
- After public accounting, corporate accounting is where graduates with bachelor's degrees in accounting choose to start their careers.
- Corporate CPAs generally work in management accounting, internal auditing, financial accounting, tax accounting, and information technology.
- Corporate CPAs are in growing fields such as green on environmental management accounting.
- CPAs have worked their way up from entry-level positions to CEO, CFO, and other senior positions in companies.
- Strong communication, financial, and interpersonal and other core skills, together with a high level of technical skill, are necessary for advancement.
- You need to have a solid understanding of the business and corporate world to decide whether corporate accounting is for you.

In the next chapter, we look at career opportunities in government.

Interview: Thomas J. Falk
Chairman and CEO, Kimberly-Clark Corporation

Thomas J. Falk is chairman and chief executive officer of Kimberly-Clark Corporation, a leading global health and hygiene company employing more than 55,000 people worldwide. Headquartered in Dallas, Texas, Kimberly-Clark operates in 37 countries; its global brands are sold in more than 150 countries. Falk started his career with the accounting firm of Alexander Grant & Co. He joined Kimberly-Clark in 1983 as an internal auditor. Following a series of promotions, he was elected president and chief operating officer and to the company's board of directors in 1990, CEO in 2002, and chairman in 2003. He received his bachelor's degree in accounting from the University of Wisconsin in 1980. A long time volunteer for the Boys and Girls Clubs of America, Falk has served as a national trustee since 2002 and a member of the board of directors since 2005. "My predecessor introduced me to the organization, but the kids made the sale for me," Falk said. "Having a chance to positively impact the lives of millions of children across the country is truly rewarding." In his quiet moments, he enjoys reading and spending time with his family. And he plays racquetball or squash every week as part of his regular exercise routine.

> *"Accounting is the language of business, so having a thorough grounding in the principles of accounting has helped me throughout my career."*

Why did you decide to study accounting in college?

When I started college, I planned to attend law school. In case I changed my mind, I thought I should get an undergraduate degree in a discipline that would enable me to get a job after college. So I signed up for business school. I majored in accounting because it looked like the toughest curriculum. I hadn't taken any accounting in high school and really knew nothing about accounting at the time.

Why did you decide to move from public accounting to the corporate world?

I had achieved my near-term goals of earning my CPA certificate and a promotion to audit supervisor within three years. I had also decided that public accounting was probably not consistent with my long-term career goals. The industry's emphasis on building consulting relationships with clients and developing selling capabilities were not where my interests were at that time.

How have you applied your education and experience in accounting in your career at Kimberly-Clark?

Accounting is the language of business, so having a thorough grounding in the principles of accounting has helped me throughout my career. I joined the company as an internal auditor and then quickly moved into an accounting/analysis role. Some of my early projects involved building analytical financial statement models for mergers and acquisitions work, helping guide the company's adoption of new pension accounting rules, and updating the company's internal control policies. All of these assignments relied heavily on my accounting background.

What is your advice to accounting students who are interested in careers in the corporate world? How do they get started?

There is no single "best" career path. Public accounting firms offer one set of opportunities and corporations another. It depends on what each individual wants and needs to achieve their career goals.

What does it take for someone to advance to a senior management position with a global organization like Kimberly-Clark? What skills are required?

Each of us is CEO of our own career. Successful CEO's do three things:

1. They deliver results today. Make sure you're delivering results in your current role before worrying too much about your next job.
2. They have a vision for the future. Know what you want to do next and what you want to accomplish over the next several years. You don't have to figure out the rest of your career, but you should have a three to five year plan.
3. They build capabilities in their organizations. Be accountable to yourself for building your own capabilities. Continue to learn and develop yourself throughout your career.

If you master these three things, you will be a very effective CEO of a very successful career!

Interview: Joseph Macnow
CFO, Vornado Realty Trust

Joseph Macnow is executive vice president—finance and administration, CFO, and CAO of Vornado Realty Trust, a real estate investment trust, and one of the largest owners and managers of commercial real estate in the United States. He has been with Vornado since 1981. Previously, he was employed for five years as vice president and CFO of City Stores Company. Before joining City Stores, Macnow was an audit manager with Ernst & Young for eight years. He is a graduate of the City College of New York, Baruch School of Public and Business Administration, where he majored in accounting. He completed the course work for an MBA at this school and the University of Southern California.

"As CFO, I have people to assist and advise me, but at the end of the day I have to make the hard decisions about accounting issues. I believe that CFOs should be accountants first and financial executives second."

How did you get interested in accounting as a career?

My dad, who was an immigrant from Russia, insisted that my older sisters have professions. One sister became an attorney, the other a doctor. It wasn't clear what my dad wanted me to be—he passed away before I started college. I thought accounting would make him proud, so I enrolled at Baruch.

Where did you start work after graduation?

After I graduated, I went to work for a midsize New York accounting firm, Klein Hines and Fink. I worked there for about a year. Then a travel agency I had worked for while in school made me an offer to work in California as a controller.

How long were you in California?

After one-and-a-half years, I returned to New York for personal reasons and went to work for SD Leidesdorf & Co., a prestigious accounting firm. It later merged into Ernst & Young. One of my clients was City Stores Co, a leading New York retail holding company. I became controller and later CFO of City Stores.

Where did you go from City Stores?

In 1981, I left City Stores to become CFO of Vornado, which at the time was a retailer. I was part of management team of Chairman and CEO Steven Roth and Richard T. Rowan, director of real estate, who is now retired. Within two years of my arrival we decided that Vornado was better being in real estate than being a retailer.

How did Vornado make the transition into real estate?

We closed the discount department store division, terminated 11,000 people, sold $800 million of inventory, and paid off creditors. We continued to own a large portfolio of real estate, primarily in the New York metro area, which we converted into strip shopping centers. In 1993, we converted to a real estate investment trust. (Under federal tax law, REITs receive preferential tax treatment if they distribute at least 90 percent of their taxable income to shareholders and meet other requirements.)

How can someone who aspires to be a CFO at a major company achieve that goal?

You have to be able to work with people with a variety of backgrounds. I have 300 people reporting to me, including those with advanced degrees to those that are high school graduates. Our president, to whom I report, is a Harvard MBA. You also have to stay knowledgeable and informed about accounting. As CFO, I have people to assist and advise me, but at the end of the day I have to make the hard decisions about accounting issues. You must also learn the world of finance and capital markets. I believe that CFOs should be accountants first and financial executives second.

Interview: Ted Phillips
President and CEO, Chicago Bears

Ted Phillips is president and chief executive officer of the Chicago Bears, a National Football League team. He joined the Bears in 1983 as the team's controller and advanced to director of finance in 1987, vice president of operations in 1993, and his current position in 1999. Before coming to the Bears, Phillips was an auditor and tax accountant with Ernst & Whinney (now Ernst & Young) from 1979 to 1983. He earned a degree in business and accounting from the University of Notre Dame in 1979 and a master of marketing and management degree from the Kellogg Graduate School at Northwestern University in 1989. He is the fourth person in the organization's more than 80-year history to serve as president, following Michael McCaskey, George "Mugs" Halas, Jr., and George S. Halas.

> **"If other executives in sports are like me, they look for young people with a true passion for the business."**

Where did you start at Ernst & Whinney?

I started as an auditor and switched to tax. Clients sometimes weren't happy when the auditors showed up. But they were always interested in ideas on how to reduce taxes.

How did you come to be hired by the Chicago Bears?

Both the Bears and George Halas, who owned the team, were tax clients and I was part of the client management team. When Jerry Vanisi, the controller, was promoted to general manager in 1983, he turned to the football side of the business, and I was offered the controller's job. It had less to do with my financial expertise and more to do with my being able to develop good relationships with management.

And you studied for your graduate degree at Kellogg while you were working full time?

Yes, I was a part time student at Kellogg. It took me about four and a half years to complete my studies. I studied management, with a concentration in marketing and finance. I thought a graduate degree to compliment my accounting degree would be useful in case I decided to make another career move.

What were the circumstances of your promotion to director of finance in 1987?

It happened that Jerry Vanisi was fired earlier that year, and there was no one to handle player contract negotiations. I talked to the owners and my peers in management and convinced them I could handle the negotiations. To their credit, they gave me the opportunity. In addition to negotiations, I handled club finances and certain operational matters, and I learned every aspect of the organization. Over time, I was able to build up trust with the McCaskey family. In 1999, I became the first president of the team who was not a family member. (Virginia McCaskey, daughter of George Halas, the founder of the Bears, is the current owner.)

How have you been able to use your education and experience in accounting over the course of your career?

Public accounting enabled me to work with a variety of companies and corporate structures and to learn about the real world of business, which is something you can't get from a textbook. My education and experience in accounting helped me to get my first job with the Bears, and I applied my experience as controller and later director of finance. My tax background was also helpful, due to the complex federal, state, and local tax issues that face many professional sports teams.

What the biggest challenge in your job?

Dealing with the media pressures. If you lose a game, it doesn't matter how financially sound the club is. As exciting as this business can be, you have to have a tough skin, because everyone has an opinion as to how the team should be run.

How could a young person interested in professional sports management get started? How do they get their foot in the door?

If other executives in sports are like me, they look for young people with a true passion for the business. If you're trying reach a CEO or a department head or an assistant, and not having any success, keep trying. Keep calling and sending letters and see if you can get an interview. Don't give up. There is no pattern as to when sports job opportunities may arise.

Interview: William Rhodes
President and CEO, AutoZone

Bill Rhodes is chairman, president, and CEO of Memphis-based AutoZone Inc., a Fortune 500 company and the leading retailer and a leading distributor of automotive replacement parts and accessories in the United States. AutoZone sells auto and light truck parts, chemicals, and accessories, through more than 4,000 AutoZone stores in the United States and 148 stores in Mexico. Rhodes was named chairman in 2007 and president and CEO in 2005, following more than 10

"From working with Ernst & Young clients, I began to understand what business is all about: people, relationships, processes, and sales."

years with the company during which he served in a variety of executive-level roles. Most recently, he served as executive vice president overseeing store operations and commercial. Prior to that, he served in various capacities including senior vice president, supply chain and information technology, senior vice president supply chain, divisional vice president of stores, and senior vice president of finance. Rhodes began his career with Ernst & Young, serving in various capacities from 1988 to 1994, when he joined AutoZone. A certified public accountant, he earned an accounting degree from the University of Tennessee and an MBA from the University of Memphis.

A native of Memphis, Rhodes is treasurer of the National Civil Rights Museum and vice chairman of Memphis Tomorrow. "I chose to support these organizations as a means to give back to my community," Rhodes said. "This is a core value of our company, and I believe both of these organizations have terrific missions to improve our community and beyond." He also is on the board of the Coalition for Automotive Repair Equality and is treasurer of the Retail Industry Leaders Association. "I participate in these organizations as a way to help improve our industry," Rhodes said. "If you want to effect change, you have to participate."

Why did you major in accounting as an undergraduate?

Like many students, I looked at which professions offered the best job opportunities, and accounting was one. But I found that I didn't particularly care for accounting, so I went on to study business in graduate school.

How did you get started at Ernst & Young?

While I was in graduate school, I worked as an intern for Ernst & Young, and after graduation, I took a full-time position with them. I thought it would be a good launching pad for a career and would give me an opportunity to learn about many different businesses. After I had been with the firm for about a year, I began to like working there, but it wasn't until after about three years that I really began to enjoy it. From working with Ernst & Young clients, I began to understand what business is all about: people, relationships, processes, and sales.

Why did you move from Ernst & Young to AutoZone?

In 1994, AutoZone, one of our clients, asked me to join them. At the time, there were two premiere companies based in Memphis: AutoZone and FedEx. I found AutoZone's culture and value system very appealing. Also, I had to decide whether to stay at Ernst & Young and see if I made partner, which at the time usually required being with the firm for about 15 years. I was a manager with about 6 years of experience, so I would have had to wait about another 9 years. Even so, I enjoyed public accounting, and I had a difficult time deciding whether to join AutoZone. But after thinking things over for a few weeks, I went decided to move forward with AutoZone.

Where did you start at AutoZone?

I started as a manager of inventory accounting, supervising about half a dozen people. After about six months, I was asked to take on additional responsibility, which was focused on streamlining the company's financial processes. It was a prelude to what later became an internal auditing function in the company.

Where did you go from there?

After about 15 months with the company, I went to work for the president responsible for store operations. I was part of a team that developed process improvement systems for stores, maintained financial discipline, and oversaw labor scheduling. Over the next few years I worked in different positions in different areas of the company, including assisting with acquisitions. In 1999, I was promoted to senior vice president of finance, which was similar to the controller's function. After about a year in that position, I was moved from our store support center to the field as vice president of the Midsouth division, working with about 500 stores and 8,000 people in 11 states. Subsequently, I had the opportunity to serve in various other capacities throughout the organization ultimately leading to my current position.

How has your accounting background helped you in managing a large company like AutoZone?

Public accounting gave me valuable insights into companies, both the strong and the weak, in a variety of industries. It's a great on-the-job education in how the business world works, and a great foundation for a career whether you stay in public accounting or go into the corporate world. Public accounting also taught me the value of hard work. To quote Kemmons Wilson, the founder of Holiday Inn, "Work half-days every day. And it doesn't matter which half, the first half or the second half."*

---

* "Kemmons Wilson, America's Innkeeper," Mike Brewster, *BusinessWeek*, October 11, 2004. www.businessweek.com/bwdaily/dnflash/oct2004/nf2004111_3044_db078.htm

What does it take to succeed in the corporate world?

You need a solid education in accounting, finance, management, or other business related disciplines. But more important are strong communication skills and people skills. As you progress in management, you have to be able to work with a variety of people, and to appreciate the value they bring to the organization. I take a bottom up view of our organization. I'm at the bottom. The people in our stores are the ones at the top.

Interview: David Richards

Past President, The Institute of Internal Auditors

Established in 1941, The Institute of Internal Auditors (IIA) is an international professional association with global headquarters in Altamonte Springs, Florida. The IIA defines itself as "the internal audit profession's global voice, recognized authority, acknowledged leader, chief advocate, and principal educator." Members of the IIA work in internal auditing, risk management, governance, internal control, information technology audit, education, and security. David Richards is a past president of the IIA.

> *"If you start as a rookie internal auditor, you could soon find yourself talking to the CEO or the audit committee."*

How did you get into internal auditing?

After I graduated with an accounting degree from John Carroll University in Cleveland, I worked at Cleveland Electric Co (now FirstEnergy Corp.) for 33 years until I retired. I worked for 3 years in general accounting and 8 in accounts payable. Then I moved into internal audit and advanced to director of internal audit.

What was the attraction of internal auditing?

The variety of the work—there was a whole watershed of different activities and the chance to see everything a company does from the minute to high subject matter. I learned the interrelationships of a company's missions, goals, objectives—how everything came together. And I had a chance to make a positive contribution to the organization.

When did you start with the IIA?

I joined the Cleveland chapter of the Institute while I was working. I served in a number of roles: president of the Cleveland chapter, regional director, member of the executive committee. I was chairman of the Board of Directors for 2001–2002 and later became a member of the staff as president in 2004. We are a global organization, with 160,000 members around the world in 165 countries, 150 chapters in the United States and Canada—and 95 affiliates. We set internal audit standards worldwide. And we run a global certification program. The Certified Internal Auditor® (CIA®) designation is the only globally accepted certification for internal auditors and remains the standard by which individuals demonstrate their competency and professionalism in the internal auditing field. Worldwide, we deliver over 75,000 parts of the CIA exam every year.

Are more companies creating an internal audit function?

Yes, and that's driven by more stock exchanges worldwide requiring an internal audit function for listed companies. More governments worldwide are requiring government agencies to create an internal audit function.

Are schools offering programs in internal auditing?

About 2 years ago, we started an education partnership program in internal auditing with colleges and universities. About 37 schools are participating globally, half of them U.S. schools, including Louisiana State University, which is considered to have the leading program. Participating schools sign up to provide internal audit as part of the curriculum. They provide basic internal audit courses, generally as an elective. Students get credit. Also, there are now several schools offering degrees in internal audit. It is difficult in the United States to introduce and expand internal audit offerings in business schools because there are already stringent accounting requirements—150 hours are now required by many states for a CPA license. Most of our success in working with schools to start degree programs has been at the graduate level. There is more flexibility at that level.

Besides the schools, where else do companies find internal auditors?

Most people are pulled into audit from within the company. They often have other degrees like information technology, human resources, finance, or engineering. Those degrees could work for an internal audit function because of the broad nature of work. Regardless of their backgrounds, people must take the IIA's internal audit exam to be certified. It's a rigorous exam. It has about a 30 percent pass rate. Candidates who fail can retake.

What do students want to know about careers in internal auditing?

Is the work challenging? Is there are a variety of work? What do internal audit jobs pay? Most students are very interested in internal audit because they want broad company exposure including operations, finance, technology, fraud detection and prevention, the supply chain, HR, and other areas. If you start as a rookie internal auditor, you could soon find yourself talking to the CEO or the audit committee.

Interview: Michael Roth

Chairman and CEO, The Interpublic Group of Companies

Michael Roth is chairman and CEO of The Interpublic Group of Companies Inc., a global provider of advertising and marketing services. Through 45,000 employees in all major world markets, Interpublic specializes in consumer advertising, interactive marketing, media planning and buying, public relations, and specialized disciplines. In his career, Roth has been chairman and CEO of The MONY Group, a financial services holding company; executive vice president and chief financial officer of Primerica Corporation, a life insurance and financial services company; and a partner at the public accounting firm of Coopers & Lybrand. (In 1998, Coopers and Lybrand merged with Price Waterhouse to form PricewaterhouseCoopers, a Big 4 public accounting firm.) A certified public accountant, Roth earned an undergraduate degree in accounting at Baruch College of the City University of New York. He holds an LLM. degree from New York University Law School and a JD from Boston University Law School.

> *"My background in public accounting has really enabled me to look at the world the way companies look at it, and to understand how to solve business problems."*

What interested you in studying accounting as an undergraduate?

I was one of those kids who knew what they wanted to do at a very early age—I always wanted to be a tax lawyer. My mother was a bookkeeper. My father was a lawyer. So I put the two together. I thought the best approach was to get an accounting degree and go to law school.

Why did you decide to go into public accounting after law school?

I had already been working in the tax department of one of the Big 8 firms. When I graduated, I had the opportunity to work for a law firm or continue in the tax department. I felt the experience I was getting in the tax department was better than what I would get working for a law firm.

How long were you in public accounting?

About nine years. I started as a tax accountant and subsequently made partner.

Why did you change from public accounting to business?

I liked what I was doing in public accounting, and I made partner at a very early age. But I wanted to take more ownership of my career and to expand my horizons. Then a client offered me an opportunity I couldn't refuse—a senior financial position that most Fortune 100 companies wouldn't offer a tax guy. An added plus was that the client knew me and saw me as part of their team. I started in finance and moved up to CFO.

How have you applied your skills and experience in accounting and law to senior executive positions in corporations in different industries?

My background in public accounting has really enabled me to look at the world the way companies look at it, and to understand how to solve business problems. And it's very helpful to understand a company in the context of a legal environment.

How do accounting graduates who want to go into business get started—work for a public accounting firm for a time, or go straight into the corporate world?

Working for a public accounting firm gave me exposure to different industries and clients. If you don't like doing that, then you have to think about doing something else.

What do you look for in hiring people?

It depends on the job—in finance, for example, you must have the requisite technical skills. But, in general, a job candidate must have a broad business view of the world.

So it would be valuable for students today to have an advanced degree in accounting, business, law, or another discipline?

Yes, if they want to move up to a senior level position in a corporation. If you have a strong educational background and an ability to work with people, you have the foundation for a successful career.

What do you like about your current job?

It's challenging, and interesting. I work in a high profile company in a high profile industry, and in a global environment. I have great people working for me, and great clients. What's not to like?

Chapter 6

Careers in Government Accounting

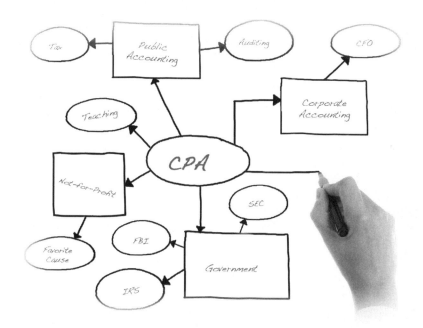

"You really have an opportunity to make a difference..."

Michele Mark Levine, Director of Accounting Services
• City of New York, Office of Management and Budget

Introduction

How is the United States governed? Let us count the ways. The United States has a federal government, 50 state governments, and 87,500 local governments, including about 3,000 county governments, 19,400 municipal governments, 16,500 townships, 13,500 school districts, and, oh, yes, about 35,100 special districts that manage airports, beaches, children's services, community and downtown development, fire control, educational and health facilities, fire control, infrastructure, libraries, mosquito control, and much more.[1]

Government is a big employer. According to the U.S. Bureau of Labor Statistics (BLS), nearly 11 million civilians worked for the federal government and state and local governments in 2006 (the latest year that BLS figures are available). Box 6-1 outlines those workforce numbers.

Box 6-1: *Government Civilian Workforce Employment 2006*

(Employment in thousands)	
Federal*	2,700,000
State**	2,424,000
Local†	5,594,000
Total	**10,718,000**

* "Federal Civilian Workforce Statistics; The Fact Book: 2007 Edition," United States Office of Personnel Management (OPM). https://opm.gov/feddata/factbook/2007/2007FACTBOOK.pdf

** "Wage and Salary Employment in State and local government, excluding education and hospitals, 2006," BLS; Career Guide to Industries. State and Local Government Except Education and Hospitals. www.bls.gov/oco/cg/cgs042.htm

† Ibid.

As discussed throughout this chapter, there is a growing need in government to recruit new employees, including CPAs, to replace the increasing number of CPAs and other government workers who will be retiring. Equally important, CPAs are needed to assist government agencies with preparing budgets and accounting for billions of dollars in government spending, and with auditing government programs ranging from far-reaching programs such as the American Recovery and Reinvestment Act of 2009, the federal government's $787 billion stimulus program,[2] to auditing spending by states, major cities, and small towns across the United States.

CPAs not only work for the government, they also are elected to government offices—from the mayor of a small town to a county assessor to a representative in a state legislature or a member of Congress. Their skills and experience in accounting, finance, tax, administration, and other disciplines make them well qualified to serve as elected officials with a range of responsibilities, such as drafting and adopting government budgets, planning and implementing public spending programs, auditing spending, or creating or changing tax laws and regulations.

Why Work for Government?

People are drawn to careers in government for a variety of reasons.

---

1 "Wage and Salary Employment in State and local government, excluding education and hospitals, 2006," Bureau of Labor Statistics (BLS); Career Guide to Industries. State and Local Government Except Education and Hospitals. www.bls.gov/oco/cg/cgs042.htm

2 "Recovery Accountability and Transparency Board," Recovery.gov

Public Service

If you want to help people, give back to your community and country, and serve the public interest, you can find a fulfilling career in government. You can work for agencies that fight global warming, protect the environment, promote education, feed the hungry, protect the country, manage transportation systems, provide housing, assist small businesses, explore space, care for the sick, the poor, the aged, veterans and others, and provide many other services to the public. Many of these agencies need the talents, knowledge, and experience of CPAs to help invest taxpayer dollars wisely, ensure fiscal integrity in government programs, assist governments to plan and prepare budgets, audit government spending, set government spending priorities, identify fraud, waste and abuse, promote transparency and accountability in government, and carry out other responsibilities.

"What's rewarding about government is that you really have an opportunity to make a huge difference in your community, at the local level, or in a much broader level in state and federal government," said Michelle Mark Levine, director of accounting services in New York City's Office of Management and Budget (OMB). (An interview with Levine is on page 234 of this book.)

Some CPAs working in the private sector decide to make a career switch into government because they are particularly drawn by the opportunities for public service. And they can apply their experience and skills in jobs such as assisting government agencies to in-vestigate money laundering and other financial crimes, or assisting government auditors to conduct audits of government spending and uncover waste, abuse, and outright fraud.

Variety of Career Opportunities

As a CPA, you can work for many different federal, state, and local agencies. Some examples include the following:

- The U.S. State Department employs accountants and auditors to meet the accounting and financing requirements for the department's worldwide operations.[3]
- The National Aeronautics and Space Administration recruits accountants to fill professional positions in its organization, for example, in the Office of the Chief Financial Officer, which is responsible for providing professional leadership for the planning, analysis, justification, control, and reporting of all of the agency's fiscal resources.
- The Federal Aviation Administration employs accountants and budget analysts to help manage the U.S. aviation system, the largest and busiest in the world.
- The Defense Finance and Accounting Service, a part of the Department of Defense (DOD), employs accountants and auditors to budget, track, analyze, and manage billions of dollars in DOD spending, ensure the accuracy of financial systems, identify problem areas, and improve the effectiveness of spending programs.
- The U.S. Department of Agriculture (USDA) recruits accountants to work in its agencies such as the Office of the Inspector General (OIG), which audits USDA programs and operations. (A USDA careers chart on its Web site shows which of its agencies employ accountants.[4])
- State auditors and comptrollers employ accountants to audit state spending. The California State Auditor from time to time recruits candidates for

---

3 "U.S. Department of State: Careers Representing America." http://careers.state.gov/civil-service/opportunities/index.html#BMF
4 "USDA Careers," U.S. Department of Agriculture. www.da.usda.gov/employ/careergr.pdf

Auditor Evaluator I, an entry level position.[5] Auditor evaluators work in teams on projects, helping to plan, conduct, and present in-depth policy and fiscal reviews of governmental entities e and programs.

- Like many cities, the City of Los Angeles employs accountants from entry level to senior management positions.[6]

Stable Employment

The recession that began in late 2007 has shown that government employees are not immune to layoffs, furloughs, reductions in hours, pay reductions, and other effects of the squeeze on government budgets. Even so, government has offered relatively stable long-term employment compared with the private sector. Where companies may be forced to lay off some or all of their workers because of profit losses, mergers, bankruptcy reorganization, or other reasons, governments are ongoing entities that generate revenue from taxes, fees, and other sources that can be used to provide pay and benefits to employees (although the number employees may fluctuate depending on the government's staffing needs, fiscal condition, or other reasons).

Public employees generally have stronger job protection than those in the private sector. In the federal government, layoffs are called reduction in force (RIF) actions. When an agency must abolish positions, RIF regulations determine whether an employee keeps his or her present position or whether the employee has a right to a different position, based on total federal service, tenure of employment, performance, and veterans' preference.[7] If employees are laid off, they are provided with benefits such as assistance in finding another position within their agency, in another federal agency, or in the private sector.[8] Many state and local governments have similar programs. Public employees represented by unions may be afforded job protection under union contracts with governments.

Opportunities for Advancement

As a CPA in government service, you will have many opportunities for advancement. (See "Need for CPAs," which follows.) But, just as in the private sector, you will have to demonstrate that you have the critical thinking, interpersonal, technical, and other skills to assume more responsibility, take on management roles, and perform well in your job.

Pay and Benefits

Some studies have found that wages and salaries of public workers, exclusive of benefits, have lagged those of private sector workers. But the picture is not clear cut. The difference between public and private worker pay varies considerably depending on the level of government (federal, state, or local), type of job, seniority, location, basis for comparing private versus public pay and a number of other factors.[9] The pay gap is most pronounced at

---

5 California State Auditor, Bureau of State Auditors, Auditor Evaluator I. www.bsa.ca.gov/opportunities/auditor

6 "City of Los Angeles Personnel Department: Career Opportunities for Accountant" www.ci.la.ca.us/PER/eeo/career/Accountant.pdf

7 "Summary of Reduction in Force under OPM's Regulations," OPM. www.opm.gov/rif/general/rifguide.asp#1

8 "The Employee's Guide to Career Transition," OPM. www.opm.gov/rif/employee_guides/career_transition.asp#intro

9 "Managing Your Government Career: Success Strategies That Work," Stewart Liff, AMACOM Books, a division of the American Management Association, 2009.

the senior management level: senior executives in the private sector earn substantially more than executives at comparable management levels in government.[10]

When benefits are factored in, the compensation of government employees usually equals or exceeds that of private sector workers. The value of government health and benefit plans is equivalent to as much as 25 percent to 35 percent of an employee's salary.[11] For an employee with a base salary of $40,000 annually, such benefits would add $10,000 to $14,000, for total compensation of $50,000 to $64,000 annually. Governments have tried to compensate for lower pay scales with attractive benefit programs. Furthermore, they often bear more of the cost of benefit programs than private employers. As a result, government employees have a higher rate of participation in benefit plans than those in the private sector. A report by the Employee Benefit Research Institute found that most employees in state and local governments participated in some type of retirement and savings plan compared with only about half of the employees in the private sector.[12]

Opportunities to Move From Government to Private Sector

For various reasons, some CPAs leave government service to work in the private sector. Some CPAs nearing retirement after 20 or more years of government service may re-

ceive attractive compensation packages from public accounting firms, companies, or other organizations that comes on top of their government retirement benefits. Some CPAs may be attracted by offers of senior positions such as partner and director of tax services of a public accounting firm or director of government relations for a large corporation. Other CPAs may fulfill longtime desires to go into teaching, take executive positions with nonprofit organizations or professional societies, start businesses, or pursue other careers.

Other Benefits

The College Cost Reduction Act of 2007 established a student loan forgiveness program for people in public service including government. Any qualified loans (those that qualify under the Act) that have not been paid off after 10 years of public service will be forgiven in their entirety. (Public service employees must have made at least 120 monthly payments on the loan while in a qualifying job for their remaining debt to be erased. Payments made on or after Oct. 1, 2007, count toward the 120 minimum.[13])

What CPAs do in Government

Just as in the private sector, CPAs (and other accountants) in government work in financial reporting, management accounting, auditing,

---

10 Ibid.

11 "Government Jobs in America," By the Editors of Government Job News, Partnerships for Community Publication, Louis R. VanArsdale, Publisher, 2009.

12 "Benefit Cost Comparisons Between State and Local Governments and Private-Sector Employers," Employee Benefit Research Institute *Notes*, June 2008. www.ebri.org/pdf/EBRI_Notes_06-2008.pdf

13 "Who Benefits from the College Cost Reduction and Access Act," House Committee on Education and Labor, George Miller, Chairman. http://edlabor.house.gov/who-benefits-from-the-college-cost-reduction-and-access-act/index.shtml

tax reporting and compliance, and other areas. CPAs can be found at every level of government, working in many different departments and agencies. Among other responsibilities, CPAs advise and assist government agencies and officials with the following.

- *Budgeting*
  Every government entity from a rural school district to the DOD must consider budget proposals, prepare a budget that determines revenue sources (taxes, fees, and so on), estimates costs of government services, sets spending priorities, allocates money to agencies and departments, and determines the amount and timing of public expenditures.
- *Reporting*
  Governments must track how taxpayer dollars are being spent, provide accountability and transparency in public expenditures, ensure that expenditures are within budget, and identify possible cost overruns or other problems.
- *Auditing*[14]
  Governments use a variety of audit procedures including the following:
  — *Performance auditing*: Independent evaluation of an organization's operation with an eye towards making it work better, faster, and cheaper.
  — *Financial audits*: Examination and verification of information provided through an entity's financial statements.
  — *Compliance Audits*: Determine whether an organization is following provisions of laws, regulations, and contractual grant or loan agreements; identify noncompliance; seek corrective action.
  — *Investigative Audits*: Investigate allegations of improper activities by government employees or agencies.
- *Tax*
  CPAs assist and advise governments on all matters tax: writing tax laws and regulations; determin-

ing tax levies, fees and assessments; tracking tax revenue; enforcing tax compliance; and other tax concerns.

Core Skills

CPAs use the same core skills in government as in public accounting, corporate accounting, and other sectors of accounting. These include the following:

- *Analytical*: Whether it's analyzing a budget, new legislation or regulations, proposed spending programs or government tax structures, or other issues, you are able to see the large picture. You understand the whole through an analysis of its components and how they fit together. You are able to interpret and explain complex information.
- *Communication*: You are able to speak and write effectively, impart information or ideas, listen carefully, and understand others.
- *Interpersonal*: You have a real interest in other people; you get along with people of diverse backgrounds; and you are able to work effectively with others at every level of an organization.
- *Leadership*: Although you may not step into a leadership role in your first job with a government agency, you will need to develop and show leadership qualities in order to advance in an organization. That means that you are self-aware—you know your strengths and weaknesses; you understand the interests of others; you are able to influence people; and you act decisively to solve problems.
- *Learning*: You are inquisitive and eager to learn; you are able to acquire and apply knowledge; learn from experience; and learn from others.
- *Teaming*: You work well in teams; you are sensitive to the interests of others; understand roles and responsibilities; share credit; put the group's priorities before your own; and know when to lead and when to follow.

---

14 "Career Paths: Government," American Institute of Certified Public Accountants (AICPA). www.aicpa.org/Becoming+a+CPA/CPA+Candidates+and+Students/Career+Paths.htm#govt

- *Job specific skills*: Government operates by its own playbook—the myriad, complex laws, regulations, policies and procedures that direct or guide the operations of every level of government. You do not need know nor would you want to know everything about government laws and regulations. But you do need to stay well informed about the laws and rules and policies and procedures covering the federal, state, or local government agency where you are working. If you are working as an auditor in the federal government, for example, you will need to be well versed in federal auditing standards known as generally accepted government auditing standards (GAGAS), (See "CPAs assist with federal reporting and auditing," later in this chapter) If you are an auditor at the state or local level, you will need to know generally accepted accounting standards (GAAS) for state and local government. (See the sidebar "Governmental Accounting Standards Board," later in this chapter). Most important, you must have the skills specific to the job. These skills are detailed in the job announcements of government agencies.

How to Learn About Careers in Government

With thousands of federal, state, and local government agencies, the public sector offers many career paths and job opportunities. But how do you decide if you might be interested in working in government? And if you are interested, how do you find a job that's right for you? Here are some ways:

- *Read up on careers*
  There are a variety of books, articles, Web sites, social networks, and other sources that provide information about and insights into careers in government. (The appendix lists some of these sources.) From these, you can learn more about what government does, career opportunities in government, finding a government job, government pay and benefits, planning a career in government, and much more. (The American Institute of Certified Public Accountants [AICPA] has produced a video, "CPAs in Government: Shaping the Future," on career opportunities for CPAs in government. It can be accessed online at the AICPA's Government Resources Center.[15])

- *Talk to people in government*
  Talk to people on the inside. Perhaps someone in your family, a colleague or friend, a professor at your school, a student studying for a career in government, or other people you know might be able to put you in touch with someone in government. You can also talk to people who have worked in government: retirees, people now working in the private sector, and others.

- *Talk to government recruiters*
  Recruiters for some government agencies visit college campuses. Check with your career counseling service or other campus sources to see whether recruiters will be visiting your school.

- *Talk to teachers and students at your school*
  If your college has a school or department that prepares students for careers in government, you can talk to the school's teachers and students about career opportunities in government.

- *Join professional societies*
  Join a professional society such as the AICPA where you can meet professional accountants, including those working in government. The AICPA has a membership program specifically for students and CPA candidates.[16] Many state CPA associations offer student memberships. (The AICPA has a "State Information" web page with links to associations in each state as well as other state information such as colleges and universities offering accounting programs.[17])

- *Visit government Web sites*
  Government Web sites provide a wealth of information about federal and state and local

---

15 AICPA Government Resources Center. http://fmcenter.aicpa.org/Resources/Government+Resource+Center/Careers+Recruiting

16 "AICPA's Student Affiliate/CPA Candidate Membership." www.aicpa.org/Becoming+a+CPA/CPA+Candidates+and+Students/The+Benefits/

17 "State Information," AICPA. www.aicpa.org/Legislative+Activities+and+State+Licensing+Issues/State+News+and+Info/States/info/index.htm

governments generally, specific agencies and departments, and career opportunities with particular agencies. Many suggestions for sites to visit are found throughout this chapter.

- *Internships*
  Federal, state, and local government agencies offer a variety of student internships that provide opportunities for students to learn about government, decide whether they want to pursue a career in government, and decide if they might want to join the agency sponsoring the internship. Internships may lead to job offers from sponsoring agencies.

Government Career Opportunities

The following is a look at career opportunities for CPAs (and other accountants) in federal and state and local governments.

Federal Government

The federal government is the largest employer in the United States. Most of the federal government's civilian employees work for the executive branch, which consists of the Office of the President (whitehouse.gov) and 15 cabinet departments. The departments include the following:

- Agriculture (usda.gov)
- Commerce (commerce.gov)
- Defense (defense.gov)
- Education (ed.gov)
- Energy (energy.gov)
- Health and Human Services (hhs.gov)
- Homeland Security (dhs.gov)
- Housing and Urban Development (hud.gov)
- Interior (doi.gov)
- Justice (justice.gov)
- Labor (dol.gov)
- State (state.gov)
- Transportation (dot.gov)
- Treasury (ustreas.gov)
- Veterans Affairs (va.gov)

In addition, the executive branch includes numerous independent agencies. They are called independent because they are not part of a cabinet department. They include agencies such as the Environmental Protection Administration, Federal Reserve, Peace Corps, and Social Security Administration. For information on the executive branch, go to the White

---

AICPA "Outstanding CPA in Government Award"

The American Institute of Certified Public Accountants sponsors an "Outstanding CPA in Government Award" that recognizes the achievements of CPAs employed in government and promotes the CPA designation as the premier professional credential for accounting, auditing, and finance professionals in government. The award is given annually to three CPAs working in the federal government, and state and local governments. The 2009 award winners were Robert Dacey, chief accountant of the U.S. Government Accountability Office; Thomas H. McTavish, auditor general of the state of Michigan; and Lena Ellis, financial services manager and CFO of the city of Forth Worth, Texas.* For information on the "Outstanding CPA in Government Award," and other AICPA awards, go to the AICPA home page (aicpa.org). Click on "About the AICPA" and "Membership Information" and "Member Awards."**

---

* "AICPA Names Recipients of 2009 Outstanding CPA in Government Award," AICPA press release, August 10, 2009.

** www.aicpa.org/About+the+AICPA/Membership+Information/ Member+Awards.htm.

House Web site (whitehouse.gov). Click on "Our Government" and "Executive Branch." Information on the other branches of the federal government and federal agencies also can be found under "Our Government."

Need for CPAs

Every level of government is in need of CPAs (and other professionals) to replace those who are leaving the public workforce.

Among government employees, more baby boomers are reaching retirement age, including CPAs who have spent part or all of their careers in government. Indeed, there is growing concern inside and outside of government about a looming shortage of CPAs and other career civil servants in government—and the implications for government and the people it serves.

Table 6-2: *Federal Civilian Workforce Employment 2006**

(in thousands)	
Legislative branch	29,400
Judicial branch	33,700
Executive branch	
Department of Defense (DOD)	675,700
Non-DOD	1,203,900
Total	1,942,700
U.S. Postal Service	757,400
Total	2,700,100

* Source: OPM. Latest year for which figures are available.

Fast Facts About Federal Employment

Of the 15 cabinet departments, Defense, Veterans Affairs, and Homeland Security employ more than half of the civilian workers in the executive branch. (Federal employment figures exclude intelligence agencies, such as the CIA, that do not disclose the number of their employees.)

More than half of federal civilian employees work in professional, management, business, and financial occupations versus less than a third in the private sector.*

The federal government has a higher percentage of college-educated employees than the private sector.

Although Washington, D.C., is the headquarters of the federal government, five of six federal employees work outside the Washington metropolitan area, in locations across the United States and even abroad.**

* "Managing Your Government Career: Success Strategies That Work," Stewart Liff, AMACOM Books, a division of the American Management Association, 2009.

** BLS, "Career Guide to Industries, Federal Government Excluding the Postal Service." www.bls.gov/oco/cg/cgs041.htm

Employee retirement is a particular problem for the federal government. Partnership for Public Service (PPS), a nonprofit organization whose mission is to inspire people to serve in government, said in a report that, between 2008 and 2012, about one-third of the federal government's full-time permanent workforce will leave government, the majority through retirement. "By 2012, federal agencies will lose nearly 530,000 employees, many of whom hold leadership and critical skills positions,"[18] the report noted. "This challenge is intensified for the federal government because downsizing in the 1990s reduced the size of

---

18 "Partnership for Public Service; Issue Brief: Brain Drain 2008." www.ourpublicservice.org/OPS/publications/viewcontentdetails.php?id=126

Box 6-2: *Top 10 Federal Agencies With Highest Percentages of Employees Projected to Retire by 2012*

Agency	Percent Retirements
Federal Aviation Administration	26%
Department of Housing and Urban Development	26%
Social Security Administration	23%
Department of Education	22%
Department of Energy	22%
National Science Foundation	22%
General Services Administration	22%
Department of the Interior	21%
Department of Labor	21%
Department of Treasury	21%

* "Partnership for Public Service; Issue Brief: Brain Drain 2008." www.ourpublicservice.org/OPS/publications/viewcontentdetails.php?id=126

the federal workforce by nearly 400,000 positions and left agencies with critical skills gaps." Box 6-2 outlines those agencies with highest project retirement rates by 2012.

The retirement wave comes at a time when federal agencies face unprecedented challenges from fighting terrorism to revitalizing and restructuring the U.S. economy to training workers to compete in a global economy to rebuilding America's infrastructure to improving U.S. education to shoring up Society Security and Medicare. The Association of Government Accountants (AGA), a professional organization, warned that federal agencies could be at risk of "mission failure" if they fail to address the exodus of federal workers.[19]

Need to Recruit More Career Employees

The severe U.S. recession that began in late 2007 could cause some federal workers to delay retirement; however, this would simply give the federal government temporary relief from having to address the long-term issue of worker retirements. According to "Where the Jobs Are 2009," a Partnership for Public Services report, the federal government will need to hire 270,000 workers in the fiscal years 2010 through 2012,[20] The PPS estimate was based on a survey of 35 federal agencies that represent nearly 99 percent of the federal workforce.

The PPS report lists the federal government's job requirements by professional field. It said that the government will need to hire more than 16,000 people in the "accounting and budgeting" category in the fiscal 2010–2012 period. Occupational areas and positions in this category include financial management/administration, accounting, auditing, revenue agent, tax specialist, and budget analysis. But CPAs could work in many other places in government, such as in compliance and enforcement.

You can view the report online at wherethejobsare.org. Links to hiring demand in various job categories can be found under "Jobs by Professional Field."

---

19 "Action Needed if Federal Agencies Are to Avoid 'Mission Failure,' Warns Study," PR Newswire, May 15, 2008. www.reuters.com/article/pressRelease/idUS45578+15-May-2008+PRN20080515

20 The federal government's fiscal year begins Oct. 1 and ends Sept. 30; for example, fiscal 2010 runs from October 1, 2009, to September 30, 2010.

Competition with Private Sector

In recruiting talent, federal agencies face tough competition from the private sector, which itself faces a long-term talent shortage because of the retirement of the baby boomers, slower population growth, and slower rate of growth in new workers coming into the U.S. labor force. "The war for today's talent is fierce, and the federal government is at a distinct hiring disadvantage with its often slow and antiquated hiring practices," the PPS said.[21]

To attract talent, the Obama administration has called for a reform of the federal hiring process. It described the current process as "lengthy and encumbered by burdensome requirements and outdated technology systems."[22] Others share that view. "Making the federal government an attractive place to work requires, as a first step, making it easier for superior candidates to enter federal service," Donald F. Kettl, dean of the University of Maryland School of Public Policy, told a congressional committee.[23]

Among other steps, the administration said agencies need to determine the effectiveness of hiring efforts and reforms such as posting brief, clear job announcements in plain language and providing timely notification to applicants on the status of their applications.

CPAs Assist with Federal Reporting and Auditing

Another reason CPAs are in demand in the federal government is to advise and assist federal departments and agencies in complying with federal reporting and auditing standards. The Chief Financial Officers Act of 1990 (CFO Act, as amended by the Government Management Reform Act of 1994) requires annual, audited financial statements for the U.S. government and its departments. Each department has a CFO who is responsible for the development of integrated agency accounting and financial management systems, including financial reporting and internal controls. These controls must comply with applicable accounting principles, standards, and requirements and internal control standards.[24]

Along with passage of the CFO Act, the Federal Accounting Standards Board (FASB) was established to develop accounting standards and principles for the U.S. government. In October 1999, the AICPA recognized FASB as the board that promulgates generally accepted accounting principles (GAAP) for federal entities.

Federal accounting standards and financial reporting are used to assess the federal government's accountability, efficiency and effectiveness. They help the President, Congress, federal agencies, and the public to

---

21 "Partnership for Purlic Service; Issue Brief: Brain Drain 2008." www.ourpublicservice.org/OPS/publications/viewcontentdetails.php?id=126

22 "Building a High Performance Government," White House Office of Management and Budget, "The President's Budget; www.whitehouse.gov/omb/budget/fy2010/assets/building.pdf

23 "State of the Federal Workforce: Re-engineer for the 21st century, says UM expert; statement of Donald F. Ketti, incoming dean of the UM (University of Maryland School of Public Policy, to the U.S. House Subcommittee on the Federal Workforce, Postal Service, and the District of Columbia Committee on Oversight and Government Reform on April 22, 2009. http://www.newsdesk.umd.edu/culture/release.cfm?ArticleID=1872

24 "FASAB Facts," Federal Accounting Standards Board. http://www.fasab.gov/aboutfasab.html.

understand the economic, political, and social consequences of the allocation and use of federal resources.

Audit Standards

The CFO Act requires federal inspectors general to comply with the U.S. Comptroller General's GAGAS for audits of government organizations, programs, activities, and functions, as well as audits of government assistance received by contractors, nonprofit organizations, and other nongovernment organizations. These standards pertain to auditors' professional qualifications, the quality of audit effort, and the characteristics of professional and meaningful audit reports.[25] (The AICPA has published an Audit Guide that provides the latest information on auditing issues affecting entities that are subject to Government Auditing Standards, also referred to as the Yellow Book.[26])

Learning about Careers and Jobs in the Federal Government

The Web sites of the federal government and its many agencies provide detailed information on career opportunities and employment. Most jobs require U.S. citizenship.

A good place to start your online research is with sites that are portals to career and job information. These include the following:

- STUDENTJOBS.GOV
  This is a one-stop portal that provides information on federal job opportunities for high school and college undergraduate and graduate students. It includes resources for assessing your career interests and skills, links to federal (and some state and local) agencies with student internship and job opportunities, information on federal hiring processes, and an "e-scholar" section on scholarships, fellowships, grants, and other educational opportunities. You can register online, create a personal account, create and post your resume, search for jobs, sign up for job alerts, apply for jobs, and manage your account.

- USAJOBS.GOV
  USAJOBS, the official job site of the federal government, is an easy-to-use portal for anyone seeking a job with the federal government. It is where most federal agencies post job openings. At any time, tens of thousands of jobs are listed, including many jobs for accountants. Job announcements are updated daily. You can create an account on the site, post your resume, search for jobs by occupation, agency, location and other criteria, sign up for email job alerts, and apply for a job online. You can get tips on writing your resume and create a single uniform resume that provides all of the information required by government agencies— there is no need to create multiple resumes in different formats for use by different agencies. You can use the site's tutorials, guides, and FAQ section for help with creating a resume, searching and applying for jobs, and other uses.

- Office of Personnel Management (opm.gov).
  The OPM Web site provides information for students, job seekers, federal employees and retirees on job opportunities, finding a job, federal salaries and benefits, job training, retirement information and much more. The OPM site features a "New to the Federal Government FAQs" that covers a range of topics from finding information about government jobs to applying for a job

---

25 "Government Auditing Standards," Government Accounting Office. www.gao.gov/govaud/ybook.pdf

26 "Government Auditing Standards and Circular A-133 Audits—AICPA Audit Guide." www.cpa2biz.com/AST/AICPA_CPA2BIZ_Specials/ MostPopularProductGroups/AuditAccountingGuides/PRD~PC-012743/PC-012743.jsp

to qualification standards for a job to whether you will be invited to an interview. It includes information for veterans seeking jobs in the federal government and veteran's preference in hiring.[27] It provides information on federal employment of people with disabilities.[28]

- USA.GOV

  This is the official Web site of the federal government. Here you can find an alphabetical listing of every department and agency in the federal government.[29] These include better known agencies such as the BLS and some you may not have heard of such as the Bureau of the Public Debt.[30] It's a small agency with a big job: borrowing the money needed to operate the federal government and to account for the resulting debt. (Its Web site has a careers section.)

In addition to the portals, the following sections offer other examples of where you can find information about career opportunities with the federal government.

Executive Office of the President

The Executive Office of the President consists of various agencies that provide support for the President in addressing a range of issues. For information on these agencies, go to the White House Web site (whitehouse. gov). Click on "The Administration" and "Executive Office of the President." One agency, the OMB, provides detailed informa-

---

United States Government Manual

Where would the government be without a manual? The U.S. Government Printing Office (GPO) annually publishes the United States Government Manual, which provides comprehensive information on the agencies of the legislative, judicial, and executive branches. It also includes information on quasi-official agencies, international organizations in which the United States participates, and boards, commissions, and committees. More information can be found on the GPO's Web site.*

* "U.S. Government Manual: About," U.S. Government Printing Office. www.gpoaccess.gov/gmanual/about.html

---

tion on careers with the OMB on the OMB home page (whitehouse.gov/omb), click on "Jobs with OMB" at the very bottom of the screen.[31] Click on "Careers with the Office of Management and Budget." Jobs with the Executive Office of the President are posted at USAJOBS.

Congress

The U.S. Senate publishes a Senate Employment Bulletin for senate offices choosing to advertise Senate vacancies. In addition, the Senate Placement Office maintains a resume bank for unadvertised positions.[32]

---

27 "Veterans employment information," OPM. www.opm.gov/veterans/

28 "Federal Employment of People with Disabilities," OPM. https://www.opm.gov/disability/

29 "A-Z Index of www.usa.gov/Agencies/Federal/All_Agencies/C.shtml

30 Bureau of Public Debt. www.publicdebt.treas.gov/index.htm

31 www.whitehouse.gov/omb/assets/omb/recruitment/careers_with.pdf

32 To become registered, applicants must complete the Senate Employment Application Form accessible at www.senate.gov/employment and participate in an information interview.

The House of Representatives has an "Employment Opportunities Web Site" where job openings are posted.[33]

Individual members of the House and Senate may recruit accountants (and other professionals) to serve on their staffs.[34]

Government Accountability Office

The Government Accountability Office (GAO), an independent nonpartisan agency that works for Congress, employs financial auditors who participate in a wide range of engagements with the overall objective of strengthening accountability for the federal government's assets and operations.[35] Auditors typically perform financial analyses, promote financial management best practices, assess internal controls, and identify and suggest improvements in a variety of financial areas. A financial auditor must have an undergraduate or graduate degree that includes 24 semester hours, or equivalent, of coursework in accounting and related subjects. Other requirements also apply. (See the Careers section of the GAO Web site.[36])

Judiciary

The Administrative Office of the United States Courts employs accountants to help provide a broad range of legislative, legal, financial, technology, management, adminis-

trative, and program support services to the federal courts.[37]

Executive Branch
Internal Revenue Service

Accountants can find many different career opportunities with the IRS, one of the largest single employers of accountants.[38] These include internal revenue agents, who examine and audit individual, business, and corporate tax returns to determine federal tax liability and ensure federal tax law compliance. To meet the educational requirements for an entry level position, you must have the following:

- A bachelor's degree in accounting at an accredited college or university, or
- Have 120 hours or study, including 30 semester hours of accounting at an accredited institution, or
- Be a CPA.

Accountants may also work in the law enforcement arm of the IRS as criminal investigation special agents, forensic accountants who investigate complex financial crimes associated with tax evasion, money laundering, narcotics, organized crime, public corruption, and much more. To meet the educational requirements for an entry level position, you must have the following:

---

33 "Vacancy Announcements," U.S. House of Representatives www.house.gov/vacancies/vacancieslist.aspx

34 The House of Representatives web site has a directory of members, with links to their Web sites. www.house.gov/house/MemberWWW.shtml. The Senate has a similar directory at www.senate.gov/general/contact_information/senators_cfm.cfm

35 Government Accountability Office: Careers. www.gao.gov/careers/financial.html

36 Ibid.

37 "Careers: Working for the Federal Judiciary," U.S. Courts. http://www.uscourts.gov/careers/

38 "Careers at IRS," IRS, Department of the Treasury. http://jobs.irs.gov/careers.html

- Completed a 4-year course of study or bachelor's degree in any field of study that included, or was supplemented by, at least 15 semester hours of accounting, plus an additional 9 semester hours in finance, economics, business law, tax law, or money or closely related fields, or
- At least three years of successful, responsible accounting and business experience, or be a CPA. There are additional requirements for these positions. (For more on IRS careers, see the Careers section of the IRS Web site.[39])

Federal Bureau of Investigation

There are two main career paths at the FBI: special agent and professional staff.[40] The FBI recruits special agents with specific critical skills including accounting. To qualify under the accounting critical skills program, a candidate must be a CPA or possess, at minimum, a four-year degree with a major in accounting and three years of progressively responsible accounting work in a professional accounting firm or comparable public setting, such as state comptroller or the General Accounting Office. Special Agents work on matters including terrorism, foreign counterintelligence, cyber crime, organized crime, white-collar crime, financial crime, bribery, bank robbery, extortion, drug-trafficking and other violations of federal statutes. The FBI also recruits forensic accountants and auditors to join its professional staff—people with a variety of professional backgrounds and skills. There are additional requirements for these positions. (For more on careers with the FBI, visit the Careers section of the FBI Web site.)

Office of the Comptroller of the Currency

The Office of the Comptroller of the Currency (OCC) charters, regulates, and supervises all national banks. The OCC's nationwide staff of examiners conducts onsite reviews of national banks and provides sustained supervision of bank operations. The OCC recruits recent college graduates, including those who majored in accounting, for entry level bank examiner positions. It also recruits CPAs with significant public accounting experience to work as senior policy accountants. (For more information, go to the OCC home page at www.occ.treas.gov.)

U.S. Department of Energy

An example of the careers available in the U.S. Department of Energy (DOE) is auditor in the OIG, Office of Audit Services, which conducts performance and financial audits for DOE's operations and programs, including those performed by contractors. To qualify for an entry level position as an auditor, you must have a degree in accounting, or related field such as business administration, that included 24 semester hours in accounting or at least 4 years of experience in accounting, or an equivalent combination of accounting experience, college-level education, and training that provided professional accounting knowledge. Your background must also include at least 24 semester hours in accounting or auditing courses, or a certificate as a CPA or a Certified Internal Auditor obtained through a written examination. (For more information

---

39 Ibid.
40 "Career Paths," FBI. www.fbijobs.gov/1.asp

on careers as an auditor with the DOE, visit the agency's Web site.[41])

Federal Pay Scale

Pay for white collar employees including CPAs is based on the general schedule pay system (GS), which has 15 pay grades and 10 steps within each pay grade and is adjusted annually. In addition to a base salary, every federal employee receives locality pay, which varies by location. To see the GS and locality pay, click on "Salaries and Wages" on the Office of Personnel Management (OPM) home page (opm.gov).

Annual raises for federal workers typically have been 2.1 percent annually.[42] (Compounded, that amounts to 10.45 percent after 5 years.[43]) In 2009, the GS included a 2.9 percent increase.

Employees in certain occupations or geographic areas may receive higher rates of pay than GS and locality rates. Some agencies administer their own pay systems for their employees, and, in certain situations, agencies may offer recruitment, relocation, or retention incentives.

The Senior Executive Service (SES) includes most managerial, supervisory, and policy positions classified above GS grade 15 or equivalent positions in the executive branch of the federal government. Compensation for SES positions is based on a pay-for- performance system.

Federal Benefits

According to the federal OPM, benefits available to federal employees include the following:

- Widest selection of health plans in the country for employees, retirees, and survivors. Includes comprehensive dental and vision plans. Employees can pay health plan premiums and costs with pre-tax dollars.
- Three-tier retirement plan consisting of social security, a 401k type (defined contribution) plan,[44] and a defined benefit plan[45] based on salary and years of employment.[46]
- Choice of several life insurance programs, covering employees, retirees, and family members.
- Long-term care insurance for federal employees and their parents, parents-in-law, stepparents, spouses, and adult children.
- Leave program that allows time off for personal, health care, or other needs.
- 10 paid holidays annually.
- Up to 13 days of sick leave each year (that accumulate until you use them).
- From 13 to 26 days of vacation a year, depending on length of service.

---

41 Department of Energy, "Career Paths: Auditor." www.ig.energy.gov/auditor.htm

42 "Government Jobs in America," by the Editors of Government Job News, A Partnerships for Public Service Community Publication, Louis R. VanArsdale, publisher; 2009.

43 Ibid.

44 A defined contribution plan, on the other hand, does not promise a specific amount of benefits at retirement. In these plans, the employee or the employer (or both) contribute to the employee's individual account under the plan, sometimes at a set rate, such as 5 percent of earnings annually. These contributions generally are invested on the employee's behalf.

45 A defined benefit plan promises a specified monthly benefit at retirement. The plan may state this promised benefit as an exact dollar amount, such as $100 per month at retirement. Or, more commonly, it may calculate a benefit through a plan formula that considers such factors as salary and service. (Source: U.S. Department of Labor. www.dol.gov/dol/topic/retirement/typesofplans.htm).

46 The OPM provides various retirement tools such as a "Federal Ballpark E$timate" to help federal employees determine how much they will need in federal pension benefits and personal savings and investments to fund their retirement.

Federal agencies may offer a variety of other programs including flexible work schedules; telecommuting, child care, and elder care assistance; adoption information and support; child care support including subsidies and pretax spending accounts; tuition assistance; and employee personal assistance. Agencies also offer a variety of career assessment and planning, training, learning and knowledge management resources for employees. The GAO, for example, assigns entry level financial auditors to a professional development program in the Financial Management and Assurance team. In their first two years with GAO, financial auditors receive a combination of on-the-job and classroom training, regular feedback and coaching, and exposure to different projects and management styles.[47]

Finding Work with the Federal Government

What's it like to work for a federal agency? Where are the best places to work in the federal government? What kinds of jobs are filled by accounting graduates? This section addresses these questions and also looks at how to get started on the job search.

Internships

Internships are an excellent way for you to learn about the federal government and gain experience working for a federal agency; furthermore, an internship might lead to a job offer. The federal government's intern pro-

gram, known as The Federal Career Intern Program, is designed to help agencies recruit and attract exceptional people into a variety of occupations.[48] It is intended for positions at grade levels GS-5, 7, and 9. (See "Federal Pay Scale," earlier in this chapter.) In general, individuals are appointed to a two-year internship. Upon successful completion of internships, interns may be eligible for permanent placement within an agency. Individuals interested in this program should contact specific agencies directly to determine whether the agency is participating in the program and how to apply.

Examples of internship programs include the following.

- White House internships: The White House offers internships to students and recent graduates as well as veterans who have recently served on active duty. Information about the internship program and the highly competitive selection process can be found on the White House Web site. On the White House home page (whitehouse.gov), click on "About the White House" and "White House Internships."
- The Central Intelligence Agency offers student work programs, including undergraduate internship and co-op programs and a graduate studies program. Students have an opportunity to participate in the agency's work, meet agency professionals, and gain practical work experience.[49]
- The Federal Deposit Insurance Corporation's Division of Finance offers a variety of internships including accounting internships. Accounting interns assist with the monitoring of accounting standards and guidelines, the establishing of corporate accounting policy and positions, and the financial statement compliance with GAAP.[50]

---

47 U.S. Government Accountability Office, Professional Development Program, www.gao.gov/careers/pdp.html

48 "Federal Career Intern Program," OPM, www.opm.gov/careerintern/

49 Central Intelligence Agency: "Careers: Student Opportunities." www.cia.gov/careers/student-opportunities/index.html#gradprograms

50 Federal Deposit Insurance Corporation, Division of Finance Internship Program. www.fdic.gov/about/dofinterns/index.html

- The Drug Enforcement Administration's Office of Finance has a two-year accounting internship program for qualified candidates.[51]

In addition to internships offered by the agencies themselves, some professional societies and other organizations sponsor internships. The Hispanic Association of Colleges and Universities has partnered with some federal agencies (and private companies) to offer internships to high achieving Hispanic students.[52]

Student Employment Programs

Some agencies such as the Department of the Treasury have employment programs for qualified students. The Treasury's Student Educational Employment Program is a one-year program that provides an opportunity for students to work in a section of the Treasury.[53]

Best Places to Work

Once you've done some research on the federal governments and its departments and agencies, and the pay and benefits available to federal employees, you may ask: where are the best places to work in government? The PPS and American University's Institute for the Study of Public Policy Implementation produce a biannual report, "The Best Places to Work in the Federal Government." It's based on an employee satisfaction survey of

federal employees as well as various other criteria such as effective leadership and work/life balance. The survey data for 2009 is summarized in box 6-3.

Jobs Filled by Accounting Graduates

According to USAJOBS, the following federal jobs are most often filled by college graduates who majored in accounting.[54]

Contract Specialist: Prepare, review, issue and monitor bid documents; review and evaluate bid proposals; prepare, review and issue contract documents; monitor the performance of contracted parties.

Box 6-3: *The Top Ten Best Places to Work in the Federal Government 2009*

1. Nuclear Regulatory Commission
2. Government Accountability Office
3. National Aeronautics and Space Administration
4. Intelligence Community
5. Department of State
6. Environmental Protection Agency
7. Department of Justice
8. General Services Administration
9. Social Security Administration
10. Department of Commerce

* "The Best Places to Work in the Federal Government 2009," The Partnership for Public Service and American University's Institute for the Study of Public Policy. http://data.bestplacestowork.org/bptw/index

---

51 "DEA Jobs," U.S. Drug Enforcement Administration. www.usdoj.gov/dea/resources/job_applicants.html

52 Hispanic Association of Colleges and Universities, National Internship Program www.hnip.net/opportunities/)

53 Department of the Treasury, "Employment—Student Employment Opportunities." www.ustreas.gov/organization/employment/internships/step.html

54 "Federal Jobs by College Major," USAJobs. www.usajobs.opm.gov/ei23.asp

Financial Manager: Responsible for budgeting, financial planning, record-keeping, cash flow management, developing or maintaining standards for financial performance.

Financial Administrator: Assist and support financial managers in budgeting, financial planning, and so on.

Financial Institution Examiner: Assist in conducting examinations of commercial banks and other financial institutions.

GAO Financial Auditor: Assist the GAO with audits of government agencies and programs.

Intelligence Specialist: Collect, record, analyze, and disseminate tactical, strategic, or technical intelligence information.

Internal Revenue Agent: Assist the IRS in collecting taxes and enforcing internal revenue laws.

Accounting graduates are not limited to these jobs. They work in many other areas of government, for example, as staff accountants for the Securities and Exchange Commission.[55]

Of course, the most important question is: What's the best job for you in the federal government? To decide, you can search for jobs that interest you.

Searching for Jobs

Most of the jobs in the federal government are in the competitive civil service, meaning that—just as in the private sector—you must compete with other applicants for the position. Some agencies are excluded from competitive civil service procedures. Known as excepted service agencies, they use their own criteria in evaluating and hiring people. They include agencies such as the CIA, the Department of State, the Federal FBI as well as Congress and the judicial branch. (For more information on excepted service agencies, check the USAJOBS Web site.[56]) Some jobs are open only to current federal employees and some only to employees of an agency.

To find out what jobs are available, start with USAJOBS. This is where all agencies are required to post announcements of openings for competitive civil service jobs. Excepted service agencies are not required to post job openings on USAJOBS, although they may do so. In any case, you may want to check the web pages of the excepted service agencies for job listings.

On the USAJOBS home page, you can search for jobs by category and location, for example, keying in "auditor" and "New York City" pulled up auditor jobs listed at the time. One was for an auditor in New York with the Department of Homeland Security, Immigration and Customs Bureau. You can also search for jobs by occupation or location or agency. For example, a search in

---

55 "Opportunities for Staff Accountants With the SEC," Securities and Exchange Commission. http://sec.gov/jobs/jobs_accountants.shtml
56 USAJOBS, "Excepted Service Agencies." www.usajobs.gov/EI6.asp

occupation, the accounting, budget and finance category, pulled up a list of accounting and auditing jobs. One listing at the time was for an accountant in the Department of Education, Office of the Chief Financial Officer, in Washington, D.C.

Searching from the USAJOBs home page, however, can produce broad search results. At the time of the search, the accounting category ran to 19 pages, each with about 50 jobs listed. Many of the jobs, locations, or agencies listed may not interest you, and you would have to check the site everyday to find updates.

Personal Account

To search more efficiently and productively, and make full use of the site's many career and job hunting tools and resources, you can click on MyUSAJOBS and set up a personal account. Then you can create job search agents (customized job searches) based on job category, occupational series, location, agency, salary range, and other criteria; sign up for automated emails that alert you of new job openings based on your interests and qualifications; create and post your resume; and attract employers by allowing agencies searching for job candidates to search your resume. You can use the site's information center for assistance with every step of the job hunting process, including tips on improving your search results.

When you do a customized search on USA-JOBS, you will get a list of jobs. Each listing has the job's title and a summary of the position including the agency, location, whether the job is open to the public (U.S. citizens), salary, and other information. Pay particular attention to the closing date or the date that a job must be submitted. It's best to submit the application in advance of the closing date to avoid the agency's not receiving your last minute application for whatever reason.

To learn more about a job on the list, click on its title for a link to the vacancy announcement. This provides a detailed description of the job responsibilities and duties, qualifications required for the job, and additional information such as the promotion potential, or the top grade level to which you can be promoted in the job. Most importantly, it has the application information, or how to apply for the job. You will be asked to provide information about your knowledge, skills and ability, or what's known as a KSA, to perform the job. You can apply for many jobs using your online USAJOBS resume builder—check the "How to Apply" tab in the vacancy announcement. Some agencies require that you use their resume builder. Some may let you fill out a form, known as the Optional Application for Federal Employment (OF-612), instead of a resume. (You can download the form at USAJOBS. Click on "Forms.") Today only a few positions require a written test as part of the job application.

Hearing from Prospective Employers

Once you've submitted your application, you should receive confirmation from the agency to which you've applied. Although each agency is different, generally, you will hear from the hiring agency in about 15-30 days after the vacancy announcement closes

Library of Congress Auditor Job Announcement

Let's take a look at a federal job announcement. This was for a full time, permanent auditor position in Washington, D.C., with the Library of Congress, the world's largest library, and the home of the U.S. Copyright Office, the Congressional Research Service, and the Law Library of Congress.

Auditor (Vacancy #: 090118)
GS-0511-13—Office of Inspector General—$86,927.00 - $113,007.00
Opening Date: Jul 1, 2009
Closing Date: Jul 16, 2009

This position is within the Office of Inspector General (OIG), an independent office within the Library of Congress. The position is supervised by the Assistant Inspector General for Audits.

Vacancy #: Every job announcement is assigned a number, which you would reference in applying for a position.

GS-0511-13: GS is a job that comes under the federal government's GS. It is in the government's 0500 occupational series: accounting and budget group, and, within that series, in 0511, audit.* The "-13" is the promotion potential. You would be hired at the GS-11 level. You would be eligible for promotion to the GS-12 level at the end of your first year of employment. Once promoted to the GS-12 level, you would be eligible for promotion to the GS-13 level at the end of a year. More important to you than these numbers are the ones with the $ sign in front of them. This job starts at $86,927 (GS-11) and has a promotion potential of $113,007 (GS-13), including the location differential for the Washington D.C. area.**

Note that there was only a two week window in which to apply for the position. Other jobs also have relatively short application periods. Because job announcements can turn over fairly quickly, you have to regularly check on new announcements by visiting agency web sites or signing up for email alerts for new openings (if a government provides this service).

Further on, the announcement explains what the OIG does:

The OIG is responsible for conducting or overseeing all audits relating to programs and operations of the Library of Congress.

Auditing includes planning, conducting, and reporting on findings and recommendations to increase economy, efficiency, and effectiveness, by preventing and detecting fraud, waste, abuse, and mismanagement in the administration of the programs and operations of the Library of Congress.

This position is responsible for performance and financial audits related to the Library of Congress, its contractors, and grant recipients. Work at this level is characterized by broad and complex assignments that affect the direction of Library programs and operations over a number of years and can result in changes to Library policies and the laws and regulations that govern its activities. Audits will also evaluate the Library's compliance with applicable laws, regulations, and its programmatic goals.

That's the big picture. The announcement goes on to describe what you would do as an auditor in this job:

- Assesses the performance of a government organization, program, activity, or function.
- Performs or assists in the systematic examination and appraisal of the economy and efficiency of department or agency operations, effectiveness in achieving program results, compliance with applicable laws and regulations, and the adequacy of reporting.

(continued)

Library of Congress auditor job announcement *(continued)*

- Analyzes work related to the development and execution of audit policies and programs. Conducts activities related to the detection of fraud, waste, and abuse.
- Evaluates the effectiveness of programs and management practices in areas such as program objectives; program results; factors impacting performance; the adequacy of management controls; and the validity and reliability of program reporting.
- Writes and/or edits material for publications, exhibits, reports, etc.

According to the job announcement, the "basic requirements" for the job are:

- Degree: accounting; or a degree in a related field such as business administration, finance, or public administration that included or was supplemented by 24 semester hours in accounting. The 24 hours may include up to 6 hours of credit in business law, or
- Combination of education and experience—at least 4 years of experience in accounting, or an equivalent combination of accounting experience, college level education, and training that provided professional accounting knowledge. The applicant's background must also include one of the following:
    - 24 semester hours in accounting or auditing courses of appropriate type and quality. This can include up to 6 hours of business law.
    - A certificate as a CPA or a Certified Internal Auditor, obtained through written examination; or
    - Completion of the requirements for a degree that included substantial course work in accounting or auditing.

The announcement then goes into more detail about meeting the degree requirements.

* OPM, Handbook of Occupational Groups and Families. www.opm.gov/FEDCLASS/GSHBKOCC.pdf
** OPM, Salaries and Wages. www.opm.gov/oca/09tables/indexGS.asp

regarding whether you are on the agency's list of qualified job candidates. If you have not heard from the agency, you should contact the agency to inquire about the status of your application. The contact information is provided in the job announcement.

If you qualify for a position, you are ranked against other qualified applicants based on your education, experience and other criteria. Depending on how high you rank, you may be called in for an interview with the hiring agency. You may have to wait awhile before you hear about an interview, so be patient. Meanwhile, you can prepare for the interview just as you would with any other interview. (For interviewing tips, see Chapter 11, Finding That First Job.) If you are hired,

you may have to serve a probationary period, and if you perform satisfactorily, you become a permanent employee.

State and Local Government

Collectively, state and local governments are among the largest employers in the United States, employing a total of about 8 million people.

Just as at the federal level, the recession that began in late 2007 has caused some state and local government workers to postpone retirement. In a 2009 survey of government managers, the Center for Excellence in State and Local Government said half the managers

Table 6-1: *State and Local Government: Employment of Accountants and Auditors**

	2006	2016 (forecast)	% Increase
State	39,011	42,109	8% (rounded)
Local	42,296	52,267	24%
Total	81,307	94,376	16%

* BLS, "National Employment Matrix, employment by industry, occupation, and percent distribution, 2006 and projected 2016, Accountants and Auditors." ftp://ftp.bls.gov/pub/special.requests/ep/ind-occ.matrix/occ_pdf/occ_13-2011.pdf

responding to the survey reported that 20 percent or more of their workers are eligible to retire over the next 5 years. However, most of these workers—about 85 percent—are delaying retirement.

In the short term, at least, governments can benefit from the delayed retirements of these experienced workers, according to the National Association of State Personnel Executives, which participated in the survey. It noted that when the economy recovers and retirement-eligible employees do start to retire, the retirement wave coupled with the layoffs that governments are implementing could cause a tremendous strain on their ability to deliver services.[57] Just like the federal government, state and local governments will find themselves in growing competition with the private sector for talent, including CPAs.

According to the BLS, about 13,000 new jobs for accountants and auditors will be created in state and local governments over the 10-year period from 2006 to 2016. Table 6-1 outlines those employment numbers by year.

As in the federal government, CPAs work throughout state and local government, assisting with budgeting, reporting, auditing, tax, and other functions and services. At the state level, they work in the executive, legislative and judicial branches, and in many departments and agencies, and at the local level, in the offices of the mayor, city manager, city administrator, or the city council (or other local legislative body), in city departments and agencies, and elsewhere in local government.

Learning about Careers and Jobs in State and Local Government

The Web sites of most state and local governments provide information about careers and jobs with the government and its departments and agencies. You can access government Web sites through a Google search or through portals such as State and Local Government on the Net (statelocalgov.net). It provides links to state, regional, county, and local government Web sites as well as independent boards and commissions and other agencies.

57 "A Tidal Wave Postponed: The Economy and Public Sector Retirements," Center for State and Local Government Excellence. www.slge.org/index.asp?Type=B_BASIC&SEC=%7B22748FDE-C3B8-4E10-83D0-959386E5C1A4%7D&DE=%7BE2CBB7DB-0A62-48FA-9F61-3F4AD2BAA54B%7D

Governmental Accounting Standards Board

To work as an accountant or auditor in state or local government, you will need to know generally accepted accounting standards for state and local government. The standards are established by the Governmental Accounting Standards Board (GASB), an independent body created to improve governmental accountability through better financial reporting. GASB issues standards and other communications that are intended to provide useful information for users of government financial reports including owners of municipal bonds, members of citizen groups, legislators and legislative staff, and oversight bodies. According to GASB, those standards also help government officials demonstrate to their constituents their accountability and stewardship over public resources.

GASB is recognized by governments, the accounting industry, and the capital markets as the official source of generally accepted accounting principles (GAAP) for state and local governments.

It is an operating component of the Financial Accounting Foundation,* which is a private sector not-for-profit entity that is responsible for the oversight, administration and finances of the GASB, FASB, and their advisory councils.

GASB's standards are not federal laws or regulations and the organization does not have enforcement authority. Compliance with GASB's standards, however, is enforced through the laws of some individual states and through the audit process, when auditors render opinions on the fairness of financial statement presentations in conformity with GAAP.

* The Financial Accounting Foundation is an independent, private sector organization with responsibility for the oversight, administration, and finances of the Financial Accounting Standards Board, the Governmental Accounting Standards Board, and their advisory councils. www.fasb.org/faf/index2.shtml

Many state and local governments have online tools for searching for jobs at the state and local levels. On StateJobsNY (statejobsny. com), you can search for jobs in New York state by keyword, job title, occupational category, region, salary, and other criteria. A search using the keyword "auditor" found, among other job announcements, an opening for a tax auditor/tax auditor trainee, doing field audits of business and individual taxpayers. CalJOBS (caljobs.ca.gov) provides information on finding jobs in California. Illinois has a Workforce Information Center with links to careers and job services. Ohio has a "career opportunity page" with similar links. Many Web sites require you to set up an account before you can view job listings, exams, and so on. Before you start searching, check the general requirements for working for a state or city, for example, whether you must be a resident to apply for a job, or become a resident if you are hired.

Internships

Some states and cities have paid or unpaid internship programs for college students. The state of Indiana has a Summer Internship program that provides full time, paid summer jobs to students who have completed one year of college. Interns will spend at least 50 percent of their time on a predetermined project that enhances college-level skills and abilities.[58] The city of Kansas City has an internship program that exposes college students to career opportunities in local government and helps them to develop professional skills in providing services to citizens. These are volunteer

58 "Summer Internships," Indiana State Personnel Department. www.in.gov/spd/2335.htm

(unpaid) internships where students work 10–20 hours a week during the semester. Internships are open to all students regardless of their major.[59]

How Jobs are Filled

Like the federal government, state and local governments recruit for both competitive civil service positions and exempt positions. These recruiting policies differ by state and local jurisdiction. In Pennsylvania, for example, about 70 percent of state employees work in civil service jobs, which are filled based on a person's skills, experience, and education, and test results. The rest are noncivil service (exempt) jobs.

Pennsylvania along with California, New York, and some other states require job applicants to take a civil service test for some positions. Some cities such as New York City require civil service examinations for most jobs. Information on upcoming exams, applying for and taking exams, exam results, interviewing for jobs and other information is provided on state and city Web sites. The California State Personnel Board Web site posts announcements of upcoming exams. You can search for exams by occupational group, title, department, and other criteria; for example, California has exams for the entry level position of Auditor I, Employment Development Department; Tax Auditor, Franchise Tax Board; and Tax Auditor, Board of Equalization. If you are interested in a job, meet the minimum job requirements and pass the test,

your name is placed on a list of eligible job candidates (eligible list) for that job, and you are ranked based on your score. The California Personnel Board posts lists of eligible candidates on its web site, using Candidate ID numbers. Depending on your ranking, you may be invited to an interview with the hiring agency, but again, be patient: it could be some time before you hear about an interview. If you are hired, you may have to serve a probationary period, usually a year.

Pay and Benefits

Like the federal government, states and cities usually have pay scales for civil service employees. As might be expected, pay scales vary depending on the government. Pay scales usually are posted on government Web sites, for example, you can look up pay for different accounting and auditing positions with the state of California on its Web site.[60] Pay for a state's exempt employees is usually determined by the office, department or agency where they work, the particular job, or other criteria.

Many states and cities offers benefit programs similar to the federal government's including base pay, annual raises, longevity increases (based on time with the government or in the job), permanent jobs (usually following a probationary period), pension plans, various voluntary employee savings and retirement plans, different health plans, life and long term disability insurance, long term care insurance, college savings plans, and other

---

59 City of Kansas City, City Manager's Office, "Internships and Fellowships With the City." www.kcmo.org/manager.nsf/web/internhome
60 "State of California: Civil Service Pay Scale—by Class Title."

benefits.[61] Just as with pay schedules, benefits vary, and you should check a state's or city's Web site for benefit information.

A Career in Government: Is it for You?

Demand for CPAs at all levels of government will continue to grow, offering many career opportunities for CPAs just starting on their careers as well as CPAs who may be interested in making a career switch into government. But is a career in government for you? Do you have a strong desire to help people, to give back to your community and country, and to serve the public? Public service is what draws people to government, along with the many career choices, opportunities for career growth, job security, and benefits that match or exceed those in the private sector. But as in other careers, government has its drawbacks. As you advance up the pay the scale, the gap between your pay in government vs. the private sector can widen. And working in a government, bureaucracy, with its rigid structure, and its many rules and regulations, can be frustrating. So before you decide whether you want to work in government, you need to learn more. Here are some things to consider:

The job: There are many different jobs available for accounting graduates or experienced CPAs in government. Study the job announcements of government agencies, and job descriptions on government web sites, to see what might interest you. Of course, you cannot consider every possible job, but you can look at enough that you have a sense of what's available.

Location: Are you set on working in one city or one region of the country, or are you willing to work anywhere in the United States? A related question is whether you are willing to relocate. If you work for a local government, you can expect to stay put. If you work for a state government, you might have to move if the job requires it, but only within the state. If you join the federal government, you could have to move to take a new job, and you might be asked—indeed, required—to relocate from time to time. You could even have an opportunity to work in other countries. Then again, you might relocate infrequently, or not at all. In any event, it's best to ask in a job interview about any relocation requirements.

Career advancement: In the federal government, you have multiple career paths. You could work in one part of a single agency, rotate through different parts of an agency, or transfer between agencies. At the state level, career choices may not be as plentiful as at the federal level, but you could still have a number of alternatives in jobs and agencies. Depending on where you work in the local level, such as in New York or Los Angeles, you could have a number of career opportunities in

---

61 "Government Jobs in America: U.S. States & Cities; Federal Agencies," The Editors of Government Job News; A Partnerships for Community Publication; Louis VanArsdale, Publisher.

city government. In a small town, the opportunities are more limited, but there are trade-offs; for example, you could learn all about local government compared learning about only a part of a larger city government. There may also be opportunities for faster advancement in a small town government.

Career development: In looking at job opportunities, consider the career development programs that are available in the governments and agencies that you are interested in. For various reasons, such as their size and resources, some agencies may have extensive training and career development programs that enable you to work with senior people in the agency, have the advice and guidance of a mentor, rotate through different units in an agency or different agencies, attend inhouse training programs, and so on. Other agencies may have more limited programs. In any event, it's a good idea to ask about such programs during a job interview.

Pay and benefits: As previously noted, pay and benefits of the federal and state and local governments vary widely. You can research the competitive service pay scales that cover many employees, and are available online. In addition, pay and benefits usually are described in job announcements of government agencies. The California Public Employees Retirement System offers its more than one million members retirement plans, health

---

Career Ladder

Just as in the federal government, the career ladder for CPAs in state and local government depends on the particular employer. In the city of Los Angeles, accountants may start as accountants or auditors in a city department, or as tax auditors, and advance to senior accounting or auditing positions, and then to top management positions in a department or agency such as chief internal auditor or chief accountant.*

* "City of Los Angeles Personnel Department: Career Opportunities for Accountant." www.ci.la.ca.us/PER/eeo/career/Accountant.pdf

---

and long-term care benefits, death benefits for survivors and beneficiaries, and disability benefits as well as a home loan program.[62]

Looking Ahead

Remember one thing about considering a career in government—start early. Start early in your college career to research career opportunities not only in government but also in public accounting, corporate accounting, nonprofit accounting and other sectors of accounting. Think about your career aspirations: where do you want to be five or ten years after you graduate? If you are considering a career in government, you can research the descriptions of high level positions in government that have been filled by CPAs, read their bios, and think about whether you would like to follow a similar career track.

If you are interested in government, you might see if you can work as a volunteer or

---

62 "CalPERS Benefits Overview." www.calpers.ca.gov/index.jsp?bc=/about/benefits-overview/home.xml

intern for a government agency, or even get a summer or part time job with an agency, which will enable you to learn about government from the inside. Even entry level positions in government can require some experience, and, depending on the employer, your internships and jobs along with your education could help to meet the experience requirement. For example, here was part of a job announcement by the city of Boston for an auditor to conduct audits of companies and businesses on Cape Cod:

MINIMUM ENTRANCE REQUIREMENTS:

Applicants must have at least (A) two years of full-time, or equivalent part-time, professional experience in accounting or auditing, or (B) any equivalent combination of the required experience and the substitutions below.

Substitutions:

I. A Bachelor's degree with a major in accounting, business administration or business Management may be substituted for a maximum of one year of the require experience.*

II. A Graduate degree with a major in accounting, business administration or business management may be substituted for the required experience.*

* Education toward such a degree will be prorated on the basis of the proportion of the requirements actually completed.

The bottom line is this: More opportunities for CPAs in government exist today than ever before, and with more CPAs expected to retire from government, even more opportunities will exist in the future. So the question is whether you might want to work in government, and if you think you might, where you want to work.

Another thing to consider is that you don't have to go into government right out of school. You could work in public accounting for a few years, and then decide if you want to go into government. Conversely, you might start in government, and then decide to move into public accounting or corporate or nonprofit accounting or teaching. You might decide to move within government, from state government to a position in the federal government, for example. As a CPA, you have portable skills, and it's a matter of where you want to apply your skills. If your choice is government, you can find a rewarding, meaningful and satisfying career in government.

Wrap-up

In this chapter, you learned the following:

- CPAs are in demand all levels of government: federal, state, and local.
- CPAs are needed to help government agencies with a variety of responsibilities such as preparing budgets, planning spending programs, or investigating waste and fraud.
- CPAs are drawn to careers in government by a desire for public service, opportunities for advancement, government benefits, and other reasons.
- There are many government jobs for CPAs in budgeting, reporting, auditing, tax, and other areas.
- CPAs work for many different federal agencies such as the FBI, the IRS, or the Government Accountability Office.
- CPAs work in a variety of state and local government positions such as a member of the staff of a state auditor or a mayor.

- CPAs use the same analytical, communication, and other skills in government as in other sectors of accounting.
- You can learn about careers in government from reading, talking to people in government, visiting government Web sites and other research.
- You can learn about jobs in the federal government through USAJOBS or the Web sites of government agencies. Generally you apply through USAJOBS.
- You can learn about jobs in state and local governments on state and local government Web sites.

- You can decide whether you want a job in government depending on where you would work (location), the pay and benefits, the opportunities for career advancement and development, and, of course, the job itself.

In the next chapter, we look at career opportunities for CPAs in the not-for-profit sector.

Interview: Ernest A. Almonte
Former Auditor General, State of Rhode Island

Ernest A. Almonte was the Auditor General of the State of Rhode Island at the time that this interview was conducted. He served as Auditor General from 1994 to 2009.

The Office of the Auditor General (OAG) is the State of Rhode Island's legislative audit agency. It conducts financial and performance audits to provide independent and reliable information to the General Assembly on a variety of topics including the State's financial condition, its use of federal funds in compliance with federal law and regulations, and whether programs are operating efficiently and effectively. From 1982 until 1994, Almonte had his own CPA firm in Smithfield, RI. From 1989 to 1994, he was Chairman of the Board of the Rhode Island Clean Water Finance Agency. He holds both a Bachelor of Science Degree in Business Administration and a Master of Science in Taxation Degree from Bryant University, a private college in Smithfield, Rhode Island. Almonte is a graduate of the Senior Executives in State and Local Government program at the John F. Kennedy School of Government at Harvard University. He was Chairman of the American Institute of Certified Public Accountants for 2008-09.

In February 2010, he joined the Rhode Island firm of DiSanto Priest & Co. as a partner.

> *"You have to be able to handle multiple jobs. On a given day, for example, we could simultaneously be doing an audit of the lottery, the prison system, and the governor's travel expenses."*

Why did you decide on accounting as a career?

I majored in business at Bryant University, and the program included a few accounting courses. I found that I liked accounting and decided to study it.

Where did you work after graduation?

I started with a small public accounting firm in Rhode Island, and then started my own accounting practice. I also taught college classes in accounting.

Why did you start your own firm?

I always liked the idea having my own business. My father and grandfather owned their own businesses. If you own your own firm, you can lead it in the direction you want to go. In the beginning, clients pretty much came to me. A lot of other accounting firms would hire me to work on complex tax issues. I also belonged to a lot of different organizations like the Chamber of Commerce, and I served on boards of nonprofit entities. It gave me exposure to people and some asked me to do their accounting.

How did you become state auditor general?

My predecessor was retiring, and one of our state representatives asked me if I would be interested in the position. I had been serving as the volunteer chairman of a quasi-public government agency for several years, and people in government knew me. The state did a national search, and the joint committee on legislative services—five leaders in the state legislature—interviewed me and selected me in 1994. So I sold my accounting firm.

Could you describe your job?

There are several main functions. Our office is responsible for the financial audit of the state of Rhode Island, a $7 billion operation. I sign off on the state's financial statements, just like an auditor signs off on the financial statement of Google or Yahoo or another company. My signature means you can rely on the state's financial statements, for example, if you are an investor in buying the state's bonds.

A second function is compliance. The federal government provides money to the state of Rhode Island with a lot of strings attached. We have to conduct an audit and issue a report to the federal government that the state has spent the money properly in accordance with federal requirements.

A third function is performance audits, or efficiency studies, which are concerned with whether the state can do things faster, better, cheaper. We compare state functions with those of other governments and businesses and make recommendations on how to improve Rhode Island state government.

A fourth function is oversight. We oversee the audits of every city and town in Rhode Island. If they have financial problems, we assist them to take steps to achieve fiscal stability.

Fifth is fraud investigations. We work with the FBI, Secret Service, US attorney, state attorney general, state police and other agencies to investigate fraud in government.

The last piece is information technology. We audit the state's IT system and controls. We also test the security of the system. We hack into systems and issue reports to the governor and agency directors on how to tighten controls and protect against outside threats from criminals and others.

How has your job as auditor general changed from when you started?

One of the biggest changes is that today you are asked to do more work with less money and fewer people. Federal, state and local governments have serious financial problems, which restricts their ability to provide services, pushes up the costs of borrowing, and increases the risks of fraud.

Another change is accelerated turnover in government. In the next five years alone we will lose probably 25% of our state work force because of retirements. That means there will be fewer senior people to share their knowledge and experience with people who are moving up in the organization. But that also means someone going into government will have an opportunity for rapid growth and advancement.

What do you like about your position?

There is a tremendous opportunity to deliver nonpartisan, nonideological, fact based information along with recommendations. We can throw light on a problem through publicity. For example, if a newspaper or local television station does a story on a report we produce, that can help to bring a problem to the attention of the public and our leaders. That is how things get fixed. The "heat" to correct problems can come from anywhere, not only the media but also the governor, the legislature, or the public.

What do you look for in hiring people?

We look for the same skills as public accounting firms, such as strong technical knowledge and good communication skills. You have to be able to handle multiple jobs. On a given day, for example, we could simultaneously be doing an audit of the lottery, the prison system, and the governor's travel expenses.

Do you visit campuses?

We participate in an event called campus gatherings around the country. We bring professionals from government, public accounting, nonprofits and other organizations to meet with students and talk about our jobs. I usually bring along some young staff people from my office. It's amazing how many students have no idea what we do in government.

Do you have an internship program?

Yes. We recruit students at Rhode Island schools—we also have had some out of state students contact us. We put our interns in the field with our auditors to give them an idea what it would be like to work in government auditing. That gives us a chance to evaluate our interns.

What are your goals for your office?

I want it to be well positioned for the future. By that I mean that the governor, the legislature and others will continue to rely upon our office as a trusted advisor. When they are making policy decisions, I want them to look to our office for high quality, nonpartisan reports that they can trust. We have and intend to maintain that trust.

Interview: Michael Cuff
Federal Bureau of Investigation

The mission of the Federal Bureau of Investigation (FBI) is "to protect and defend the United States against terrorist and foreign intelligence threats and to enforce the criminal laws of the United States." It has three national security priorities: counterterrorism, counterintelligence, and cybercrime; and five criminal priorities: public corruption, civil rights, organized crime, white collar crime, and major thefts and violent crime. As of July 31, 2009, the FBI had a total of 32,709 employees.

"You must have an analytical mind set, and a high degree of professional skepticism. You have to be willing to take the extra step to probe financial records or find hidden assets."

That includes 13,249 special agents with critical skills including accounting as well as 19,460 support professionals, such as intelligence analysts, language specialists, information technology specialists, accountants, and other professionals. Investigations are at the heart of FBI operations, and forensic accountants play important roles in assisting the FBI to conduct investigations.

Michael Cuff is a Supervisory Special Agent with the FBI and the Unit Chief, Forensic Accountant Unit, Financial Crimes Section, Criminal Investigative Division.

How do the FBI's forensic accountants assist with investigations?

Forensic accountants work on the financial aspects of our national security and criminal investigations, for example, in tracking down secret bank accounts or hidden assets. The information they uncover helps to support cases for prosecution and/or to address national security priorities.

How did the position of forensic accountant come to be established at the FBI?

Back in the 1970s the FBI started hiring accounting technicians to perform basic accounting work. As time went on there was a need for accountants with specialized experience to work as financial analysts, for example, in helping to investigate fraud in the widespread failure of savings and loan associations in the 1990s. More recently, the subprime mortgage crisis, corporate fraud, the problems in the financial markets and other issues have created a need for accountants with more sophisticated investigative skills. In response, we have created a new program to recruit CPAs to work as forensic accountants.

Who are you trying to recruit?

We are hiring or trying to recruit individuals with a bachelor's or master's degree in accounting, at least several years of professional experience in auditing or forensic accounting, and a CPA license. The Forensic Accountant is a professional support position who essentially functions as an investigator without a gun—someone in this position is not required to carry a firearm.

What makes for a good forensic investigator?

You must have an analytical mind set, and a high degree of professional skepticism. You have to be willing to take the extra step to probe financial records or find hidden assets. You must have the knowledge and experience to participate in highly complex financial investigations. And you need strong computer skills, good communication and interpersonal skills, and the ability to work on teams and in a professional environment.

Do you have a training program for forensic accountants?

We are in the process of establishing a forensic accounting training program. Plans call for those joining the program to participate in a two or three week training program.* The rigorous training curriculum will focus on the FBI investigative programs and priorities and will provide the basic fundamentals necessary to conduct a forensic financial investigation. Intermediate and advanced programs are being developed for forensic accountants who have more experience with the FBI, with a focus on expert witness testimony, advanced financial tracking techniques and asset forfeiture procedures.

What is the career path for a forensic accountant at the FBI?

Placement within the Forensic Accountant career path continuum will depend on your background, education, professional experience and other criteria. The current Forensic Accountant career ladder is a GS-9 through a GS-13.** From there you could qualify for promotion to higher grade levels, move into supervisory and management positions, take on more responsibility, and work on more complex cases.

Do you recruit on college campuses for the forensic accountant position?

No, but we plan to do so in the future. We want to make students aware that once they earn their degree and CPA license, and have a few years of experience, they might want to consider applying for our forensic accounting program.

---

* The FBI Academy at Quantico, Virginia.

** For information on federal pay scales, see "Salaries & Wages" on the U.S. Office of Personnel Management web site. http://www.opm.gov/oca/09tables/index.asp

How did you come to join the FBI?

I worked in public accounting as an auditor for about four years, and then joined the FBI, a career I aspired to for years. My experience in public accounting was immensely valuable. It helped me to begin to develop the investigative skills that are essential in forensic accounting.

To learn more about the work of the FBI's forensic accountants, see a 2007 presentation by Joseph L. Ford, Associate Deputy Director of the FBI, at the AICPA's National Conference on Fraud and Financial Litigation. It's on the FBI web site at http://www.fbi.gov/pressrel/speeches/ ford092707.htm. And to learn about the FBI's role in combating white collar crime, see a 2009 presentation by FBI Director Robert S. Mueller, III, at the Economic Club of New York. http://www. fbi.gov/pressrel/speeches/mueller060209.htm. Information about careers with the FBI also can be found on its web site (fbi.gov).

Interview: Shannon Dickerson
IRS recruiter

Shannon Dickerson, CPA, is a revenue agent for the Internal Revenue Service. She currently is on temporary assignment as an IRS corporate recruiter. She got interested in accounting in high school, where she participated in an IRS-sponsored business co-op program that included basic courses in accounting, business law, and other subjects. After she graduated from high school, the IRS hired her as a secretary. While working full time, she earned a business degree from a community college, and went on to earn a bachelor of science in accounting degree through the University of Maryland's night school program.

> *"I think our strongest selling points are the opportunities for public service and career advancement, the variety of career paths in the IRS, our excellent training programs, and our competitive benefits."*

Where did you start with the IRS after you earned your accounting degree?

I started in 1994 in a compliance position, which is similar to an auditor position in public accounting. In 1998, I became a revenue agent and have been in that position since then. The IRS rotates agents through recruiting positions, and I was taken out of the field to work for 3 years as a full time recruiter. I'm 1 of 23 IRS recruiters nationally. I work in the Washington, DC, Maryland, Delaware, and Virginia area. After I complete my tour as a recruiter, I'll return to work as an agent. I've spent my career at the IRS because it is such a great place to work.

Where do you recruit?

I recruit mostly on four-year college campuses, but we reach out to a wide group of people including military veterans, diversity groups, and the disabled, as well as the general public. We also recruit at two-year community colleges.

What are your selling points—what gets the attention of prospective employees?

I think our strongest selling points are the opportunities for public service and career advancement, the variety of career paths in the IRS, our excellent training programs, and our competitive benefits. In addition, we have numerous locations throughout the United States, and there may be opportunities for people to move around for personal or professional reasons.

What are some of the questions that students most often ask about the IRS—what do they want to know?

As with any job, the first question usually is, "Will I like it?" People also want to know if the IRS is a good fit for them. One hurdle we have to help people get over is how to apply. You have to go through our hiring process, which could take six months.

What does the IRS look for in hiring college graduates—who would be a good fit?

We look for people with good communication skills, an interest in customer service, and a commitment to public service. Today's graduates won't stay with a single employer for their entire careers unless they have a compelling reason. The opportunity for public service provides a strong motivation.

Where would a graduate of a four-year college start at the IRS? What types of positions are available?

Entry level positions for college graduates include revenue agent, revenue officer, tax compliance officer, and special agent—these are typical starting positions. There are descriptions of these positions on our Web site. The career paths for accounting graduates include revenue agent, who deals with civil examinations, and special agent, who focuses on criminal investigations. Career paths for nonaccounting majors include tax compliance officers, revenue officers, IT specialists, or contract specialists.

Where do you have the greatest need currently?

Revenue agents and revenue officers are in greatest demand, particularly with more of our senior agents and officers retiring.

Interview: Jeanette Franzel
U.S. Government Accountability Office

Jeanette Meixner Franzel is managing director of the Financial Management and Assurance Team of the U.S. Government Accountability Office (GAO), the investigative arm of Congress charged with examining matters relating to the receipt and payment of public funds. She heads up the GAO audit unit responsible for oversight of financial management across the federal government. Her team is responsible for the financial audit of the government's consolidated financial statements, numerous financial audits of large federal agencies and programs, and overseeing the efforts of the Department of Defense to achieve an auditable status. Franzel's unit also performs reviews of internal control, financial management systems, cost management, improper payments, and the full range of accountability and corporate governance issues across the federal government. Franzel also directs GAO's work in establishing Government Auditing Standards (The Yellow Book), and has responsibility for GAO's work in the accounting and auditing profession. She represents GAO in coordinating with accountability and standards-setting organizations in the United States and at the international level. Before joining the GAO, she worked in public accounting, providing auditing and accounting services to not-for-profit clients and clients that received government funding. Franzel has a master's degree in business administration from George Mason University and a bachelor's degree in accounting and Spanish from the College of St. Teresa. She also completed the Senior Executive Fellows program at Harvard University. Prior to her career in accounting and auditing, she taught elementary school and high school in South America.

> "All of the work we are doing right now associated with the financial crisis and economic downturn has been fascinating, because these are completely new situations that we are dealing with in 'real time.' We often get involved whenever there is a national crisis or emergency."

How did you get interested in accounting?

I took an accounting class at the College of St. Teresa (Winona, Minnesota), and liked it so well that I decided to major in accounting.

Where did you go after school?

I decided to take a year off and teach in South America. Before I left, I applied to GAO, and I was hired when I returned. I had always been interested in public affairs, politics, and community issues. When I read the mission of the GAO, which was to review the effectiveness of government programs and use taxpayer funds effectively, I decided to join them. I started in 1986 as an entry level auditor. An added attraction was that I had the opportunity to work in Washington, DC.

What were your entry level job responsibilities?

A little of everything. We were out interviewing people, looking at accounting records and supporting documentation, and trying to answer the questions that Congress had given us. The entry level position is very similar today. Our entry level staff does a lot of data mining, data analysis, and a whole lot of interviewing to figure out what is happening, and corroborating data and oral responses with other sources of evidence.

To figure out where and how the public money is being spent?

Yes. The job gets more involved when something goes wrong. Then we have to figure out the magnitude of the problem, the root causes, and what types of corrective actions are needed. When you think of someone in the accounting profession, you don't think of someone who is out interviewing, writing, putting together a story, and helping to bring about constructive improvements.

From auditor, where did you go in the GAO?

I became a senior auditor, then left to work in public accounting for three years, and returned to GAO as an audit manager. I subsequently moved up to assistant director, then director, and now managing director. It's a progression similar to that in a public accounting firm. A director in the GAO is the equivalent of a partner in a public accounting firm and a managing director is similar to a managing partner.

Was your experience in public accounting helpful to your work in the GAO?

Yes, because in public accounting I got to dig into a lot of accounting data and accounting systems in a smaller environment compared with the larger entities that we audit at GAO. Once I learned how things were supposed to work in a smaller environment, it was easy for me to apply that knowledge to a much larger environment. Without my experience in public accounting, it would have been harder for me to get my arms around a large federal entity spending billions of dollars a year.

What is the scope of your responsibilities at the GAO?

I am currently responsible for GAO's oversight of financial management across the federal government. Our work includes financial audits of large agencies, as well as the audit of the consolidated financial statements of the government. We also perform internal control reviews, financial systems reviews, financial analyses, and provide input related to the cost of government programs. Some of our major new responsibilities include providing close oversight of the recently established Troubled Asset Relief Program (TARP) and the new economic stimulus programs being implemented in response to the current economic downturn. I also direct GAO's work in establishing *Government Auditing Standards*, and coordinate with accountability and standards-setting organizations in the United States and at the international level. In the past at GAO, I've led many different engagements dealing with financial management of the civil agencies, internal controls over grants and, procurement, as well as evaluating governance structures. I am also responsible for GAO's issuance of government auditing standards and GAO's relationships with the accounting profession. I work very closely with the AICPA, the PCAOB, and other organizations. I also represent the GAO internationally with the International Organization of Audit Institutions.

What have been some of the most interesting investigations you've done?

All of the work we are doing right now associated with the financial crisis and economic downturn has been fascinating, because these are completely new situations that we are dealing with in "real time." We often get involved whenever there is a national crisis or emergency. In terms of specific projects, last year we completed a report on the financial condition of five hospitals in New Orleans before and after Hurricane Katrina to assist the congress in making decisions about whether those hospitals needed special funding. This type of job had never been done before under those circumstances. Many of our jobs are unique. We did the first financial audit of the SEC's financial statements in 2004. And we reported material weaknesses. It was obviously a difficult and sensitive job. We are still auditing the SEC annually, and have provided numerous recommendations to help SEC management fix the problems. After the attacks of September 11, 2001, there were numerous emergencies and crises, and Congress needed many reports on short notice. I was on a team that looked at how to help the airline industry survive the drastic slowdown in air travel. During the 1990s, I spent years auditing savings and loans that failed in the S&L crisis. We looked at what the government could recover after liquidating failed S&Ls and paying off depositors—it was a fascinating experience.

What do you look for in interviewing people for positions with the GAO?

I tell them we need people with a very solid accounting background plus many other skills such as the ability to achieve results, think critically and perform unique types of analysis, and strong written and oral communications skills. Our work is accounting and auditing "plus"—you need to do a whole lot of things besides accounting and auditing, and you need to be able to put them all together.

Do schools offer courses to prepare students for work as government accountants?

Most schools offer a course that combines government and nonprofit accounting. We look for graduates of schools that emphasize case studies, writing reports and presenting findings—similar to the Harvard Business School approach.

For someone interested in a career with GAO, can they join out of school? Or would it be helpful to work first in public accounting or for state or local government?

There are various entry points to the GAO. We do have a very heavy recruiting program on college campuses, and we have an internship program. Students can work as interns between their junior and senior year, and if they are good performers we can offer them a job—they will have a job when they graduate. That's a tremendous way to bring staff in because we can find out whether they are a good fit. A lot of people come in with master's degrees, and they are studying or preparing to study for the CPA exam. We want people who are eligible to take the exam or almost so. If someone has another 10 classes to take towards the 150-hour requirement, it may be hard for them to catch up with their peers. We also have a professional development program for entry-level staff and those who are entering GAO at the beginning stages of their careers. We also recruit people who are making mid-career changes, but we don't have the same structured training program for them.

Interview: Michele Mark Levine
Director of Accounting Services, City of New York, Office of Management and Budget

Michele Mark Levine is director of accounting services in the City of New York Office of Management and Budget (NYC OMB). Born in New York City, and raised in suburban West Nyack, New York, she comes from a family that placed a high value on helping others. While attending the State University of New York Binghamton, she was actively involved in student advocacy and student government. "That experience opened my eyes to the importance of participating in public discourse, and to understanding the great potential for government to affect peoples' lives—positively or negatively," she said.

> "Because I'm the internal resource person for accounting, I have been involved in all sorts of policy and planning issues related to a very broad array of city services and functions just because they have some sort of accounting, audit, or financial reporting aspect."

After earning a bachelor of science in management degree, with a major in accounting, she accepted a position with Coopers & Lybrand (now PricewaterhouseCoopers) in Manhattan. After two years in public accounting, she enrolled in the Masters of Public Administration program with a concentration in public finance at the Maxwell School of Citizenship and Public Affairs at Syracuse University. Following her graduation from Maxwell, Levine worked for two years in the New York City Council's Finance Division, a budget and finance analytical and policy office, where she worked closely with several city agencies and the NYC OMB and learned how budgets and other laws are introduced, analyzed, and negotiated. She then joined NYC OMB, where she has worked since 1995. The NYC OMB is charged with developing, administering, and overseeing one of the largest municipal budgets in the world.

Was any one in your family an accountant?

Both my grandfathers were accountants—one was a CPA, the other was a tax auditor.

Why did you decide to earn a master's in public administration?

When I worked at Coopers, I had a variety of clients. I found that I liked the nonprofit and government clients the best—I had an affinity for what they were trying to accomplish.

After you earned your master's, why did you go to work for the City of New York?

After I graduated, I did some temporary work because my husband was planning to go to graduate school, but hadn't decided where. After he selected New York, I began to look for a job there. Through my connections from grad school I got a job with the New York City Council's finance division. It was a fascinating education in government. After a couple of years there, I was asked to join the City of New York Office of Management and Budget.

Could you provide a capsule description of your current job?

The core of my job is to be an expert and internal consultant on governmental GAAP (generally accepted accounting principles) as it applies to local and state government. As a result of New York City's fiscal crisis in the 1970s, New York state law requires the city to have a balanced budget. The city's budget—both its planned budget and its actual results of operations—must be balanced in accordance with GAAP. We literally have to follow GAAP definitions of revenues, expenditures, etc., in balancing our budget. Also, we are only permitted to borrow money, (i.e., issue city bonds) for the acquisition or construction of assets that would be considered capital assets under GAAP. As a result, there is a great need for an understanding of GAAP rules as they apply to the budget.

How does your position fit into city government overall?

In New York City, there is an independently elected comptroller. Overall responsibility for the city's accounting and financial reporting functions, and most of the accounting expertise in the city government, is within the comptroller's office; however, proposing and administering the city's budget is a mayoral function. Therefore, the mayor's budget office needs someone with governmental GAAP expertise. That's the core of my job.

What else does your job entail?

It also has entailed a variety of other responsibilities over the years, some related to the budget, and some related, post 9/11, to dealing with the Federal Emergency Management Agency. Also, for about three years, I have been serving as the assistant comptroller for several financing entities that have issued debt on behalf of the city. In February 2008, I became the comptroller of those organizations when the previous comptroller retired. I now have a split role—one is providing GAAP and government auditing and consulting expertise for the internal budgeting process, the other is the actual accounting and reporting for these entities.

What would you say are the biggest challenges in those two roles?

There are political and power dynamic issues that are always found in government. For the city, the final arbiter of its accounting policies is another elected official, the city comptroller, but I don't work for the city comptroller's office, I work for the mayor's office. Sometimes there are hang-ups over technical issues that really should have nothing to do with politics but become politicized. Another issue is that in terms of technical expertise, at times I have been sort of alone within the organization. The person to whom I report directly does not have a background in accounting and auditing. So I have to develop strong relationships with colleagues outside of my organization to engage them in the normal give and take over technical issues. But my job also has been a real opportunity. Because I'm the internal resource person for accounting, I have been involved in all sorts of policy and planning issues related to a very broad array of city services and functions just because they have some sort of accounting, audit, or financial reporting aspect. I work with people in a wide variety of agencies such as the police department, education, and libraries and cultural institutions, social services and health and hospital organizations, among others.

This sounds like a job that requires good communication skills.

Yes. I don't consider myself a wonderful communicator, and I have had to challenge myself in that regard. I will never be invited to be a dinner speaker, but I do feel more comfortable in public forums. For example, as comptroller, I participated in some meetings of the board of directors of the New York City Municipal Water Finance Authority of New York and New Jersey. By law, those meetings are required to be Webcast. So there I was in a public speaking role, on a Webcast. It wasn't something I envisioned when I graduated with a degree in accounting.

Interview: Kamile Narine
Federal Bureau of Investigation

When the FBI was created in 1908, it started with a budget of about $6 million. Since then it has grown into an organization with a fiscal 2010 budget totaling more than $10 billion. The FBI's Finance Division manages the Bureau's budget as well as all financial and procurement activities. This responsibility is divided among the Accounting, Budget, and Procurement Sections. Kamile Narine is the Accounting Section Chief reporting to the FBI's Chief Financial Officer.

> *"Working in the Accounting Section gives you great insight into how the FBI's financial operations work and how it uses its financial resources to meet its many responsibilities."*

How did you get interested in accounting?

In college, I originally studied engineering. I happened to get a part time job with a CPA. He asked me to help him with his books and records. That got me interested in accounting. I changed majors and earned bachelor's and master's degrees in accounting. After graduation, I joined UPS and worked in financial systems. The work interested me so much that I got a second masters degree, in Management Information Systems, and worked in IT and accounting for UPS. As time went on, I began thinking about new career opportunities where I could apply my knowledge and experience in accounting and systems, and that would also fulfill my desire for public service and helping my country. In 1998, I decided to join the FBI, which was growing and had many career opportunities. I started in a field office doing audits and improving IT controls, and advanced to my current position in headquarters, where there was greater opportunity for advancement.

What are the responsibilities of the Accounting Section?

Every fiscal year the FBI submits a proposed budget to Congress, which has final authority over the budget. After Congress decides on the budget, the FBI has to account for how it spends the money it has been allocated. That is where the Accounting Section comes in. We prepare quarterly and annual financial statements and other financial reports for Congress. We assist our internal and external auditors to conduct audits and prepare audit reports and we carry out various other duties. We make all the payments for and collect funds due to the Bureau. We track and account for all the Bureau's assets. We provide financial information needed to run operations. Working in the Accounting Section gives you great insight into how the FBI's financial operations work and how it uses its financial resources to meet its many responsibilities.

Who are you interested in recruiting to join the Accounting Section?

People with strong accounting backgrounds who are interested in careers with the FBI and in helping to run the FBI's financial operations. I especially look for job applicants who are CPAs or Certified Government Financial Managers or Certified Information Systems Auditors. Having two or all three of these credentials is a plus.

Equally important are strong analytical abilities, excellent communication and interpersonal skills, and the ability to work on teams.

What is the career path for an entry level accountant in the Accounting Section?

Your career path would be accountant, senior accountant, and lead accountant, then running a unit of people performing a specific accounting function such as accounts receivable, and, ultimately you could become the section chief or deputy section chief overseeing all accounting functions. Along the way, you would advance in the federal grade and pay scale.* Depending on the FBI's needs and your interests, you could follow other career paths, for example, in internal auditing or forensic accounting. For example, an employee in the Accounting Section started as an intern in the unit that produces financial statements. In a few years she would like to start working as an investigator. With her experience in our section, she will have a solid foundation for investigative work.

---

* For information on federal pay scales, see "Salaries & Wages" on the U.S. Office of Personnel Management web site. http://www.opm.gov/oca/09tables/index.asp

Interview: Kathy Petronchak
Retired IRS Commissioner for
Small Business

In high school, Kathy Petronchak took business classes including accounting, and she worked part time while in college at a bookkeeping and tax preparation firm. That sparked a lifelong interest in accounting and small business. Her last public service job was as IRS commissioner for Small Business/Self-Employed. In 2008, she retired from the IRS and joined Deloitte Tax LLP as director of tax controversy. In an interview, she talked about her 29-year career with the IRS.

> *"When you work as an agent, it's almost like being self-employed, but you draw a regular paycheck from the IRS. You have to be self-directed, manage your time, and take the initiative in working your caseloads."*

Did you originally plan on a career in accounting?

In college, I initially planned on being a teacher majoring in business, but after my first year I switched to accounting. I liked working with numbers.

Where did you study accounting?

I attended a community college for two years and then transferred to Virginia Commonwealth University, where I earned a degree in accounting.

Did you work in accounting while you were in college?

I worked for an accountant whose clients included small businesses and nonprofit organizations. We were a jack-of-all trades. We did bookkeeping for some clients and basic payroll for others as well as other functions that would assist them. Back then, everything was manual. We had big old heavy books everywhere. Our clients used to bring in receipts in bags and dump them on our desks.

How did you get interested in working for the IRS?

When I was working for the accounting firm, revenue agents would come in to do audits of our clients. I talked with them at lunch about their jobs, and what they did. Also, I had a great tax instructor in college who got me interested in taxes. So I decided to apply to the IRS and got hired.

When did you join the IRS?

Right after I graduated from college in 1979. I started as a revenue agent in the Richmond, Virginia, office.

What was it like to work in the field as a revenue agent?

When I went out on my first field audit, the taxpayer dumped a bunch of paperwork on his desk. That was nothing new—I was used to it. In most cases we went out to a representative's office or a business site to inspect a taxpayer's books and records. One time I was dressed in a suit and high heels and went to see a client who had a portable lumber mill right out in the woods. I didn't realize where he was located and found myself hiking through the woods to his job site.

How did you move from revenue agent to your first managerial position?

I worked as a revenue agent for about seven years. We had after work sessions for those who were thinking about pursuing our interest in management. I attended some of those, learned about positions that were available, and was encouraged to apply.

Where did you start as a manager?

I went into a managerial position in an office that assisted field office managers in obtaining their workloads based on the resources they had available. This was in Richmond, Virginia, and I was responsible for the workload for all offices within the state. It helped me to learn more about the IRS and to have a broader perspective of the organization.

What skills did you have to develop as a manager vs. an agent?

When you work as an agent, it's almost like being self-employed, but you draw a regular paycheck from the IRS. You have to be self-directed, manage your time, and take the initiative in working your caseloads. As a manager, you're responsible for a team of people. Then it's a question not only of what you can do but how you lead others in getting things done.

What was your next management position?

In 1989, I was promoted to chief of the quality review section in Richmond as well. We reviewed cases for quality control and provided feedback, such as whether better documentation might be needed in some areas. We reviewed trends to see if further training might be needed, for example, to improve the probing of taxpayer income.

Where did you go from there?

In 1991, I started work for the IRS National Office of Penalty and Interest. At the time, this was a task force trying to establish a service wide perspective on penalty administration. It was eye opening working in our national headquarters. It gave me a much better understanding of how the IRS is organized, and of all its components. I had been working there for about nine months when my husband's job required him to move to California.

What did you do?

I asked for a transfer, moved to California in 1992, and went back to being a front line manager. Although I stepped back in the career ladder at the time, it was right for me personally. I worked in the Long Beach office, managing revenue agents in the field, and helping them to work cases. In 1995, I moved to Laguna Niguel, California, as a branch chief, responsible for multiple groups that performed audits. In 1998, I moved to Los Angeles, where I was the exam division chief. Then I applied for the IRS executive development program and was selected. I spent four months in a training program in 2000.

Where did you go after training?

I applied and was accepted for a position in Laguna Niguel with the large and midsized business division. I was responsible for managing agents who conducted audits of retail, food, and health care taxpayers in the western half of the United States. I also interacted with outside stakeholders such as organizations of CPAs or tax executives in communicating our vision, how we perform our work, and so on. Then I moved back to Washington in 2002.

In what position?

I was assigned to the pre-filing and technical guidance office for large and midsized companies, responsible for providing technical advice on issues such as the research tax credit and reportable transactions. We provided recommendations that were put on a priority plan used by the chief counsel and the Department of Treasury to issue needed guidance to taxpayers. I was then asked to serve as the IRS commissioner's chief of staff. In that position, I coordinated the activities of the commissioner's office and attended meetings with the Secretary of the Treasury and representatives in Congress. It gave me a view from the top. I could see the breadth and depth of the organization, and how people performed. From there I moved into my last position. I was once again working with small business taxpayers, just as I did when I was in college.

Why did you decide to join Deloitte?

I had planned for a number of years to move to public accounting once I had achieved all the goals I had set for myself at the IRS. The opportune time came in 2008. I retired from the IRS and started my second career. As a member of Deloitte Tax LLP, I use what I learned at the IRS to resolve tax controversies. I recommend approaches to be used in resolving tax disputes or the use of alternative resolution techniques available to our clients.

Chapter 7

Careers in Nonprofit Accounting

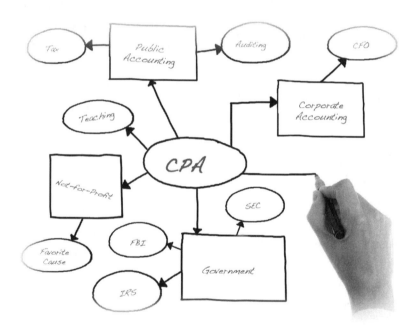

"Education and experience are essential, but without leadership, education and experience can only take you so far."

Allan Golston, President of U.S. Programs • Bill and Melinda Gates Foundation

Find a Rewarding Career as a CPA Working for Nonprofit Organizations

In your hometown, the city, or community where you attend school—indeed, all across the United States—not-for-profit organizations provide food, clothing, and shelter to those in need, day care for children of working parents, literacy programs for adults, job training for unemployed workers, after school programs for elementary and high school students, scholarships for college-bound students, and hundreds of other services to the public.

National Student Partnerships (NSP) was founded in 1998 by two Yale undergraduates, Kirsten Lodal and Brian Kreiter. They designed a program in which college student volunteers work 1-on-1 with community residents, coordinating access to employment opportunities and social services, including job training, housing, health care, child care, and transportation. Based on the organization's early success in serving the New Haven, Connecticut, neighborhood surrounding Yale, the founders decided to expand their vision to other communities, and today NSP operates in 11 cities.[1]

You may have some experience with a not-for-profit, perhaps serving as a volunteer for a not-for-profit organization or as the recipient of a scholarship or other financial aid from a not-for-profit. If you are a student, you might be considering whether to find a job with a not-for-profit organization after you graduate, or, if you are a practicing CPA, perhaps you are thinking of making a career change to the not-for-profit sector. This chapter examines the career opportunities for CPAs with not-for-profit organizations. CPAs are much in demand to advise and assist not-for-profits in developing programs, preparing budgets, managing spending, controlling costs, administering internal controls, improving transparency and accountability, and realizing the most value from every dollar spent on the organization's programs and services. Many CPAs are in senior positions with not-for-profit organizations. Allan C. Golston, CPA, started his career in public accounting. Today, he's financial director of the Bill and Melinda Gates Foundation. (An interview with Golston appears on page 268.)

Today's not-for-profit organizations have their antecedents in the philanthropic organizations that were started in the United States before the Revolutionary War. Benjamin Franklin and 50 friends started one of the earliest such organizations in 1753 with The Library Company of Philadelphia, the first successful circulation library, so people of moderate means could better themselves through reading.[2] From modest beginnings, the not-for-profit sector today has grown into 1.5 million organizations that are registered with the IRS as tax-exempt organizations. Today, not-for-profits reach into every corner of society and touch the lives of most Americans.

---

1 "About NSP: History & Founders." www.nspnet.org/about/about_history.htm

2 "A Chronological History of Philanthropy in America," National Philanthropic Trust, http://74.52.60.18/~npt/index.php?page=1700-s

In 2006, not-for-profits contributed $666 billion to the U.S. economy.[3] They accounted for 5 percent of gross domestic product (GDP); 8 percent of the economy's wages; and nearly 10 percent of jobs. Health not-for-profits dominated the not-for-profit sector, accounting for 45 percent of its total expenses and nearly 24 percent of its assets. Education was second largest, with nearly 12 percent of total expenses and 19 percent of total assets.[4]

Many not-for-profits are small organizations with modest budgets. About 93 percent of nonprofits have incomes of less than $1 million, according to the Urban Institute's National Center for Charitable Statistics (NCCS [nccs.urban.org]), a national clearinghouse of data on the nonprofit sector in the United States. The nation's more than 60,000 small foundations are led entirely by volunteer boards or operated by just a few staff.[5] Other not-for-profits are national or global organizations with large staffs and multi-billion dollar budgets.

Not-for-profits rely heavily on volunteers, with about 25 percent of Americans contributing their time and talents. In 2006 (the latest year that figures are available), about 61 million volunteers contributed 12.8 billion hours to not-for-profit organizations, or about 207 hours per volunteer. At an assigned rate of about $16 an hour, those volunteer hours had a value of about $215 million.[6]

In 2008, during the worst recession in decades, donations to charitable causes in the United States fell 2 percent to an estimated $308 billion, from $314 billion the previous year, according to *Giving USA*, an annual report of the Giving USA Foundation (which was researched and written for the Foundation by the Center on Philanthropy at Indiana University). That was only the second decline in donations since Giving USA began publishing reports in 1956.[7] (To put that $308 billion figure in perspective, it was more than South Africa's 2008 GDP of $300 billion.)[8]

What are Nonprofits?

The term nonprofit (or not-for-profit) doesn't begin to describe the breadth, depth, and reach of these organizations—it says more about what they are not than what they are. They are not profit making organizations like corporations and businesses, nor do they pay dividends to shareholders or investors. They are not part of government.

So what are they?

3 "Research Area: Nonprofit Sector," Urban Institute. www.urban.org/nonprofits/more.cfm

4 "New Edition of Nonprofit Almanac Offers Detailed Portrait of an Expanding Sector," The Urban Institute, press release, May 2, 2008. www.urban.org/publications/901164.html

5 Association of Small Foundations, "About Us," www.smallfoundations.org/site/pp.asp?c=fvKRI7MPJqF&b=2309715

6 "The Nonprofit Sector in Brief: Facts and Figures from the Nonprofit Almanac 2008; Public Charities, Giving and Volunteering; Table 5: Number, Hours and Dollar Value of Volunteers," Urban Institute National Center for Charitable Statistics (NCCS). nccsdataweb.urban.org/kbfiles/797/Almanac2008publicCharities.pdf

7 "U.S. charitable giving estimated to be $307.65 billion in 2008," Press Release, Giving USA Foundation, June 10, 2009. www.givingusa.org/press_releases/gusa/GivingReaches300billion.pdf.

8 "The World Factbook, Field Listing: GDP," Central Intelligence Agency. www.cia.gov/library/publications/the-world-factbook/fields/2195.html

First and foremost, not-for-profit organizations exist to serve the public. Every not-for-profit is dedicated to a mission, whether that mission is to alleviate hunger, promote alternative energy, conserve natural resources, or achieve many other goals. Not-for-profits accomplish this by generating revenue from fund-raising, grants from foundations, fees from providing certain goods and services, government contracts, and other sources. Their *surplus revenue*—the revenue that remains after expenses for staff salaries, rent, office equipment, and supplies and other expenses—goes to support the organization's mission. Not-for-profits are sometimes described as "double bottom line" organizations: the first bottom line is their financial performance, measured by their income and other financial benchmarks; the second is their social performance or their contribution to the public good. Not-for-profits are independent, self-governing organizations, with boards of directors and volunteer or paid staffs.

The NCCS says there is no "one size fits all" way to think about the 1.5 million not-for-profits in the United States. They include soup kitchens and traditional charities that serve the poor as well as local churches, synagogues or mosques, the Chamber of Commerce, environmental organizations such as the Sierra Club, labor unions such as the United Steel Workers, cultural organizations such as New York's Metropolitan Opera, and professional organizations such as the American Institute of Certified Public Accountants (AICPA).

In contrast with taxpaying corporations, organizations that qualify as not-for-profits under Section 501(c) of the Internal Revenue Code are tax exempt, and donations to not-for-profits may be tax deductible. According to the NCCS, not-for-profit organizations can be grouped into three categories: public charities, private foundations, and other exempt organizations.

Public Charities

The IRS defines *public charities* as those that

- are churches, hospitals, qualified medical research organizations affiliated with hospitals, schools, colleges, and universities,
- have an active program of fund-raising and receive contributions from many sources, including the general public, governmental agencies, corporations, private foundations, or other public charities,
- receive income from the conduct of activities in furtherance of the organization's exempt purposes, or
- actively function in a supporting relationship to one or more existing public charities.[9]

Public charities generally are required to register as tax-exempt organizations with the IRS. (Those whose annual gross receipts normally are less than $5,000 are generally exempt from registration.[10])

According to the NCCS, 956,760 public charities were registered with the IRS in 2008.[11]

---

9 "Public Charities," IRS. www.irs.gov/charities/charitable/article/0,,id=137894,00.html

10 IRS.gov, "Application for Recognition of Exemption." www.irs.gov/charities/article/0,,id=96109,00.html

11 "Quick Facts About Nonprofits," Urban Institute NCCS. http://nccs.urban.org/statistics/quickfacts.cfm

The nation's approximately 350,000 religious congregations are considered public charities, but they are not required to register with the IRS, although about half have chosen to do so.[12]

Public charities with more than $25,000 in gross receipts are required to annually file Form 990, *Return of Organization Exempt From Income Tax*, with the IRS. Those whose gross receipts are normally $25,000 or less must file Form 990-N, *Electronic Notice (e-Postcard) for Tax-Exempt Organizations not Required To File Form 990 or 990-EZ*.[13] Box 7-1 outlines some of the largest U.S. public charities.

Private Foundations

In contrast with public charities, private foundations typically have a single major source of funding (usually gifts from one family or corporation rather than funding from many sources) and most have the making of grants to other charitable organizations and to individuals, rather than the direct operation of charitable programs, as their primary activity.

All foundations must register and file with the IRS. In 2008, 112,959 private foundations were registered.[14] Box 7-2 reflects a list of the top 10 foundations.

Box 7-1: *Largest Public Charities in the U.S. 2007*[*]

Name	Total Assets
President and Fellows of Harvard College	$57,850,842,000
Yale University	28,324,069,000
Stanford University Board of Trustees	25,887,631,118
Southwest Louisiana Business Development Center	24,000,086,595
Howard Hughes Medical Institute	21,676,241,456
Kaiser Foundation Hospitals	20,878,470,177
Trustees of Princeton University	17,987,893,000
Massachusetts Institute of Technology	14,924,101,000
Common Fund for Non-Profit Organizations	14,168,224,254
Harvard Management Private Equity Corporation	12,273,938,683

* Urban Institute NCCS: Largest Public Charities http://nccsdataweb.urban.org/PubApps/showOrgs ByCategory.php?ntee=A

12 Ibid. 503(c)(3) Public Charities," Urban NCCS.http://nccsdataweb.urban.org/PubApps/nonprofit-overview-segment.php?t=pc

13 IRS.gov, Form 990 N (e-Postcard): Who Must File www.irs.gov/charities/article/0,,id=177783,00.html

14 "Quick FactsAbout Nonprofits," Urban Institute NCCS. http://nccs.urban.org/statistics/quickfacts.cfm

Box 7-2: *Top Ten Foundations by Total Assets**

Name	Total Assets
Bill & Melinda Gates Foundation	$38,921,022,000
The Ford Foundation	11,045,128,000
J. Paul Getty Trust	10,837,340,620
The Robert Wood Johnson Foundation	10,730,549,952
W.K. Kellogg Foundation	8,058,127,639
John D. and Katherine T. MacArthur Foundation	7,052,165,312
The Andrew W. Mellon Foundation	6,539,865,000
Gordon and Betty Moore Foundation	6,409,252,816
The William and Flora Hewlett Foundation	6,289,035,000
Lilly Endowment Inc.	5,722,416,949

* "The Top 100 Foundations, by Total Assets," Foundation Center. http://foundationcenter.org/focus/economy/forecast.html

Other Nonprofit Organizations

These are organizations that do not fit into the first 2 categories. Among them are large health maintenance organizations (HMOs), labor unions, and business and professional organizations. In 2008, 443,464 of these other organizations were registered with the IRS.[15]

Nonprofit Classification by Mission

To provide an in-depth look at U.S. not-for-profits, the NCCS uses two classification systems. One is known as the National Taxonomy of Exempt Entities (NTEE) system, which is used by the NCCS and the IRS. It divides not-for-profits into nine broad categories. (Not-for-profits that did not provide enough information to be classified or otherwise do not fit in the nine categories are labeled as "Unknown, Unclassified.")

The nine categories are:

1. *Arts, Culture, and Humanities*, including museums, performance venues such as concert halls; performance groups such as ballet; arts councils; conservatories and historical societies; and distribution channels such as public television.

2. *Education*, including early childhood; elementary and secondary school; higher education; supplemental programs such as academic programs, career centers, workforce development; educational materials; and libraries.

15 "Quick FactsAbout Nonprofits," Urban Institute NCCS. http://nccs.urban.org/statistics/quickfacts.cfm

3. *Environment and Animals*, including environmental protection (conservation of land, water, energy, and forests); parks and gardens; environmental education; and animal welfare including wildlife and endangered species preservation and protection; veterinary services; and zoos.

4. *Health*, including hospitals, centers and clinics; mental health services; health insurance including HMOs; and research and organizations devoted to the treatment of diseases such as cancer.

5. *Human Services*, including family and children services; public safety and emergency assistance; housing and shelter; crime prevention and legal services; employment; food and nutrition; recreation; sports and leisure; youth development; and advocacy.

6. *International, Foreign Affairs*, including cultural and student exchange; development such as microfinance and small business loans; health care; nutrition; education; disaster relief; and human rights. (Not-for-profit organizations that work globally are sometimes known as nongovernmental organizations or NGOs or international nongovernmental organizations or INGOs.)

7. *Public, Societal Benefit*, including civil rights and social action; civic engagement such as voter education; advocacy; community improvement, and philanthropy; volunteerism; and grantmaking (including private foundations, community foundations, and fund-raising federations such as United Way.)

8. *Religion Related*, including care for members; social services such as soup kitchens; affordable housing; assistance for first time home buyers; education and community support such as tutoring; job training; and substance abuse programs.

9. *Mutual/Membership Benefit*, includes some professional societies, labor unions, political groups, trade associations and other groups that primarily serve the interest of members and are member-run.

On the NCCS Web site, you can research any of the 9 categories and 26 subcategories that interest you and obtain additional information such as a listing of not-for-profits by state. An FAQ page covers a number of questions about not-for-profit organizations, for example, which are the largest public charities in the United States, based on total assets and other criteria, or which are the largest in a category such as education or human services? Alternatively, you can do a Google search of the NTEE data base, for example, "NTEE arts, culture and humanities" pulls up a list of the largest organizations in this category (as of publication the leader is New York's Metropolitan Museum of Art with $3.6 billion in assets) as well as a random sampling of other not-for-profits in this category, such as the Community Playhouse of Lancaster County (in Pennsylvania) with total assets of about $33,000.

In addition to the NTEE system, NCCS has developed the Nonprofit Program Classification System (NPC) for classifying the programs of nonprofit organizations. The NPC system generally covers the same broad areas, but it has a higher degree of specificity in its use of more subcategories. Regardless, both systems are very useful in learning about the not-for-profit sector. (On the NCCS home page, click on "Classification" for links to the two systems and tools for using them.)

Nonprofits as Major Employers

In regard to the total wages they pay and the total number of people working for them, not-for-profits are major employers. In 2006, the latest year that figures are available, not-for-profits including public charities, private foundations, and other organizations accounted for $1 of every $8 in wages and salaries paid in the United States.[16] According to the Bureau of Labor Statistics, 1 in 6 American workers was employed in the not-for-profit sector in 2007, compared with 1 in 4 in 1994. Over that 13-year period, the number of not-for-profit workers increased to 8.7 million from 5.4 million.[17]

Why CPAs are in Demand at Nonprofits

Demand for CPAs in the nonprofit sector is increasing as regulators and not-for-profit boards, executives, and donors push for stronger corporate governance, increased transparency and accountability, and, in particular, tighter internal controls. A frequent criticism of not-for-profit organizations has been the perceived weaknesses in their controls, largely due to chronic understaffing, insufficient resources, or poor training.[18] The need for strong controls has become even more evident in the aftermath of the Bernard Madoff scandal when some foundations reportedly lost billions of dollars[19] and by financial improprieties in not-for-profits such as the diversion of funds to insiders.[20]

The Sarbanes Oxley Act of 2002 (SOX) includes specific internal control requirements for public companies and their auditors, and although it does not apply to them, not-for-profits are using it as a guide to strengthen their internal controls. And some states have enacted not-for-profit laws similar to SOX, for example, California requires large not-for-profits to establish audit committees and conduct annual audits.[21] The AICPA has created the "AICPA Audit Committee Toolkit: Not-for-Profit Organizations" to assist audit committees of not-for-profit organizations to ensure that strong controls are in place and address other audit issues. Not-for-profit associations also are providing advice and guidance. The Independent Sector, a coalition of

6 The Urban Institute, NCCS, *Nonprofit Almanac* 2008. http://nccs.urban.org/statistics/quickfacts.cfm

17 "Wages in the Nonprofit Sector: Management, Professional and Administrative Support Occupations," Bureau of Labor Statistics. http://www.bls.gov/opub/cwc/cm20081022ar01p1.htm

18 "The AICPA Audit Committee Toolkit for Not-for-profit Organizations," Reviewed by Julie Lynn Floch, *The CPA Journal*, February 2006. www.nysscpa.org/cpajournal/2006/206/perspectives/p9.htm

19 "Madoff and America's (Poorer) Foundations, Nicholas Kristof, *The New York Times*, January 29, 2009. http://kristof.blogs.nytimes.com/2009/01/29/madoff-and-americas-poorer-foundations/

20 Advising Nonprofit Organizations: the CPAs Role in Governance, Transparency and Accountability," Claudia L. Kelley and Susan Anderson, *The CPA Journal*, August 2006 issue. http://www.nysscpa.org/cpajournal/2006/806/infocus/p20.htm

21 "Nonprofit Integrity Act of 2004: Summary of Provisions," California Registry of Charitable Trusts. http://www.ag.ca.gov/charities/publications/nonprofit_integrity_act_nov04.pdf

not-for-profit organizations, has created a "Checklist for Accountability" to help organizations strengthen their transparency and governance.[22] Not-for-profit boards and executives are dedicating more resources to accounting and financial and administrative functions as well as other areas such as board oversight and executive compensation.[23]

Talent Shortage

Just as in business and government, a leadership exodus will ripple through not-for-profit organization as more baby boomers retire. The Conference Board said in a 2007 report that "widespread executive-level and leadership skill shortages currently affecting many nonprofits are predicted to get much worse as the sector expands and experienced executives retire."[24] The recession that began in late 2007 may have caused some not-for-profit executives to temporarily delay retirement; however, the talent shortage will continue to worsen over the long term.

In a 2006 study of not-for-profit organizations with revenue of more than $250,000, the Bridgespan Group said that over the next decade (2006-2016), these organizations will need to attract and develop some 640,000 new senior managers. "The leadership deficit looms as the greatest challenge facing nonprofits over the next 10 years," Bridgespan said, noting that not-for-profits need to take

action to address the problem, such as investing more in building skilled management teams.[25] Bridgespan is a not-for-profit organization "that helps nonprofit and philanthropic leaders to make strategic decisions and to build organizations that inspire and accelerate social change."

To help meet the need for talent, not-for-profit board members and executives are reaching out to CPAs, public accounting firms, state CPA societies, the AICPA and other organizations to recruit CPAs to serve on their boards or in staff positions from entry level accountant to CFO. Not-for-profits are looking to their CFOs not only to provide financial management but, increasingly, to help provide strategic direction. The CFOs role is not just to crunch numbers, but to help guide the organization's future.[26]

Why Work for a Nonprofit?

If you are passionate about helping others, serving the community, or promoting a cause, you can fulfill your altruistic ambitions by working for a not-for-profit organization. The benefits include the following:

- *Work with like-minded people*
  You can work with energetic, resourceful, dedicated people who share your passion for the organization's mission.

21 "Checklist for Accountability," Independent Sector. http://www.independentsector.org/issues/accountability/checklist/checklist_full.pdf

23 "The Nonprofit Career Guide: How to Land a Job That Makes a Difference," Shelly Cryer, Fieldstone Alliance, St. Paul, MN, May 2008.

24 "Non-Profit Firms Face Many Challenges And Some Opportunities With Advent of Retirement of Baby Boom Generation," The Conference Board, release, May 2007.

25 The Nonprofit Sector's Leadership Deficit: Executive Summary," Thomas J. Tierney, The Bridgespan Group, www.bridgespan.org/LearningCenter/ResourceDetail.aspx?id=948

26 "Nonprofit CFOs: Visionary Protectors of the Bottom Line, or Myopic Bean Counters?," Russell Pomeranz, *The CPA Journal*, February 2008 issue. www.nysscpa.org/cpajournal/2008/208/perspectives/p6.htm

My Experience with Not-for-Profits

You may be among the many people who support a cause. Whatever the cause, your support often is defined by personal experience. You may have a relative who was seriously ill with cancer, and you decided to support an organization doing cancer research or providing assistance to cancer patients. You may have been inspired by a teacher, and decide to support an organization that provides counseling and financial support to college bound students from low income families. Sometimes your early support becomes a lifetime commitment to a cause, and you may provide pro bono services to a not-for-profit organization dedicated to that cause, serve on the organization's board of directors, or raise or donate money. That has been my experience.

When I was very young, I took up my first cause: raising money in support of statehood for Israel. I got interested in this cause because my parents and many of my relatives had immigrated to the United States, while other relatives had immigrated to Israel. When Israel became a state in 1948, I continued to help raise funds to send to Israel to support its schools and health care system, its fledgling military, and the thousands of refugees who were coming to Israel from all over the world. That early experience instilled in me a lifelong desire to help others. I went on to other philanthropic endeavors that could produce tangible results, just as my early support of Israel, however modest, had contributed to Israel's statehood.

Contributing Professional Skills

Early in my career, I didn't have a lot of money to contribute to not-for-profit organizations. But I found that organizations had a real need for people with accounting knowledge, financial acumen, tax skills, and, equally important, an ability to communicate with the organization's board members, staff and others who were not CPAs. I was asked by not-for-profit organizations to help put together budgets, financial statements, and business plans that could be easily understood by the board and others. I saw firsthand how not-for-profit funds were accounted for, but more important, how they were used—how much went for an organization's administrative and other expenses and how much actually went to its cause.

Serving in Senior Positions

As I advanced in my career, I became closely involved with organizations such as the Urban Land Institute (ULI), an international organization of real estate professionals, planners. and others. I served as the ULI's treasurer for a number of years. I was responsible for working with the organization on budget, planning, review of financial statements, and other areas. In addition, I served on the Board of Trustees of Baruch College, providing advice on financial and other matters. I also was treasurer and a member of the Executive Committee and Board of Directors of the American Jewish University (AJU). Later on in life, I became a major financial contributor to the ULI, the AJU, and Baruch College and the University of Southern California (USC). I contributed to the City of Hope, a comprehensive cancer research, treatment and educational organization.

My deepest involvement has been with USC, where I am chairman of the board and a senior fellow of USC's Lusk Center for Real Estate, a center of research, educational programs, and professional development in real estate. As an adjunct professor, I have taught a class or two. I have organized programs for industry leaders and our students, and I have mentored numerous students.

My Experience with Not-for-Profits *(continued)*

My most satisfying experience at USC has been working with the Lusk Center to establish the Ross Minority Program in Real Estate, which my wife Marilyn and I endowed. The program is designed to provide real estate professionals, not-for-profit and community leaders, entrepreneurs, and others with the skills to influence the redevelopment of minority and underserved communities, either by completing development projects or by participation in the development and planning process. Many of the program's students come from inner city areas, and they have a strong interest in the development of new residential, commercial, or retail projects and the redevelopment of existing buildings.

In a sense, the not-for-profit has been a second career for me. Although I have never worked for a not-for-profit organization, I have had the opportunity to contribute professionally and financially to worthy organizations, to be directly involved in the raising and use of funds for a cause, and to meet and network with others in the community who were philanthropic, actively involved in causes, and share the same philosophy and principles that I do. And my first career as an accountant made it all possible.

- *Work in a collegial environment*
  Not-for-profits tend to be informal, collaborative, supportive communities. People can freely share ideas and participate in decision-making, and feel that their work is valued.

- *Realize personal fulfillment*
  Maybe you're dissatisfied with your current job or where you are in life. Maybe you want a new and different experience, or a real sense of accomplishment. Working for a not-for-profit can bring you a sense of personal fulfillment.

- *Learn new skills*
  Particularly in a small organization, where the lines between job positions are not always well defined and responsibilities overlap, you could have the opportunity to learn new skills, for example, in developing, implementing, and managing a program.

- *More opportunities for career advancement*
  Not-for-profit organizations need to recruit, train, and promote a future generation of leaders to replace those who will be retiring or leaving for other reasons. This will open up more opportunities for people to advance in their careers, either in their current organization or by moving to another organization.

- *More career choices*
  The recession that began in late 2007 temporarily slowed but will not stop the continued growth of not-for-profit organizations, both in number and size. This will offer more choices for people going into the not-for-profit sector.

- *Not-for-profits value business skills*
  At one time not-for-profit organizations would have looked askance at hiring people from the for-profit sector. In recent years, however, not-for-profit organizations have come to realize that CPAs and others from the for-profit sector bring valuable experience and skills to their work, for example, in helping not-for-profits to stay on a solid financial footing.

- *Not-for-profits are innovative*
  Like entrepreneurs in the for-profit sector, the founders and leaders of not-for-profit organizations are innovators who have creative ideas for new services. SingleStopUSA (singlestopusa.org) was started as a not-for-profit because the organization found that billions of dollars in government benefits for the nation's working poor go unclaimed because people are unaware of or don't know how to claim them. SingleStop began in New York, operating from storefronts in low income neighborhoods where residents could drop by and meet with counselors. Using software programs with up-to-the-minute information on government benefit programs, counselors could quickly inform people about their eligibility for

benefits such as Medicaid, child care, welfare-to-work programs, housing assistance, and food stamps as well as tax credits. Counselors then assisted them through the process of claiming their benefits. The program has worked so well that SingleStop rolled it out nationally.

* *Relationship-building opportunities*
Serving on the staff of a not-for-profit, you may have the opportunity to meet and perhaps build relationships with volunteer board members, fundraisers, CPAs and other professionals, community leaders, and others who support the organization. You can build professional connections and networks that could help you advance in your career. Some of the people you meet could become mentors, provide referrals if you decide to seek a new job, or hire you somewhere along the line.

Disadvantages

Like every sector where CPAs work, not-for-profit has its drawbacks, such as the following:

* *Pay compared with for-profit sector*
Pay in not-for-profit organizations generally does not match that of for-profit companies because not-for-profits are under pressure from donors to invest every possible dollar to meet the needs of clients and to keep operating costs including salaries at a minimum, among other reasons.[27] This is an issue for prospective employees. A 2008 survey of not-for-profit job seekers by Commongood Careers, a recruiting firm for the not-for-profit sector, found that salary schedules made 70 percent of the respondents hesitant about pursuing long-term careers in the not-for-profit sector. Even so, not-for-profits can compete if they have a mission that excites prospective employees, Commongood noted, and if they are diligent about providing vacation time and offer flexible work programs, both of which are important to job seekers.

* *Burnout risk*
The turbocharged people who work for not-for-profit organizations are willing to put in long hours and sacrifice personal time for the organization's mission, but they are also at risk of burning out and leaving. As the Commongood study noted, not-for-profits must be conscientious about giving employees time away from the job.

* *The work environment*
One of the attractions of not-for-profit organizations is their collaborative environment, and one of the drawbacks is, well, their collaborative environment. Everyone is consulted, ideas are deliberated, discussions go on, meetings stretch out, and decisions are slow to be made, a process that can be frustrating.

* *The pressure to service clients*
The clients of not-for-profits depend on them for food, shelter, health care, job training and placement, and other essential services. That puts enormous pressure on not-for-profits to deliver. If they fall short, clients may not receive immunizations, or have difficulty finding shelter, or miss an opportunity to get a job.

* *Differences in measuring success*
For-profit companies measure results in profits, share prices or other commonly accepted benchmarks. Not-for-profit organizations have different measures of success, some that may only be evident over time. Is helping illiterate adults to acquire basic reading skills a success? Or is it in helping them to read well enough to get a job or take a driver's license exam. Or to read well enough to take a college admissions exam and earn a college diploma? Depending on how success is measured, it could be years before the outcome is known.

* *The pressure to raise money*
For-profit companies make money from selling products and services. Not-for-profit organizations have to constantly raise money to deliver services to their clients. And the better they are at providing services, the more the demand, and the greater the need for money. To achieve their revenue

---

27 "Transitioning to the Nonprofit Sector," Laura Gassner Otting, Kaplan Publishing, New York, 2007.

goals, some not-for-profit units have established profit-making subsidiaries that generate income from the sale of goods or services. Although revenue from such profit-making ventures is taxable, they can still generate significant after-tax income.

- *The squeeze between need and resources*
  Many not-for-profits are constantly squeezed between the need to serve their constituencies and the limited resources to meet those needs. Organizations constantly have to make do with less-than-optimal resources. This has inspired creativity and innovation in ringing the most value from limited funds, but it can also be frustrating to constantly scrimp.

Positions in a Nonprofit

Just as in the for-profit sector, the structure of an organization in the not-for-profit sector depends on its size. A large not-for-profit has a formal hierarchy, defined roles, and large staffs. Professionals in a large organization may include not only CPAs but also lawyers, economists, and other professionals. A small organization has a more informal structure, overlapping roles and responsibilities, and a limited staff.

The following are among the positions in a large organization. Most could be filled by CPAs, such as CEO or CFO, whereas some such as a marketing director are likely to be filled by professionals with other backgrounds.

Executive director (CEO or President): Provides leadership in accomplishing the organization's mission, develops and implements the strategic plan, and oversees the budget, program development, fund-raising, communications, human resources, and other operations. Appointed by the organization's board of directors, and, depending on the organization's policies, may be a member of the board.

Associate Director (or Assistant Director, Deputy Director, or COO): Collaborates with the executive director on strategy, programs, fund-raising and other activities. Manages day-to-day operations of organization. Fills in as needed to allow executive director to focus on specific issues such as fund-raising.

Director of Development (Director of Fundraising): Collaborates with executive director in planning, implementation, and evaluation of fund-raising programs. Responsible for raising funds through major gifts, capital campaigns, events, phone and direct mail, membership solicitations, and other sources.

Director of Programs: Advises executive director in development of the organization's programs for the delivery of its services. Responsible for creating, designing, implementing, prioritizing, and evaluating programs.

CFO (or Director of Finance): Assists executive director with strategic and business planning, fund-raising plans and strategies, program implementation and evaluation, and other strategic functions. Handles banking relationships, financing, and cash flow requirements. Oversees accounting and reporting processes and procedures, internal audits, budgeting, payroll, accounts payable and receivable, and tax filings. Oversees grant disbursement (in a foundation).

Director of Marketing/Communications: Advises executive director on strategic communications planning. Oversees the organization's marketing, public relations, public affairs, publications, web development and design, and external communications with donors, clients, and the public.

Director of Human Resources: Assists and advises executive director in addressing the organization's human resources issues and needs. Develops and implements strategic plan for the recruiting, hiring, training and retaining of managers and employees. Administers personnel and compensation policies. Manages recruitment and training of volunteers. Ensures compliance with government laws and regulations

In many small not-for-profits, and some large ones, some of these functions may be combined. In a small not-for-profit, the executive director or president may directly manage development, programs, finance, human resources, and other functions with the assistance of a few staff people. The organization may employ part time workers for jobs such as bookkeeping or it may outsource such work. In some large organizations, the CFO or finance director may be responsible for administration, human resources, and information systems as well as finance.

Managers: Managers assist directors in overseeing programs, development, human resources and other functions, for example, a manager may be assigned to a single large program or a select number of smaller programs. In small not-for-profits, a single manager might assist a lone director with a range of activities. Other organizations may be too small to have managers.

Associates (or assistants): People joining a large organization as associates, an entry level position, work for managers on accounting and finance, programs, development, communications, or other activities. In small not-for-profits, associates do a little of everything.

Example of Job Listing for Accounting Associate

The following is part of a job listing for an accounting associate, in this case with a large conservation organization.

Accounting Associate

Reports to: Accounting Manager

Position Summary: The Accounting Associate will be responsible for providing general support to the accounting team. S/he will be responsible for data processing, posting, reconciliation, and filing in accordance with organizational documentation procedures. S/he will also assist the Accounting Manager with special projects.

Qualifications:

- Bachelor's degree in Accounting or comparable work experience;
- 2-5 years' experience working in an accounting department with demonstrated experience working with an accounting system;

- Strong computer skills (MS office with advanced proficiency in Excel required); knowledge of Solomon accounting software a plus;
- Ability to interact professionally with culturally and linguistically diverse staff and clients;
- Ability to work within a team structure as well as independently, take initiative and be attentive to detail;
- Dependability and excellent organizational skills

Salary: Commensurate with experience. Competitive benefits package provided.

Work of CPAs in Nonprofit Organizations

Only through sound planning, budgeting, and financial management, will not-for-profit organizations have the financial resources to accomplish their goals, and that is where CPAs come in. They assist with or manage accounting, internal auditing and tax reporting, and other financial activities, work with people at every level of an organization, and serve in every capacity from CFO to entry level accountant. In small not-for-profits, they may be a one person finance department, managing all aspects of the organization's finances, and they may be called on to help in other areas as well, such as writing a grant proposal or planning a fund-raising drive.

If you joined a not-for-profit from a company or business, you would see that some of the work CPAs perform is similar to what you find in the corporate world. But as tax-exempt entities, and organizations that derive much of their revenue through donations and grants, not-for-profit organizations

> ### Not-for-Profits Myths
>
> *"The nonprofit sector is for people who could not make it in the business world."*
>
> This is one of the most common myths about not-for-profit organizations, according to Idealist—Action Without Borders, a Web site (idealist.org) that facilitates connections between individuals and institutions that are interested in improving their communities.
>
> In fact, according to Idealist.org, "nonprofit organizations are full of intelligent people with a passion for their work (many with graduate degrees and years of experience in the sector). Many people switch between the nonprofit, government, and private sectors during their careers."
>
> For more not-for-profit myths and myth busting, visit the Idealist Web site at www.idealist.org/ioc/learn/scc/Myths.pdf.

also have unique accounting, auditing, and tax reporting requirements. The Financial Accounting Standards Board (FASB) is the primary standards setter for not-for-profits. FASB's *Accounting Standards Codification*™ is the source of authoritative generally accepted accounting principles (GAAP) for not-for-profit organizations. Although the codification does not change GAAP, it introduces a new structure—one that is organized in an easily accessible, user-friendly online research system.[28] The federal Office of Management and Budget has standards and guidelines for not-for-profits that receive federal grants. And the IRS has its reporting requirements. To manage all of their reporting and compliance responsibilities, many not-for-profit organizations use accounting and tax software programs designed for nonprofit use.

---

28 "FASB Approves Accounting Standards Codification™; Launched July 1," *The CPA Letter*, AICPA, July 2009. www.aicpa.org/download/cpaltr/2009_07/cpaltr-jul09.pdf

Among other responsibilities, CPAs assist not-for-profits with the following:

- *Cash management*
  Like businesses, not-for-profit organizations prepare cash flow statements that look at cash received less cash spent. They also prepare cash flow projections. Together, the cash flow statement and projections enable an organization to manage its cash.
- *Account management*
  Not-for-profit organizations use accounts to track program activity or transactions directly related to providing services to clients and members. They also use accounts to track supporting activity or transactions common to all programs such as general administrative costs. Not-for-profits are particularly concerned with trying to minimize costs for support services and using any cost savings to help fund programs.
- *Budgeting*
  Not-for-profit organizations prepare operating budgets, or annual budgets, of planned revenue and expenses for the coming year as well as various other budgets including cash budgets, capital budgets (for major assets such as equipment and buildings), proposal budgets (for fund-raising), and program budgets to plan the costs of delivering services to clients. Each program has a separate budget to enable the not-for-profit to track its investment in individual programs. This is especially important with restricted grants, or those dedicated to specific programs, that require the nonprofit to closely monitor spending for that program.
- *Financial statements and analysis*
  CPAs prepare a not-for-profit organization's cash flow statement, income statement (statement of activities), balance sheet (statement of financial position) and other statements. They may also prepare reports for lenders or donors to provide assurances that loans will be repaid or donations are invested as the donor expected. They are called upon to evaluate the financial feasibility of projects and the cost effectiveness of achieving goals. Sometimes they are asked to help write grant proposals.

- *Internal audit*
  CPAs conduct or assist with internal audits to evaluate the operating effectiveness of an organization's internal controls, examine and verify information provided through an entity's financial statements, and detecting and preventing fraud and abuse. CPAs may work with independent auditors in conducting audits of a not-for-profit organization.
- *Tax*
  CPAs advise and assist not-for-profits with tax reporting and compliance under IRS regulations and applicable state tax laws. They also ensure that an organization complies with applicable tax laws in raising capital from donors and financing its investments in its various programs. They may work with donors (and the donors' accountants) to create structures such as annuities to fund the organization. They also may assist outside public accounting firms in conducting audits of not-for-profits.

Skill Sets

One of the benefits of being a CPA is that you have portable skills: you can use many of the same skills in working for (or volunteering for) a not-for-profit organization that you would use in public accounting or government. These include the following:

- *Analytical:* You are able to interpret and explain complex information.
- *Communication:* You are able to speak and write effectively, impart information or ideas, listen carefully, and understand others.
- *Interpersonal:* You have a real interest in other people, you get along with people of diverse backgrounds, and you work effectively with others.
- *Learning:* You are inquisitive and eager to learn, you are able to acquire and apply knowledge, learn from experience, and learn from others.
- *Teaming:* You work well in teams, you are sensitive to the interests of others, understand roles and

responsibilities, share credit, put the group's priorities before own, and know when to lead and when to follow.

- *Leadership:* You show leadership qualities that will help you advance in an organization. You are self-aware—you know your strengths and weaknesses. You understand the interests of others. You are able to influence people and you act decisively to solve problems.
- *Sector specific skills:* As a CPA working for (or volunteering for) a not-for-profit organization, you must be knowledgeable not only about GAAP generally but also about GAAP as it applies to not-for-profit organizations, for example, in accounting for fund-raising, or money spent on programs. (The appendix lists some books about GAAP for not-for-profits.) In addition, you have to be knowledgeable about federal tax law and IRS regulations governing not-for-profit organizations as well as applicable state tax laws.
- *Adaptable:* While you would bring these portable skills to your work for a nonprofit, you would have to adapt them to the not-for-profit environment. CPAs and other professionals who come from the for-profit sector or right out of school sometimes have difficulty communicating with professionals who come from not-for-profit backgrounds. CPAs are focused on the numbers, which measure results, and, ultimately the organization's financial performance. Professionals in not-for-profits are focused, above all, on the mission. To communicate effectively with people in the organization, CPAs need to fully understand and appreciate the organization's mission and strategic goals.[29]

How to Learn About Careers in the Nonprofit Sector

With more than a million not-for-profit organizations of all sizes in the United States, and organizations providing many different educational, environmental, health, social, and other services, the not-for-profit sector offers multiple career and job opportunities. But how do you decide if you might be interested in a career in this sector, and, if so, how do you find a job that's right for you?

To answer these questions, you first need to do some research to learn more about the not-for-profit world. Here are some suggestions:

- *Read up on the not-for-profit sector:* Many books, articles, Web sites, social network sites, and other sources of information cover not-for-profits. (The appendix lists some sources.) From these, you can learn about the overall not-for-profit sector, individual organizations, careers with not-for-profits, and much more. As noted earlier in this chapter, the NCCS provides in-depth information on the different not-for-profit categories such as public and societal services and other information. The Nonprofit Almanac (updated annually), available from the Urban Institute or bookstores, details not-for-profit revenues by type and amount, contributions, employment, expenses, and outlays as well as other essential facts about not-for-profits.
- *Talk to the insiders*
  Talk to the people who work for not-for-profits, especially CPAs. Perhaps someone in your family, or a friend or colleague, might be able to put you in touch with someone working for a not-for-profit. You can also talk to people who have previously worked for not-for-profit organizations: retirees, people now working in the for-profit sector or government, and others. Also talk to CPAs who volunteer to provide accounting services to not-for-profits.
- *Talk to teachers and students at your school:*
  If your college has a school or department or offers some classes that prepare students for careers in the not-for-profit sector, you can talk to the school's teachers and students about career opportunities.

---

29 "CPAs, Nonprofits, and the Art of Communication," James Sullivan, CPA, AICPA *CPA Insider,* June 8, 2009. www.cpa2biz.com/Content/media/PRODUCER_CONTENT/Newsletters/Articles_2009/CPA/June/Art_of_Communication.jsp

- *Join professional societies*
  Join a professional society such as the Young Nonprofit Professionals Network (ynpn.org). It was created to help develop the next generation of leaders in the not-for-profit sector.
- *Volunteer*
  One of the best ways to learn about the not-for-profit sector is to work for a not-for-profit. An organization in your community could use help with setting up a bookkeeping system, or preparing a budget, or other accounting needs. Organizations might also need help in providing services to their clients, such as helping low income wage earners file tax returns and claim refunds. Contact local not-for-profit organizations where you live or attend school about volunteer work. Or contact national organizations for not-for-profit volunteers such as Accountants in the Public Interest, an organization that matches up CPAs, retired CPAs, recent accounting graduates, and accounting students with not-for-profit organizations and others who need but cannot afford accounting services. Another option is to join a student organization such as Students Consulting for Non-Profit Organizations (scno.org), a national organization of undergraduate students committed to developing communities through pro-bono consulting engagements with nonprofit organizations.

Is a Career in the Nonprofit Sector for You?

After you have done some research, you can start thinking about whether a not-for-profit career may be right for you. You can begin with a rigorous self-assessment of your personal and career aspirations. Some questions to consider:

- What issues matter the most to you?
- Who are the people you most admire? Why?
- How could you achieve greater personal fulfillment and satisfaction?

- What volunteer work have you done?
- What organizations have you actively participated in?
- What extracurricular activities, workshops and public meetings have you been involved in?
- What would you like to change in your community, the nation, and the world?
- If you had $100,000, how would you spend it to affect change?
- If you were to start a not-for-profit organization, what would be its mission?

If, upon thoughtful consideration of these questions, you think you might be interested in a not-for-profit career, the next question is where you might want to work in the vast not-for-profit sector. The following questions will help you narrow your search:

What area of the not-for-profit sector do you want to work in?

Somewhere in the vast and diverse not-for-profit sector, you may find an organization whose mission and goals align with your interests in a advancing a social cause, solving a social problem, and effecting change.

But where?

As previously described, the NCCS has two systems, the NTEE, and the NPC System for classifying not-for-profit organizations, and you can use them to learn about different not-for-profit subsectors, missions and programs and decide which interest you. On the NCCS home page (nccs.urban.org), click on "Classification" and "Tools."

For example, in the NPC program, the "Education" category has dozens of subcategories such as Early Childhood Education, Adult Education, After School Enrichment, and much more, together with descriptions of

The Not-for-Profit Board

A not-for-profit is governed by a board of directors, usually unpaid volunteers who contribute their time and talents to promote the organization's mission, and usually make a financial contribution to the organization. Many CPAs serve on not-for-profit boards. Board members have a legal and fiduciary responsibility for the organization's governance, and they are accountable to the people served by the organization, its members and other constituents, as well as the public. The board sets the direction for the organization, ensures it has the resources to carry out its mission, oversees the affairs of the organization, and works closely with the organization's chief executive to accomplish the organization's mission. Among other responsibilities, board members are expected to stay informed about the organization's mission, services, policies, and programs, be well prepared for board and committee meetings, suggest possible nominees to the board, keep up-to-date on developments in the organization's field, and follow conflict-of-interest and confidentiality policies. Members also are expected to assist the board in carrying out its fiduciary responsibilities, such as reviewing the organization's annual financial statements.

What does it take to be an effective board member? *BoardSource*, a not-for-profit organization "dedicated to building exceptional not-for-profit boards and inspiring board service," suggests the following qualities:*

- Ability to listen, analyze, think clearly and creatively, and work well with people individually and in a group.
- Willingness to prepare for and attend board and committee meetings, ask questions, take responsibility and follow through on a given assignment.
- Contribute personal and financial resources in a generous way according to circumstances.
- Open doors in the community.
- Evaluate oneself.
- Have or develop certain skills such as the ability to solicit funds or recruit board members and other volunteers.
- Possess honesty, sensitivity to and tolerance of differing views, a friendly, responsive, and patient approach, community-building skills, personal integrity, a developed sense of values, concern for the organization's development, and a sense of humor.

Whereas some not-for-profit organizations prefer members with years of experience in business or other fields, others may be interested in recruiting young CPAs and other professionals who can contribute new expertise, fresh ideas, a different perspective, enthusiasm, and a strong commitment to the organization's mission. You may want to consider serving on a not-for-profit board sometime in your career. It's an opportunity to give back to the community, to gain experience as a board member and to build relationships and networks.

* "BoardSource Knowledge Center; Q&As: What are the responsibilities of individual board members?" www.boardsource.org/Knowledge.asp?ID=3.369.

each. "Dropout Programs" covers programs that provide educational services for school dropouts or which seek to prevent students of compulsory school age from dropping out of school.

What type of organization do you want to work for?

In the not–for–profit sector, you can work for public charities, the primary employer in this sector, for foundations or for other types of not–for–profits such as advocacy groups, unions, or business and professional organizations.

Public charities provide services directly to the public: a new arts program for the community, a homeless shelter, a center for abused women or children, a clinic offering free healthcare services, an adult learning program, a program to assist minority entrepreneurs start their own businesses and much more.

Foundations provide grants to institutions or individuals for programs in education, health, human services, societal benefits, arts and culture, and other categories. There are two types: private foundations and public foundations. In a private foundation, most of the funds come from one source, whether an individual, a family, or a corporation. A public foundation receives funds from multiple sources, which may include private foundations, individuals, government agencies, and fees for service.

Compared with jobs in public charities, foundation jobs are difficult to land. Less than 10 percent of all not-for-profit organizations are foundations, and they employ only a small percentage of the total number of people working in the not-for-profit sector. They have little turnover, and tend to hire and promote from within. So if you are set on working for a foundation, it may take longer to find work than with a public charity. You can learn more about foundations generally and individual foundations on the Web site of the Foundation Center (foundationcenter.org), a leading national authority on philanthropy.

Other types of not-for-profits are a mix of different organizations including advocacy groups, or organizations that work to influence the public or elected officials to support or oppose new legislation or change existing policies. These include organizations such as the American Teacher's Union and the National Association for the Advancement of Colored People. Depending on your interests, advocacy groups may be another source of employment.

Where do you want to work?

Do you want to work in your hometown, where you're attending school, or elsewhere? Do you want to job search in a state or region, or nationally? Or would you be interested in working for an international not-for-profit organization that has offices or is headquartered in the United States? In deciding on the scope of your search, consider the tradeoffs. Focusing on a single city or town can help you narrow your search; however, it also narrows the job possibilities. Alternatively, you can search nationally, but you will have to relocate if you find a job in another city.

What compensation do you want?

You may not earn as much as in the for-profit sector, but you do need to make enough to cover your living expenses, put some money in savings and investments, maybe pay off college loans, and take a vacation. And party occasionally.

Do you want to work for a small or large organization?

Do you want to work for a small not-for-profit such as a community-based organization that provides services to a local community? In a small organization, the environment may be more informal and collegial, with more contact among people at all levels, and more of a family feeling. You may have more flexibility, more responsibility, and do a variety of jobs. But the pay and benefits may not be as much as in a larger organization, and the job security may not be as great. Or would you prefer to work for a large organization? They usually have higher salaries and better benefits, a more formal work environment, clearly defined jobs, more opportunities for advancement, and a formal career ladder. But a large organization can be more formal, the job more narrowly defined, with less multitasking, and less contact between junior staffers and senior management and the board.

What is the organization's culture?

What's it like to work in an organization? Not surprisingly in a sector as large as not-for-profit, the culture of organizations varies widely. Some are dynamic, high energy organizations with a clear sense of mission, a passion for accomplishing the mission, a plan of action to achieve the organization's goals, and benchmarks for measuring success. Some may have lost their way: the mission is ambiguous, progress in accomplishing the mission has been slow, and people are losing their enthusiasm. Some not-for-profits are startups with dynamic leaders and energetic people. Others are long-running organizations that have ossified. Still others are long-established organizations that have redefined themselves, with a new sense of purpose.

Unless you actually work in an organization, it can be difficult to know its culture. But you can get a sense of the organization from talking to people in the not-for-profit community who are knowledgeable about the organization, and, if you can, by speaking

with people in the organization. You can also learn from studying the organization's Web site, checking not-for-profit Web sites and blogs, reading news reports about the organization, and reviewing the Form 990 tax return that registered not-for-profits are required to file with the IRS. It's available on the Web sites of some not-for-profits or on the Web site of Guidestar, (www.guidestar.com), a database of not-for-profit information. You can register and do a search of basic information about a not-for-profit free-of-charge (and a more detailed search for a fee). You could also check a library to see if it subscribes to Guidestar's information services for libraries.

Finding a Job

Now you're ready to start looking for a job. Decide on your priorities. Is geographic location most important? Then you can look for jobs in the location of your choice. Or is the field you work in the most important? Maybe you want a job in human services, and you're willing to work in a city that may not be your first choice. Once you have your priorities set, you can start your search. Here are some places to look:

- *Directories of not-for-profit organizations.* Gale, an information services provider, annually publishes *The Directory of Nonprofit Organizations*, which provides detailed information on the largest not-for-profits in the United States. It's available in print and online. You can see if your local library has it. And while you're at the library, you could also check out books, articles, and other sources of information on careers in the not-for-profit sector.
- The *Nonprofit Times* publishes a compensation and benefit report, available by subscription. See if it's available at a local library.

Not-for-Profit Educational Programs

If you plan a career in the not-for-profit sector, of if you simply want to learn more about not-for-profits, you could take a college course. According to the Bureau of Labor Statistics, in 2006 (the latest year that figures were available at publication) more than 250 colleges and universities offer courses on the management of nonprofit organizations.*

In addition:

- About 70 college programs offered noncredit courses in fund-raising and nonprofit management.
- More than 50 programs offered continuing education courses.
- About 119 schools offered at least 1 course for undergraduate credit.
- About 160 colleges and universities had at least 1 course related to management of nonprofits within a graduate department.

If you are interested in certification, American Humanics (humanics.org) offers the American Humanics Certificate in Nonprofit Leadership/Management program in collaboration with some colleges and universities. American Humanics, a not-for-profit organization, describes itself as "an innovative course of study that equips college and university students to become skilled professionals and leaders in America's nonprofit organizations." Its certification program is open to any college student, regardless of major. Among other requirements, you must earn a baccalaureate degree from any academic department, complete 17 nonprofit competences, and complete 300 or more hours of not-for-profit internships. Check the American Humanics Web site for more information on the certification program, and which colleges offer it.

* "Career Guide to Industries: Advocacy, Grantmaking and Civic Organizations," Bureau of Labor Statistics. www.bls.gov/oco/cg/cgs054.htm

- Idealist–Action Without Borders (idealist.org) has an online job listing service. You can search by state and city, area of focus such as energy conservation and green living (and many other areas), and job category (accounting and finance).
- *The Chronicle of Philanthropy*, a newspaper that covers the not-for-profit sector, has a career section where you can search for jobs by zip code and other criteria. (philanthrophy.com/jobs).
- Commongood Careers (commongoodcareers.org), a search firm for the not-for-profit sector, has a job listing service.

Other sources of not-for-profit career and job information are listed in appendix 1 of this book. Chapter 11 has more on the job hunting process.

Final Thoughts

As with careers in public accounting, government or other sectors of the profession, you owe it to yourself to research a career in the not-for-profit sector. Only then can you consider all the options and make an informed career choice. In any event, you might want to consider working as a volunteer for a not-for-profit organization while you are in college. Besides helping your community, you will get an inside look at a not-for-profit organization. In addition, not-for-profits often require several years of experience for even entry level positions, but some are flexible in defining experience. This is part of a job listing for a staff accountant with a not-for-profit:

Minimum Qualifications:

Bachelor's degree from an accredited college or university in Accounting, Finance or a related field. Two years progressively responsible accounting experience or any equivalent combination of training and experience which provides the required knowledge, skills and abilities."

Your service as a volunteer can help demonstrate to prospective employers that you are interested in the not-for-profit sector and that you have the experience for the job.

After due consideration, you may decide that you want to start your career in public accounting, but you are interested in the not-for-profit sector. You might get a job with a CPA firm whose market niche is in providing services to not-for-profit organizations. Do an online search on Yahoo or Google or other search engine for such firms in your area. If you want to start in government, you might find an agency that partners with not-for-profit organizations, for example, in building low income housing.

Then again, you don't have to go into the not-for-profit sector right out of school. You might decide to work first in public accounting, and make a switch into the not-for-profit sector sometime during your career, or when you retire. You might start with one of the largest CPA firms, which frequently provide services to not-for-profit organizations for a fee, and also may do some pro bono work. And during your career, you might volunteer to provide accounting services to a not-for-profit whose mission and programs interest you or serve on a not-for-profit board. Along the way, you may even decide that you want to start a not-for-profit organization.

In conclusion, there are many ways for you to find personally satisfying and professionally rewarding connections with the not-for-profit sector, whether you work full time in the sector, volunteer your services, or start a not-for-profit organization. As a CPA, your knowledge and experience will be highly valued by not-for-profit organizations, and your services will be much in demand.

Wrap-up

In this chapter you learned the following:

- If you have a passion for a social cause, and a deep desire to help others, you can find a rewarding career as a CPA with a not-for-profit organization.
- CPAs assist not-for-profits with a variety of activities from developing programs to preparing budgets to managing spending.
- CPAs are much in demand in not-for-profit organizations, particularly in helping them to become more transparent and accountable.
- If you join a not-for-profit organization, you will work with people who share your passion for a cause, work in a collegial environment, realize personal fulfillment, and enjoy other benefits.
- Working for a not-for-profit has its challenges, such as the constant pressure to provide services to people who depend on the organization, limited budgets, or the lower pay vs. the private sector.
- You can learn about the not-for-profit world from reading, online research, talking to people who work for nonprofits, volunteering to work for a nonprofit, and other ways.
- You can decide where to work based on an organization's mission, size, type (public charity, foundation, or other organization) and other criteria.
- If you do your research, you can find the not-for-profit that's right for you.

Interview: Amy Coleman
Vice President of Finance and Treasurer, Kresge Foundation

Amy Coleman is vice president of finance and treasurer of The Kresge Foundation (www.kresge. org), a $ 2.8 billion private, national foundation headquartered in the Detroit suburb of Troy, Michigan. The foundation was established in 1924 by businessman and philanthropist Sebastian Spering Kresge, founder of the S. S. Kresge Company, the first chain of five-and 10-cent stores, now known as Kmart and owned by the Sears Holding Corporation. The foundation is not affiliated with the corporation.

> *"If joining a nonprofit organization fits with your goals, then find an organization whose mission you're passionate about—you must have a strong belief in the organization and what it is trying to accomplish."*

The Kresge Foundation supports non-profit organizations in six fields of interest: health, the environment, community development, arts and culture, education and human services. "Working with our grantees, we endeavor to improve the life circumstances and opportunities for poor, disadvantaged and marginalized individuals, families, and communities," the foundation states on its Web site.* "The strong desire of our founder, Sebastian Spering Kresge, 'to promote human progress,' continues to be our guiding light." In 2008 the foundation awarded 342 grants totaling $181 million.

Coleman holds an associate degree in business from St. Clair Community College, Port Huron, Michigan, and a bachelor of business administration degree in accounting from Troy's Walsh College.

How did you get interested in accounting?
I took accounting classes in high school and at St. Clair, and found that I really enjoyed it. When I transferred to Walsh College, I decided to pursue a business degree with a major in accounting, and to obtain CPA certification.

Where did you start your career?
At PricwaterhouseCoopers in Detroit. After five and a half years there, I joined the Kresge Foundation in 1995 as director of finance.

---

* "What We Do," Kresge Foundation web site. http://www.kresge.org/index.php/what/index/

What interested you in moving from public accounting to the nonprofit sector?

At PWC, I worked on audits of several private foundations, which enabled me to learn about the nonprofit world. I always had an interest in giving back to the community, and then the opportunity to join the Kresge Foundation came along. The foundation's mission greatly appealed to me. So did its strong support of community development in the Detroit area.

What are your responsibilities?

In addition to my position, our finance group consists of a controller, accounting manager, staff accountant, and administrative assistant. We are responsible for formulating financial policy and plans and for providing overall direction for the accounting, tax, insurance, budget, and treasury functions. We direct activities associated with the security of the Foundation's assets and ensure that financial transactions, policies and procedures meet its objectives and regulatory body requirements.

What do you like about your job?

It continues to change as the foundation grows and evolves. Historically, the foundation has supported fundraising campaigns to build capital projects such as libraries, hospitals, schools, museums and community centers. In 2007, we began a long-term program to expand our grant making, and we have since started a number of new programs. Recently, for example, we introduced a Community Relief Fund to make interest-free loans to human service organizations providing food, shelter, and other emergency services. We also announced two new grant award funds to directly support community health organizations in addressing critical needs for underserved populations.

What should students and practicing CPAs consider in deciding whether to join a nonprofit organization?

You need to put the question in the context of your career. What are your long-term career goals? Is community service—giving back to the community—among your goals? If joining a nonprofit organization fits with your goals, then find an organization whose mission you're passionate about—you must have a strong belief in the organization and what it is trying to accomplish.

Is public accounting experience useful if you plan to join a nonprofit?

Absolutely. Working in public accounting, even for a few years, helps you develop strong analytical skills and gives you broad exposure to different industries and companies and to different people. Likewise, in the nonprofit world, you will work with everyone from donors to grant applicants to board members, and in many different areas such as health care, education, or human services. You must have technical and analytical skills, which you can obtain by obtaining CPA certification. The CPA certification enhances your credibility with prospective employers, and prepares you for a career in many industries, including the nonprofit sector.

Interview: Allan Golston

President of the United States Program, Bill and Melinda Gates Foundation

Allan C. Golston is president of the United States Program—Bill and Melinda Gates Foundation. He leads the foundation's efforts to reduce inequities and increase access to opportunities for low income and disadvantaged Americans. He oversees the United States Program's major areas of grantmaking—education, U.S. libraries, Pacific Northwest, special initiatives, and advocacy. Golston, who joined the foundation in 1999, most recently served as the foundation's chief financial and administrative officer. Golston's professional background is in public accounting, finance, and health care. He holds a master's degree in business administration from Seattle University and a bachelor's degree in accounting from the University of Colorado. He is an active community volunteer and serves on the boards of regional and national organizations.

> *"I had an amazing accounting professor. . . . She opened a window into accounting that I never realized existed."*

Why did you study for an undergraduate degree in accounting?

I intended to get a degree in mathematics and computer technology, but in my freshman year, I took an accounting course out of curiosity. Fortunately, I had an amazing accounting professor. She was smart, pushed us hard, and made it fun and interesting. She opened a window into accounting that I never realized existed. By the end of that course, I was hooked. I signed up for as many accounting courses as I could.

Why did you decide to earn an MA in business administration?

I worked in business for over 15 years before going back to grad school, so I had a strong base of experience. I chose an MBA because I wanted to learn more about the underlying theories behind all my work experience in a more advanced and rigorous way, and I wanted to learn from and contribute to the learning of others that had similar backgrounds and interests.

Why did you start your career in public accounting?

Two reasons. First, what was then "The Big Eight" was the aspiration of almost every accounting student—including me. Second, and most importantly, I recognized that in public accounting, I would be exposed to an array of business challenges across many industries through the lens of my profession. I realized that I couldn't buy that type of experience in that compressed amount of time. I realized that I would learn more at a public accounting firm than I would learn in going directly into industry in an equivalent time frame. All that was true for me. It was hard work, it was full of stress, and I learned more about business, leadership, solving problems and management than I even hoped. I wouldn't trade the experience for anything.

How has your education and experience in accounting helped you in your career?

It has been a huge factor. As I mentioned, I got a compressed amount of experience and knowledge from my public accounting experience, and my education provided the underlying theories and pushed my thinking and knowledge even farther. It has made a huge difference in affording me opportunity. I will also mention that I have worked for—both in public accounting and in industry—some incredible leaders. I always showed up as a contributor and a willing student, and the leaders that I have worked for were a significant influence on me. Education and experience are essential, but without leadership, education and experience can only take one so far.

What is your career advice to students who are thinking of studying accounting in college?

It is both a great career, and one of the best preparations you can get to work in business. Mastery of concepts matter, so study hard and make sure you not only have the conceptual knowledge, but the practical application of the knowledge. Don't think of it in terms of accounting only, but as a window into how organizations work. That will keep you thinking strategically. With this education and experience, it creates amazing opportunities. You can run anything—from the private to the public to the nonprofit sectors.

Chapter 8

Sole Practitioner: Starting Your Own Business

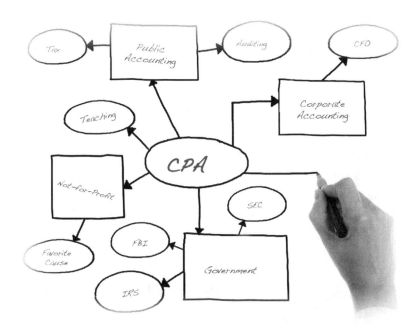

> "You have to be passionate about what you do."
>
> DeAnn Hill, Founder • DeAnn Hill CPA

Introduction

Eugene Price, CPA, started an accounting firm in 1971 after he graduated from New York's Baruch College. Today, he's the senior partner of the firm he founded, now known as RRC Price CPAs, located in Bardonia, New York, north of New York City.

DeAnn Hill worked for CPA firms for a few years, and then in 1983, founded DeAnn Auman Hill CPA, a small firm in Baxter, Kansas, that she has owned and managed ever since.

Ronald Durkin, CPA, worked a total of 30 years as a special agent for the FBI and a partner with a Big 4 firm. In 2008, he founded Durkin Forensic Inc., a forensic accounting firm with offices in San Diego and metropolitan Los Angeles. (Interviews with these three CPAs can be found on pages 288, 285, and 342, respectively.)

As these examples show, CPAs have started their own firms right out of school, after only a few years in public accounting, or after many years in public accounting, and, in Durkin's case, government service as well.

Thousands of small CPA firms are located across the United States—you can find them in just about every city and community. Starting a small firm is an exciting—and extremely challenging—career choice for a CPA, and this chapter discusses why you might want to start such a firm, some questions to consider before going out on your own, and how to get started.

Small CPA Firms

Although there is no hard and fast definition of a "small" CPA firm, one way of categorizing such firms is by their number of employees. According to the U.S. Census Bureau, there were more than 53,000 CPA firms in the United States in 2006 (the latest year that figures are available). These ranged from firms with no employees (sole proprietorship) to the largest firms with 2,500 employees or more.

Table 8-1 presents a breakdown of the number of U.S. CPA firms employing up to 99 employees. The smallest firms, numbering 36,725, accounted for about half the total number of U.S. CPA firms.

Table 8-1: *U.S. CPA Firms by Employment Size 2006*[*]

Employment: Size of Enterprise	Firms	Paid Employees	Annual Payroll
0-4 employees	36,725	63,593	2,495,625,000
5-9 employees	10,368	67,127	2,654,033,000
10-19 employees	4,286	56,025	2,786,885,000
20-99 employees	2,062	74,446	4,657,784,000

[*] U.S. Census Bureau: Statistics of U.S. Businesses; 2006; Offices of certified public accountants United States; U.S.—Offices of Certified Public Accountants—by Employment Size of Enterprise. www.census.gov/epcd/ susb/2006/us/ US541211.HTM

Services of Small CPA Firms

As a group, small CPA firms provide many of the same assurance, tax, and advisory services as the largest CPA firms. Individually, however, small firms usually focus on certain clients, services, industries, and geographic markets. Clients of small firms include individuals, private corporations, small businesses, partnerships, not-for-profit organizations, government agencies, professional services firms (such as law firms), professional or trade organizations, and others. Some firms may work mainly with small businesses or not-for-profit entities, in industries such as real estate, and serve clients mainly in a particular city, community, or region.

The services provided by small firms include:

- *Assurance services:* The firm attests to the reasonableness of disclosures, freedom from material misstatements, and adherence to generally accepted accounting principles in the financial statements of a company, small business, or other organization. A firm may provide different levels of assurance services, such as the following:
  — *Compilation:* The firm prepares a client's financial statements without any assurance about the information provided by the client.
  — *Limited assurance:* The firm, through a series of inquiries and analyses, provides a limited form of assurance concerning a client's financial statements.
  — *Audit:* The firm conducts a complete audit of a client's financial statements and the transactions behind them. (The audit function was discussed in Chapter 1.) For various reasons, many small firms do not provide audits of SEC-registered companies, for example, if the firm does not want the liability risk of an audit or to commit time and resources to performing audits.

Within the broad assurance area, small firms may provide specific services. For example, a firm may advise and assist a company with managing special purpose audits. These are designed to help a company bring a systematic, disciplined approach to evaluating and improving the effectiveness of risk management, control, and governance processes. Better risk management can help a company with mitigating risks ranging from excessive costs in doing business to inaccuracies in financial reporting to fraud. Another example of a service provided by a firm is to conduct an audit of a specific aspect of a business, such as an employee benefit plan. A third example is a financial analysis. A firm analyzes a company's financial statements and other information to prepare reports for senior management. These reports are used in making business decisions, such as whether to seek a bank loan or acquire another business.

- *Tax services:* These are designed to assist companies to minimize tax risks such as underreporting of taxes and to maximize tax opportunities such as the use of tax incentives. Among them are the following:
  — *Tax preparation and reporting:* A firm assists businesses, individuals, and other clients with preparing and filing federal, state, and local tax returns.
  — *Tax compliance:* Advise companies in managing the complexities and risks of federal, state, and local tax compliance.
  — *Tax efficiency:* Assist companies to manage their tax functions more efficiently, such as improving the use of computer software and systems in preparing tax returns.
  — *Tax planning:* Develop the appropriate tax structure (for example, limited liability corporation, subchapter S corporation, C corporation). Design tax deferral strategies (for example, exchanges, installment sales, mergers, and reorganizations).

- *Advisory services:* In addition to assurance and tax services, CPA firms provide a variety of advisory services to companies, businesses and other clients. These include the following:
  — Bankruptcy reorganization: Advise a company in reorganizing in bankruptcy proceedings in order to achieve strategic goals such as resolving outstanding debt, settling legal disputes, or securing new investors in the postbankruptcy company.
  — Business advisory: Advise businesses on their plans and strategies, for example, to launch new products or provide new services, buy or sell assets, raise capital, or form alliances or partnerships.
  — Business interruption: Natural disasters such as floods as well as electric power or telecommunications disruptions and other events can interrupt a company's operations. A CPA firm can assist a company to estimate the financial costs to the company and prepare claims.
  — Business valuation: Assist companies to value their businesses, for example, in preparation for a merger or sale, or to obtain bank financing.
  — Due diligence: Assist with preparing and ensuring accuracy of financial information required for an acquisition, merger, sale, or other transaction.
  — Develop systems: Assist companies in developing and selecting systems and technology for financial information and books and records.
  — Estate planning: Assist individuals in the planning, administration, and orderly disposition of their estates, including steps to minimize estate taxes.
  — Expert opinion: Provide companies, shareholders, attorneys, courts, and others with an independent, expert opinion for the valuation of an asset or business in order to resolve a commercial dispute, a dispute with investors, or other purposes.
  — Financial planning: For individuals, this could include assisting with establishing financial goals, budgeting, investment planning and other services. For companies and businesses, this could include assistance with preparing financial forecasts, including the cash required for future operations and investments and how it will be raised.
  — Forensic accounting: Conduct forensic investigations to identify vulnerabilities and manage risks, uncover fraud and support companies and their attorneys in investigations, mediation, lawsuits, and other work.
  — Human capital: Advise on recruiting, training and retaining talent; complying with employment laws and regulations; structuring compensation and benefits; and other employer issues.
  — Information technology: Install, maintain, and advise on accounting, auditing, and tax software and systems.
  — Restructuring: Assist companies to restructure their business operations and balance sheets to mitigate the adverse impact of such problems as cash flow shortages, falling share prices or diminished margins, or underperforming operations.
  — Succession planning: Assist family owned businesses to plan the handover of the business from one generation to the next.
  — Workouts: Assist companies in loan workouts (loan restructurings) with their lenders. These workouts are intended to avoid defaults and keep financing in place.
  — Venture capital: Assist an entrepreneur to obtain capital to start a business or an established company to secure financing for research and development of new products.

In addition, clients may outsource certain work to CPA firms such as bookkeeping, payroll processing, and quarterly tax filings, bill payment, customer invoicing and other work. Some firms maintain the books and records of small clients. Firms may also provide accounting staff to work temporarily at a client's facilities on certain projects such as helping to prepare year-end financial statements or assist with a business valuation.

Why Start a CPA Firm?

To start a CPA firm, you must have startup capital, technical skills, and skills in managing a business, marketing your services, and building and maintaining client relationships. When you are just getting started, you can expect to work long hours without the benefit of a paycheck from an employer. The demands on your time and energy are enormous. And sometimes you may wonder what you are getting into. You must be organized, disciplined and committed. You should develop a formal business plan (discussed subsequently). Starting a business is not easy, and it's not for everyone, but that hasn't discouraged CPAs from going ahead. These are some of the reasons why CPAs are drawn to entrepreneurship:

Take charge: Starting a business is all on you. You most likely will seek advice and assistance from others, but you make the decisions, and you're accountable for them. You decide everything from how you will line up financing to how you will market your services and bring in clients to how much you will charge. And that's the way you want it.

Provide services that clients value: Through the services you provide, you help clients to solve business problems, capitalize on business opportunities, address tax issues, plan their estates, and much more. You can't bill and collect unless you provide value added services.

Build client relationships: Over time, you develop strong relationships with clients, who come to see you not simply as a service provider but as a trusted business advisor. These are clients who could be with your firm for years.

Build your business: You slowly build a stable, growing business that has a solid client base, a strong balance sheet, and consistent cash flow. You may take on new clients, hire employees, and perhaps bring on a partner.

Secure your financial future: Over time, you invest some of your profits from the business in building your investment and retirement portfolio, planning your estate, and perhaps funding an endowment for a not-for-profit institution in healthcare, education, or other fields.

Achieve work and life balance: As your business grows, you gradually cut back from your frenetic pace at the start to a normal work week. Sure, you put in more hours during tax season, but you take time off during other parts of the year. And you spend more time with family and friends, enjoying recreational activities, reading a book or perhaps taking a class.

Work where you live: You decide to start a business in the city or community where you live. You may start by working at home, and with a few clients, and eventually open an office and take on new business.

Give back to your community: As a business owner, you develop strong ties with your community. You may provide pro bono services to a not-for-profit organization and join the board of another. You join local civic, professional, and community organizations and participate in their activities. You may teach an accounting class at a local community college. Through getting to know people in your community, you build professional and personal networks, win new clients, and find new employees for your company.

Starting a CPA Firm: Is It Right for You?

Do you think you might be interested in starting your own firm? Before you can answer that question, you need to learn more about what's involved. You can start by reading books and articles, and perusing Web sites, for information on starting a business generally, and starting a CPA firm specifically.

For information on starting a CPA firm, go to the "PCPS Practice Center" on the American Institute for Certified Public Accountants (AICPA's) Web site (pcps.aicpa.org) and search for "Starting Your Own CPA Practice Planning Checklist."[1] This is a detailed list of what you need to do to get started. The AICPA also publishes "The Management of an Accounting Practice Handbook," or MAP Handbook, which includes guidance on starting your own firm. You could see if your local college or other library has a copy.

In addition to your own reading and research, you might take a class on starting a business, possibly through a community college, the local offices of the Small Business Administration, or another source. (For links to local SBA offices, go to the SBA Local Resources page at http://sba.gov/local resources/.)

Also, take a look at the Web sites of some small CPA firms. Learn about their people, services, and the value they provide to their clients. You can look up firms in your area through online directories such as yellowpages.com.

Most importantly, talk to CPAs who have started their own businesses. Ask them how they got started, what challenges they had to overcome, and what they learned from the experience. Ask for their advice on how you can start your business.

To connect with the owners of small firms, ask people you know—family, friends, current or former teachers or classmates, people you work with, and others—if they know any owners. You could also meet them through your membership in professional organizations such as state CPA societies and the AICPA.

Small Businesses: The Hot Sector of the U.S. Economy

If you decide to start your own CPA firm, you will be part of the hottest sector of the U.S. economy—small businesses. According to the U.S. Small Business Administration, most U.S. businesses are small businesses, or those employing fewer than 500 workers. They employ just over half of all private sector employees, and account for about 44 percent of total U.S. private payroll. Small businesses have generated nearly two-thirds of net new jobs over the past 15 years.[*]

* Small Business Administration Office of Advocacy, *The Small Business Advocate*, Frequently Asked Questions, August-September 2009. www.sba.gov/advo/aug-sep09.pdf

---

1 http://pcps.aicpa.org/Resources/Starting+a+CPA+Practice

It's not uncommon to work for someone and start your own practice on a part-time basis (discussed under "Getting Started").

Self-assessment

If you think you might be interested in starting a firm, you need to do a candid self-appraisal to test your readiness to go out on your own. Here are a few key questions to consider:

Do you have the motivation and personality to start and manage a CPA firm?

Starting a business will be a real test of your character. So talk to people who know you well—your spouse, partner, family, friends, classmates, and others—and ask them whether they think you're ready to go out on your own. Now look in the mirror, clean off the smudges, and ask yourself the same question. Others can offer their insights, but only you can decide whether it's "go" or "no go."

Do you have the experience to start a CPA firm?

You could start a firm right after you graduate from college, but experience is a great teacher. Working for a CPA firm for at least a few years would give you a practical understanding of how a firm works.

Do you have the ability to market your firm?

No matter how good your technical skills, you must be able to sell your professional services. To do this, you have to develop professional relationships, build a network of people who can refer business to you, communicate effectively, and persuade prospects to do business with you. You have to close the sale.

Do your spouse or partner and your family support your decision to start a business?

It's important to know, because you may not see your loved ones much while you're toiling at the midnight hour trying to get your business started. And when your business does take off, be sure to buy them a nice dinner at their favorite restaurant. It's the least you can do.

Do you have the financial means to weather a start up period?

Before you can answer that question, you need to estimate the costs of starting up and running your business, and how long it will take to bring in clients. It could take awhile. Be prepared to go four to six months without any income from your fledgling business.[2] Then you need to prepare an estimate of how much revenue your firm will generate—not much at first, but presumably more over time. Once you've prepared cost and revenue forecasts, you can determine how much capital you will need to get started.

Next question: Are you willing to risk most of your money from savings and investments to start your business? Can you borrow from your family? Can you can tap some of your friends for startup capital. At least you'll find out who your friends really are. Are there other ways to finance your startup? Should you take out a home equity loan? Arrange a business loan from your bank? Many entrepreneurs use credit cards to help finance their startup businesses. These usually are easier to obtain than bank loans, and not subject to as many conditions; for example, credit card

---

2 "Do You Have What It Takes to go Solo?," Trina Steward Quinn, CPA, PhD, assistant professor of accountancy, Arkansas State University, Jonesboro, Arkansas, *The Practicing CPA*, March 1999.

users do not have to account for where the money went. But entrepreneurs also run the risk of taking on too much credit card debt that could put the business at risk.[3] Wherever the money comes from, make sure you will have enough. You don't want to find yourself running severely short of startup capital before the revenue starts to flow.

Are you prepared to make financial sacrifices while you get your business up and running?

Can you cut your spending on food? Entertainment? Skip that vacation to Bali? Wait a year before trading in your clunker for a new car? Stop buying lottery tickets? Whatever savings you realize can go into starting your business.

Can you overcome hardship?

Inevitably, you will run into problems in trying to start your business. Do you have the perseverance to overcome whatever difficulties come your way? Think back on problems you've encountered in the past. How did you deal with them?

These are a few questions to consider in starting a business. For more help with your self-assessment, go to the Small Business Administration's (SBA's) home page (www.sba.gov). Click on "Starting a Business" for a link to the SBA's "Small Business Readiness Self-Assessment Tool."[4] This is an online questionnaire you can complete in a few minutes and send to the SBA for immediate scoring. You'll get back an evaluation of your readiness and suggestions on using SBA resources to help you prepare to start a business.

Getting Started

Like any entrepreneur, you start with a plan for your business. The following discusses the elements of your plan.

Solo, Partnership, Strategic Alliance, or Buyout?

Do you plan to start a firm on your own, using your own capital and that of other investors and perhaps a lender? You would take all the risks, but you would also have all of the profits. Rather than jumping from a full-time job with a CPA firm into starting a business, you could work evenings, weekends, and vacations in starting your business, for example, by providing tax preparation and tax planning services to a few clients. You would need to ensure that you are not competing with your employer for clients, and at some point you probably would inform your employer of your plans to start your own firm. Once you're on your own, there may be opportunities to collaborate with your former employer in pursuing business and providing services to selected clients.

Another option is to partner with another CPA in a startup. You could share ideas and knowledge and leverage your experience, for example, you might have expertise in tax, and your partner in auditing, or you might have experience in working with information technology companies, and your partner with small businesses. And with a partner, you could share the risks of starting a business. But you have to find the right partner, someone you trust, whose knowledge and experience

---

3 "Credit Card Debt Sinks Many Startups," Ohio Society of CPAs, updated 8.25.09. www.ohioscpa.com/Content/45010.aspx
4 Small Business Administration, "Small Business Readiness Self-Assessment Tool." http://web.sba.gov/sbtn/sbat/index.cfm?Tool=4

you value, and with whom you can work in building a business. Furthermore, you would have to share the profits with your partner. Then again, you might be able to build your business and increase your profits faster than on your own. As an alternative to entering into a formal partnership with another CPA, you could form an alliance with another firm. This is an informal agreement to share knowledge, certain clients, and specific costs. You might fill in gaps in the other firm's knowledge and expertise, and vice versa. For example, you might be knowledgeable in tax, the other firm in providing services to small businesses. Together you might provide tax planning and reporting services to small businesses. Just as in entering into a partnership, you need to give careful consideration to forming an alliance, and look at the benefits and the risks. An alliance could help to generate more business, but there is also risk in working with another firm. Is there mutual trust? Can you work together? How will you resolve disagreements? What is your liability?

Finally, you might buy an existing CPA firm. With more baby boomers reaching retirement age, more CPAs might decide to sell their firms. Buying a firm is a complex process, however, and a number of issues must be addressed. For example, you and the owner would have to agree on the price and other terms. Although the firm would come with an established client base, you would have to develop good relationships with these clients. To smooth the transition, the former owner might stay on for a time as a consultant, helping to maintain client relationships.

Leaving a Firm to Start a Business

If you are currently working at a CPA firm, and decide to start your own business, you may be able to take one or two clients with you, but you have to be careful about this. These clients might want to join you at your new firm because they highly value the work that you have done from them and want to continue working with you. But you may not be able to do this if you have a noncompete agreement with the firm you're leaving that says, in essence, that you are not permitted to take clients from them, although in some cases you may be able to do so if you agree to compensate them in return.

In any event, don't burn your bridges with your former firm. There may be opportunities to collaborate in the future in pursuing business opportunities. The same is true with other firms. For example, for various reasons a large firm may not be interested in working with a particular client, and might refer the client to your firm. At Kenneth Leventhal & Company, not long after our firm got started, we had the opportunity to take on a Securities and Exchange Commission (SEC)-registered company as a client. Up to then, we had worked with private companies that did not have to register with the SEC, but this particular client wanted to use us. We went to one of the Big 4 firms that did a lot of work with SEC-registered clients. The firm took on a support role, mentoring us in working with our client, teaching our people about working with SEC-registered clients, and providing technical input, especially on SEC matters. That really established our firm's ability to handle SEC-registered clients. The Big 4 firm did this as a professional courtesy and to develop a good relationship with our firm, which might result in future referrals from us.

What Legal Structure Will You Use?

Will your firm be a partnership, C corporation, S corporation, limited liability partnership or corporation, or other structure? You also need to know and comply with local, county, and state licensing requirements; for example, not only you but your firm may need a license in order to do business or you may be precluded from using a corporation to practice. In Ohio, for example, all CPA firms must register with the Accountancy Board of Ohio, a state agency.[5] You might want to consult and retain an attorney in deciding upon and setting up a legal structure for your business and addressing other legal questions as they arise.

Depending on your services, you also need to check with state and national rule making bodies as well as the AICPA as to any applicable requirements, for example, if your firm conducts audits, compilations or reviews, your firm may be subject to peer review, or a review of your accounting and auditing practices conducted by a peer firm. All CPA firms that are AICPA members are required to have a peer review.[6]

What is Your Firm's Mission (Business Philosophy)?

Writing a mission statement will help you to crystallize your thinking about your firm. Simply put, it covers who you are, what you offer, to whom, and, most important, why

they benefit. What value do your clients receive from your services? How do you differentiate yourself? This is a question about perspective—the client's. If you think you're delivering more value than the client does, the client may not come back.[7] Conversely, if you are able not only to meet to but to exceed the client's expectations, you could have a longtime client.

What Skills and Experience Do You Offer?

If you've been a tax partner with a large accounting firm, you bring years of experience in advising clients on tax issues to starting a firm. Likewise, if you've worked in government, you could get your firm going by offering services to government agencies. If you have experience in a particular industry, you could have an edge. (See the sidebar on page 281 that tells how we developed a real estate specialty at Kenneth Leventhal & Co.) But what if you don't have much experience? You might start by offering basic services such as tax preparation or bookkeeping, and, once these are generating steady income, you might begin to offer additional services and build your business.

Who Are Your Clients?

To decide on your prospective clients, you first determine the market for your services. Do you plan to concentrate in the city or community where you've set up your business? The region or state where you are based?

---

5 "Starting a CPA practice guide," Ohio Society of CPAs. www.ohioscpa.com/Content/39629.aspx

6 "Peer Review of CPA Firms: an Overview." From the *AICPA Audit Committee Toolkit*. www.aicpa.org/audcommctr/toolkitsnpo/Peer_Review_of_CPA_Firms.htm

7 "At Large: What's the 'Secret' Sauce for CPA Success?," Rick Telberg/At Large, American Institute of Certified Public Accountants (AICPA), *CPA Insider*, October 5, 2009. www.cpa2biz.com/content/media/PRODUCER_CONTENT/Newsletters/Articles_2009/CPA/Oct/SecretSauce.jsp

Why Should You Specialize?

You might do fine as a generalist firm, providing the same accounting and tax services as your competitors, but I really believe that to stand out from the competition, you need to specialize.

I joined Kenneth Leventhal & Company, a startup CPA firm in Southern California, in its early years. We decided to specialize in real estate, an industry where we could grow our business with little or no competition from other firms. We found opportunities to provide accounting, tax, and consulting services to a number of commercial property development and homebuilding companies that had been founded by young, ambitious entrepreneurs.

To develop a deep and broad understanding of the real estate industry, our partners and senior managers participated in in-house and external training programs in all sectors of the industry, including finance. Sometimes we would bring in outside speakers who were knowledgeable and experienced in some aspect of real estate. As part of this training, we would pick accounting and tax issues that deeply affected the industry such as capitalization of interest and taxes, depreciation, partnership allocation of income, and tax free exchanges. Then we would discuss these issues and how we could add value in helping clients to address them. For example, we would recommend that, for tax purposes, a company expense interest and taxes to minimize their tax liability, but for financial reporting, especially for financing, they capitalized these costs, which resulted in higher earnings.

We assigned people to become actively involved with every single professional association in real estate such as the National Association of Homebuilders and the Urban Land Institute (ULI). They attended meetings, served on committees, participated in panels, and spoke at industry events. They wrote articles for the publications of industry associations. They served as a technical resource on accounting issues for the staff and members of real estate organizations. Our people were so active that we created the impression we were a much larger firm than we actually were at the time. I became a lifetime trustee of the ULI and also served as a governor. I also participated in the International Council of Shopping Centers, a professional association for businesses in retailing, and the Real Estate Roundtable, an organization of industry leaders, and many others. Although our firm's participation in these organizations was a big investment on our part, it allowed us not only to learn about current issues in the industry but also to network and meet with our potential clients. It was a phenomenal way of marketing our firm. We also hired a public relations firm early on to help get our name out.

In our marketing, we emphasized our technical expertise in accounting, tax, and consulting, and our knowledge of the real estate industry. It was that combination of accounting and real estate expertise that distinguished us. Our people had excellent opportunities to market our services because they had a deep knowledge and understanding of real estate, spoke the language of real estate, and were comfortable in meetings with people in the industry. Equally important, we were able to explain technical accounting terms in ways that real estate clients—and other clients—could understand. Along the way, we also began doing work for government agencies, something that a lot of other firms didn't do. We started by answering government request for proposals, or RFPs. This was a time consuming, difficult process, and very costly if we didn't submit a winning bid. But we won enough work to justify our investment, and providing services to government was a major practice of our Washington, DC, office, which was staffed with CPAs and others experienced in working for government clients. Among other jobs, we were a major contractor for the Department of Housing and Urban Development and the Resolution Trust Corporation, an agency created to liquidate and sell the assets of a number of thrift institutions that failed in the late 1980s and early 1990s because of a recession and other reasons.

(continued)

Why Should You Specialize? *(continued)*

Finally, we developed creative concepts and ideas that helped our clients achieve faster growth and meet other strategic goals. Whenever there was a new development in the industry, we developed strategies to help our clients capitalize on the opportunities or minimize the risks. When mortgage backed securities first came on the market, we were there in developing financial models and the appropriate tax and financial reporting for our clients. When there was a wave of mergers and acquisitions in real estate, we were there with tax strategies, such as tax free exchanges and income deferrals. And when the real estate industry slid into a recession, and many companies began to fail, we became experts in reorganizations and restructures. I went to many bankruptcy meetings with lawyers and others, and I usually was the only accountant in the room. Finally, when the U.S. real estate industry began to go global, with more companies developing and investing outside their home markets, we formed a global alliance with other CPA firms that helped us to follow our clients overseas, for example, we were very active in Japan and Germany, among other countries in Asia and Europe.

Because we were recognized for our expertise in real estate, and our ability to deliver value for our clients, we were able to charge premium fees. Our clients were willing to pay for value. This would not have been possible if we had not decided to specialize.

Our specialization enabled us to become national, then international, and hire high quality CPAs who wanted to be trained in real estate. Many went on to work for real estate companies or other employers, and many of them ended up hiring us as their accountants.

So as you build your practice, think about whether to specialize. I know from experience that there is great value in specializing—both for you and your clients.

Within your market area, how will you establish a market niche? In a specific industry or sector? If you have experience in working for not-for-profit organizations, then these organizations might be your market. You might also uncover business opportunities through market research.[8] Perhaps there is a need for services that is not completely met by established firms; for example, there may be a concentration of small businesses that need assistance with particular tax issues, systems, or new technology.

As you build your firm, solicit more clients, and have clients referred to you, the question is, which clients to accept? You don't want to take on prospective clients just because they have a pulse. You only want clients who are ethical, competent, and understand the services you provide, need your services, and will pay your fees. Consequently, you may want to establish a system for qualifying prospective clients (client acceptance system).

What Are Your Firm's Goals?

Once you've established your target market, you can decide on your goals—and how you will reach them. Do you want to become a leading provider of tax services in your market area within five years? A leader in solutions for companies in real estate or health care? How will you achieve these goals? For example, if you want to position your firm

---

8 "Start Your Own Practice," Randy Myers, *Journal of Accountancy*, April 2006. www.journalofaccountancy.com/Issues/2006/Apr/StartYourOwnPractice.htm

in services to healthcare organizations, you might hire a CPA from one of these organizations, perhaps someone who, with the right pay and other incentives, would be willing to make a change from a large organization to a startup firm.

How Will You Bring in Clients?

It's a given that you have to market your firm to bring in clients. But how will you market? Just like looking for a job, you can find clients through networking. Join community organizations, get active in community affairs, serve on the boards and committees of not-for-profit organizations, and find other ways to meet people, build networks, and contribute to the community. Get a listing in local business directories, join associations, make speeches, and write articles. Consider whether to hire an outside marketing consultant to help you plan and implement a marketing campaign. Depending on your budget, your market and other considerations, this could include direct mail, telemarketing, and print advertising. It could also include Internet marketing through creation of your firm's Web site, use of social media to network and reach prospective clients, and online advertising.

What Fees Will You Charge?

At the start, you may be tempted to try and charge lower fees than your competitors just to bring in business. But you could fail to bring in enough money to cover your overhead and make a profit. Better to price your services competitively, but based on your experience, skills and the value you can deliver. You can test your fee schedule with prospective clients. If you start getting feedback that your fees are too high, you can adjust accordingly. But prospects may be willing to pay your fees if they feel assured that you can provide quality service on schedule, and that you maintain good communications with them, meaning you quickly respond to their phone calls and emails, answer questions promptly, and are otherwise attentive to their needs. Once you've established your fees, you need to set up a system for billing clients, receiving payments, and so on.

What Insurance Will You Require?

Before you start marketing your business and finding clients, you need to consider your insurance needs. Professional liability insurance is critical (but may be costly) in protecting your practice and your personal assets against legal liability resulting from errors or omissions in providing professional services. If you hire employees, employment practice liability insurance protects you against charges of discrimination in hiring, wrongful termination, and other workplace liabilities. And as a benefit to employees, you may want to offer group life insurance and perhaps health insurance. For more information on insurance, see "Starting Your Own CPA Firm" on the AICPA's Web site.

When Will You Need to Start Hiring Employees?

As your business grows, you will reach the point where you need help. You may hire an administrative assistant or contract with an outside firm for administrative services. You may hire CPAs full time or part time, or use

CPAs who are independent contractors or work for staffing agencies, to help work with your growing number of clients. And now that you're an employer, you need to establish pay schedules, work hours, employee benefit plans, tax withholding, and reporting schedules and so on. This will begin to take up your time, and you may want to consider whether to get the assistance of an outside human resources firm to help deal with employee matters so you can concentrate on your clients.

Where Will You Locate?

At least initially, you could set up a home office. You would not have to pay to rent an office, and you could set up your office for a modest investment in a computer, photocopier, scanner and fax machine, and a telephone line and Internet connection. Home-based businesses are so common that clients might not mind your working from home. Then again, if you rent office space right from the start, clients might see your business as more established and professional, and you might be able to charge higher fees. A solution might be to start at home and rent office space after your business has grown to the point that you start hiring people.

Wrap-up

Here's a recap of what we covered in this chapter:

- Starting a CPA firm is an exciting but very challenging career choice for CPAs.
- CPAs are drawn to entrepreneurship by the opportunity to run their own business, deliver services that are highly valued by clients, and build a secure financial future.
- CPAs usually have at least a few years of experience working for a CPA firm before they go out on their own
- You need to do a candid self-assessment and seek the advice of others before deciding whether to start your own firm. Do you have what it takes?
- Your first step in getting started is to write a business plan that details how you will raise capital, find clients, and determine what services to provide.
- Specialization could help you to stand out in the market for CPA services.
- Your success depends on your ability to consistently deliver services that clients value.
- You inevitably will face difficulties in starting a business, but if you persevere, you may enjoy the rewards that can only come from being an entrepreneur.

At some point in your career, you might be interested in joining a college faculty to teach the next generation of CPAs. The next chapter discusses teaching as a career.

Interview: DeAnn Hill
Founder, DeAnn Hill CPA

DeAnn Hill graduated from Pittsburg State University (PSU), Pittsburg, Kansas, in 1980, with a bachelor's degree in business administration (major in accounting). After passing the CPA Exam and working for two CPA firms, she founded her own firm (deannhillcpa.com) in 1985 in Baxter Springs, Kansas. She has been an active member of and held many offices with several national and state professional organizations. In 2003, she was named Outstanding Alumni of Pittsburg State University. She is very active in PSU's business school and advisory council.

> *"You can get to the point where your business consumes you. I wanted to maintain a balance between my personal life and my business."*

After you graduated, how did you begin your career?

I worked for the summer after I graduated as an intern for a public accounting firm. I was then hired full time. I worked for them 2 years. One of the partners left to start his own firm and I went with him. Since he took several major clients with him, the practice was pretty well established at the onset. I was in charge of many client projects and much of the office in general. It was challenging, but it was also a learning opportunity. I learned what to do and what not to do in working with clients and employees as part of managing a small CPA firm. I worked for him for 2 years. After that I left to start my own firm, at age 24.

How did you get started?

I began with some clients of my former firms—I hadn't signed agreements not to compete with them. I had amicable relationships with my previous firms, and I did some subcontract work for them. I also took on some new clients, but I was careful to screen clients. I didn't take just anybody who walked through the door. At the start, I did mostly tax returns.

How did you develop your network of peers, business associates, and potential clients?

Early on I joined the AICPA, the Kansas Society of CPAs, and other professional organizations. I was actively involved in these organizations, and served in various leadership positions, including president of the Kansas Society. I've met and gotten to know a lot of people over the years. Today, I can call other firms and organizations all over the country if I need some guidance or backup on a certain area or position. Since I do not have any partners, I would have a hard time existing without my network.

How did you finance your startup?

I didn't want to take on any debt, so I invested about $10,000 of my own money, mainly for a computer and other office equipment.

Did you develop a specialty practice?

For a time I did a lot of work for machine shops in my area, and a lot of audits for local non-profits and governmental units. I have mostly abandoned the audit area and now concentrate on services to small businesses. I help clients to build their businesses, and if needed, to take them apart for estate or other purposes. At present, we provide a full range of accounting services, accounting software selection and implementation, estate, gift, and trust tax return preparation, financial reporting, general business consulting, tax return services and planning, and other services.

Who have been your clients?

Mickey Mantle's* children's charities were a client at one time. Mickey played baseball as a young boy in my home town of Baxter Springs, Kansas. He lived in Commerce, Oklahoma, which is 10 miles away. The charity hosted celebrity golf tournaments to raise funds. I did accounting work for the tournaments. I have some unique memorabilia autographed by Mickey and some of his sidekicks that used to frequent the tournaments—Stan Musial and Yogi Berra, to name a few. Since my family has always been a big baseball family, that was a very exciting time for me.

Did working for small business clients help you in learning to manage your business?

Yes. I have learned a lot from clients, in particular a man who founded a printing business. He didn't have a formal education, but was very business savvy. He started his company in a barn. It grew to several hundred employees and several million dollars a month in revenue. The company had an accounting department but not a CPA. So I worked as their outside controller. Eventually he sold his business to a public company. He really had an impact on my life and still does to this day. I hold him and his family in the highest regard.

Have you continued to build your business?

At one point my business had grown to where I employed eight people. Now I have three. Some left at my encouragement to go back to school or take other jobs or for personal reasons. There were specific areas of practice I did not enjoy. As my staff lightened, I culled practice areas that I no longer wanted to be involved in, so I would not have to replace them. I still make a good living.

---

* New York Yankee Hall of Famer Mickey Mantle was born in Spavinaw, Oklahoma, and grew up in Commerce, Oklahoma. He died in 1995.

Why did you scale back?

I didn't want to spend more and more of my time building my business, possibly buying another firm, and hiring and managing more people. You can get to the point where your business consumes you. I wanted to maintain a balance between my personal life and my business. I currently have a daughter in college, and a son at home, and when they are out of school, I plan to build my business again. I have the experience to do that.

What does it take to succeed in accounting?

My daughter is majoring in accounting in college. I've told her that you have to be passionate about what you do—whether it's accounting or another profession. You have to be persistent, starting with the CPA exam. If you don't pass it the first time, try again. As you run into challenges in your career, figure out how to deal with them. Don't give up. You have to be professional and able to get along with people.

Any advice for women going into accounting?

Have confidence in yourself. Don't sell yourself short. You don't have to act or dress like men. Be confident. Even today, when I walk into a room full of strangers, I'm a little nervous, but that goes away as soon as I strike up a conversation. Bottom line ... be yourself.

Interview: Eugene Price
Founder and Senior Partner, RRC Price CPAs

Eugene Price is the founder and senior partner of RRC Price CPAs, an accounting firm based in Bardonia, New York.

Where did you go after school?

I thought about joining a big CPA firm, or a corporation, but decided against it. In a big firm, you can get stuck in a niche. I wanted more diversity and control. Therefore, I started my own firm in 1971, and I've been happy ever since. Today, the firm is one of the largest in Rockland County, with about $3 million a year in revenue. We have 2 offices in Rockland County, one in Bardonia and one in Nanuet, which are owned by the firm, and one in Goldens Bridge in Westchester County. We have 4 partners, in different specialties, and about 20 employees.

"Helping others has turned out to be good for the soul and good for the image of the firm."

Who are your clients?

Rockland County is very service oriented. Many of our clients are doctors, lawyers, computer specialists, and other service providers. We also have a variety of additional clients including small businesses, restaurants, not-for-profits, and others. You never know who will walk through the door or how you will get your next client. A very special client developed when I volunteered to do the accounting for the Juvenile Diabetes Foundation charity in Rockland County, at its inception, pro-bono. The president's son had juvenile diabetes, while my children were lucky enough not to have this disease. He was so impressed by my offer to help that this led to a great business and personal relationship. I have been the treasurer for Big Brothers in Rockland County for over 25 years. Helping others has turned out to be good for the soul and good for the image of the firm.

What services do you provide?

We provide a range of accounting, audit, and tax services. However, our emphasis is on taxes. We prepare several thousand tax returns every year. We do tax planning and IRS representation and assist clients with various tax issues. Some of our clients have lost money in "mini-Madoff" Ponzi schemes, and have had to file for extensions and address unique tax reporting questions.

Being a "small" firm enables close contact with our clients. Therefore, personal service becomes a by-product of this and I become the client's business advisor and friend. This is evidenced by the many personal events I am invited to such as weddings.

What do you like most about your work?

I like meeting and getting to know my clients. As far as duties are concerned, I especially like representing clients with the IRS. Knowledge of the federal tax code is important in dealing with the IRS. However, I have found over the years that building a rapport with the IRS agent is even more important. It gives me the latitude I need to talk and explain my client's situation when questions arise. Therefore, I do better for my client and it is a win-win for everyone. This is my strong suit. Years ago, I had an audit with an agent who, like me, grew up in the Bronx. We spent as much time talking about the Bronx as the audit. This proved very beneficial to my client.

How do you develop business?

I've gotten to know people by joining professional and business organizations and serving on the boards of not-for-profit organizations. I know most of the local politicians and government leaders. I've been longtime friends with quite a few lawyers practicing in the county. They send me business, and I reciprocate. I like to market—to meet people and network. We have a solid reputation and reputation is everything, especially in a small community.

What are your retirement plans?

There is an agreement in place to buy me out and have me consult with the firm for a period of time when I retire. I also will stay involved with bringing in new business, as this I truly enjoy and find personally rewarding. My wife, who worked on Wall Street for 22 years, asked me what I'm going to do when I retire. I told her I still plan to come into the office. I like it there.

Chapter 9

Careers in Teaching

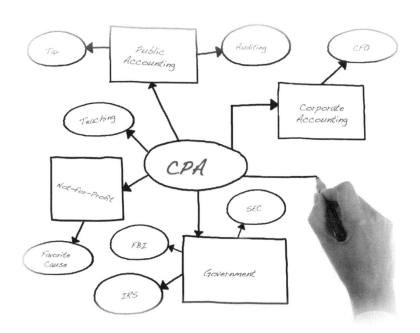

"To succeed as an academician, you must have a passion for teaching and for researching interesting questions."

Doyle Z. Williams, Executive Director • Accounting Doctoral Scholars Program

Passion for Teaching and Research Could Lead to Success

Kenneth Baggett originally planned to study architecture in college, but decided he didn't have the creative ability. "So I wandered down to the business school, took an accounting class, and said to myself, 'This is something I really want to do.'" Today, he's managing principal and CEO of the Reznick Group, one of the largest CPA firms in the United States.

Janet Franzel took an accounting class at the College of St. Teresa, Winona, Minnesota. "I liked it so well that I decided to major in accounting." Today, she's the managing director of the Financial Management and Assurance Team of the U.S. Government Accountability Office, the investigative arm of Congress.

Amy Coleman took accounting classes in high school and college. "I found that I really enjoyed accounting. I decided to pursue a business degree with a major in accounting, and to obtain CPA certification." Today, she's vice president of finance of the Kresge Foundation (kresge.org), a $3.1 billion national foundation. (Interviews with Baggett, Franzel, and Coleman can be found on pages 125, 228, and 266, respectively.)

Many CPAs decided on careers in accounting because of their first encounter with accounting in a college or a high school class. They may not remember the names of long ago teachers, but they do remember that the teacher had a talent for making the class interesting, engaging, and challenging, and for that they are appreciative. Was it not for such teachers, some CPAs might not have gone on to successful careers in public accounting, business, government, not-for-profit organizations, or other fields.

Indeed, some CPAs follow in their teachers' footsteps and become teachers themselves. Some go into teaching right out of college, whereas others move into teaching at some later point in their careers or when they retire.

This chapter looks at careers in teaching accounting, the educational requirements, why people go into teaching, and how to get started in teaching.

PhD Faculty

If you were to check the faculty directories of universities offering undergraduate and graduate accounting programs that are accredited by the Association to Advance Collegiate Schools of Business (AACSB), you might notice that many professors are PhDs. You might ask, why do they have PhDs? Then again, you might not, but we'll tell you anyway.

The AACSB accreditation standards define 2 types of accounting faculty: academically qualified (AQ) and professionally qualified (PQ). Most full-time accounting faculty are AQ, which generally requires a PhD in accounting.[1] The AACSB standards require that at least 50 percent of faculty be AQ. PQ faculty are discussed later in this chapter.

Accounting professors are in demand not only because of the accreditation requirement,

---

1 "A Profession's Response to a Looming Shortage: Closing the Gap in the Supply of Accounting Faculty," Michael Ruff, Jay C. Thibodeau and Jean C. Bedard, *Journal of Accountancy*, March 2009, www.journalofaccountancy.com/Issues/2009/Mar/AccountingFaculty.htm

A Note of Thanks to My Teachers

When I took math in high school, our teacher was extremely enthusiastic about the subject. Instead of putting us to sleep with a discussion of abstract numbers, he used examples to bring math into the real world. To this day, I still remember a question about two trains traveling at different speeds, with the faster train making several stops, and the slower train not stopping, and how long did it take each train to reach its destination? Our teacher helped us think through this problem. In the process, he helped us develop our analytical skills, although, being high school kids, we probably didn't appreciate it at the time. Nobody went home to report they had a great day developing their analytical skills.

Keepers of the Numbers

In college, I got my first exposure to accounting in a freshman class. Most of us didn't understand accounting or what CPAs did. Our teacher put it in simple terms: accounting is a numbers game, and CPAs are the keepers of the numbers. They know how to track, report, interpret, and communicate numbers. He went on to provide examples of the use of numbers in preparing financial statements or corporate business plans and strategies. He introduced us to double entry bookkeeping, the foundation of modern accounting. He told us debits were by the window and credits were by the door, and we were to make sure we were always sitting in a room that had windows. He taught us the significance of balancing, reconciling, and keeping track of accounts. If we didn't balance our accounts properly on homework assignments, we wouldn't get a passing grade.

New Hampshire Mill

One of the most interesting classes I had was cost accounting. We were taught how to account for and aggregate all the costs to produce a product. This information could help a company decide whether it was profitable to manufacture and sell the product. If the cost to produce a widget was, say, 70 cents, and a company could sell it for $1, then the product's margin was 30 cents, and the company might go ahead with widget production. If the cost was 90 cents, but the company couldn't sell it for more than $1 because of competition, it might decide the 10 cents per widget margin was too low to justify production. CPAs were essential to this process because they had to accurately calculate the costs.

We didn't just sit around in class. Our teacher took us to a textile mill in New Hampshire where we watched the weaving process. He explained how we could estimate the cost of the thread, the color and dye, and all the other costs of weaving, including depreciation for plant and equipment. He covered the costs of the whole process from raw material to finished goods. It was exciting to learn this in an actual manufacturing operation.

During my time in school, our professors brought the world into the classroom. Visitors from the New York Stock Exchange, the Securities and Exchange Commission, other regulatory agencies, and public accounting firms, talked to us about audits of public companies. Corporate CEOs and CFOs would discuss their respective company's operations, financial management (such as planning a budget), internal control issues, and other topics. Our professors demonstrated real world applications of accounting; for example, how CPAs applied accounting principles in preparing financial statements and how investors used those statements to make decisions about whether to buy or sell a company's stock.

So to all my teachers—from my high school teacher to the professor who taught the very last accounting class I took in college—thank you. If it wasn't for all of you, I might never have gotten interested in math and accounting and decided on accounting as a career.

but also because of the needs of accounting programs at colleges and universities. PhDs are highly valued for their intellectual acumen, academic knowledge and training, scholarship, research experience, teaching skills, professional experience (if they have worked as practicing CPAs), and the recognition and prestige they bring to accounting programs. The problem is that there are not enough of them in such programs.

Faculty Shortage

In recent years, an increase in enrollments in undergraduate and graduate accounting programs, coupled with an increase in retirements of accounting faculty, has resulted in a severe faculty shortage.

In a 2008 report, the American Accounting Association (AAA), an organization dedicated to promoting worldwide excellence in accounting education, research, and practice, said that the number of full-time, tenured,[2] or tenure-eligible accounting faculty at U.S. institutions offering baccalaureate and higher degrees, declined more than 19 percent between 1993 and 2004.[3] The report, which was co-sponsored by the American Institute of Certified Public Accountants (AICPA), went on to note that accounting faculty were aging—the number of faculty over the age of 55 increased, while the number under the age of 40 declined by half. Furthermore, fac-

ulty were retiring faster than they could be replaced. An estimated 500 faculty members retired annually during the study period, but only about 140 new accounting PhDs were awarded each year. Finally, about half of the PhD degrees were awarded to non-U.S. citizens, and, the study said, many of them might not stay to teach in the United States.

The report also looked at the faculty employment trend from a broader perspective—the total number of faculty eligible for tenure, on track for tenure, and not eligible for tenure at all types of institutions, including 2-year colleges. That number declined more than 13 percent between 1993 and 2004. Table 9-1 compares total estimated accounting faculty with tenure-eligible accounting faculty.

The faculty shortage remains just as serious today. "It's an acute problem that will only worsen," said Ira Solomon, CPA, PhD, head of the department of accountancy at the University of Illinois at Urbana-Champaign. "There is a very real prospect of accounting programs not having enough faculty for classes." (An interview with Solomon is on page 72 of this book.)

Why the shortage of accounting faculty?

As noted in chapter 2, enrollments in accounting programs have been increasing. This, in turn, has increased demand for accounting faculty. But schools are not turning out enough graduates with accounting PhDs to keep up with demand.

---

2 *Tenure* is the right of academics not to have their positions terminated without just cause.

3 "Accounting Faculty in U.S. Colleges and Universities: Status and Trends, 1993-2004; A Report of the American Accounting Association (AAA), February 2008;" report prepared by David S. Leslie, Chancellor, Professor of Education, The College of William and Mary. Based on the National Study of Postsecondary Faculty, National Center of Education Statistics, U.S. Department of Education. http://aaahq.org/temp/phd/Accounting FacultyUSCollegesUniv.pdf

Table 9-1: *Estimated Number of Accounting Faculty**

	1993	2004	% Change
Estimated Number of Full-Time, Tenure-Eligible Accounting Faculty at Institutions offering baccalaureate degrees	6,331	5,121	−19.11%
Estimated Number of All Accounting Faculty at All Types of Institutions	20,321	17,610	−13.3%

* "Accounting Faculty in U.S. Colleges and Universities: Status and Trends, 1993-2004; A Report of the American Accounting Association (AAA), February 2008;" report prepared by David S. Leslie, Chancellor, Professor of Education, The College of William and Mary. Based on the National Study of Postsecondary Faculty, National Center of Education Statistics, U.S. Department of Education. http://aaahq.org/temp/phd/AccountingFacultyUSCollegesUniv.pdf

Part of the reason is that schools would have difficulty finding the funds to expand doctorate programs in accounting and graduate more PhDs. In 2003, a Doctoral Faculty Commission submitted a report titled "Sustaining Scholarship in Business Schools" to AASCB International's board of directors. The commission was composed of college deans, a business executive, the not-for-profit foundation of a global accounting firm, and an AACSB executive. (Many university and college accounting programs are part of an institution's business school.) The commission reported that, based on a survey of U.S. PhD program directors and deans, about 80 percent of funding for doctoral programs derives from business schools' own resources. Endowments and university sources, such as fellowships and assistantships, constitute the remainder. Federal and corporate funding supports only a small fraction of the costs.

"Unlike other business school programs, such as the MBA, there are few financial or reputational incentives to invest in PhD pro-grams," the commission report said. "The advantages to enlarging a PhD program are intangible—increased faculty satisfaction, for example."

Finally, the commission noted that four out of five of the largest doctoral programs are in public institutions, which will face repeated budget contraction and rescission. (Since the report was published, some private institutions also have experienced budget cuts because of losses on their endowment portfolios during the U.S. recession that began in late 2007, among other reasons.)

Another reason for the shortage of PhD accounting faculty is the opportunity cost to students of enrolling in a PhD program. During the 4 or 5 years usually required to study for a PhD, a student foregoes the potential income of working for, say, a public accounting firm or a corporation. Some students may not want to make that sacrifice. In addition, students face the substantial costs of earning a PhD. Most PhD programs provide stipends, generally $10,000–$20,000 for 9 months,[4]

___

4 "Making a Difference: Careers in Academia," Nancy Bagranoff, Dean, Old Dominion University, and Stephanie Bryant, Beta Alpha Psi, 2007 Beta Alpha Psi annual meeting, http://aaahq.org/temp/phd/index.cfm

and waive tuition, but these measures do not completely offset students' costs.[5] For some students, the combination of coursework, research obligations, and teaching duties can be extremely stressful, and some drop out.[6]

PhD Accounting Program Graduation Rates

In a 2007 survey of schools with accounting PhD programs, the AAA asked, among other questions, about schools' graduation rates. For example, what percent of students who entered the schools' PhD program went on to graduate?[7] The response from 89 schools are shown in Table 9-2.

As noted in Table 9-2, 5 schools, or 6 percent of the total, graduated 50 percent to 59 percent of the students who entered the PhD program, while 25 schools, or 27 percent of the total, graduated 90 percent to 100 percent of these students.

Since the Doctoral Commission report was published in 2003, the accounting profession, schools, businesses, and educational organizations, have started various programs and initiatives to try to address the PhD shortage. These include the Accounting Doctoral Scholars Program and other scholarship programs, and an AACSB "bridge" program, discussed later in this chapter. The bridge program prepares experienced business ex-

Table 9-2: *PhD Accounting Program Graduation Rates*

Number of schools	% of total schools	% of students graduating
5	6%	50-59%
3	3%	60-69%
16	18%	70-79%
23	26%	80-89%
25	27%	90-100%
17 no response	20%	—
89	100%	—

ecutives, CPAs, and other professionals who have master's degrees to teach college classes.

What Do Professors Do?

So why do students spend so much time in a PhD program, make the financial sacrifice, cope with the stress, and face the challenges of a demanding program of study to earn a doctorate and become professors? Before addressing that question, let's first address consider another question: What, exactly, do professors do?

If you're currently in college, you see your professors in a lecture hall or classroom, perhaps meet with them occasionally in their offices, work for them as a teaching assistant,

---

5 "Help Wanted: Accounting PhDs," Marge O'Reilly-Allen, CPA, PhD, chair of the accounting department at Rider University in Lawrenceville, N.J., and David Wagaman, CPA, a professor at Kutztown University of Pennsylvania in Kutztown. accountingweb. July 27, 2009. www.accountingweb.com/topic/education-careers/help-wanted-accounting-phds.

6 Ibid.

7 "Information on Accounting PhD Programs," as of 11/13/2007, AAA Summary Data. http://aaahq.org/temp/phd/StudyMaterials/Questionnaire Summary.pd

or work under their direction on a research project. In the process, you get a glimpse into the busy academic life of a professor. That life generally can be segmented into research, teaching, and service.[8,9]

Research

How much time a professor spends on research depends partly on the school. Professors at universities tend to spend more time on research than those at four-year or two-year colleges; faculty at four- and two-year colleges may spend more time on teaching. Professors may find it difficult to conduct research during the school year because of the demands of teaching and other duties, and they may do much of their research during the summer or while on sabbatical. Their research involves collecting and analyzing data, examining original documents and source material, performing experiments, developing concepts or ideas, commenting upon issues and questions of interest to other scholars in the field, and conducting research studies and publishing the results in *peer reviewed* journals (journals with articles validated for quality by other scholars), as well as in books or in electronic media. Research often is a collaborative process. Professors attend outside lectures, colloquia, and conferences, and share and discuss works in progress.

Teaching

Professors prepare and give lectures to students in large classrooms, direct teaching assistants in large classes, and lead small seminars. They grade exams and papers, advise and work with students individually, and supervise graduate students' teaching and research. They evaluate existing courses and introduce new course material. They plan, develop, and introduce new courses, for example, in international accounting issues. This is a growing field of study, and one that is creating more demand for teachers knowledgeable and experienced in international accounting issues, such as the possible U.S. adoption of International Financial Reporting Standards (IFRS). Professors also spend time on administrative work: office hours, academic advising, supervising independent studies, thesis reading, and writing letters of recommendation for students.

Service

Professors serve on academic or administrative committees that deal with the policies of their institution, departmental matters, or academic issues, curricula, budgets, equipment purchases, and hiring. Some work with student and community organizations. Some professors serve as chairs of accounting departments, which could mean they teach fewer classes because of their departmental responsibilities. One possible academic career path is illustrated in Figure 9-1.

Why Study for a PhD?

So to go back to our original question: Why do students study for PhDs in accounting and become professors? What motivates them?

---

8 "What Do Professors Do All Day?" Kirsten Silva Gruesz, University of California Santa Cruz. January 25, 2008. http://people.ucsc.edu/~ksgruesz/whatdo.html

9 "Teachers—Postsecondary," Occupational Outlook Handbook, 2008-2009 edition, Bureau of Labor Statistics, U.S. Department of Labor. www.bls.gov/oco/ocos066.htm#earnings

Figure 9-1: *Possible Academic Career Path*

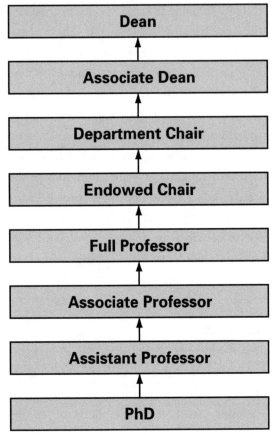

Strong Interest in Research

Accounting PhD candidates and professors enjoy the intellectual challenge of research, the opportunity to contribute new ideas and concepts to accounting theory and practice, and the relevance of research to the major areas of accounting: financial accounting, managerial accounting, and auditing and tax accounting.

In financial accounting, professors have conducted research in, among other areas, accounting standard setting, financial regulation, international accounting, company valuation and financial statement analysis, earnings management, stock markets and market efficiency, earnings forecasting, and financial analyst behavior.

In management accounting, research has included performance evaluation and compensation, budgeting and other control issues in organizations, and strategic management accounting.

Auditing research has included auditing and corporate governance, audit markets, auditor independence, auditor behavior and decision making, and corporate governance issues.

Tax accounting research has included such topics as tax planning and tax policy and its effects on businesses. In addition, accounting researchers have made important contributions to other disciplines such as economics, finance, law, strategic management, and information systems.

Solomon said research appeals to him because "I always want to figure out not only how but why things work" and, he added, "why things are as they are in the world of accounting."

Passion for Teaching

"Teaching is very satisfying—and challenging," said Igor Vaysman, associate professor in the Zicklin School of Business at New York's Baruch College. "As a teacher, you have an opportunity to prepare students for careers in accounting and business, improve their analytical and other abilities, and add to the pool of qualified accountants."

"(At Baruch) many of our students are the first in their families to attend college," said Masako Darrough, a Baruch professor, and chair of the Stan Ross Department of Accountancy. "I take great satisfaction in knowing that I help students by teaching accounting and economics."

My Experience in Teaching

I was not a tenured professor of accounting during my career; I worked in public accounting. However, I came to appreciate the passion that professors have for teaching and helping students. I felt the same enthusiasm for education, teaching, and learning as a result of my experience as a teacher and my association with the accounting program at Baruch College in New York, and the real estate program at the University of Southern California's (USC's) Lusk Center for Real Estate.

My experience in teaching began in the home of Kenneth Leventhal, who founded a CPA firm Kenneth Leventhal & Company (KL&CO) in Los Angeles in 1949 and went on to build a nationwide firm. (It merged with Ernst & Young in the mid-1990s.) I joined KL&CO in it's early stages in 1961. A small group of our partners held our own continuing education classes on Saturdays at Ken's home. Each week a partner was assigned to prepare and give a presentation on a particular topic and then gave the other partners an exam. I made some of the presentations, along with the other partners, and we all learned together.

From those meetings in Ken's living room, I went on to give lectures on various topics to accounting and real estate groups, the California State Society of CPAs, and other organizations. I also taught classes at various universities including USC; the University of California, Los Angeles; Stanford; and Harvard.

My biggest commitment to teaching occurred after I retired from Ernst and Young in 1999. I became chairman of the board and senior distinguished fellow for the USC Lusk Center for Real Estate, and the equivalent of an adjunct professor at the school. There, I was involved in teaching specific programs under the Masters of Real Estate Development (MRED) program and the MBA program at the USC Marshall School of Business. This was a totally different experience from my occasional teaching in the past because at USC I was teaching regularly. I got to know the students in my classes better than I had in previous classes, and I got to know many of the faculty in the MRED and MBA programs.

I taught classes on a variety of real estate, tax, finance, and other topics. In one of my classes, I helped the students read real estate company financial statements. I showed them how to analyze those statements from the perspective of a potential investor in a company—what were the company's strengths and weaknesses? This was a lot of fun for me. The students were not accounting majors, but they enjoyed learning how to use financial statements. That class, which I continue to teach, has had significant demand and interest.

I also ran what was known as a Seminar Series program. To be considered for admission, students had to write a paper on any real estate topic that interested them, and I only admitted 12 students. I did not plan the curriculum. Instead, students planned it, based on our first class meeting when we spent a couple of hours discussing topics that we would like to explore, study, and discuss further, such as the environmental impact of development, student housing, or senior assisted living. The top 4 or 5 topics were assigned to student teams, and each team had to do their own research and write a 3- or 4-page summary. The summary was circulated to the other students and we discussed it in class. The program helped students in doing research, planning, writing, communication, and teamwork, and they also acquired new knowledge.

Teaching has given me an opportunity to gain a new perspective on a topic that I know well or to learn about a new topic. I get to observe the thinking processes and logic of young people (and begin to feel young again!). I get to know the students in my classes. In fact, I've also served as a mentor for some of them. Outside the classroom, I meet with them, discuss their concerns, talk about their long-term plans and perhaps give some career guidance. I have kept in touch with many students after they graduated, and I have had the joy of watching them grow personally and professionally, pursue their dreams, and achieve their career goals.

Opportunity to Give Back to the Accounting Profession and the Community

Professors help to educate the next generation of accountants for careers in research and teaching, public accounting, government, the not-for-profit sector, and other fields. They also contribute their academic and professional experience, and their time, to community service.

Flexible Schedules

Professors work long hours, but they have flexible schedules that enable them to better balance their professional and personal lives. They must be present for classes, faculty and committee meetings, and student consultations during regular office hours. Otherwise, they are free to decide when and where they will work, and how much time to devote to course preparation, grading, study, research, graduate student supervision, and other activities.

Pay and Benefits

Although salaries and compensation of professors may not match those of senior corporate executives or partners in large CPA firms, the compensation nevertheless is attractive. According to the 2008-2009 faculty compensation survey of the American Association of University Professors (AAUP), the average compensation of full professors in all disciplines totaled more than $155,000 (see table 9-3). Professors add to their income by publishing books, consulting, serving on corporate boards, advising entrepreneurs on starting businesses, and other income-generating activities.

According to the AAUP, professors' average salaries increased nearly 4 percent at all schools in 2008-2009, from 2007-2008; 3.4 percent at public schools; 5 percent at private institutions; and 4.7 percent at church-related schools.

Accounting salaries

In a separate report, the AACSB looked specifically at accounting salaries (table 9-4). It compared the mean (average) salaries of recent PhD graduates in accounting with those of graduates in other disciplines. At $127,400, the salary of accounting/taxation graduates was the highest.

PhD Programs

If you were to study for a PhD in accounting, where could you attend school?

Table 9-3: *American Association of University Professors 2008–2009 Faculty Compensation Survey: Average Salary and Average Compensation Levels**

Professor	All schools combined	Public	Private	Church-related
Salary	$123,785	115,509	151,403	129,615
Compensation	155,543	145,462	189,368	161,679

* Survey Report Table 4. www.aaup.org/NR/rdonlyres/4041489A-90C4-4312-9BA4-135F82D3CD4E/0/tab4.pdf

Table 9-4: *New Doctorate Salaries by Field/Discipline: 2008 Mean (Average) Salary*

Field/Discipline	Mean	% change from 2007
Accounting/taxation	$127,400	2.2%
Finance/banking/real estate/insurance	119,900	0.2%
Marketing	108,800	6.3%
Production/Operations Management	102,800	−4.4%
Management/Behavioral Sciences/ International Business Strategic Management	101,800	0.4%
CIS/MIS	101,700	8.5%
Quantitative Methods/Operations/Research/Statistics	91,700	11.2%
Economics/Managerial Economics	85,800	3.6%

More than 90 universities and colleges in the United States offer accounting PhD programs. A list of these schools (along with schools offering such programs worldwide) can be found on the Web site of the AAA.[10] Schools with PhD accounting programs range from large public universities such as the Wharton School of the University of Pennsylvania, the University of Michigan, and the University of Missouri–Columbia, to other state schools, such as the University of South Florida, to private universities, such as Stanford University, Harvard University, and USC. Schools define the missions of their PhD programs differently, but generally the focus is on research and academic careers. For example, the goal of the University of Michigan's program "is to develop the next generation of accounting scholars capable of pursuing academic careers at leading research-oriented universities."[11]

Although admission requirements vary by school, most look at academic background, undergraduate and graduate transcripts, recommendation letters, an applicant's research interest and potential, application essays, and scores from the Graduate Management Admissions Test (GMAT) or the Graduate Record Examination (GRE). The GMAT is required by MBA programs; the GRE is the standard for graduate schools in general.[12] Schools may also consider a candidate's professional work experience and credentials, such as CPA.

---

10 "Directory of Accounting PhD Programs," AAA, http://aaahq.org/ATA/public-interest/PhD-programs/phdschools.cfm

11 University of Michigan Ross School of Business, Doctoral Program, Accounting Area Program, http://bschool.washington.edu/phd/accounting.shtml

12 "The GRE. vs. the GMAT," Christine Lagorio, *The New York Times*, December 23, 2008, www.nytimes.com/2009/01/04/education/edlife/strategy-t.html

Table 9-5: *Top Accounting Doctoral Programs*

Doctoral Rank	University	Degree Program	School
1	University of Chicago	PhD Program in Accounting	The University of Chicago Booth School of Business
2	Stanford University	PhD Program in Accounting	Stanford Graduate School of Business
3	Wharton School of the University of Pennsylvania	PhD Program in Accounting	Wharton School of the University of Pennsylvania
4	University of Texas-Austin	Doctoral Program in Accounting (PhD)	McCombs School of Business
5	University of Michigan	PhD	Stephen M. Ross School of Business
6	University of Illinois at Urbane-Champaign	PhD	College of Business at Illinois
7	Cornell University	PhD in Accounting	The Johnson School
8	University of Washington	PhD	Foster School of Business Department of Accounting
9	University of Iowa	PhD Program in Accounting	Tippie College of Business
10	Harvard University	Doctoral Program in Accounting and Management	Harvard Business School
11	University of Georgia	PhD	J.M. Tull School of Accounting
12	University of Southern California	Juris Doctor/Master of Businss Taxation* PhD	Leventhal School of Accounting
13	Massachusetts Institute of Technology	PhD in Accounting & Control	Sloan School of Management
14	Pennsylvania State University	PhD in Business Administration— Accounting	Smeal College of Business
15	University of Mississippi	PhD in Accountancy	Patterson School of Accountancy
16	Oklahoma State University	PhD in Business Administration: Major Field in Accounting	Spears School of Business
17	Ohio State University	PhD in Accounting & MIS	Fisher College of Business
18	Texas A&M University	PhD in Accounting	Mays Business School
19	Indiana University Bloomington	PhD in Accounting	Kelley School of Business
19	University of Missouri-Columbia	PhD	Robert J. Trulaske, Sr. College of Business

Source: Public Accounting Report 27th Annual Professor's Survey 2008

* Dual degrees

Many schools limit the number of candidates accepted into PhD programs each year, and the admissions process is highly competitive. The University of Chicago PhD program admits about 20 students each autumn.[13] (Some schools admit even fewer students each year.) A list of the top accounting doctoral programs in 2008 can be found in table 9-5.

What Schools Look for in Students

What qualities do schools look for in PhD candidates?

In a 2007 survey of schools with accounting PhD programs, the AAA asked, among other questions, what qualities they look for in students applying for admission. The responses from 89 schools can be found in table 9-6 (responses total more than 89 because some schools checked off more than 1 quality).[14]

Based on the survey, schools are especially interested in a student's general academic ability and intelligence as well specific quantitative and other skills. But communication and writing skills also are important. So is a student's research potential. Given the challenges of a PhD program, schools want motivated students who are prepared to work hard. Although not ranked as high, teaching potential is important, too. A successful career as a professor depends not only on one's research skills but also on teaching ability.

Table 9-6: *2007 PhD Candidate Admission Metrics*

Student Qualities	# of Responses	%
Intelligence/Academics	39	13%
Communication/Writing	35	12%
Quantitative/Economic/ Other specific skills sets	33	11%
Work Ethic/Motivation	32	11%
Outstanding Research Potential	30	10%
Intellectual Curiosity	26	9%
Experience/Accounting Background	21	7%
Collegiality/Positive Attitude/Personality	20	7%
Commitment	15	5%
Outstanding Teaching Potential	12	4%
Creativity	8	3%
Desire/Keen Interest	10	3%
Ability to Work Independently	2	1%
Willingness to Learn	7	2%
Maturity	6	2%
Professional Certification	1	–
Interest in International Focus	1	–
Total	**298**	**100%**

---

13 The University of Chicago Booth School of Business, PhD Program, Admission Requirements, www.chicagobooth.edu/phd/admissions.aspx

14 "Information on Accounting PhD Programs," AAA, November 13, 2007, http://aaahq.org/temp/phd/StudyMaterials/QuestionnaireSummary.pdf

Course of Study

The first two years of a PhD program are primarily devoted to coursework and students work with an advisor and the program faculty in planning a course of study. Students usually chose either of two tracks: economics (also called archival) or behavioral.[15] Courses in the economic track are primarily based in economics and finance, and a strong background in mathematics is necessary. The behavioral track is primarily based in psychology. Students study how and why people make decisions; for example, how CEOs and CFOs make business decisions as well as other psychology-based topics. For an example of the two-track curriculum, visit the Web site of the PhD program in the Leventhal School of Accounting at USC's Marshall School of Business at www.marshall.usc.edu/leventhal/curriculum/phd-accounting/. Click on Program Overview.

In addition to selecting a study track, students also focus on a particular functional area. These include financial, auditing, managerial, tax, and information systems. Students usually must complete only a few required courses, and they have considerable flexibility in selecting their tracks and functional areas.

Students typically decide on their area of interest for a dissertation and choose their dissertation advisor sometime in the second year. At the end of that year, they take a written and oral general examination, and if they pass, they enter the dissertation phase of their study. The student proposes a dissertation, and, if it is approved by a dissertation committee, the student proceeds to write and defend the dissertation before the committee. During the dissertation period, students continue to take some courses and usually work as faculty research assistants. They may also work as teaching assistants. In some programs such as USC's, this may include a semester as an independent instructor so students get hands-on teaching experience. But students' main focus is on completing their dissertation. Students usually start looking for jobs in their fifth (or other final) year of the program.

Is a PhD Program For You?

If you're an undergraduate, a PhD program in accounting might seem like something on the far horizon, but your undergraduate years are the time to start thinking about studying for a PhD and a career in research and teaching—and careers in accounting, generally. Here are a few questions to consider about a PhD program:

Do You Have the Intellectual Curiosity—and Ability—to Pursue Studies for a PhD in Accounting?

Your classroom studies will, as previously noted, cover a broad range of subjects that provide the intellectual foundation for research, scholarship, and teaching. One way to test your interest and ability to master these subjects is to take undergraduate courses that lay the groundwork for more advanced studies. For example, you could take an undergraduate course in economics to test your interest in the subject. But it's not just a matter

---

15 "Pursuing a PhD in Accounting: Walking In With Your Eyes Open," Jason Bergner, Journal of Accountancy, March 2009, www.journalofaccountancy.com/Web/PursuingaPhDinAccounting.htm

Learning More about Accounting Programs

To learn more about accounting PhD programs, talk to professors in the accounting department at your school, or, if your school doesn't have a department, contact the departments at other schools, or see if someone—your teachers, CPAs, others—can put you in touch with accounting professors. They can tell you about why they chose careers in accounting and academia, their experiences in studying for the PhD, what it's like to be a professor, and answer your questions about PhD programs. Current students in accounting PhD programs would be another good source of information. If your school has a chapter of Beta Alpha Psi (bap.org), an honorary organization for financial information students and professionals. you might consider joining. Members include accounting students, some who may be planning to enter PhD programs, and you could talk to them about why they are interested in academic careers.

Also check out Web sites with information on PhD programs. They include:

The American Accounting Association (aaahq.org): Organization that promotes worldwide excellence in accounting education, research, and practice. From the AAA home page, click on "Issues and Resources," and "Future Accounting Faculty and Programs" for information on PhD programs, the faculty shortage and other information.* Also from the home page, click on "Links and Organizations" for more sources of information.

Association to Advance Collegiate Schools of Business (aacsb.edu): Organization that accredits college programs including accounting and business. From the home page, click on "Accredited Institutions" and "Schools Accredited in Accounting—by Country/ Region." You will pull up a list of accredited U.S. schools (plus a few outside the United States), including those that have PhD programs. (Not all accredited schools do—many have only bachelor's and master's programs.)** For schools with only accounting PhD programs, check out the AAA's *Directory of Accounting PhD Programs.*†

James R. Hasselback (Jrhasselback.com): Another source of information is the *Hasselback Accounting Faculty Directory*, edited by James R. Hasselback, PhD, professor of accounting at the University of West Florida. Prentice-Hall, Inc., publishes the directory and distributes it free to accounting faculty, CPAs, and various other individuals and organizations.‡ A link to active PhD accounting programs offered by U.S. schools can be found on the Hasselback Web site (Jrhasselback.com) On the Hasselback home page, click on the link to the "Accounting Doctoral Information" page. It also has frequently asked questions on PhD accounting programs, a listing of accounting PhD graduates by school, and other information.§

School Web sites: Schools that offer accounting PhD programs are excellent sources of information. Because there are only 90 or so schools with these programs, a search of the Web sites of these schools is more manageable than if you were reviewing the countless number of sites of bachelor's and master's programs in accounting. Also, contact the PhD program director at schools that interest you. Talk to them about the school's program and any questions you may have about admissions, course content, the dissertation, financial aid, and other concerns.

(continued)

Learning More about Accounting Programs (continued)

AICPA Accounting Education Center (*http://ceae.aicpa.org*): Provides information and resources on accounting education, including the 2009 *Supply of Accounting* graduates report, as well as information on education and curriculum development and links to AICPA educational news. A companion site, startheregoplaces.com, is dedicated to careers in accounting. It includes information about college scholarships. (Log in required.)§§

Journal of Accountancy (*journalofaccountancy.com*): Published by the AICPA, it includes articles about accounting careers, degree programs, including the PhD, the accounting profession, and other topics.

The CPA Journal (*cpajournal.com*): Published by the New York State Society of CPAs, it includes articles on careers in accounting, degree programs, including the PhD, and other topics.

---

* http://aaahq.org/temp/phd/index.cfm
** www.aacsb.net/eweb/DynamicPage.aspx?Site=AACSB&WebKey=5E69A86E-6455-457E-A159-D89A31C7FF73
† http://aaahq.org/ATA/public-interest/PhD-programs/phdschools.cfm.
‡ Vita of James R. Hasselback, PhD, www.jrhasselback.com/
§ www.jrhasselback.com/AtgDoctInfo.html.
§§ To log in, go to www.startheregoplaces.com/futureme/sign-in/

of taking the class. You need to do well on your course examinations, term papers, and final exam.

Do You Have a Strong Interest in and a Talent for Research?

PhD programs are research driven, and as a professor, you would spend much of your time on research. You would have to write and submit for peer review papers on various topics and succeed in having them published in recognized academic journals. As an undergraduate, you could look for opportunities to do research beyond your normal coursework; for example, by assisting a teacher or teaching assistant with a research project or doing independent research on a topic that interests you. Do you like doing research? Do you think you have an aptitude for it? Do your teachers agree, based on their comments on your research papers and your grades in courses requiring research?

Do You Have a Passion and a Talent for Teaching?

From my experience as a student and a teacher, you must, above all, have a demonstrated passion for teaching—demonstrated in the sense that your students can see that you are truly passionate, and not just pretending to be. You must have the ability to communicate effectively, to make complex topics understandable to students and to pique their interest in the topic. Finally, you have to demonstrate how theoretical concepts have real world applications; for example, the effects of a new accounting principle on businesses, regulators, and accountants.

Do You Have the Drive to Complete a PhD Program?

In *A League of Their Own*, a movie about the first women's professional baseball league, a player complains to manager Jimmy Dugan (played by Tom Hanks) about how hard it is to succeed at the professional level. Dugan replies: "Of course it's hard. It's supposed to be hard. If it wasn't hard, everybody would do it. It's the hard that makes it great." Like playing major league baseball, studying for a PhD is hard, and it's not for everyone. Do you have the self-discipline, the focus, the energy, and the staying power to spend five or more years on PhD studies?

Can you work Independently?

As noted, professors have the freedom to manage their time as they wish, except for commitments to teach classes or keep office hours or show up at school meeting on various topics and issues. But they also have many responsibilities as researchers, teachers, advisors, administrators, and leaders. Consider teaching.

"To a considerable degree, teaching is a solitary profession—you design the course, deliver it, and evaluate the students," said John Elliott, dean of the Zicklin School of Business at New York's Baruch College. "So you have to be a self-starter and know how to allocate time."

Would you, as a professor, be able to manage your time effectively? One clue—how well are you managing your time now?

Deciding Where to Apply

If you decide to study for an accounting PhD, which schools should you apply to?

One of the first considerations when finding a school is the quality of the faculty. This you can learn by reviewing published ratings, such as the previously mentioned *Public Ac-counting Report*'s annual Professors' Survey of top PhD programs, by talking with accounting faculty and students at your school or other schools, and by talking to students currently enrolled in PhD programs or program graduates. Another key concern is the financial aid available in the form of tuition forgiveness and stipends. Program Web sites provide information on financial aid, and you can also discuss it with the school's PhD program director. In addition, fellowships are available through other scholarship programs. (See "Scholarship Programs" in the accompanying sidebar.) As in selecting a bachelor's or master's program, a school's location is an important concern, but even more so with a PhD program because there are only 90 schools. Fortunately, schools with these programs generally can be found in most parts of the country.

Professionally Qualified Faculty Member

For experienced CPAs who are interested in teaching, an alternative to earning a PhD and joining a school as an AQ faculty member is to become a PQ member. AACSB accreditation standards say a PQ member must (1) possess at least a masters degree (or equivalent qualification) in a discipline or field related to the area of teaching responsibilities, (2) have professional experience at the time of hiring that is significant in duration and level of responsibility and consistent with the area of teaching responsibilities, and (3) participate in continuous development activities that

Scholarship Programs

In addition to the stipends available from schools with accounting PhD programs, various accounting and other organizations provide scholarships for PhD students. These include:

Accounting Doctoral Scholars Program

To help address the shortage of PhD accounting candidates, the Accounting Doctoral Scholars (ADS) program was created in 2008.[*] The mission of the ADS program and its sponsoring organizations is to increase the supply of academically qualified accounting faculty who have recent experience in public accounting in audit and tax. Spearheaded by the largest accounting firms, the ADS program is administered by the American Institute of Certified Public Accountants (AICPA) Foundation[**] and managed by an executive director and program manager. To date, 67 of the largest CPA firms and 39 state CPA societies have committed a total of $16.5 million for the program. For more information on the ADS program, see the interview with Doyle Williams, executive director, on page 313 of this book and visit the program's Web site at www.adsphd.org.

Other Programs

In addition to the ADS program, some foundations established by CPA firms help support accounting PhD programs. The PhD Project (phdproject,org) provides scholarships for minority doctoral students in business disciplines including accounting. The KPMG Foundation (kpmg-foundation.org) is the primary funder and administrator of the project, which is supported by a number of corporate and other sponsors, including the AICPA.[†] Another program is the Deloitte Foundation Ph.D. Fellowship grants. In 2009, the foundation awarded $250,000 in fellowships to 10 doctoral students in accounting.[‡] PricewaterhouseCoopers sponsors the Faculty Initiatives, various programs to provide financial support to schools. (www.pwc.com/us/en/faculty-resource/initiatives.jhtml.) Among other programs, the Ernst & Young Foundation funds the Ernst & Young Professorships, which currently support 32 accounting professorships, allowing more than 30 schools to attract and retain the highest quality faculty.

The AICPA Fellowship for Minority Doctoral Students program is designed to ensure that CPAs of diverse backgrounds are visible in college and university classrooms to serve as role models and mentors to young people in planning their education and careers. These competitive, renewable fellowships of up to $12,000 are awarded annually to full-time minority accounting scholars who demonstrate significant potential to become accounting educators. For the 2008–2009 academic year, 22 accounting PhDs were selected as recipients. For more information, visit the program's Web site at www.aicpa.org/MEMBERS/DIV/CAREER/MINI/FMDS.HTM and see the interview with Ostine Swan, CPA, senior manager, AICPA Diversity, Work/Life & Women's Initiatives program, on page 36 of this book.

The International Management Association's Foundation for Applied Research has a financial support program for doctoral students specializing in the management accounting area. For more information, visit www.imanet.org/doctoral_student_grant.asp.

[*]   "Doctoral Scholars Program in Accounting Created by CPA Profession,"

[**] Information on the Foundation can be found on the AICPA's Web site at www.aicpa.org/About+the+AICPA/Understanding+the+Organization/AICPA+Foundation+Inc.htm

[†]   "The PhD Project" www.phdproject.org/aboutus.html

[‡]   "The Deloitte Foundation Announces 2009 PhD Fellowship Grants," Deloitte Foundation press release. February 16, 2009, www.deloitte.com/view/en_US/us/About/Deloitte-Foundation/press-release/a2251ec6f6001210VgnVCM100000ba42f00aRCRD.htm

demonstrate the maintenance of intellectual capital (or currency in the teaching field) consistent with the teaching responsibilities.[16]

To help address the shortage of PhD faculty, many accredited business schools and accounting programs are hiring CPAs with master's degrees and significant professional experience as PQ faculty. In fact, many business schools have established career tracks for PQ faculty who are CPAs, with a focus on teaching and service.[17]

James Benjamin, head of the accounting department in Texas A&M's Mays School of Business, says that a key strategy to filling its faculty needs at the school has been to utilize highly qualified professionals who do not hold a PhD. "We have full-time faculty members in accounting who have master's degrees and relevant work experience," Benjamin said. "One retired after years as a senior partner with a large accounting firm. He is very good working with students."

Although PQ faculty do not receive the same salary and compensation as AQ faculty, the PQ faculty program does provide a way for experienced CPAs to become teachers in accounting programs. And if they are interested in research and teaching as a career, they could return to school to study for a PhD and join a school as an AQ faculty member.

Bridge Program

To help support PQ programs, the AACSB has created a "bridge" program to train experienced business professionals, including CPAs as PQ faculty members. Professionals who are interested in the program submit an application to AACSB. If they are admitted, they attend courses at a designated business school and receive a certificate of completion. The AICPA Foundation has provided a grant to AACSB to provide scholarships to several outstanding bridge program applicants who have significant experience in the field of accounting (audit or tax, or both) and are CPAs. For more information on the bridge program, see "Connecting Senior Executives to a Career in Academia" on the AACSB Web site at www.aacsb.edu/bridge/about.asp

High School Accounting Teachers

The first impression that a student has of a profession may come not in college, but in high school. That's when students may first learn something about accounting—maybe in an accounting class, maybe in a different class that touches on accounting. Depending on the school, students may learn about accounting as a vocation; that is, how they can complete high school and perhaps study accounting at a community college, graduate with an associate's degree, and find work as

---

16 "Deploying Professionally Qualified Faculty: An Interpretation of AACSB Standards," Association to Advance Collegiate Schools of Business (AACSB) White Paper, January 2006, Revised February 2008, www.aacsb.edu/accreditation/papers/DeployingProfessionallyQualifiedFaculty.pdf

17 "Profession's Response to a Looming Shortage: Closing the Gap in the Supply of Accounting Faculty," Michael Ruff, Jay C. Thibodeau & Jean C. Bedard, *Journal of Accountancy*, 1 March 2009, www.aacsb.edu/media/articles/Journal%20of%20Accountancy%20-%20Profession's%20 Response%20-%20AACSB%20Bridge.pdf

a bookkeeper or an office assistant. Those are perfectly good jobs, but high school students would have a much broader view of accounting if it were presented as a career, with multiple job opportunities in many different fields. In the accounting profession, accounting organizations such as the AICPA, state accounting societies, and some college accounting teachers, have been reaching out to high schools and teachers, to inform them about accounting as a career and how it can be presented as such in the classroom. One of the leaders in this endeavor is Dan Deines, an accounting professor at Kansas State University, who has developed and implemented an accounting recruitment program aimed at counteracting what he says are the negative stereotypes of accounting among high school students. Deines was also involved in designing and implementing a nationally recognized revision in the college accounting curriculum. You can read an interview with Deines on page 66 of this book.

Wrap-up

In this chapter, you learned the following:

- Teaching and research offer different career paths for college students who plan careers in accounting.
- This is an excellent time for students to study for a PhD in accounting.

- Because of a shortage of PhD faculty, graduates of PhD accounting programs are in demand.
- Students pursue an accounting PhD because they enjoy the intellectual challenge, are deeply interested in research, have a passion for teaching, like the flexible schedule, and have a strong desire to give back to the accounting profession and their communities.
- Colleges and universities offer attractive salaries and compensation, and recent PhD accounting graduates have commanded higher salaries than those in other disciplines.
- The best time to start thinking about whether you may be interested in a career as a professor of accounting—and careers in accounting generally—is while you are an undergraduate.
- First, consider why you may want study for a PhD and join a faculty. Do you really enjoy research? Teaching?
- Second, consider whether you have what it takes to complete the rigorous PhD program of advanced classes, research, teaching, and the writing and review of a dissertation.
- If you have a strong interest in, and the demonstrated ability to complete, a PhD program, you will receive strong support from the accounting profession, accounting faculty, and the AICPA and other professional organizations in the form of financial assistance, guidance, and mentoring. All have a vital interest in your success.

Now that we've discussed careers in teaching, public accounting, government, corporations and businesses, and the not-for-profit sector, as well as starting your own business, we will help you consider in chapter 10 which career path might be right for you.

Interview: Masako Darrough
Baruch College, City University of New York

Masako Darrough is a professor and chair of the Stan Ross Department of Accountancy at Baruch College, Zicklin School of Business, City University of New York. Her area of expertise is in the strategic use of information within the firm and the capital markets. She has taught at a number of universities including the University of California at Davis, University of California at Los Angeles, and Columbia University. She holds a BA in economics from International Christian University, Japan, and a PhD in economics from the University of British Columbia.

"College education can be a life-changing experience. I take great satisfaction in knowing that I help students in that process by teaching accounting and economics."

How did you get into teaching?

I went to a liberal arts college in Japan, which provided a very good educational foundation. When I moved to the United States, however, I didn't know what to do with a BA from a Japanese college. So I enrolled in a PhD program in economics, and studied accounting as part of that program. When I finished my PhD, becoming a professor was the most natural thing.

When did you start teaching accounting?

Although I started my teaching career in economics, after a while I decided to switch into accounting since I was interested in information economics. At British Columbia, I taught a course in cost accounting, which was an eye-opening experience. I decided to approach cost accounting from the economics perspective and viewed it as a tool in managerial decision making.

What do you teach at Baruch?

At Baruch, I teach managerial accounting at the undergraduate, master's, and PhD levels. The undergraduate class is called cost accounting but I think of it as a course on decision making using accounting information. In addition to teaching, I also serve as the chair of the department.

What do you like about teaching?

At Baruch, many of our students are the first in their families to attend college. So, college education can be a life-changing experience. I take great satisfaction in knowing that I help students in that process by teaching accounting and economics. We help them prepare for careers in accounting, business, or other fields. I feel that professors really make a difference here. At some other schools, students would have done well regardless.

What does it take to succeed in accounting?

I believe that one of the most important things is a passion for accounting. Some students might be in accounting because they were pushed by their parents, but they are not really excited about it or have no feel for numbers. If so, accounting is not for them. I don't know if we can instill passion in students, but I think, as teachers, we can show our passion, and try to make accounting interesting by demonstrating how it relates to the real world.

For a student interested in a career teaching, what is the path to the PhD in accounting?

First, get into a school that has a good PhD program—the school you attend makes a difference. Once enrolled, you will take a range of courses in finance, accounting, econometrics, and other fields. After two or three years, you will take a comprehensive exam to show that you have mastered the knowledge to go into academic accounting. You will write a dissertation, which should include something new that contributes to a body of knowledge on accounting issues, and, hopefully, is publishable. It usually takes five years to obtain a degree, so it is important that one has curiosity, patience, and strong work ethic.

What's the attraction of being a professor in a program such as Baruch's?

At many schools, research is an important component of what professors do. In a large program like Baruch's, you have the opportunity to do research on subjects that interest you. You also have the opportunity to teach undergraduate or graduate students in areas that interest you. At Baruch, we have students with diverse backgrounds. So, it is fun to find out about our students. Demand for PhDs in accounting is strong. So, most professors have good jobs. You are eligible for tenure after several years. You periodically are able to take sabbaticals or leaves to visit other universities. Although pressures to publish and teach well are strong, all in all, being a professor is a very rewarding career for most of us.

Interview: Doyle Z. Williams
Executive Dirctor, Accounting
Doctoral Scholars Program

In 2008, the CPA profession created the Accounting Doctoral Scholars (ADS) program (www. adsphd.org). The mission of the ADS Program and its sponsoring organizations is to increase the supply of academically qualified accounting faculty who have recent experience in public accounting in audit and tax. Spearheaded by the largest accounting firms, the ADS Program is administered by the American Institute of Certified Public Accountants (AICPA) Foundation* and managed by an executive director and program manager. To date, 67 of the largest CPA firms and 39 state CPA societies have committed a total of $16.5 million for the program.

"My message to those interested in an academic life is: If a kid like me from a Louisiana Bayou can earn a PhD and find a rewarding career as an accounting educator, so can you."

Doyle Z. Williams, PhD, CPA (inactive), is executive director of the ADS Program. He is a senior scholar in the School of Accountancy at Kennesaw State University, Kennesaw, Georgia. Williams retired in 2005 as dean of the Sam M. Walton College of Business at the University of Arkansas, where a chair in accounting was established in his honor.

Earlier, Williams was the founding dean of the School of Accounting at the University of Southern California (USC). He also served for two years as interim dean of the USC School of Business Administration. He has served on the faculty and as coordinator for the area of accounting at Texas Tech University. He was chairman of the Accounting Education Change commission for its inception in 1989 to 1993. He is a recipient of the American Institute of Certified Public Accountants Gold Medal for Distinguished Service, the AICPA's highest award, as well as its Outstanding Accounting Educator Award. He has served as a vice president and board member of the AICPA and has held leadership positions with several national and regional accounting organizations. Williams earned his bachelor of science degree in accounting from Northwestern State University of Louisiana in 1960 and his master of science and PhD in accounting from Louisiana State University in 1962 and 1965, respectively.

---

* Information on the Foundation can be found on the American Institute of Certified Public Accountants (AICPA's) Web site at: www.aicpa.org/ About+the+AICPA/Understanding+the+Organization/AICPA+Foundation+Inc.htm

How did you get interested in accounting as a career?

I grew up on a small cotton and hay farm in the Ajax community in rural northwest Natchitoches Parish, Louisiana. There were 7 people in my 1957 high school graduating class. I enrolled in Northwestern State University in Natchitoches, 30 miles away from my home. I was the first individual in my family to attend a 4-year college. When I arrived on campus, I didn't know what I wanted to study. Upon the advice of my advisor, I enrolled in chemistry. After a week of classes, I quickly learned that chemistry was not for me. One of my 2 roommates was a senior in accounting. He convinced me that if I majored in accounting, I would be able to get a job. I switched to accounting, and earned my bachelor's degree in 3 years while working my way through school.

Where did you work after graduation?

Upon graduation in 1960, I joined the New Orleans office of Deloitte Haskins and Sells, one of the public accounting firms that recruited on campus. I thought I might be interested in teaching some day, and I persuaded the firm to let me apply to graduate school at several universities to attend in the summers to earn a master's degree in accounting. Upon receiving my application, Louisiana State University responded by offering me a full scholarship that would pay for my room, tuition, books, and all other expenses for a master's in accounting, but I would have to attend full time during the fall and spring semesters. I talked to the office managing partner, and he said that this offer was an opportunity I shouldn't pass up. I could return to the firm after receiving my master's degree. At LSU, my roommate was a first year doctoral student. He encouraged me to enroll in the doctoral program and become a professor. I received my PhD in 1965 at age 25.

Where did you start teaching?

Upon graduating from LSU, I accepted a faculty appointment at Texas Tech University, where my former roommate was a faculty member. In the summer of 1966, I traveled to New York to grade CPA exams for the AICPA. Upon returning to campus, I was recruited by the AICPA for a two-year appointment to join the staff as manager of special educational projects beginning in the fall of 1967. In 1969, I returned to the faculty at Texas Tech University and in 1973, was named coordinator for the area of accounting. In 1978, I was recruited by the University of Southern California to chair the department of accounting with the goal of establishing and leading a school of accounting. In February 1979, USC's trustees approved the establishment of the school of accounting, now the Elaine and Kenneth Leventhal School of Accounting. In 1986, I was thrust on short notice into the position of interim dean of the USC School of Business Administration, a position I held for two years. In 1989, I was named chair of the newly formed Accounting Education Change Commission. I left USC in 1993 to join the University of Arkansas as dean of the College of Business—now the Sam M. Walton College of Business Administration. I retired from the University of Arkansas in 2006.

What interested you about taking the position as executive director of the ADS Program?

The program was being developed to help address an issue of critical importance to the future of accounting education and the accounting profession. There was a growing shortage of doctorally qualified faculty to teach the future generations of accounting graduates. The

ADS Program is designed to recruit and support working accounting professionals to make a career change, obtain their doctorate, and become accounting professors. This program had the potential of making a difference to the next generation of accounting professionals.

How does the program work?

The program began in July 2008. Each year for 4 years, beginning in the fall 2009, up to 30 program applicants who have at least 3 years of recent public accounting experience in auditing and tax, are selected as ADS Program Scholars. They receive a stipend of $30,000 for up to 4 years to be full time doctoral students at universities participating in the program. (Participating universities are listed on the ADS Program Web site). Participating universities have agreed to waive tuition for ADS Program Scholars.

How do students apply for the program?

Information on the application process, eligibility requirements, and an application packet can be found on the ADS Program's Web site at adsphd.org. The application must be completed online. The complete application packet must include a completed eligibility statement, letters of reference, official transcripts, official GMAT test score (must be within the last five years), and a written essay.

How are students selected?

It's a two-step process. First, we review applications based upon the applicant's academic and professional achievements and potential for successfully earning a doctorate in accounting. Applicants whose profiles are deemed to be competitive for admission to several doctoral programs at participating universities are invited to a one-day fall orientation conference held near O'Hare Airport in Chicago.

What do you discuss at the conference?

At the conference, applicants learn what life is like as faculty member, the nature and content of doctoral programs, and have the opportunity to visit with doctoral program representatives from participating universities. We are very clear with them about the number of hours involved in earning a PhD, the research and other requirements, the process for finding a position on a university faculty, the obligations for research and teaching, and qualifying for tenure.

What is the next step in the application process?

Following participation in the conference, applicants are asked to confirm their commitment to apply for doctoral study in accounting at one or more participating universities for the following fall enrollment. A committee that includes selected representatives from the participating universities selects from the remaining pool of candidates the 30 ADS Program Scholars. ADS Scholars must commit to a career in teaching and research in auditing or tax at an AACSB International** accredited university in the United States.

** AACSB International—The Association to Advance Collegiate Schools of Business—is an association of educational institutions, businesses, and other organizations devoted to the advancement of higher education in management education. www.aacsb.edu

What's been the response to the program?

We were very pleased with the response to the program during its first year. We received well over 100 completed applications and had an excellent pool of candidates for selecting ADS Program Scholars. For example, the average GMAT score for those selected for funding was 718. Several applicants for whom ADS Program funding was not available found placement with university funding at participating and other universities. There is a consensus that the existence of the ADS Program has stimulated increased interest among working professionals considering a career change. In May 2009, as we began the second year of the program, the ADS Program Web site received almost 5,000 visits. As the word has spread, we expect twice the number of applicants this year as we received in the first year of the program. (Check the program's Web site for the filing deadline.)

What does it take to succeed at the PhD level?

I maintain that for anyone to reach their fullest potential in any endeavor, they must have a passion for what they are doing. Besides, life is too short for you to be in a career that you don't enjoy. To succeed as an academician, you must have a passion for teaching and for researching interesting questions. You must communicate that passion to your students—they can tell whether you are excited about your role as a college professor. You must have a sense of moral responsibility and a commitment to making ethical choices through your teaching, research, and personal conduct. After all, you will be preparing the next generation of professionals.

What are the research requirements?

You must produce published research in order to qualify for tenure and promotion as a faculty member. To be an effective researcher, you need to have an inquisitive mind, strong quantitative and writing skills, a high level of technology skills, and the ability to apply your research skills to advance the accounting profession. You should select research issues in which you have a strong interest, for example, how to measure audit quality more effectively or develop more effective means for achieving a higher level of tax compliance. Research is highly quantitative, so as a student, you need to load up on courses such as advanced statistics, calculus, matrix algebra, or econometrics to sharpen your quantitative skills. You should be able to bring your institutional knowledge and professional experience to the classroom and your research. That experience will clearly show in your teaching compared with someone who does not have the same experience.

Final thoughts?

You can repay the profession, and those who have helped you to advance in your career, by encouraging other professionals to pursue careers in teaching. You can leave a legacy of learning that can make a difference. You, too, can be a difference maker. My message to those interested in an academic life is: If a kid like me from a Louisiana Bayou can earn a PhD and find a rewarding career as an accounting educator, so can you.

Chapter 10

Career Paths: What's Right for You?

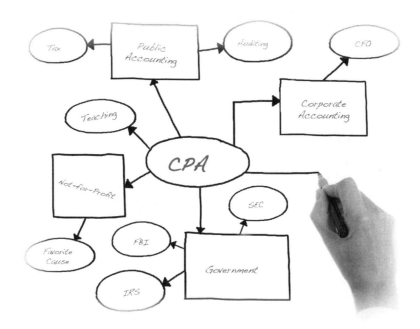

> "There is no single 'best' career path."
>
> Thomas J. Falk, Chairman and CEO •
> Kimberly-Clark Corporation

Guidance for Deciding on a Career Choice in Accounting

Previous chapters have examined careers for CPAs in public accounting, corporations and businesses, government, the not-for-profit sector, teaching, and owning a CPA firm (sole practitioner). Within each of these sectors, there are many career paths. In public accounting, for example, you could work for a Big 4 firm or one of the many other CPA firms in the United States. You could develop expertise in audit or tax, and in a particular industry such as health care or real estate. In the corporate world, you could work for a large or small corporation, in management accounting, internal audit, financial accounting, or tax accounting. The choices go on. There are so many choices that they may seem overwhelming, and leave you staring blankly at a wall, paralyzed by indecision. Then your friends will rush you to the emergency room, where a doctor will treat you for "career confusion," a common ailment.

So how do you decide on a career that's right for you? It's a dynamic question, one that you will often ask yourself as you advance in your career and your aspirations change as the result of your professional experience, personal interests, the opening of new career opportunities in accounting (such as in forensic accounting or in green building design and development), and changes in the big wide world, such as continuing advances in information technology that are transforming business and accounting itself and creating demand for CPAs with IT skills, or the increas-

ing globalization of business that will mean more opportunities for CPAs to work overseas (especially if you have foreign language skills). In all likelihood, you will pursue not one, but multiple careers in accounting over time, and perhaps find careers beyond accounting. For example, maybe you'll partner with a friend to start a software firm, or perhaps volunteer to work in a developing country where you use your accounting skills to advise a not-for-profit organization that provides micro loans to budding entrepreneurs.

In considering possible careers in accounting, you can begin with a broad perspective. The following is a summary and brief description of the principal career options.

Public Accounting Firms (chapter 4)
Big 4
  Audit and assurance
  Tax
  Advisory
  Industry Specialty
  International Networks
Other Firms
  Audit and assurance (some firms)
  Tax
  Advisory
  Industry specialty (some firms)
  Some have international affiliations

Corporation/Business, Public or Private; Large or Small (chapter 5)
  Management accounting
  Internal audit
  Financial accounting
  Tax accounting
  Information technology

Public Accounting

Big 4

Because of their size and resources, the Big 4 are able to offer the most extensive training programs for new college recruits as well as other staff. Their pay equals or exceeds that of other firms, and their benefits packages are among the most generous in corporate America. They have expanded and refined their flexible work programs to try to give employees a better work and life balance and compensate for the long hours that employees work during tax season and sometimes at other times of the year. If you work for a Big 4 firm, you will receive support and guidance from supervisors, colleagues, mentors, and others to help you get started and advance in your career. Initially, you would work in audit and assurance, or in tax, or both. You might also do some work in advisory. After you have a year or two of experience, you may concentrate in audit or in tax. Your area of concentration will depend on the firm's needs as well as your interests.

In audit, you could find yourself participating in audits of some of the world's biggest corporations as well as other companies. In tax, you likewise could assist in providing tax services to some of the largest corporations as well as other companies. Big 4 firms provide many services, including consulting and advisory, to clients in a number of industries, and over time you could develop experience and expertise in an industry from working with clients in it. Because the Big 4 have offices all over the United States and the world, you may be able to work in different offices for personal or professional reasons and, if you really stand out, to work overseas. You will meet, work with, and get to know a variety of people. While the environment in a Big 4 firm is very supportive, it also is very competitive, and you are expected to perform at the highest level. You will face strong competition from other talented people for raises, promotions, and opportunities to advance in the organization.

Other Public Accounting Firms

Besides the Big 4, there are thousands of other public accounting firms, ranging from large to mid-sized to small firms based on their revenue, number of partners and employees, number of clients, and other criteria. These firms include some of the fastest growing CPA firms in the United States. Although many of these firms do not offer training on the scale of the Big 4, many have very good training programs. Their cultures are friendly and less formal, and their pay and benefits are competitive. Like the Big 4, they have worked to improve their benefits programs in areas like flex time. In smaller firms, you are likely to meet and work with many of the people in the organization, including senior management. Some of these firms conduct audits of public companies (those not audited by the Big 4) as well as private companies, and many provide tax services. Many of them do the work for exciting and new start-up companies. Some also provide various types of assurance services. Most do not have formal programs to rotate you through audit and tax; instead, you would learn through on-the-job training, working for audit and tax clients.

Some of these firms specialize in selected industries such as real estate, and you could develop an industry specialization, although the number of industries in which you could work will be limited compared with a Big 4 firm. You could also develop experience in working with small businesses, which constitute most of the businesses in the United States and are a core client base of many firms, as well as with individuals, for example, in personal financial and estate planning. Depending on the firm, you may have a chance for faster advancement than in a Big 4 firm.

Companies

In the corporate world, you could work for public or private companies that range from the Fortune 500 to small businesses. In a large company, you usually would start as a staff accountant, and you might work in management or corporate accounting (including general accounting, cost accounting, and bud-

geting), internal auditing, financial accounting, tax accounting, or information technology, or for a specific division. Depending on the company, you might rotate through some of these functions in your first year or so with the organization. Large companies offer competitive salaries and attractive benefits, although these vary by company, and they usually pay performance bonuses that, in public companies, may be partly in company stock (and the rest in cash). Your first promotion usually would be from staff accountant to senior staff accountant, and, after a few years with the organization, you might move up the financial accounting track; for example, your next promotion might be to supervising financial analyst. Alternatively, you might move up the management accounting track, with your next promotion to accounting supervisor. (See the Corporate Career Ladder in chapter 5, page 165.) Alternatively, you might work in a specialty area such as tax. In smaller companies, the accounting functions might not be as formalized, and you might work in general accounting, cost accounting, budgeting and many other accounting activities. The pay and benefits might be less than in a larger organization, but there are trade-offs, for example, you could learn about all aspects of the company's operations, take on more responsibility more quickly, and work in a less structured, more informal environment. And some small companies might offer ownership interests to employees based on their performance, years with the company, or other criteria.

Working in Corporate Versus Public Accounting

What's the difference between working as a CPA in a corporation and a public accounting firm? A public accounting firm provides audit, tax, and other services to corporations and other clients. To maintain its independence as an auditor, the firm cannot maintain the client's books and records or prepare its financial statements or other financial documents. To be sure, CPAs in a public accounting firm work with their counterparts in a corporation in gathering, analyzing, validating and preparing information for an audit. But it is the corporation's management team, not the CPA firm, that creates the financial statements and other documents. For its part, the public accounting firm examines the company's financials and issues an audit report. These are two separate but interrelated functions. Likewise, the company's management team and staff prepare the company's tax returns, while its public accounting may assist and advise in preparing the returns. The firm may also advise the company on tax issues, for example, the impact of new tax laws or regulations on the company's business.

Industry Experience

Another difference between public and corporate accounting is that CPAs in public accounting firms usually work for many companies and other clients in the same or different industries. At some point, they may elect to specialize in servicing clients in a particular industry. In doing so, they develop in-depth knowledge of that industry.

By contrast, CPAs in corporate accounting work for a single company in a particular industry, and they usually do not have the same broad industry exposure as those working for public accounting firms. From working in their companies every business day, corporate CPAs have a depth of knowledge about and experience in their organizations that generally is unmatched by the CPAs that audit their companies.

What corporate CPAs and some public accounting CPAs have in common is industry knowledge. Corporate CPAs are highly knowledgeable about the industry of which their company is a part, and so, too, are public accounting CPAs who specialize in that industry.

Government

If you're interested in government, there's a job for you. CPAs are in demand at all levels of government—federal, state, and local. Depending on the agency, you could step into a challenging job right out of school or with a few years of experience in accounting. You could work as a revenue agent for the IRS, a special agent for the FBI, join the CIA, help the Government Accountability Office audit billions of dollars in government spending, or serve on the accounting staff of a big city agency. If you want to give back to the community and help others, you can work for government agencies whose missions are to alleviate poverty, provide social services to those in need, assist military veterans, protect the environment, or promote education. With increasing numbers of government employees scheduled to retire,[1] workers joining the government will have more opportunities for advancement. Salaries of government employees are usually less than those for similar positions in the private sector, but when government benefit programs are factored in, the

---

1 This subject was discussed in chapter 6, Careers in Government Accounting.

total compensation of government employees usually equals or exceeds some private sector compensation. Depending on the government, employees may have stronger job protection than in the private sector.

Not-for-Profit

If you would like to work for a not-for-profit organization, you won't have to look very far. Not-for-profit organizations can be found in most cities and communities across the United States. They include public charities that provide services and programs that reach many Americans, foundations that provide funding for other nonprofits, and other not-for-profit organizations such as health maintenance organizations. Among other areas, not-for-profits support the arts, education, environmental causes, human services (such as family and children services), and social action organizations. From among the broad range of not-for-profits, you could find some whose missions and goals appeal to you and are organizations where you would like to work. In a large not-for-profit, you could start as an associate, an entry level position, working for managers on accounting and finance, programs, development, communications, or other activities. You could advance to manager, supervising specific programs. In a small not-for-profit, functions are not as structured and you might be responsible for financial reporting and internal auditing and assist with program management, marketing, fund-raising, and other activities.

Starting a CPA Firm (Sole Practitioner)

Rather than working for someone else, you could start you own firm. It's an appealing idea, being on your own. But you would require a solid business plan, startup capital, a high degree of technical skill, and skills in managing a business, marketing, and finding clients. Starting and operating your own firm is not easy. It requires focus, discipline, and persistence to be successful and, because of the risks, CPAs usually go out on their own only after they have at least a few years of experience working for a CPA firm. If the risks are high, so are the rewards—the satisfaction of providing services that clients value, using some of the profits from your business to build your personal wealth, having flexible work hours (once your business is established), and maybe giving back to your community by providing pro bono services to low-income families or volunteering to teach a class in personal financial planning at a community college.

Teaching

If you have a strong interest in research and a passion for teaching, you could earn a PhD and join the accounting faculty of a university. There is a shortage of PhD faculty in the business schools and accounting departments of universities and colleges nationwide, and it is expected to intensify as more accounting faculty retire. While your salary as an accounting professor might not be as much as a partner's in a Big 4 firm or a corporate CFO's, your pay plus your benefits would provide for an attractive compensation package. And you might supplement your income with outside consulting work, publishing books, or other activities. Furthermore, you would have more flexible hours, and perhaps a better work/life balance, than you might find in the private sector. Because of the shortage of PhD faculty, many schools are hiring CPAs with a master's degree and significant professional experience. If you meet these and other qualifications, you might get a teaching position. Alternatively, with a master's degree, you could teach in the accounting program at a community college.

What Career is Right for You?

So what career in accounting is right for you? As noted at the start of this chapter, it's not a question you consider once. ("I will go forth, accounting degree in hand, and work in corporate accounting to the end of days.") Rather, it's a question you will consider often as you advance in your career, and your career aspirations change with time and experience. As a CPA (or future CPA), you have highly portable technical and professional skills and are much in demand in business, government, not-for-profit organizations and academia. So you could move from one public accounting firm to another, or from public accounting to the corporate world, or wherever your interests take you.

But you don't want to become some sort of accounting nomad, bouncing aimlessly from one job to the next. You need a career plan, beginning with a vision for your career.

Where do you see yourself in five years, and ten? As a manager with a Big 4 firm? A partner in a small CPA firm? A special agent with the FBI? Supervising IRS revenue agents? CFO of a Fortune 500 company? CEO of a not-for-profit? Starting your own business? Professor of accounting at a university? First CPA on Mars? Forget that last one. Shows you've got a great imagination, but your vision needs practical grounding. Here on Earth.

Next, think about your goals—your big, audacious goals, or whatever you want to call them. While you will pursue different careers and job opportunities, your career choices should be based on your core set of goals that will guide your decision making throughout your career. The following is a list of goals I've compiled based on talking about careers with a number of students at different universities and colleges across the United States as well as CPAs in every sector of accounting and at every level of experience in the profession. This is not intended as a comprehensive list but as a simple guide—a starting point—in your career planning. You can refine and adapt it to your expectations and prioritize it depending on what's most important to you.

- Your work
  - Interesting: Work with a variety of clients, on different projects, in the field or in the office, using the latest technology
  - Enjoyable: Work that you like doing, that gets you out of bed in the morning
  - Challenging: Help clients to solve difficult problems, work on complex projects
  - Meaningful: Have a sense of accomplishment personally and as part of an organization.
  - Flexible: Work in the field, in the office, at home; work different hours depending on your employer's and your personal needs

- People you work with
  — Diverse: Work with people of diverse background, experiences, perspectives
  — Teamwork: Work with others toward common goals
  — Camaraderie: Work with people who enjoy working together, helping one another
  — Connections: Develop professional relationships with others
- Career development
  — Opportunities for advancement
  — Progressively assume more responsibility
  — Move to leadership positions
- Learning opportunities
  — On the job
  — Employer training
  — Employer funded outside training (classroom or online)
  — Employer support of CPA, other certification (pay exam expenses, allow time off to study)
- Security
  — Financial: Build wealth, finance retirement, create estate
  — Career: Achieve a stable career in the accounting profession
- Give back to community
  — Work for profit-making company whose products and services have social benefit
  — Volunteer through employer-sponsored volunteer programs
  — Work for not-for-profit organization
  — Work for government agency focused on community services (for example, education, housing, services for the homeless)
  — Educate the next generation of CPAs (teaching, mentoring, training, and so on)

Next, you can prioritize your goals however you want, such as "1" for most important and "5" for least important. In setting your priorities, consider that it takes time to achieve a goal. So you need to take the long view. Consider the "Your work" category, for example. Particularly with entry level jobs, there is bound to be a certain amount of routine work—grunt work. But if that work will lead to a promotion and more interesting work, then it may merit a high rating, not as an end in itself, but as a means to an end.

Inevitably, in setting your priorities, you will have to make trade-offs. If you work for a small CPA firm, for example, your might take on responsibility faster than in a large firm. But in a small firm, your training might be mainly on the job, compared with a combination of on the job and classroom training in a large firm.

Once you have an idea of your priorities, you may need to do some research. If you're just starting college, and are interested in a career in accounting, you may not know enough about the different career choices to decide on a career path. To learn more, you can start with the best sources of information—CPAs who are currently working in public accounting, the corporate world, and other sectors. You may be able to connect with them through your network of friends, current and former classmates, teachers, recruiters who visit your campus, and so on. You can also research online for articles and other information on careers and check out books on the topic at a library (some sources on careers are suggested in appendix 1.)

Early career planning can also help you make decisions about your education. For example, you could earn an undergraduate degree in accounting, and if you have an interest in real estate, you could study for a graduate degree such as a master's of real estate development. If you think you might go into corporate accounting, you might consider earning an MBA. Figure 10-1 maps out one process for evaluating accounting as a career path.

Figure 10-1: *Career Evaluation*

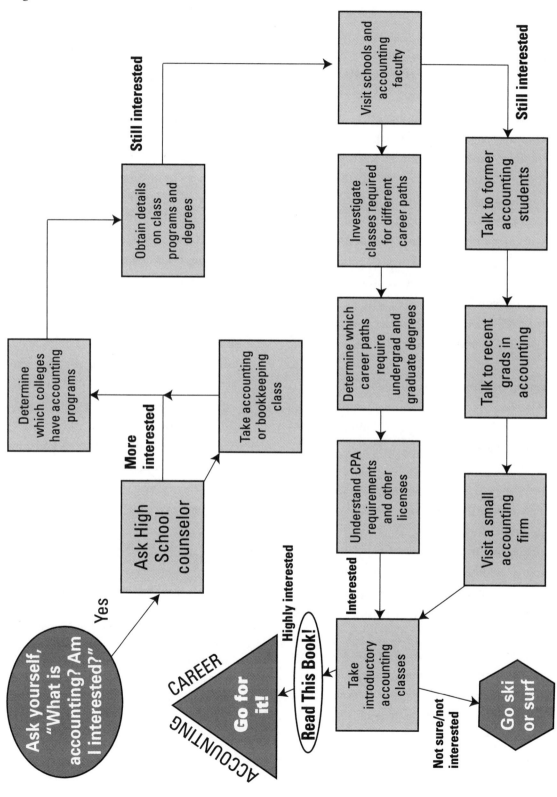

So where should you start in accounting? Having spent my career in public accounting, I strongly recommend that you start with a public accounting firm, whether a Big 4 firm or other firm. If you talk to CPAs or read the interviews in this book, you will find that many CPAs began their careers in public accounting. By working for a public accounting firm, you will develop a deep understanding of accounting, learn how a firm operates, and learn about business, the not-for-profit sector, government and other sectors from working with the firm's clients. Public accounting will provide a strong foundation for whatever career path you choose.

After you have some experience working for a CPA firm, for example, you could decide whether you want to continue in public accounting, and, if so, whether you want to remain with the same firm or change firms. Alternatively, you could move into another sector such as corporate accounting or government accounting.

To be sure, public accounting is not the only starting point for your career, and you may decide that you want to work for a corporation, for example. You could work in management accounting, financial accounting or another accounting area, and develop the skills and experience to advance in the company or, if you choose, to change jobs. For example, for better pay and benefits, and other reasons, you might move from management accounting in one company to a similar position in another company. In government, you might start with a federal agency and develop skills in auditing or budgeting that would enable you, if you choose, to work in state or local government. If giving back to the community is a high priority, you could start with a not-for-profit organization. Your skills as a CPA would be highly valued by an organization in planning investments in programs and services, ensuring that it gets the most value from its investments, and maintaining strict accountability for its investing.

Regardless of your career path, accounting provides a relatively stable career. To be sure, demand for CPAs can fluctuate with changes in the economy, but demand will continue to grow over the long term.[2]

And whatever career path you choose, it is important for you to develop and refine your skills. You should develop a high level of technical skill in audit, tax, or advisory services, acquire knowledge and skills in one or more industries, develop outstanding communication (written and oral) skills, work well with people, and demonstrate leadership skills. The better your skills, the more you will be in demand, and the greater your career opportunities.

Wrap-up

In this chapter, you learned the following:

- As a CPA, you have a choice of careers in public accounting, corporations and businesses, government, and the not-for-profit sector, as well as in teaching. Alternatively, you could decide to start your own business.

---

2 Demand for accountants is discussed in chapter 1.

- Your career aspirations will change as the result of your professional experience, personal interests, and the opening of new career opportunities in accounting.
- Most likely you will pursue not one, but multiple careers in accounting over time and perhaps find careers beyond accounting.
- You need to have a vision of where you want to be in your career in 5 or 10 years and create your own career goals. Your vision and goals will guide you in your career choices.

- Public accounting can provide a solid foundation for whatever career paths you choose.
- As a CPA, you have portable skills that you can use anywhere in accounting, but you need to develop a high skill level in order to create the best career opportunities for yourself.

In the next chapter, we look at what employers want when hiring CPAs.

Chapter 11

Finding that First Job

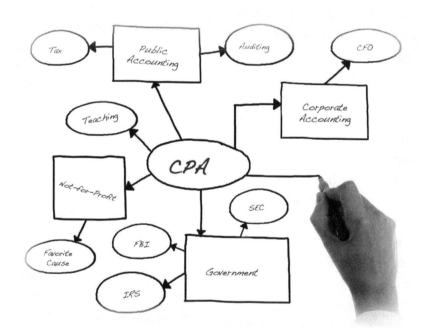

"You have to be open to learning, regardless of how much experience or education you have."

Ed Nusbaum, CEO • Grant Thornton International Ltd.

Search for the Job You Want

The key employers of graduates with bachelor's and master's degrees in accounting or related fields (such as a business degree with an accounting minor) are public accounting firms, corporations and businesses, government agencies, and not-for-profit organizations.[1] CPAs work in a variety of jobs with thousands of organizations in these sectors. But how did they find a job? It was through a process of deciding upon the sector in which they wanted to work, the location where they wanted to work, and the employers they wanted to work for, and then applying for and landing a job with a target employer.

Easier said than done, you may think, perhaps feeling a little overwhelmed at the prospect of the job hunt. For guidance, you could consult a fortune teller. Or put on a blindfold and throw a dart at a list of employers. But what would you say in a job interview? "How did you decide to apply to our company?" "The dart landed on your name."

There are, of course, far better ways to find a job than leaving things to chance. This chapter offers guidance when deciding who you want to work for and landing a job with the employer of your choice. The following are key points to consider.

Location

In earlier chapters, you learned about careers in the different sectors of accounting and, in chapter 10, about how to decide upon the sector you want to work in. Now you're ready to look for a job in your target sector.

Regardless of which sector you choose, you can narrow your job search by deciding where you want to work—in a large metropolitan areas like New York or Los Angeles? Other major cities? A small town?

Let's say you decide to work in public accounting, as many graduates do (although some go on to work in other sectors).[2] The Big 4 firms have offices in most major cities in the United States. The major firms have offices in particular regions, and some have a national presence. In addition, there are thousands of small CPA firms or sole practitioners in cities and town across the country. You can compile a list of prospective employers in your target city from the Web sites of public accounting firms, online and print directories, and other sources. Likewise, many major corporations have offices in various locations and you can go through the same process of researching companies and compiling a list of employers in the city where you want to work. In government, most federal agencies are headquartered in Washington, DC, but many have offices in other cities. Although

---

1 Some accounting graduates start their own businesses, but usually only after acquiring experience working for CPA firms. Some go on to study for a PhD in accounting and go into teaching and research, but these are a relatively small number of graduates compared with those who go to work in public accounting and other sectors.

2 Chapter 4 discusses careers in public accounting.

state governments are headquartered in capital cities, they also have offices in other cities across the state. And city and county governments are major employers. You can develop a list of prospective government employers from information on their Web sites and government career and job sites like USAJobs.

In the not-for-profit sector, some large, national organizations have offices in different locations, but many not-for-profits are small and concentrate their services in a particular community. So although you may find a job with a large not-for-profit in your target city, you are more likely to work for a small organization. You can compile a list of not-for-profit organizations in your target market using resources such as the Urban Institute National Center for Charitable Statistics, The Foundation Center, or doing an online search. (The chapters on the different sectors and appendix 1 are additional sources of information on researching organizations.)

If you focus your job search on a particular city, however, you may not find an employer you want to work for or a job that interests you. So you might consider expanding your search parameters somewhat, for example, by deciding on the 3 top cities where you want to work and searching there. But stay within limits. You don't want to start scouring the entire country and barging into every CPA or corporate office looking for work. Of course, persistence could pay off. After visiting your 9,000th office, you might be offered a job, but by then, decades may have gone by, and you'd be 80 years old. Just tell your co-workers you're a late bloomer. But I digress. Back to the job hunt.

Organization Size

Regardless of the sector, large organizations tend to have common characteristics—as do small ones. Large organizations have a formal hierarchy with defined job roles and career paths. They provide a variety of job orientation and training programs and other resources to support you on the job and help you advance in your career. They may pay more than smaller organizations and usually have greater benefits. But their more formalized structures may limit you in pursuing your professional and career interests within the organization. A small organization has a more informal structure and you may not have the same support and benefits, but you might have more responsibility, the opportunity to work on different types of jobs, as well as the opportunity to advance more quickly.

Of course, these are generalizations about organizations, and you need to research a particular organization to understand its work environment. For example, some large organizations, in efforts to attract and retain talented employees, are trying to adapt the more flexible approach of small companies in giving new employees more responsibility early on, and more experience in working in different parts of the company rather than being pigeon holed in a single department. Additionally, some small companies are trying to provide more support to new employees through training or mentoring programs.

Public or Private

If you decide to work in the corporate sector, you could work for a public or private company. Public companies that are registered with the Securities and Exchange Commission (SEC) must file financial reports and comply with the Sarbanes-Oxley Act (SOX), and as part of your job you might assist a company to prepare these reports, and to conduct internal audits to ensure the company is SOX compliant. Private companies are not subject to the same reporting requirements as public companies; however, many private companies have chosen to adhere to the same SOX reporting procedures as public companies. In working for a private company, you may still be involved in SOX reporting to some degree. The same is true if you work for a not-for-profit that follows SOX reporting.

Another consideration in working for a public company is compensation. At the entry level, you might participate in some type of profit sharing plan that pays you a year-end bonus in stock, for example. And if you move into a senior position in a company, your incentive compensation plan could provide for a stock payment, depending on the company's performance, and yours. To stay competitive in attracting talent, private companies may pay some form of cash bonus. And who knows? Maybe you'll find a company that will throw in free movie or concert tickets, and that will clinch your decision to join them. R-i-g-h-t.

Corporation or Partnership

"Are you a C corporation, S corporation, partnership, limited liability company (LLC), or limited liability partnership (LLP)?" Probably not the first question you'd ask an employer in a job interview, but it is good to know the differences in the structure, organization, ownership interests, voting rights, legal authority, and responsibility of corporate executives and partners, compensation plans, and other aspects of these different entities. Large companies usually are C-corporations. Other companies may use the S corporation structure. (The various ownership structures were covered in chapter 5.) Public accounting firms and other professional services firms usually are partnerships or, more commonly, LLPs or LLCs. The ownership structure may not matter when you join an organization in an entry level position, but it would matter if you advance to an ownership position in a partnership or senior executive level in a corporation. If you become a partner in a CPA firm that is a partnership, you would have legal authority to bind the firm, for example, in a contract with a client, and you would be liable for the company's debts and other obligations along with the other partners. If the firm is an LLC or LLP, your liability would most likely be limited to what you have invested in the firm. If you work for and own shares in a corporation, your exposure is limited to your shareholder interest. In a partnership, you receive a percentage of the firm's income, and your share depends on how much income the firm generates. You may also receive some base amount of compensation. As a senior executive in a public corporation, part (and sometimes a substantial part) of your compensation is in company stock, which fluctuates in value on the stock exchanges where it is listed.

Your Interests

If you want to work in the corporate sector, think about the industries that corporations are in, which industries interest you, and then about companies to target in that industry. If you plan to go into public accounting and join a Big 4 or other firm, you could work for clients in different industries. By contrast, if you join a small firm that specializes in an industry such as health care or real estate, you would be working mainly with clients in those industries. Do you want broad exposure working for multiple clients, or perhaps more in-depth exposure to clients in a few industries? If you plan to join a not-for-profit organization, consider whether it provides services mainly to organizations in the arts, education, health care, or other fields, and decide which fields interest you. And if you want to go into government, consider the services that an agency provides, or whom it regulates.

Creating a Target List of Employers

After considering where you want to work, the size of the organization, and so on, you can start to develop a list of prospective employers. If the employers are large, well-known public accounting firms, companies, or other organizations, you can develop a list fairly easily. For example, suppose you decide you want to work in New York for one of the Big 4. You probably already know who they are. Or you may decide to work for a large public company in New York. You can check a list such as the Fortune 500.[3] If you're interested in a large private company in New York, you can check the Forbes "America's Largest Private Companies."[4]

Other information sources can help in your research. Bigbook.com (www.bigbook.com) lists businesses by industry, state, and city. For example, on its home page, in keyword, type in "accountants," and in location, type in New York, NY, to pull up links to lists of accountants, public accountants, and CPAs in New York. Crain's New York Business sells a "Book of Lists" containing the top public accounting firms, companies, not-for-profit, and other organizations in New York. Your library may have a copy. American City Business Journals sells books of lists of the top companies, accounting firms, and so on, in a number of

---

3 On the Fortune 500 home page, click on "Near You" and "Cities." http://money.cnn.com/magazines/fortune/fortune500/2009/

4 On the Forbes "America's Largest Private Companies" home page, under "Sort List By," click on "State." A short list of companies, and the state, comes up. Click on "NY" to pull up New York state companies, including those in New York City, such as Bloomberg, ranked number 52 on the Forbes 2009 list. www.forbes.com/2009/10/28/largest-private-companies-business-private-companies-09_land.html

cities such as Los Angeles. Again, through a library, you may be able to find a particular city book that interests you. Some subscription services offer free resources. Hoovers (www.hoovers.com) publishes detailed information on companies in many industries. Although a subscription is required for in-depth company research, Hoovers does allow a free look at limited company information. Local chambers of commerce are another source of information about companies. If you're interested in a government job in New York City, various directories help you learn which government agencies have offices there, for example, CitiDex New York City (citidex.com) is an online directory and guide to New York City. Click on "G" (Categories Starting with the Letter G) for links to United States, New York State, and New York City offices. And, of course, you can use Google, Yahoo!, or other search engines to track down information about prospective employers.

What to Learn

In the course of your research, learn as much as you can about an organization. What are its goals? What challenges does it face? What are its strengths? Its weak points?

Equally important, learn about the organization as a place to work and start a career, using the career goals in chapter 10 as a guide. Among the questions to consider are the following:

- *Reputation.* What is the organization's reputation in the industry with its customers, employees, competitors, the public?

- *Culture.* What is the organization's culture? Is it a culture in which you would find satisfying work and perform up to your expectations—and the organization's?
- *Management.* What is the organization's management style? Would management provide the right level of supervision and support?
- *Work environment.* Do employees enjoy working at the organization? Would you?
- *Work/life balance.* Would you have a life besides work?
- *Training.* What training does the organization provide?
- *Opportunities for advancement.* Where could you expect to be in the organization in a year or two? Or in five years?

With the wealth of research resources available, you can develop a list of public accounting firms, companies, or other organizations in your target market—whether it's a short list, such as the New York offices of the Big 4, or a much longer list, such as a list of CPA firms in New York. Next, you can start doing research on individual organizations to develop a list of prospective employers.

Learning About Individual Employers

So how do you learn about individual employers?

Go to the Source

You can learn a lot about companies from their Web sites, which typically include their mission statements and goals, business lines and services, news about the organization, newsletters, reports, and career opportunities. The career section of Crowe Horwath, one of the largest public accounting firms, has two starting points—one for university hires and the other for experienced professionals. The university hire section includes reasons to join the firm, internships, career paths, events, and how to apply. Clifton Gunderson's site includes a list of frequently asked career questions.

Internships

You can also learn a lot about an organization by working as an intern. Many large organizations, and some small ones, have internship programs and information about these programs usually can be found in the careers section of a firm's Web site. If an organization doesn't have a formal intern program, you could contact it to see if you could work as an intern.

What Others Have to Say

A wealth of information is available from others within the accounting profession that may help you decide on your career in accounting. Consider the following sources of information:

- *The traditional media.* A wealth of news and analysis can be gleaned from coverage of organizations in print and online media, including general and business newspapers, magazines and newsletters, trade publications and industry journals, and other outlets.
- *Social media.* Many organizations have sites on Facebook, YouTube, LinkedIn, and other social media that provide information about careers with the organization. Some are robust sites with informative, creative content that communicate the organization's story in print, video, and other ways.

- *Blogs.* Blogs written by an organization's current or former employees, college faculty members, business consultants, journalists, industry analysts, and others provide insights into public accounting firms, corporations, government agencies, and not-for-profit organizations.
- *Your network.* You've developed a network of friends, colleagues, associates, teachers, mentors, and others in college, and, before that, in high school, grade school, and so on. People in your network may be knowledgeable about some of the companies you're targeting, or know someone who does, or know someone who knows someone. Through your network, you might be able to connect with current or former employees of the company who could give you insights into the organization.
- *Student and professional organizations.* If you have a student membership in the American Institute of Certified Public Accountants and perhaps a state CPA society or other professional organization, or belong to a student organization such as Beta Alpha Psi,[5] you can attend the organization's meetings, participate in its activities, and get to know people in the profession, including some who may work for a public accounting firm, company, not-for-profit organization or government agency where you are interested in working. Such memberships also are a way to build long-term business and professional relationships.
- *Campus activities.* Public accounting firms, companies, and other employers visit some campuses for career days or other recruiting events, and CPAs, business people, government executives, and others often visit campuses. Take advantage of opportunities to meet representatives of organizations and develop connections that might lead to future employment.

---

5 An honorary organization for financial information students and professionals

Skills Assessment

Let's assume that, as a result of your research, you've narrowed your list of prospective employers to, say, five public accounting firms, companies, government agencies, or not-for-profit organizations. What are these organizations looking for in a job applicant? In addition to the accounting, audit, tax, or other skills required for a particular job, organizations evaluate prospective employees based on a core set of skills. These skills were discussed in chapter 5, so there's no need to go into detail here. They include communication, analytical, interpersonal, leadership, learning, teaming, financial (understanding money and finance), and personal integrity.[6] To learn more about the skills that employers require, you can check the Web sites of employers themselves. The career sections of some employers include a list of what they are looking for in job applicants. For example, on Ernst & Young's home page, click on "Careers" and "Students" and "Applying to Ernst & Young."

In considering your skills, don't overlook your reading skills. I mention reading because as a CPA or other professional, you will be required to read, comprehend, analyze, and interpret vast amounts of information such as accounting pronouncements, laws and regulations, a variety of reports, communications from people inside and outside your organization, and much more. Usually you have to accomplish this under the constant pressures of your job—so much to read and never enough time. No lying in a hammock and reading a novel on a lazy summer afternoon here. I took a speed reading course that helped me to improve my reading ability, although my wife claims I never remember anything I read.

If there is one area in which graduates could improve, it is in their communication skills. I know this from my own experience in managing people, in interviewing senior people in public accounting, corporations and other sectors for this book, and in talking to other executives. It is also evident in the efforts of schools with accounting and business programs to strengthen the communications component of their curriculums. So whether you are in school or working in public accounting or elsewhere, do an assessment of your communication skills as part of your overall skills assessment. A teacher, mentor, or other person might help you to evaluate your strengths and which skills need improvement; in addition, you might use software programs designed for this purpose. And, as a simple evaluation tool, you could list your skills on a spreadsheet and assign a value to each, with "10" for the highest skill level and "1," the lowest.

Applying for Jobs

Besides the core skills that are required in most jobs, you must also have the skills specific to the job itself. Again, you can check the Web sites of prospective employers to see

---

6 Chapter 2 includes the American Institute of Certified Public Accountants' recommended course of study in college for CPAs to become well rounded professionals.

if they list any jobs in which you are interested, the job requirements, and how to apply. The IRS career Web section[7] includes an explanation of its hiring process, a 10-step job application process, and a link to search for and apply for jobs.

Even if an employer doesn't happen to list a job you're interested in, you can get a sense of what the requirements might be by doing a search for jobs on the Web sites of similar employers. For example, if you are interested in an entry level audit job with a particular Big 4 firm, but none are available, you could check the sites of each of the other Big 4 firms for similar positions.

Many organizations are interested in hearing from prospective employees even if they don't happen to have an immediate job opening. On Hewlett Packard's Web site (hp.com), for example, you have the option of creating a profile that the company's recruiters can use to match your qualifications with future job openings.[8]

More and more organizations are advertising jobs on online job sites such as career-builder.com (appendix 1 lists some of these sites.) Staffing agencies that are hired by companies to recruit CPAs and other employees also post jobs online. Some professional organizations also list jobs online. You can check these various sites to see if they list any jobs and employers that interest you. Typically, you can search by keyword (such as accountant or auditor), location, and other criteria. Some organizations provide detailed job descriptions, others a short description. Some online sites also provide guidance on writing resumes, preparing for job interviews, and other career help.

Experience Requirement

One of the first things you should check on an online job posting is the experience for a position. Many public accounting firms hire graduates right out of school, and by joining such a firm, you can acquire the experience required to get a CPA license. This varies by state, but generally is two years. (See chapter 3.) Depending on the firm, you might be given (paid or unpaid) time off to study for the exam and the firm might pay for you to take a CPA exam study course. Outside of public accounting, employers may require that you have some level of experience, for example, two years of public accounting experience, or they may require you to have a CPA license, which, as noted, includes an experience requirement. Some job posting may have a specific experience requirement, for example, two years of audit experience with a health care organization. Some organizations may be flexible about the experience requirement, for example, experience is "preferred" rather than "required." And if you don't have the requisite experience, the firm might consider other factors, such as whether you were an outstanding student, participated in extracurricular activities, held leadership positions in student organizations, and worked in various jobs while in school. In any case, if you have a question about the experience part of a job posting, you might try calling

---

7 On the IRS home page, scroll to the bottom, click on Careers. That will take you to the "Careers at IRS" page. Click on Search/Apply for Jobs.

8 On the Hewlett Packard home page (hp.com), under "HP Corporate," click on "Jobs." This will take you to the "Jobs at HP" page. Under "Go Local," pull up "United States." This will take you to the HP United States recruiting Web site.

or e-mailing the organization. Keep in mind, however, that while the Internet is a powerful tool for job searching, it does have its limitations. You may not find a job that excites you and meets your career expectations, or you may find a job posted, but not with a CPA firm, company or other employer that interests you. You will compete directly with others who are applying for the same job. And an employer may not list a job online because it does not have the time or resources to screen applications, among other reasons. Thus, your primary job hunting approach should be to identify prospective employers and contact them directly.

Letter of Recommendation

When applying to an organization, see if you can get a letter of recommendation from a teacher, professional or business associate, mentor, or other person, written to a senior executive in the organization. The executive, in turn, may suggest to a hiring manager or human resources director that you be asked to come in for a meeting. Such requests carry a lot of weight inside an organization. I personally have written letters of recommendation for countless students—letters that often resulted in a meeting being scheduled. And even if the organization doesn't have a job for you at the moment, you could get serious consideration when a job opportunity is available. And if you are particularly well qualified, the organization may even create a position for you.

Resumes

If you decide to apply for a job listed online, or apply to an organization directly, you will have to submit a resume as part of the application process. Some organizations have an online resume that you fill out; others ask you to upload a resume. Otherwise, you could mail your resume and a cover letter to an employer.

Advice on writing resumes and cover letters is readily available online. (Type in "how to write a resume" in a search engine such as Google.) There are a number of books on resume writing. (Do a search on Amazon or other online book seller.) So let me offer just a few thoughts on preparing your resume:

What do you want to do with the organization?

If you're contacting the organization to let it know of your interest in employment (rather than responding to a specific job announcement), explain the type of job you're interested in, and why.

Why do you stand out?

What skills, experience, and personal and professional characteristics do you have that differentiate you as a prospective employee? Say what you've accomplished, not what you've done. Don't say you were the membership chair of a student organization, say you helped to increase its membership 40 percent.

Don't overlook what you've accomplished. If you were on a team that beat five other schools in an accounting case study competition, say so.

Include your job experience.

If you worked a summer driving a forklift in a warehouse, that may not have much to do with your studying accounting, unless you happened to learn something about inventory management. But include it on your resume. Shows you have experience in the real world of work.

Highlight all of your experiences.

Employers realize that you may have little job experience (other than driving that forklift). They want to know about your other experiences. If you did volunteer work or participated in extracurricular activities, such as serving as an officer of a student organization, include these in your resume.

Ask a mentor, advisor, or colleague to review your resume before you send it in. They may offer suggestions as to how you might improve the resume. Be sure to carefully proofread your resume—check for grammar, spelling, typing errors, and so on. Ask someone to proofread it—they may catch mistakes that you don't.

Interviewing for a Job

Suppose your diligent job hunting efforts have resulted in an organization's contacting you about a job. Depending on the company, a representative may initially interview you over the phone or on a day when they are scheduled to visit your campus. Next, you may be called in for one and perhaps two interviews with the organization, including the person you will work for. Some companies describe the interview process in the career

---

Talk about Chutzpah

At a college graduation, I was sitting on stage with a prominent businessman. The graduates were routinely walking up to the stage to shake hands with school officials, receive their diplomas, and depart. This had been going on for awhile when a graduate, upon being handed his diploma, didn't leave. With the entire audience watching him, he walked over to the businessman and said, "Here's my business card, sir. It's a tough job market out there. If you need someone, please give me a call."

Was that the right thing for the graduate to do? It was questionable. But it worked. After the graduate left the stage, the businessman turned to me and said: "That's the kind of kid we want to hire—aggressive, confident, and willing to take risks." His company hired the graduate.

Note to future graduates: Please don't get the idea of handing out your business card to the dignitaries who are on the stage at your graduation ceremony. It may have worked once, but if everybody did it, it wouldn't mean anything, it would take all night to finish the ceremony, and I'd be hearing about it.

---

sections of their Web sites; if not, ask the company representative who initially contacts you about the process.

To prepare for the interview, you need to have a thorough knowledge of an organization—its mission, goals, lines of business, products or services, clients and customers, business issues, and so on. Look at the organization in a broader perspective. If your target employer is a company, read up on the industry it's in, the issues facing that industry, and so on. If it's a public accounting firm, research the general issues facing accounting firms. Read up on recent pronouncements of the SEC, Financial Accounting Standards Board, and other agencies concerning accounting issues like whether and when the United States should adopt international financial reporting standards. Read about new laws or regulations impacting public accounting firms, companies, or not-for-profit organizations. You can't know everything, of course, but you can learn enough to demonstrate to prospective employers that you're attuned to current issues.

Questions for Job Candidates

You need to prepare for questions that you could be asked in an interview.

As with resumes and cover letters, many sources of information are available on the Internet about questions that you might be asked. You can do a search on Google or other search engine, or the online job listing services like monster.com. Some employer Web sites cover in a general way questions you might be asked. That said, I will offer a few questions that might be included in an interview:

Why did you decide on accounting as a career?

Why are you interested in our company?

Why do you want this job?

Why are you the best qualified person for this job?

What are your strengths? Your weaknesses?

Give me an example of a project that you managed. What challenges did you overcome?

Remember to listen carefully to a question. If you're not sure you answered the question to the interviewer's satisfaction, ask.

Questions to Ask Employers

The job interview also is your opportunity to ask questions, learn more about the company and the position, and decide whether you will accept if the employer makes a job offer. Here are some questions to ask:

What are the major responsibilities of the job?

What qualities will be key to success in this position?

Would you describe a typical day in this position?

What are some of the more difficult problems I would face in this position?

Please tell me about the people with whom I would be working most closely.

What are the opportunities for advancement?

Will you allow me paid time off to study for the CPA examination?

Will you pay part or all of my examination costs, such as a fee for a CPA exam study course?

Compensation

If you applied for a job in response to an online job posting, the employer may have included the salary or salary range in the job description. If you sent a resume and a cover letter inquiring about a position with the company and were called in for an interview, you may be asked what compensation you have in mind. As with other questions, it's important to do your homework and be prepared to discuss compensation. You can research salaries through online sites such as salaries.com.

Robert Half International, a staffing firm, has a salary calculator on its Web site that you can use to determine salaries for financial positions in your location. You can also request its salary guide, which has starting salaries for accounting and other positions. You could also talk to your current or former teachers, people you know in public accounting firms or other organizations you want to work for, and other people to see what you can learn about salaries and compensation.

Until you have a job offer, however, try not to discuss salary. If the organization presses you on a salary range, provide a polite but vague answer, such as wanting to discuss the position further. When it does make a job and salary offer, ask for time to think about it. If the salary is less than you expected, you can come back with a counteroffer. It's part of the negotiating process. But don't get so absorbed in salary issues that you lose sight of the larger picture. Are you prepared to invest your career in this organization?

On the Job

From your first day on the job, you can start to demonstrate the leadership skills and other qualities that will make you stand out as an employee and help you to advance in the organization. Show that you know how to organize your work, manage your time effectively, work well with other people, and communicate effectively; for example, keeping your supervisor well informed of your activities. Put all your energy into excelling

at your job and building your reputation in your organization. Learn not only your job but the job just above you so you'll be prepared to move up if there's an opening. Continue to network, build relationships, and stay tuned to career opportunities. Take continuing education courses. If you are licensed as a CPA, consider studying for certification in areas that interest you such as forensic accounting. Always keep working to learn and grow in your job—and in your career.

Wrap-up

In this chapter, you learned the following:

- By addressing questions such as where you want to work, you can identify potential employers and job opportunities from seemingly endless possibilities.
- You can develop a list of target reporters from online research, your network of friends, teachers, mentors and others, employer Web sites, accounting blogs, and other sources.
- You need to do an assessment of your professional skills, preferably with the assistance of a teacher, mentor, or someone else who can give you a candid evaluation of your strengths and where you need improvement. More employers are recruiting online through their own Web sites or the Web sites of job listing services or staffing services.
- Although the Internet is a powerful tool for job hunting, your primary strategy should be to identify prospective employers and contact them directly.
- Many resources are available, online and in print, to help you prepare your resume, write a cover letter, and prepare for a job interview. Make full use of these resources to land an interview and excel during the interview.

Interview: Ronald Durkin
Founder and Senior Managing Director, Durkin Forensic Inc.

Ronald L. Durkin, the founder and senior managing director of Durkin Forensic Inc., is a CPA with more than 30 years combined experience as a special agent with the FBI, and in public accounting. During his tenure with the FBI, he was responsible for investigations involving white collar crime, political and public corruption, money laundering, organized crime, labor racketeering, racketeer-influenced and corrupt organization statute violations, and narcotics matters. He left the FBI to join KPMG, where he was the national partner in charge of the fraud and misconduct investigations practice and served as the western region's forensic practice leader as well as the office coordinating partner for the Los Angeles office's forensic practice. He retired from KPMG in 2008 and founded Durkin Forensic, a forensic accounting firm that focuses on solving fraud and fraud-related issues for its clients. He has assisted clients in matters involving fraud prevention, detection, and internal investigations. He has worked on cases involving Foreign Corrupt Practices Act, employee embezzlement, management fraud, financial statement fraud, conflict-of-interest, check kiting, bankruptcy fraud, money laundering, and Ponzi schemes.

"Accountants are needed to investigate a broad range of cases such as white collar crimes, money laundering, corruption, drug trafficking, and much more. CPAs with forensic accounting experience are particularly in demand."

Durkin is a frequent speaker at the FBI Academy and at the American Institute of Certified Public Accountants (AICPA) National Fraud Conference as well as the California, and other state, CPA societies. He has served in leadership positions on AICPA committees concerned with business valuation and forensic litigation services, anti-fraud programs and controls, and litigation and dispute resolution services. In 2006, he was honored with the AICPA's Distinguished Achievement Award for his long time commitment to the AICPA. In 2007, he was awarded the AICPA's first-ever FLS (Forensic and Litigation Services) Lifetime Achievement Award. Durkin has co-authored or contributed to AICPA and other publications on forensic accounting, fraud investigations, internal controls, and other topics. He holds a bachelor of science degree in accounting from California State University, Sacramento, and an MBA (emphasis in accounting) from California State University, Sacramento. He is a certified fraud examiner and certified insolvency and restructuring advisor, and he is certified in financial forensics.

How did you get interested in joining the FBI?

I had always been interested from as far back as I can remember. I studied accounting in school because accountants were in demand at the FBI, and there was intense competition for jobs with the bureau. I contemplated a career with the FBI before I went into the Air Force in 1966. After serving my country for nearly four years, and working as an accountant for over three years, I joined the FBI as a special agent. One interesting fact about my entrance into the FBI was that I was assigned to a new agents class that was comprised of all accountants. This was the first time in the history of the FBI that an all-accountant class went through new agents training.

Where did you start work with the bureau?

I started my career as a special agent in the Los Angeles Field Office working fugitive deserters. It was one of the most high risk jobs in the bureau because not only the fugitive, but his friends and relatives, would resist his being put into custody. After a few months, I was assigned to investigate white collar crimes. One of my first assignments in that squad was a major Ponzi scheme. I did all of the forensic accounting work, and eventually testified in court. After that, I worked on a variety of cases, including several where I served as an undercover CPA.

What were examples?

One difficult case involved an FBI agent who sold secrets to the Russians. After bringing my wife home from the hospital with our second child (on a Friday night), I got a phone call from my bureau supervisor who asked that I leave home that evening to lead a team that was being assigned to conduct a physical surveillance on the Russian agent. I worked double shifts on this case and, 35 days later, got a day off. Needless to say my wife was not a happy camper. In another assignment, I worked in an undercover capacity against a felon who was running a scam from prison, working with his girlfriend on the outside. The convicted felon was able to fraudulently transfer title in undeveloped land to an alter ego of his, using fake notary stamps. Once he was released from prison, he worked feverishly to get bank loans against the land. We were able to arrest the felon (his third foray into the criminal system) prior to his securing any loans with financial institutions. After serving a search warrant at his residence, we recovered over 100 notary stamps that could have been used to transfer title on other real property.

How long did you work on an investigation?

Sometimes these investigations can take a year or several years because you have to prove your case beyond a reasonable doubt, and it has to stand up under heavy cross examination by a defense attorney. It takes a lot of digging, a lot of pick and shovel work, and good presentation skills.

What's the demand for accountants in the bureau?

Accountants are very much in demand—the bureau has about 900 CPAs out of 13,000 agents. If all those CPAs were in a public accounting firm, it would be one of the biggest in the country. Accountants are needed to investigate a broad range of cases such as white collar crimes, money laundering, corruption, drug trafficking, and much more. CPAs with forensic accounting experience are particularly in demand. In fact, the bureau recently started a program to hire and train forensic accountants to work for the FBI in roles other than special agents. I have been asked to assist the FBI with the forensic accounting training program.

If you are a recent accounting graduate, how can you get the experience the bureau is looking for?

You could work for a CPA firm for a few years to learn about business and work on audits. The bureau is looking to hire people with audit expertise—in my opinion, the best forensic accountants are auditors. It also helps if you develop experience in an industry such as real estate by auditing mortgage or real estate companies since mortgage fraud appears to be one of the hottest areas for the FBI today. Many federal investigations require you to have knowledge of an industry, for example, in investigating mortgage or health care frauds. Having that specialized knowledge is a plus.

Interview: Howard Rosenkrantz
Senior Manager, UHY Advisors FLVS Inc.

Howard Rosenkrantz is a senior manager in the New York office of UHY Advisors FLVS Inc (uhy-us.com), a firm that provides business and tax consulting services. He is a CPA and a certified fraud examiner (CFE).

How did college help you prepare for a career?

For one, the SUNY Albany Business School had an excellent reputation. Highly regarded schools attract the top companies, providing graduates with the best job opportunities. All of the major accounting firms recruit at SUNY Albany. Another thing that helped me to prepare for a career was playing first base for the Great Danes, SUNY's baseball team. I was able to convince my coach that although I was only five-foot-six, I could play the position. From baseball, I learned about working with others, sharing common goals, and staying focused. The team unity and camaraderie developed over my four years was a big reason why the team made it to the playoffs. This experience taught me how important it is to be able to work together in a team environment.

> *"In addition to forensic knowledge and experience, you must have superior communication skills."*

Where did you go after you graduated?

I started with Kenneth Leventhal & Co., a firm specializing in real estate, where I had worked as an intern while in college. (The Leventhal firm merged with Ernst & Young in 1995.) I reviewed the audits of other accountants that were to be included in initial public offerings, performed due diligence procedures in connection with acquisitions, and did other audit, review and agreed upon procedure type work. In the process, I learned about the real estate industry, and the practical applications of accounting.

Where did you go from there?

I joined Rubin & Katz, a New York CPA firm, as an audit supervisor. Like Leventhal, it specialized in real estate, but it was a smaller firm at the time. I performed audits and reviews of the development and operation of residential and commercial buildings. The firm started giving me forensic accounting projects, such as an audit to find out how much a commercial property manager had stolen from a property. More stories were appearing in the media about investigations of corporate malfeasance. It appeared that forensic accounting was a growth market, with expanding career opportunities. I decided to take some classes offered by the Association of Certified Fraud Examiners to learn more about forensic accounting, and went on to earn my CFE certification.

What was your next move?

I joined Kroll, a global risk consulting firm, as a manager in financial advisory services. I worked on a variety of projects, for example, conducting damages and financial analyses in a breach of contract dispute for a large telecommunication company. Then I moved to Aon, a provider of risk management and other services, as a manager in financial advisory and litigation consulting services. Again, I worked on different projects such as intellectual property infringement disputes and forensic investigations involving kickback schemes and embezzlement of funds. I joined UHY in November 2007.

What type of work do you do for UHY?

I do intellectual property infringement consulting and work on forensic investigations. For example, in an intellectual property infringement suit, we are hired to provide an economic damages analysis assessing an appropriate amount to compensate the infringed upon company.

What's your advice for students who might be interested in careers in forensic accounting?

First and foremost, get your CPA certification. Work in auditing for a public accounting firm, on as many different engagements as possible. Then try to get into forensic work, either with your current firm or another firm. Consider getting CFE certification. It will demonstrate that you have the professional knowledge to work in the forensic field. In addition to forensic knowledge and experience, you must have superior communication skills. In an investigation, you ultimately have to write a report of what you learned. If the investigation results in a case that goes to trial, you will have to give a deposition, and to testify. You have to be comfortable speaking to people. Forensic accounting requires a high level of knowledge, experience and skill, but if you can make the grade, you will find it a very interesting and rewarding field.

Conclusion

Beyond Accounting

One of the beautiful things about accounting is that your career is not limited to accounting. CPAs have gone on to many other careers. One became an actress, another a pilot of a major airline, and yet another the owner of a gentleman's club in Las Vegas. Others became judges and other government officials. Five accountants serve in Congress.[1]

Now you don't have to be a CPA to become an actress or a pilot, but these examples do show that CPAs are talented people who can succeed in a variety of careers.

Many other professionals have applied their accounting backgrounds in their work. I serve on the board of the American Jewish University. Robert Wexler, its president (and my rabbi), received his MBA from New York's Baruch College, where he took accounting classes as part of his graduate studies.

At some point in your career, you may decide to leverage your knowledge and experience in accounting to go into another career—perhaps partner with a technology professional and private investors to start and finance a software company or form an agency to represent professional athletes or start a consulting firm that provides forensic accounting services (a different business model than the traditional accounting firm).

CPAs have succeeded because they have a vision for their careers, clear goals to realize their vision, and the knowledge, skills, and experience to achieve their goals. You can start your career planning as early as high school. Check out *Start Here. Go Places* (startheregoplaces.com), a career planning guide sponsored by the American Institute of Certified Public Accountants (AICPA).

As the interviews for this book attest, people have come to their careers in accounting from a variety of backgrounds, experiences, and circumstances. What they have in common is the CPA license. As noted in chapter 3, that license is worth the effort because it leads to better career and employment opportunities, greater credibility with clients, the potential for higher earnings, peer recognition, and qualifying for membership in the AICPA and state CPA societies with all the attendant benefits. So I strongly encourage you to earn your license.

And I wish you as much success and enjoyment in your career in accounting as I have had.

---

1 "Congress and Country: Behold the Differences," Sam Roberts, *New York Times*, February 9, 2010. www.nytimes.com/2010/02/10/us/politics/10congress.html?scp=4&sq=accountants&st=cse

Appendix 1

Recommended Resources on Careers in Accounting

Careers—General

- "Best Places to Launch a Career 2009," *BusinessWeek* http://images.businessweek.com/ss/09/09/0903_places_to_launch_a_career/index.htm

- CareerOneStop (careeronestop.org). Guides to careers, education, job search, resumes and interviews, salaries and benefits, and more. From the U.S. Department of Labor.

- O*NET Online (online.onetcenter.org): U.S. Department of Labor, which hosts this site, bills it as "the nation's primary source of occupational information." Detailed descriptions of the world of work for job seekers, students, and others.

- *Occupational Outlook Handbook: 2008-2009 Edition,* Bureau of Labor Statistics, U.S. Department of Labor. www.bls.gov/oco/ocos001.htm#outlook

- "Preparing the Workers of Today for the Jobs of Tomorrow," Executive Office of the President, Council of Economic Advisors, July 2009.

- "Top Jobs for the Class of 2009," press release, National Association of Colleges and Employers, September 25, 2009. www.naceweb.org/

- "Top Employers for the Class of 2009," press release, National Association of Colleges and Employers, March 30, 2009. www.nace.org

- "Working Mother 100 Best Companies 2009." On the Working Mother home page (workingmother.com), click on "Best Companies."

- *What Color is Your Parachute?, 2010: A Practical Manual for Job-Hunters and Career-Changers,* Richard N. Bolles, Ten Speed Press, Crown Publishing Group.

- Many colleges and universities provide in-depth career information on their Web sites, usually under Career Center, Career Services, or similar titles.

Careers—Accounting

- *2009 Trends in the Supply of Accounting Graduates And The Demand For Public Accounting Recruits,* American Institute of Certified Public Accountants. Available by search at www.aicpa.org.

- "What It Takes: A Guide to Becoming a CPA," CalCPA Education Foundation. www.calcpa.org/Content/licensure/requirements.aspx

- "Why Accounting?" Start Here, Go Places, American Institute of Certified Public Accountants. www.startheregoplaces.com

- "Tax Careers for CPAs." Tax Center, American Institute of Certified Public Accountants. http://tax.aicpa.org/Community/Tax+Careers+for+CPAs.htm

- *Careers in Accounting,* WetFeet (Insider Guides), 2008.

- *Careers in Accounting,* 4th edition, Gloria Gaylord and Glenda Ried, McGraw-Hill, 2006.

- *Questions Answered on Accounting Careers,* Caitlind Alexander, Laurel Lane Publishing, 2007.

- *Vault Career Guide to Accounting,* 3rd edition, Jason Alba, Manisha Bathija, Staff of Vault; Vault Career Library, 2008.

- Many state CPA societies have career information. Links to the state societies can be found on the AICPA Web site at www.aicpa.org.

- Many CPA firms have information about careers with their organizations posted on their Web sites.

Careers—Government

- *Managing Your Government Career: Success Strategies That Work,* Stewart Liff, AMACOM Books, a division of the American Management Association, 2009.

- *Government Jobs in America*, by the Editors of Government Job News, a Partnerships for Community Publication, Louis R. VanArsdale, Publisher, 2009.

- USAJOBS (usajobs.com). Official job site of the federal government. One stop shopping for federal government jobs.

- USA Jobs: State and Local Government Opportunities. Links to job information in individual states. www.thejobpage.gov/statelocal.asp

- State and local government Web sites: information on careers and jobs with state or local government agencies.

- *Making the Difference* (makingthedifference.org). Information on federal jobs and internships.

- U.S. Office of Personnel Management (opm.gov). Includes information for federal job seekers.

Careers—Not-for-Profit

- *The Nonprofit Career Guide: How to Land a Job That Makes a Difference*, Shelly Cryer, Fieldstone Alliance, St. Paul, MN, May 2008.

- *Chronicle of Philanthropy* (philanthrophy.com). Click on "Jobs" for information on careers and jobs.

- *Philanthropy Journal* (philanthrophyjournal.org): Click on "Jobs" to access a job search engine.

CPA Exam

- The Uniform CPA Examination: Information on preparing for and taking the CPA Exam. www.cpa-exam.org

- "The CPA Exam," American Institute of Certified Public Accountants. www.aicpa.org

Diversity

- "CPAs of Color: Celebrating 40 Years," AICPA Minority Initiatives Committee, www.aicpa.org

- *Women of Color in Accounting—Women of Color in Professional Services Series*, Katherine Giscombe, Catalyst, Research Reports, 2008. www.catalyst.org

- *Retaining People of Color: What Accounting Firms Need to Know—Women of Color in Professional*

Services Series, Deepali Bagati, Catalyst, Research Reports, 2007. www.catalyst.org

- *A White-Collar Profession: African American Certified Public Accountants Since 1921*, Theresa A. Hammond, The University of North Carolina Press, Chapel Hill, NC, 2002.

- Women in Accounting and Business—"The attraction, retention and advancement of women leaders: Strategies for organizational sustainability," Mary L. Bennett, Crowe Horwath LLP, AICPA Women's Initiatives Executive Committee. www.aicpa.org

- "Building Bridges: Strategies for a Successful Off-Ramping Program," Mary L. Bennett, Crowe Horwath LLP and Harris Smith, Grant Thornton LLP.[1] www.aicpa.org

- "Employee Retention Guide: How to Keep Your Top Talent on Board," AICPA Women's Initiatives Executive Committee. www.aicpa.org

- "Share, Learn, Grow, Mentor: A how-to guide from the (AICPA) Women's Initiatives Executive Committee." www.aicpa.org

- "The White House Project Report: Benchmarking Women's Leadership," November 2009. www.thewhitehouseproject.org/documents/Report.pdf

- "What Women in the Profession Are Thinking: A Focus Group Recap," presented by Cheryl Leitschuh, Ed.D, LP. www.aicpa.org

- *Women in Accounting: Quick Takes*, Catalyst, 2009. www.catalyst.org/publication/204/women-in-accounting

Education

- American Institute of Certified Public Accountants (aicpa.org).

- *American Accounting Association (aaahq.org)*: Organization that promotes worldwide excellence in accounting education, research, and practice. On its home page, click on "Career Center" to see postings of jobs in education and research.

- *Colleges and Universities Offering Accounting Degree Programs*, American Institute of Certified Public Accountants. www.aicpa.org

---

1 http://grad-schools.usnews.rankingsandreviews.com/best-graduate-schools/top-business-schools.

- *Public Accounting Report*, a subscription newsletter published by CCH, publishes an annual professor's survey that ranks undergraduate and graduate accounting programs.

- *Schools and Courses: The Basics*, American Institute of Certified Public Accountants.

- U.S. Department of Education maintains a database of accredited postsecondary institutions and programs (www.ope.ed.gov/accreditation).

- *U.S. News and World Report* produces an annual ranking of business school graduate programs, including rankings by specialties including accounting. (From the U.S. News home page (usnews.com): Education _ Best Graduate Schools _ Best Business Schools _ Business Specialties _ Accounting.[1])

- *Collegegrad.com*: Career options, resume writing, interview preparation, job search, salaries and more.

College Selection

- "Choosing a College That's Right for You," College Board, www.collegeboard.com

- *Top Ten Rules for Selecting a College or University*, School Guides www.schoolguides.com

- *How to Select Colleges*, College Admission Services www.go4ivy.com/choosecollege.asp

- *Student Gateway to the U.S. Government.* (students.gov). Information on choosing a college, financial aid, internships and jobs, and more.

Starting a CPA Firm

- "At Large: What's the 'Secret' Sauce for CPA Success?," Rick Telberg, Editor, AICPA *CPA Insider*, October 5, 2009. www.cpa2biz.com

- "Start Your Own Practice," Randy Myers, *Journal of Accountancy*, April 2006. www.journalof accountancy.com

Interviews

- *Job Interviews for Dummies*, 2nd edition, Joyce Lain Kennedy, Wiley Publishing Inc., 2008

- *Interviewing Success*, CollegeGrad.com, www.collegegrad.com/intv

Job search

- *Finding and Applying for Jobs and Evaluating Offers*, Occupational Outlook, 2010-11 Edition, U.S. Department of Labor, www.bls.gov/oco/oco2004.htm

- *Search Smarts: Best Practices for Conducting an Online Job Search*, Robert Half International. www.rhi.com/OnlineJobSearch.

Online Job Search

- accounting.com
- business.com
- careers-in-accounting.com
- careerbank.com
- careerbuilder.com
- careercast.com
- experience.com
- hotjobs.com
- jobcentral.com
- jobs.com
- ledgerlink.com
- monster.com
- Robert Half International (rhi.com)
- salary.com
- simplyhired.com

Professional Organizations

- American Accounting Association (aaahq.org)
- American Institute of Certified Public Accountants (aicpa.com)
- American Woman's Society of Certified Public Accountants (awscpa.org)
- American Society of Women Accountants (aswa.org)
- Ascend (asendleadership.org)[2]

---

1 http://grad-schools.usnews.rankingsandreviews.com/best-graduate-schools/top-business-schools.

2 "Ascend aims to be the premiere professional organization for enhancing the presence and influence of Asian Americans in the finance, accounting and other business related professions. Individuals who share in Ascend's mission from all professional or ethnic backgrounds are welcome to become members." About Ascend, Ascend Web site.

- Association of Certified Fraud Examiners (acfe.com)
- Association of Financial Professionals (afponline.org)
- Association of Government Accountants (agacgfm.org)
- Association of Latino Professionals in Finance and Accounting (alpfa.org)
- Beta Alpha Psi[3] (bap.org).
- Institute of Internal Auditors (theiia.org)
- Institute of Management Accountants (imanet.org)
- National Association of Black Accountants (nabainc.org)
- National Association of Tax Professionals (natptax.com)
- National Society of Accountants (nsacct.org)
- National Association of State Boards (nasba.org)

CPA Directories

CPA Directory. (cpadirectory.com): Leading online database of certified public accountants.

Teaching and Research

- "A Profession's Response to a Looming Shortage: Closing the Gap in the Supply of Accounting Faculty," Michael Ruff, Jay C. Thibodeau and Jean C. Beaded, *Journal of Accountancy*, March 2009. www.journalofaccountancy.com/Issues/2009/Mar/AccountingFaculty.htm

- "Directory of Accounting PhD Programs," American Accounting Association. http://aaahq.org/ATA/public-interest/PhD-programs/phdschools.cfm

- "Help Wanted: Accounting PhDs," Marge O'Reilly-Allen, CPA, PhD, David Wagaman, CPA, accountingweb. July 27, 2009. www.accountingweb.com/topic/education-careers/help-wanted-accounting-phds

- "Information on Accounting PhD Programs," American Association of Accountants, November 13, 2007. http://aaahq.org/temp/phd/StudyMaterials/QuestionnaireSummary.pdf

- "Pursuing a PhD in Accounting: Walking In With Your Eyes Open," Jason Bergner, *Journal of Accountancy*,

March 2009. www.journalofaccountancy.com/Web/PursuingaPhDinAccounting.htm

Web sites and Publications

- *Accounting Today* (digitalaccountingtoday.com): News, opinion, special reports, practice resources, Accounting Tomorrow blog, and more.

- *AICPA Links*: American Institute of Certified Public Accountants (AICPA) gateway to other accounting-related sites on the Internet. (www.aicpa.org)

- *CPA Journal*: (cpajournal.com): Publication of the New York Society of CPAs. Coverage of news, developments, and trends in accounting and auditing, taxation, finance, management, technology, and more.

- *CPA Letter Daily*: Free AICPA e-newsletter with the daily's top economic, business, accounting, and other news, and more. Sign up at www.smartbrief.com/cpa/.

- *CPA2biz* (cpa2biz.com): Exclusive marketing arm for AICPA products and services—including publications, webcasts, conferences, continuing professional education, and member benefits programs to CPAs and financial professionals nationwide.

- *CPA Trendlines* (cpatrendlines.com): Online newsletter of accounting news, analysis, reports, and more. Published by the Bay Street Group.

- *Journal of Accountancy* (journalofaccountancy.com): Flagship publication of the AICPA. Its articles and features cover accounting, financial reporting, auditing, taxation, personal financial planning, technology, business valuation, professional development, ethics, and many other subjects.

- *Public Accounting Report*: Leading provider of competitive intelligence for public accounting firms and the profession.

- *Start Here Go Places.* (startheregoplaces.com): Why Accounting? Career Options, Getting Started, Ask a CPA, Start Here Magazine, and more.

- *WebCPA* (webcpa.com): Provider of online content for the accounting and tax professions.

---

3 International honorary organization for financial information professionals.

- *Young CPA Network* (www.aicpa.org/YoungCPANetwork/): Career planning and development, mentoring, networking, work/life balance, professional issues, and more.

- *The Student CPA* (thestudentcpa.com): Blog covering accounting education, graduate school selection and preparation, networking, and career search strategies.

- *Vault (vault.com)*: Career guides, news, career management advice, job search, resume writing, and more.

- *The Wall Street Journal* _Careers (on wsj.com, click on Careers). Career news, tips, job search, and more.

Accounting Blogs

Many individual CPAs, accounting firms, professional organizations, and others publish accounting blogs. Do an online search under "accounting blogs."

Appendix 2

Is Accounting for You? A Questionnaire That Can Help You Decide

Throughout this book, you have heard accounting professionals—people just starting out as well as leaders in the industry— talk about why they went into accounting. The questionnaire that follows can provide guidance for you in deciding whether accounting is for you.

For each question, rate your level of interest/ability on a scale of 1 to 10, with 10 being the highest level of interest and ability and 1 being the lowest.

		Rating (1 to 10)
1	Do you like to solve complex business problems?	
2	Do you have strong analytical skills?	
3	Do you like working with numbers?	
4	Can you tolerate risk?	
5	Do you communicate effectively?	
6	Can you relate to people of diverse backgrounds, experiences, and attitudes?	
7	Do you like working with others?	
8	Are you a team player?	
9	Are you a team leader?	
10	Can you see the big picture?	
11	Do you pay attention to details?	
12	Do you finish what you started?	
13	Can you multitask?	
14	Do you work well under pressure?	
15	Are you accountable?	
16	Do you like technical issues and learning new technical information?	
17	Can you work independently?	
18	Can you handle significant amount of detail?	
19	Are you an organized person?	
20	Do you have computer skills and do you like technology?	
21	Can you deal with tough deadlines?	

The highest possible score is 210. What was your score? If you were realistic in your self-appraisal (if, for example, you asked someone who knows you well to review your self-evaluation), and your score was high, you may have a future in accounting. But if you scored low, don't give up on the idea of accounting.

Use this simple questionnaire for guidance, but not for deciding. It is merely intended to help you focus your thinking. Use it with other career planning resources, including those listed in appendix 1. And talk to people in accounting and other professions, attend the meetings of real estate trade groups and professional organizations, take classes in finance and other subjects related to accounting, and seek a part-time job or an internship with an accounting firm. To make a well-informed decision about whether to go into accounting, you need to invest time and effort in the decision-making process, so use these resources to full value.

Appendix 3

Big 4 Timeline

	Deloitte	Ernst & Young	KPMG	Pricewaterhouse Coopers
1845	William Welch Deloitte opens an accountancy office in London. Charles Waldo Haskins and Elijah Watt Sells form Haskins & Sells.			
1849		Frederick Whinney joins Harding & Pullein in London.		Samuel Lowell Price establishes an accountancy in London.
1854				William Cooper establishes an accounting practice in London. Seven years later it becomes Cooper Brothers.
1865				Samuel Price enters into a partnership known as Price Waterhouse & Co.
1877			Accountancy firm Thomson McLintock opens in Glasgow.	
1890			William Barkley Peat forms an accounting firm in London.	
1894		Harding & Pullein renamed Whinney Smith & Whinney.		
1897			James Marwick and Roger Mitchell found Marwick, Mitchell & Co. in New York.	

(continued)

	Deloitte	Ernst & Young	KPMG	Pricewaterhouse Coopers
1898	George Touche establishes office in London. Touche and John Ballantine Niven establish Touche Niven & Co. in New York.			William Lybrand and partners form Lybrand, Ross Brothers and Montgomery in Philadelphia.
1903		Brothers Alwin and Theodore Ernst form Ernst & Ernst in Cleveland.		
1906		Arthur Young and his brother Stanley form Arthur Young & Co. in Chicago.		
1911			William Barclay Peat & Co. and Marwick Mitchell & Co. merge to form Peat Marwick Mitchell & Co, later known as Peat Marwick.	
1917			Piet Klynveld founds Klynveld Kraayenhof & Co. in Amsterdam.	
1924		Arthur Young allies with Broad Paterson & Co, England. Ernst & Ernst allies with Whinney, Smith & Whinney.		
1925	Two of Deloitte's U.K. and U.S. predecessor practices form a co-partnership in several countries under the name Deloitte, Plender, Haskins & Sells.			
1947	Touche, Niven & Co. merges with two other firms to become Touche, Niven, Bailey & Smart.			

	Deloitte	Ernst & Young	KPMG	Pricewaterhouse Coopers
1957				Cooper Brothers merges with two other firms to form Coopers & Lybrand.
1960	Touche, Niven, Bailey & Smart merges with two other firms to form Touche, Ross, Bailey & Smart.			
1969	Name Touche Ross adopted.			
1975	Tohmatsu Awoki & Co. becomes part of the Touche Ross International network.			
1978	Name Deloitte Haskins & Sells adopted.			
1979		Ernst & Whinney forms and becomes the fourth largest accountancy firm in the world.	Thomson McLintock forms KMG (Klynveld Main Goerdeler) a grouping of independent national practices.	
1987			Thomson McLintock/KMG and Peat Marwick formed a firm called KPMG in the United States and Peat Marwick McLintock in the United Kingdom.	
1989		Ernst & Whinney and Arthur Young merge to form Ernst & Young.		
1990	Merger creates Deloitte & Touche.		Name changed to single name globally: KPMG Peat Marwick McClintock.	
1991			Name changed to KPMG Peat Marwick.	
1993	International firm is named Deloitte Touche Thomatsu.			
1995			Name changed to KPMG.	
1998				Price Waterhouse and Coopers & Lybrand merge to form PricewaterhouseCoopers.

Glossary

The following is a short glossary of accounting terms. It is intended merely as a sample.

For a detailed glossary, go to the Web site of the AICPA at www.aicpa.org.

Or go to the home page of the New York State Society of CPAs at www.nysscap.org). In the "Things to Do" box, click on "select from menu." Scroll down to "Define a Term." A glossary will appear on your screen. Alternatively, type www.nysscap.org/glossary in your browser.

You can also search online. Type "accounting glossary" or "accounting dictionary" in your browser.

Finally, chapter 1 discusses some accounting terms such as generally accepted accounting principles (GAAP) in more detail.

Accountant's Report

Formal document that communicates an independent accountant's expression of limited assurance on financial statements as a result of performing inquiry and analytic procedures (review Report); results of procedures performed (agreed-upon procedures report); nonexpression of opinion or any form of assurance on a presentation in the form of financial statements information that is the representation of management (compilation report); or an opinion on an assertion made by management in accordance with the Statements on Standards for Attestation Engagements (attestation report). An accountant's report does not result from the performance of an audit.

Accounting Principles Board (APB)

Senior technical committee of the American Institute of Certified Public Accountants that issued pronouncements on accounting principles from 1959-1973. The Accounting Principles Board was replaced by the Financial Accounting Standards Board.

Accrual Basis

Method of accounting that recognizes revenue when earned rather than when collected. Expenses are recognized when incurred rather than when paid.

American Institute of Certified Public Accountants (AICPA)

The national, professional organization for all certified public accountants. Its mission is to provide members with the resources, information, and leadership that enable them to provide valuable services in the highest professional manner to benefit the public as well as employers and clients. In fulfilling its mission, the American Institute of Certified Public Accountants works with state CPA organizations and gives priority to those areas where public reliance on CPA skills is most significant.

Analytical Procedures

Substantive tests of financial information that examine relationships among data as a means of obtaining evidence. Such procedures include: comparison of financial information with information of comparable prior periods; comparison of financial information with anticipated results (such as forecasts); study of relationships between elements of financial information that should conform to predictable patterns based on the entity's experience; and comparison of financial information with industry norms.

Balance Sheet

Basic financial statement, usually accompanied by appropriate disclosures that describe the basis of accounting used in its preparation and presentation of a specified date, the entity's assets, liabilities, and the equity of its owners. Also known as statement of financial condition.

Capitalized Interest

Interest cost incurred during the time necessary to bring an asset to the condition and location for its intended use and included as part of the historical cost of acquiring the asset.

Cash Basis

Method of bookkeeping by which revenues and expenditures are recorded when they are received and paid.

Fiduciary

Person who is responsible for the administration of property owned by others. For example, corporate management is a fiduciary with respect to corporate assets that are beneficially owned by the stockholders and creditors. Similarly, a trustee is the fiduciary of a trust and partners owe fiduciary responsibility to each other and to their creditors.

Financial Accounting Standards Board (FASB)

Independent, private, nongovernment group that is authorized by the accounting profession to establish generally accepted accounting principles in the United States.

Forecast

Prospective financial statements that are an entity's expected financial position, results of operations, and cash flows.

Forensic Accounting

Provides for an accounting analysis that is suitable to a court of law that will form the basis for discussion, debate, and, ultimately, dispute resolution. Forensic accounting encompasses investigative accounting and litigation support. Forensic accountants utilize accounting, auditing, and investigative skills when conducting an investigation. Equally critical is the ability to respond immediately and to communicate financial information clearly and concisely in a courtroom setting.

Fraud

The use of one's occupation for personal enrichment through the deliberate misuse or misapplication of employing an organization's resources or assets. This can include the fraudulent conversion and obtaining of money or property by false pretenses.

Generally Accepted Accounting Principles (GAAP)

Financial statements are based on generally accepted accounting principles, the authoritative rules for preparing and presenting financial statements, and for disclosure of financial information. Unless they say otherwise, public companies and other companies and businesses are assumed to follow generally accepted accounting principles in their financial reporting.

Generally Accepted Government Auditing Standards (GAGAS)

Generally accepted government auditing standards—informally known as the Yellow Book—are promulgated under the leadership of the comptroller general of the United States, who heads the U.S. General Accounting Office.

Governmental Accounting Standards Board (GASB)

The current source of generally accepted accounting principles used by state and local governments in the United States.

Joint Venture

When two or more persons or organizations gather capital to provide a product or service. Often carried out as a partnership.

Limited Liability Company (LLC)

Form of doing business combining limited liability for all owners (called members) with taxation as a partnership. A limited liability company is formed by filing articles of organization with an appropriate state official. Rules governing limited liability companies vary significantly from state to state.

Limited Liability Partnership (LLP)

General partnership that, via registration with an appropriate state authority, is able to enshroud all its partners in limited liability. Rules governing limited liability partnerships vary significantly from state to state.

Litigation Support/Dispute Resolution

A service that CPAs often provide to attorneys— for example, expert testimony about the value of a business or other asset, forensic accounting (a partner stealing from his other partners, or a spouse understating his income in a matrimonial action). The lawyer hires the CPA to do the investigation and determine the amount of money stolen or understated.

Prospective Financial Information (Forecast and Projection)

Prospective financial statements that present an entity's expected financial position, results of operations, and changes in financial position.

Public Company Accounting Oversight Board (PCAOB)

Five-member board created by the Sarbanes Oxley Act that has the authority to set and enforce auditing, attestation, quality control, and ethics (including independence) standards for public companies. It is also empowered to inspect the auditing operations of public accounting firms that audit public companies as well as impose disciplinary and remedial sanctions for violations of the board's rules, securities laws, and professional auditing standards.

Sarbanes Oxley Act (SOX)

An act designed to improve quality and transparency in financial reporting and independent audits and accounting services for public companies, to create a Public Company Accounting Oversight Board, to enhance the standard-setting process for accounting practices, to strengthen the independence of firms that audit public companies, to increase corporate responsibility and the usefulness of corporate financial disclosure, to protect the objectivity and independence of securities analysts, to improve Securities and Exchange Commission resources and oversight and for other purposes.

Securities and Exchange Commission (SEC) Filings

Financial and informational disclosures required by the SEC in order to comply with certain sections of the Securities Act of 1933 and the Securities and Exchange Act of 1934. Some of the more common filings that publicly owned companies must submit are the form 10–K, form 10–Q, and form 8–K.

Special Report

A term applied to auditors' reports issued in connection with various types of financial presentations such as specified elements, accounts or items of a financial statement, compliance with aspects of contractual agreements, or regulatory requirements.